J.E. Peterson is a historian and political analyst specializing in the Arabian Peninsula. He has taught at various universities including Bowdoin College, the College of William and Mary, the University of Pennsylvania, Portland State University and Sciences Po; and has been associated with a number of leading research institutes in the United States and the United Kingdom. Until 1999, he served in the Office of the Deputy Prime Minister for Security and Defence in Muscat, Sultanate of Oman. He is currently affiliated with the Center for Middle Eastern Studies at the University of Arizona and is the author or editor of a dozen books and monographs, including most recently *Historical Muscat: An Illustrated Guide and Gazetteer; Oman's Insurgencies: The Sultanate's Struggle for Supremacy; The GCC States: Participation, Opposition, and the Fraying of the Social Contract; The Emergence of the Gulf States: Studies in Modern History* and a third edition *of Historical Dictionary of Saudi Arabia.*

'This book fills a significant gap in the available literature on Saudi Arabia. There are a number of texts that focus on Ibn Saud's reign, but most of these focus on the personal agency of his leadership and his foreign relations, while only tangentially analyzing the political economy of the time. This book goes a long way to remedying this situation. A key strength of the book is that it draws heavily on primary sources, most of which are archived US government reports. This really adds depth to the book and makes it stand out.'

Christopher Davidson, Associate Professor (Reader) in Middle East Politics, University of Durham

'This book fills a very important gap in the literature on Saudi Arabia and will add immediate scholarly and analytical value to the academic and policy debates over Saudi Arabia's attempts to transform its economy once again and move decisively into a post-oil era. The depth of primary and secondary research that has gone into the book is extremely impressive and adds up to a considerable advance in the sum of academic knowledge about the creation of economic institutions and decision-making in Saudi Arabia between the 1920s and the 1950s.'

Kristian Coates Ulrichsen, Fellow for the Middle East, Baker Institute for Public Policy, Rice University

SAUDI ARABIA UNDER IBN SAUD

Economic and Financial Foundations of the State

J.E. Peterson

I.B. TAURIS
LONDON · NEW YORK

Published in 2018 by
I.B.Tauris & Co. Ltd
London • New York
www.ibtauris.com

Library of Middle East History 75

ISBN: 978 1 78453 900 9
eISBN: 978 1 83860 904 7
ePDF: 978 1 83860 905 4

A full CIP record for this book is available from the British Library
A full CIP record is available from the Library of Congress

Library of Congress Catalog Card Number: available

Typeset in Stone Serif by OKS Prepress Services, Chennai, India

Contents

List of Illustrations

MAPS

TABLES

Preface

In recent decades, the name Saudi Arabia has become synonymous with oil and with it a presumed wealth brought about by its vast oil reserves. It is all too easy to forget that prior to the discovery, and especially the exploitation of, its crude oil the country was amongst the poorest places in the world. The early decades of the twentieth-century state that became the Kingdom of Saudi Arabia (the name was adopted only in 1932) were characterized by chronic financial shortages and economic crises. The ruler and king until 1953, ʿAbd al-ʿAziz b. ʿAbd al-Rahman Al Saʿud, was a desert chieftain who left financial matters to a single individual, ʿAbdullah b. Sulayman al-Hamdan. The latter was entrusted with nearly all of the country's early financial dealings and administrative development. The Ministry of Finance, which he headed from its inception, served as nearly the sole government agency dealing with a wide variety of matters, many of which had only a peripheral connection to finance or the economy.

This book examines the role of the Ministry of Finance and its minister, ʿAbdullah al-Sulayman, in holding the country together financially and administratively until the promise of substantial oil income was realized a few years after World War II ended. It is organized according to three distinct economic phases. Part I outlines the 1920s and 1930s when the formative period of the modern state was constituted, with the government relying most heavily on revenues from the annual *hajj* (pilgrimage) and taking the first tentative steps toward a rational administrative structure. Part II discusses how World War II marked an intensification of Saudi Arabia's financial troubles and the state's dependence on British and American subsidies. The war ended with the US supplanting Britain as Saudi Arabia's principal partner. Part III explains that while oil had been discovered in 1933, large-scale production was delayed until after the war. Although postwar oil payments increased dramatically, the country's current expenses and development needs grew even more, leaving the government nearly as destitute as ever. Throughout all three periods, the Ministry of Finance was charged with creating the strategies necessary to find enough income to cover government expenses.

The book has been organized thematically by the three epochal time frames described above. But rather than adhering to a strict chronological order, it seemed preferable to keep discussion of different subtopics such as currency matters or agriculture together to enable the reader to get a clearer picture of how the sector developed during each of the selected time frames. In addition, Part III is further subdivided into two smaller intervals as the development orientation and financial capabilities of the Saudi government were markedly different between the period of 1945 to 1949/1950 and that of 1950 to 1954. While it makes sense to keep discussion of oil developments in a single chapter, just as was done in Part I, it also seemed sensible to group treatment of other subtopics together during the half-decade periods rather than breaking the overall discussion down into an awkward year-by-year survey of events. This means that the chronological order is occasionally skewed in order to provide coherent examination of developments in individual sectors even if some subjects, such as the resignation of ʿAbdullah al-Sulayman, is mentioned briefly several chapters before the full story is covered.

I am grateful for the assistance of Shaykh Ahmad al-Sulaiman, son of Shaykh ʿAbdullah al-Sulaiman, in gathering materials for this book in connection with research for a biography of his father. This assistance enabled me to search out relevant documentation at the National Archives in London and the National Archives in Washington, DC, as well as in various collections in Saudi Arabia and private papers held in the United Kingdom and the United States. I also benefitted from discussions with a variety of individuals familiar with Shaykh ʿAbdullah in Saudi Arabia, and the country's financial development inside and outside Saudi Arabia.

Furthermore, well into my research, I became aware that another of Shaykh ʿAbdullah al-Sulaiman's sons, Shaykh ʿAbd al-ʿAziz, had commissioned a team of people from the University of Essex in about 1982 to gather available material in Western languages about his father. Over the course of five years, notes and photocopies had been gathered from the principal British and American archives, both private and public, while a series of interviews was carried out with Shaykh ʿAbdullah's remaining contemporaries and Westerners who had known and dealt with the former minister of finance. Although a multi-volume synopsis of the material was prepared, no further use was made of the collection until I came across it while researching this book, and indeed it had been forgotten. The work of this team has been of invaluable help in the writing of the present volume, particularly in the information contained in interviews as well as the collection of some additional archival material.

A brief note on terminology for the name of the country and the title of its ruler should be made at the outset. After 1902 when ʿAbd al-ʿAziz b. ʿAbd al-Rahman al-Faysal Al Saʿud recaptured the family's ancestral seat at Riyadh, he became styled as either *imam* or the *sultan* of Najd. After ʿAbd al-ʿAziz extended his control over al-Hijaz in the mid-1920s, his title was *sultan* of Najd and king of al-Hijaz and the country was known as Najd and al-Hijaz. With the incorporation of the other territories that make up the present state, the Kingdom of Saudi Arabia was proclaimed as the name of the country in 1932 and its ruler became the king of Saudi Arabia. For the sake of simplicity, the founder of the twentieth-century state generally is referred to as Ibn Saʿud, the name by which he was best known in the West, when mentioned before 1932 and as King ʿAbd al-ʿAziz or the king for references after that date.

The transliteration system employed by the US Library of Congress and the British Library has been used here, without diacritics apart from the *ʿayn* and the *hamzah*. Some exceptions have been made. Conversion of dates from the Islamic to the Christian calendar, where not present in the original source, have been made using Kingdom of Saudi Arabia, Ministry of Finance and National Economy, *taqwim umm al-qura* (Riyadh: musallahat matabiʿ al-hukumah, 1413/1992–3 and online at <http://www.ummulqura.org.sa/Index.aspx>. Dual dates in the Islamic (*hijri*; normally indicated as A.H.) and the Western (Gregorian) calendars (normally indicated as A.D.) are expressed as, for example, 1308H/1887 or simply 1308/1887. The maps were created by Hélène David-Cuny and originally appeared in J.E. Peterson, ed., *The Emergence of the Gulf States: Studies in Modern History* (London: Bloomsbury, 2016); they appear here by permission of Altajir Trust, London.

Glossary

amir	prince, commander, governor, ruler (in the smaller Gulf states)
awqaf	plural of *waqf*
bayt al-mal	treasury in a traditional Islamic state
hajj	the Islamic pilgrimage to Makkah
imam	the leader during prayers; a religious notable; the head of the Islamic community
kiswah	the richly decorated cover of the Ka'bah, the holy stone edifice around which the Great Mosque of Makkah was built
mahmal	the highly decorated ornamental litter that accompanied the Egyptian delegation on the *hajj* from Mamluk times until Ibn Sa'ud's assumption of control over Makkah
riyal	the official currency of Saudi Arabia; originally minted only in silver
sultan	a secular title for an Islamic ruler, most commonly but not always applied to the ruler of a sultanate
suq	market
'ulama' (sing. *'alim*)	the body of religious scholars or authorities in Islam
wadi	watercourse
waqf	a perpetual endowment of land or shops generally created to support a mosque or other religious institution
zakat	alms tax

Abbreviations

AIOC	Anglo-Iranian Oil Company
APOC	Anglo-Persian Oil Company
ARAMCO	Arabian American Oil Company
b/d	barrels per day
BAPCO	Bahrain Petroleum Company
CASOC	California Arabian Standard Oil Company
E£	Egyptian pound
E&GS	Eastern and General Syndicate
FO	Foreign Office (United Kingdom)
FRUS	Foreign Relations of the United States
GOVENCO	Government Engineering Company of Saudi Arabia
HMG	Her/His Majesty's Government (United Kingdom)
IOR	India Office Records (United Kingdom)
IPC	Iraq Petroleum Company
mbd	millions of barrels per day
MBJI	Michael Baker Jr. Inc.
MESC	Middle East Supply Center (United Kingdom, based in Cairo during World War II)
MT$	Maria Theresa thaler (dollar)
NARA	National Archives and Records Administration (United States)
PAB	Political Agent, Bahrain (United Kingdom)
PAK	Political Agent, Kuwait (United Kingdom)
PRC	Petroleum Reserves Corporation (United States)
PRPG	Political Resident/Residency in the Persian Gulf (United Kingdom)
RG	Record Group (used by US National Archives and Records Administration)

Rs.	rupees
SAG	Saudi Arabian government
SAMS	Saudi Arabian Mining Syndicate Limited
SATCO	Saudi Arabian Maritime Tanker Company
SOCAL	Standard Oil of California
SR	Saudi *riyal*
tel.	telegram
TEXACO	Texas Company
TPC	Turkish Petroleum Company
UKCC	United Kingdom Commercial Corporation

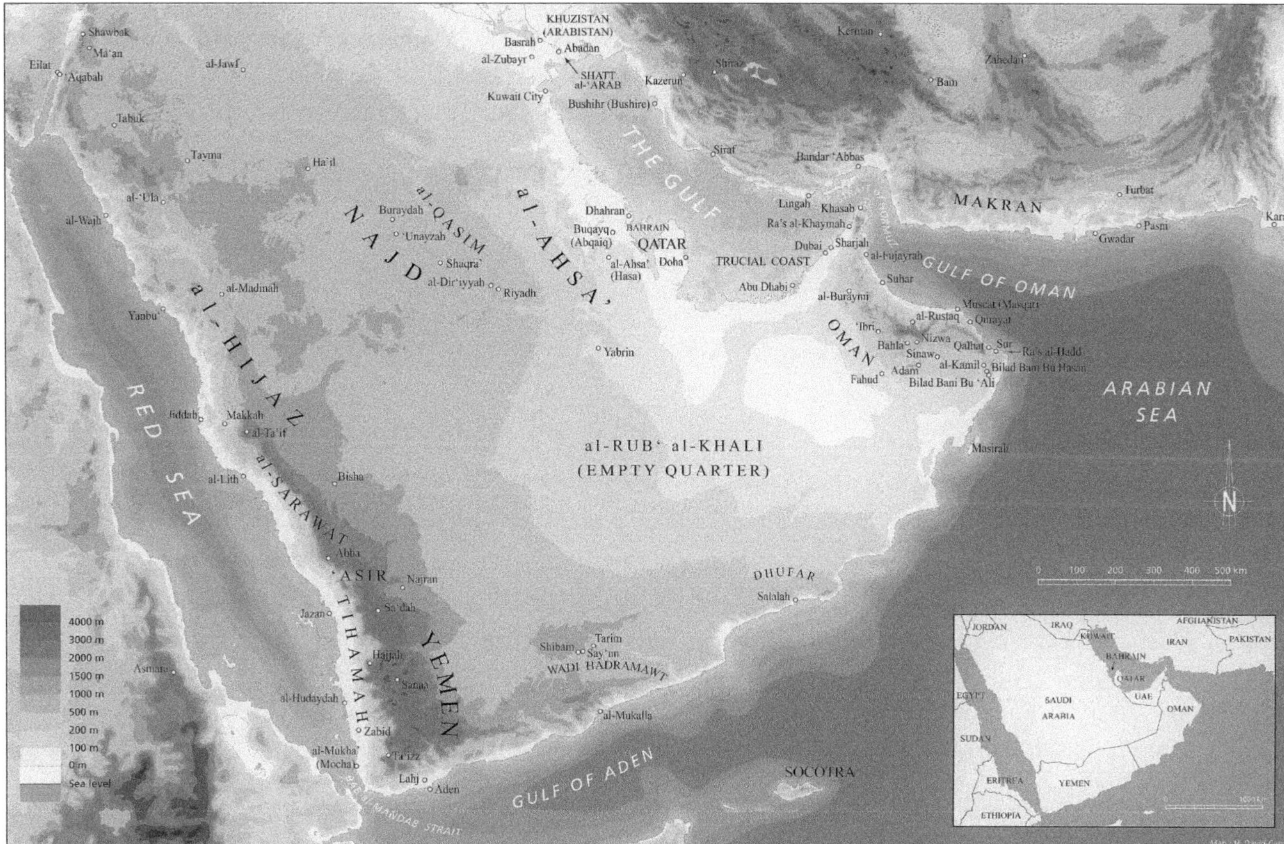

MAP 1 The Arabian Peninsula: Topography and Place Names.

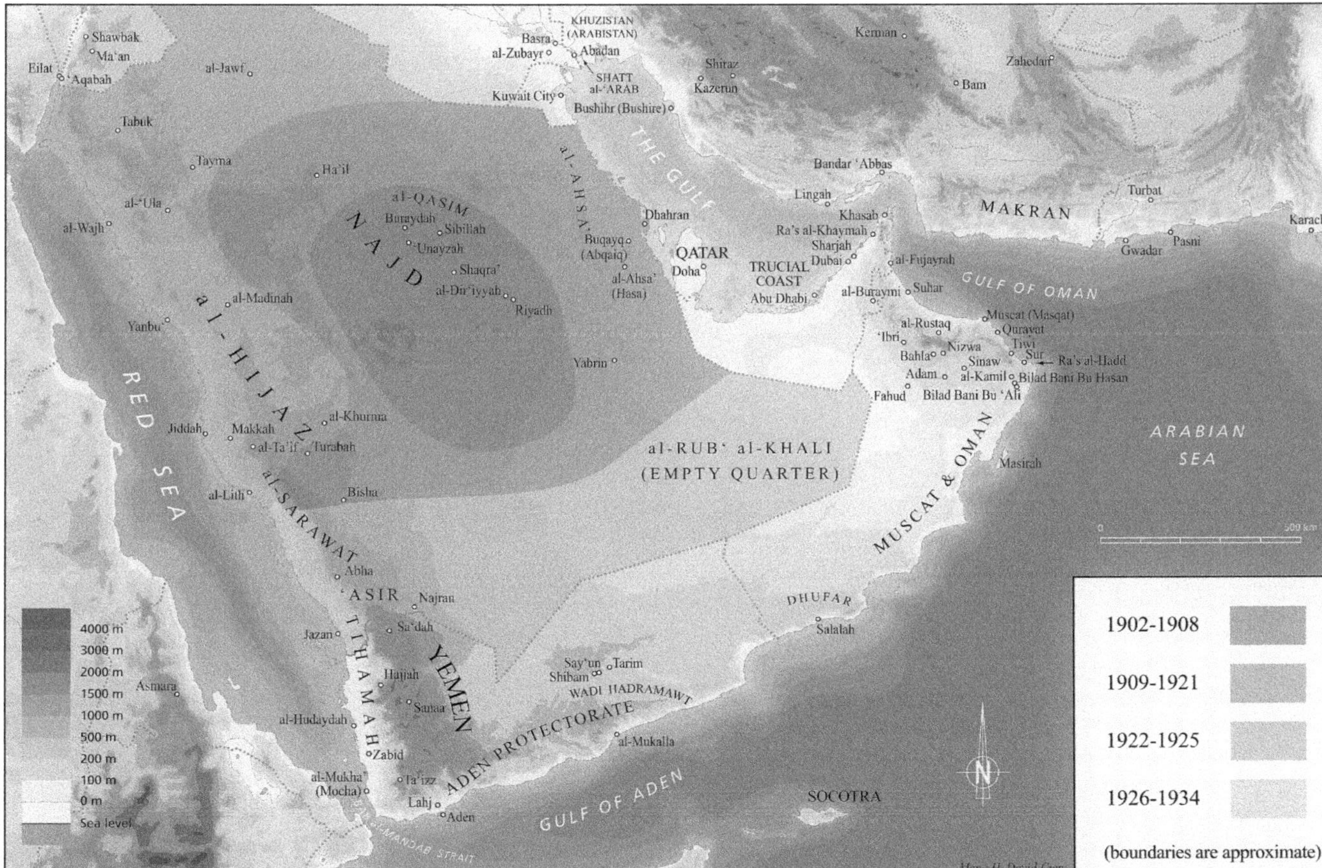

MAP 2 The Expansion of the Third Saudi State.

CHAPTER 1

Saudi Arabia in the Twentieth Century

The Arabian Peninsula was a very different place at the beginning of the twentieth century. It was not until 1902 that 'Abd al-'Aziz b. 'Abd al-Rahman Al Sa'ud, better known in the West as Ibn Sa'ud, regained control of the family's seat at Riyadh. And it was not until 1932 that Ibn Sa'ud was able to meld the pieces of the widespread territory he had united into the Kingdom of Saudi Arabia.

Not surprisingly, the formal creation of the kingdom was only the beginning of the process of creating a viable state. Most of the country was desperately poor and the new king's principal source of income was revenue from the *hajj*, the annual Muslim pilgrimage to Makkah (Mecca) in the west of the country. Even the signing of a major oil concession in 1933 with what eventually became the Arabian American Oil Company (ARAMCO) only helped the financial situation marginally. For long decades, it was absolutely necessary to seek trickles of revenue wherever possible and to allocate scarce funds carefully.

It is not an exaggeration to say that in the first half of the twentieth century the Kingdom of Saudi Arabia was in its political, administrative, and economic infancy as a state. The founder of the modern state, 'Abd al-'Aziz b. 'Abd al-Rahman, began his long and fruitful career as a tribal chieftain in southern Najd. Over three decades, he extended his control over much of the Arabian Peninsula. His authority was exerted through him directly and through his sons as was the traditional way. His eldest son and heir Sa'ud was kept in Riyadh to serve as his father's right-hand man and as viceroy of Najd while his second son Faysal served his father as viceroy of al-Hijaz, the more developed and more populated region of the new country.

Trusted assistants carried out the functions of the Diwan, his court, also as had been done traditionally. For relations with the outside world, he also depended on northern Arab advisers, such as Hafiz Wahbah, Yusuf Yasin,

'Abdullah al-Damluji, Rashad Pharaon (Fara'awn), and Khayr al-Din al-Zirkali, as well as the transplanted Englishman H. St. John B. Philby. Arab rulers for centuries had done the same.

But as the state grew in physical size and administrative complexity, 'Abd al-'Aziz required functionaries who could manage the difficult financial situation and create the initial bureaucratic machinery necessary to run the various functions of the growing state. He found his principal instrument in 'Abdullah al-Sulayman al-Hamdan. A native of 'Unayzah, an important town in al-Qasim region of central Najd, al-Sulayman had worked in India and Bahrain before joining his older brother Muhammad at the court in Riyadh. Quickly impressing 'Abd al-'Aziz with his intelligence, creativity, and loyalty, the ruler made him his treasurer and, after the incorporation of al-Hijaz, the country's first finance minister. While al-Sulayman served as minister of finance from before the creation of the Kingdom of Saudi Arabia until after the death of Ibn Sa'ud in 1953, his functions and responsibilities went far beyond just finances.

Major components of his position included maintaining charge of the treasury and making payments as ordered by the king, as well as keeping track of revenues and expenditures and producing simple budgets. An example of his work in the latter context is the detailed revenue figures he produced for the years 1355–60H/1936/1937–41/1942.[1] However, his remit covered far more than just finances. He negotiated the initial oil concession with the predecessor of ARAMCO, drummed up interest in mining, started agricultural schemes, created schools, supervised the *hajj*, served as deputy minister of defense, negotiated foreign loans and assistance, and created the country's currency and central bank, among numerous other activities. From 1917 until his retirement in 1954, al-Sulayman's fingerprints were all over the fledgling government. King 'Abd al-'Aziz trusted him fully to carry out his wishes, to a greater extent than any other of his servants.

It took several decades for the discovery of oil in 1933 to be translated into significant state income. The intervening years were marked by poverty and a desperate scramble for available resources to meet essential needs. The decline of *hajj* revenues due to the Great Depression and restrictions imposed by World War II forced the kingdom to rely increasingly on first British and then American subsidies. The consequence of Britain's straitened economic circumstances during and after the war was less willingness to extend aid. As Britain withdrew financially, the United States stepped into the breach. This assistance, when combined with the winning of the oil concession by American companies (and the subsequent formative role that ARAMCO played in the development process, particularly in the Eastern Province), inevitably shifted Saudi Arabia from reliance on Britain as its principal ally and protector to a deepening partnership with the US. Remarkably, the partnership has endured ever since, despite periodic disagreements and deeply buried incompatibilities. The following pages chronicle the early attempts to create a state administration and financial structure and then the initial gestation of Saudi Arabia's prosperity.

THE KINGDOM OF SAUDI ARABIA

Saudi Arabia shares the Arabian Peninsula with six other countries: Kuwait, Bahrain, Qatar, the United Arab Emirates, Oman, and Yemen. It occupies by far the largest proportion of the peninsula, although Yemen and Oman are relatively large countries as well. All seven states in their present form are twentieth-century creations, although some of the smaller "city-states" such as Kuwait and Bahrain in effect trace their origins back to the eighteenth century and Oman has been independent far longer.

Before the beginning of the twentieth century, Arabia had a much different political complexion, reflecting its varied and wide-flung geography. What is now Saudi Arabia is composed of three principal geopolitical regions, flanked by northern and southern areas. The Najd occupies central Arabia and forms the heartland of the present kingdom. Its principal city is now Riyadh, also the country's largest urban area, but Ha'il in the north and 'Unayzah and Buraydah in the center also have been prominent in history. The Eastern Province is noteworthy today as the source of Saudi Arabia's immense oil fields. The urban areas of Dhahran, al-Dammam, and al-Khubar are essentially recent creations, built to take advantage of the oil industry and the associated industrial and population boom that oil brought. Historically, the region's focal points were the two large oases of al-Ahsa' (Hasa) and al-Qatif, as well as several small ports on the Gulf. The Eastern Province's location on the Gulf is what gives Saudi Arabia an aspect as a Gulf state, as well as boundaries with the smaller states that form the six-member Gulf Cooperation Council (GCC).

On the western or Red Sea coast of the country, al-Hijaz is the most cosmopolitan region of the country. Jiddah is the second largest city in the kingdom and site of its most important port. But the mountainous al-Hijaz is more notable for its possession of the two holiest cities in Islam: Makkah (more formally and respectfully known as Makkah al-Mukarramah; Mecca), where the Prophet Muhammad was born and where the venerated Ka'bah (the spiritual center of Islam) is found, and al-Madinah (al-Madinah al-Munawwarah; Medina), where the Prophet Muhammad created the original Islamic state and later died. To the south lie the fertile highland regions of 'Asir and Najran, as well as the coastal plain of Tihamah. Several small provinces in the north, along the southern rim of the immense Nafud

Desert, form the borderlands with the "new" states of Jordan and Iraq. The south-eastern region of the kingdom consists of the Rubʿ al-Khali Desert or Empty Quarter, which, as its name suggests, is inhabited by only a few nomads and constitutes the largest sand desert in the world.

The agglomeration of these distinct regions into a single state is a recent phenomenon but one with roots in the eighteenth century.[2] An alliance begun in 1744 between Muhammad b. Saʿud, the head of the town of al-Dirʿiyah in southern Najd, and an Islamic reformer named Muhammad b. ʿAbd al-Wahhab soon resulted in the expansion of the so-called Wahhabi doctrine throughout much of Arabia and the establishment of the Al Saʿud dynasty. The dynasty's rule experienced a wave of expansions and regroupings through the nineteenth century. Late in the century, the Al Saʿud were forced from their new capital at Riyadh into exile in Kuwait.

It was left to ʿAbd al-ʿAziz, the young son of the family's leader, to lead a few men into Riyadh in the dark of the night and recapture the city in 1902. Following this celebrated event, ʿAbd al-ʿAziz required only a few short years to extend his control over much of Najd. When he was unable to secure British recognition, he was forced to accept nominal Ottoman suzerainty. But in 1913, following Ottoman setbacks in Europe, ʿAbd al-ʿAziz captured the Ottoman garrisons in al-Ahsaʾ and al-Qatif in eastern Arabia. This obliged the (British) Government of India to conclude a treaty with him. The principal effect of this treaty was to encourage the Al Saʿud to contend with the Al Rashid, who remained Turkish allies. But ʿAbd al-ʿAziz still did not have British favor. The Arab Bureau in Cairo championed Sharif Husayn b. ʿAli al-Hashimi of Makkah as the preferred leader of the "Arab Revolt" against the Ottomans and recognized his declaration of an independent Kingdom of al-Hijaz in 1916.

Following the end of the war, ʿAbd al-ʿAziz resumed his unification goals, conquering his arch rivals, the Al Rashid of Haʾil, in 1921. In the same year, he dropped the traditional Al Saʿud title of *imam* and adopted the secular title of *sultan* of Najd. His desire to incorporate al-Hijaz, forestalled by British intervention during the war, grew more transparent as the Hijazi kingdom's weaknesses became apparent. British concern was provoked by the first major Saudi conquest in al-Hijaz, i.e. the city of al-Taʾif in 1924, when the Ikhwan, ʿAbd al-ʿAziz's tribal army, were given free rein and civilian casualties were enormous.[3] Makkah surrendered without a struggle soon afterwards, al-Madinah followed in 1925, and Jiddah fell at the end of 1925 after a siege. With the flight of the Hashimi family, the Hijazi notables formally recognized ʿAbd al-ʿAziz on behalf of the people as their sovereign and he combined the titles of *sultan* of Najd and king of al-Hijaz. Ibn Saʿud continued to probe to the south and his sovereignty over ʿAsir, Najran, and the northern

Tihamah plain (Jazan) was recognized by his Yemeni rival, Imam Yahya, after Saudi victory in the Saudi–Yemeni War of 1934. Further expansion to the north was blocked by the British-backed Hashimi monarchies of Transjordan and Iraq, and similar obstacles were encountered on the Gulf littoral because of British protection for the shaykhdoms in Kuwait, Bahrain, Qatar, and Abu Dhabi. In 1932, ʿAbd al-ʿAziz adopted the Kingdom of Saudi Arabia as the official name of his country.

Subsequently, Ibn Saʿud turned his attention to transforming a fragile rule in Najd, based on tribal alliances, into a central state, and then to gradually integrating al-Hijaz with Najd. A principal step in this process had occurred in the late 1920s when the rebellion by the Ikhwan movement of tribal levies was finally put down. A long series of negotiations with the British over boundaries in eastern Arabia ended in stalemate when the Saudi king rejected the British "Red Line" and London rejected his "Riyadh Line." A third major concern was over the lack of finances. The signature bonus for the oil concession granted to Standard Oil of California (SOCAL) in 1933 was a major financial boon to Ibn Saʿud. Although oil was discovered at Dhahran in 1938 and production started in 1939, the first significant impact of oil came after World War II when exports began in large quantities. It was perhaps unfortunate that the rush of oil income should occur in Ibn Saʿud's declining years. Although attempts were made to create a more rational infrastructure, to expand the government and establish social welfare programs, much of the early wealth dissipated.

Financial problems continued after the death of ʿAbd al-ʿAziz in 1953 and the succession of his eldest son Saʿud. Another problem arose with the aggressiveness of the new revolutionary Arab regimes, which actively sought the downfall of all monarchies, including the Saudi one. The Arab radical threat was brought dramatically close to the kingdom when Egypt under the leadership of Jamal ʿAbd al-Nasir (Nasser) intervened in the Yemen civil war (1962–70). That war, however, ended with a compromise between the Yemeni royalists and republicans and saw the extension of Saudi support for the new republic.

However, King Saʿud's reign was also marked by an intense rivalry with his younger half-brother Faysal. Faysal had proven himself to be a capable viceroy of al-Hijaz under his father, but he accepted his father's decision to make Saʿud his successor. The exercise of power in the state shifted between King Saʿud and his prime minister, Prince Faysal, before the *ʿulama'* (religious leadership) and inner circle of the royal family stripped Saʿud of all but his title. Later Saʿud departed the country and Faysal was named as king in November 1964.

It was undoubtedly fortunate for Saudi Arabia that Faysal proved to be as strong and capable as his father. Faysal had proved himself as a military commander during the early years of conquest and then had gained considerable administrative experience as the semi-autonomous viceroy of al-Hijaz. In internal affairs, King Faysal had to establish the foundations of a political and economic infrastructure that could cope with the growing wealth of the country and expectations of its population. Under Faysal, Saudi Arabia's horizons seemed to expand beyond the Arabian Peninsula for the first time. The kingdom participated more fully in Arab councils and instituted an extensive aid program to fellow Arab states, as well as other Islamic and Third World recipients. Not surprisingly, Saudi Arabia was drawn into the arena of the Arab–Israeli conflict because of the "oil weapon," and Faysal adhered to the Arab oil boycott of 1973–4 despite his close relations with the United States. Saudi Arabia had been a founding member of the Organization of Petroleum Exporting Countries (OPEC) and, under Oil Minister Ahmad Zaki Yamani, the kingdom played an increasingly pivotal role in OPEC pricing decisions.

Many basic directions in Saudi development and policy had been set out by Faysal before his assassination in 1975. This was a considerable blessing for the future since his successor, half-brother Khalid, had a softer personality and less attention to detail and incisiveness of action. The country was also fortunate that Khalid's reign roughly coincided with the oil boom, when opportunities for many seemed limitless. Soon after another half-brother Fahd inherited the throne, the oil boom was replaced by recession and regional threats, including the Iranian Revolution, the Iran–Iraq War, and the Iraqi invasion of Kuwait, grew more intimidating. King Fahd's reign was hampered by his poor health in later years and his half-brother ʿAbdullah acted much as regent. ʿAbdullah succeeded to the throne upon King Fahd's death in 2005 and, assisted by buoyant oil prices, set out on an ambitious program of economic, social, and political development of the kingdom. He was succeeded upon his death in 2015 by another half-brother Salman, whose first years as king were characterized by the consolidation of power in the hands of his son and heir apparent, Muhammad b. Salman.

ORIGINS OF GOVERNMENT ADMINISTRATION AND FINANCIAL REQUIREMENTS

For 30 years, Imam ʿAbd al-ʿAziz was relentless in the expansion of his political realm until it assumed the borders it retains today. Although there is very little record for these formative years, there can be no doubt that ʿAbdullah al-Sulayman played at least some role in an administrative or financial capacity in many of these events. Indeed, his activity on behalf of his sovereign in some events is historically verifiable. One of these was the campaign against the Al Rashid, the dynasty that had ousted the Al Sa'ud from Riyadh, resulting in the occupation of Ha'il on 4 November 1921. 'Abd al-'Aziz chose not to enter Ha'il himself, realizing that the creation of a local administration might lessen the possibility of trouble in Ha'il. But he entrusted his promising young clerk, 'Abdullah al-Sulayman, with the task of traveling to Ha'il to inventory the *sultan*'s new possessions. Al-Sulayman spent some six months collecting information and organizing the collection of taxes and *zakat* (alms or wealth tax), before returning to Riyadh with 40,000 pounds (sterling presumably), camels, and cattle.[4]

This was the first mention of al-Sulayman's role in financial affairs but he subsequently assumed an increasingly greater control over the *sultan*'s treasury. One of his tasks was to secure the financing necessary for the military campaigns. This he did by acquiring loans for later campaigns from the leading merchant families, such as the Buqari and Dahlawi families of al-Hijaz. "They usually responded to his requests because they had faith in his word and they were usually repaid in full plus interest . . . and his word was his bond."[5]

Payment for service for those who took part in the campaigns did not come in wages but in a share of rewards from the campaign. The *sultan* reserved one fifth of the total amount for the *bayt al-mal* and the remainder was parceled out to the participants according to their role. The allocation of shares was made by the *sultan* but al-Sulayman would make the inventory of the numbers of men to be paid and how much each was to receive, and then arrange for the payments.[6]

Not long after the conquest of the Najd, incidents with the Kingdom of al-Hijaz began to escalate into war clouds by 1924. Sultan 'Abd al-'Aziz apparently placed Muhammad b. Shilhub of his Diwan in charge of organizing the Ikhwan for the campaign and relied upon al-Sulayman to collect the money for it from *zakat*, mainly in al-Ahsa', and then to distribute it among the Ikhwan.[7] This seems to have marked the beginning of al-Sulayman's long connection with al-Hijaz. Whether he replaced Hamad b. Faris, who had been in charge of the treasury (Bayt al-Mal) at the time of the tenure in the Diwan of Muhammad al-Sulayman, 'Abdullah's older brother,[8] is not known. Collecting revenues and arranging for supplies was of course a task for more than one man. In those early years, al-Sulayman relied on his younger brother Hamad, particularly in al-Qatif, as well as the al-Qusaybis in Bahrain, the al-Nafisah in Kuwait, and so on.[9]

The Najdi forces of Ikhwan swept into the Hijazi city of al-Ta'if in August 1924 and, two months later, King Husayn abdicated and left for al-'Aqabah (in present-day Jordan). He was succeeded by his son 'Ali but Saudi forces marched into Makkah less than a week later. Al-Sulayman played a quiet role in these events. In Rabiʿ al-Thani 1343 (October–November 1924), the *sultan* dispatched al-Sulayman as part of a delegation with Hafiz Wahbah and Dr. ʿAbdullah al-Damluji to al-Hijaz to either reassure the population of the *sultan*'s good intentions or to prepare for Ibn Saʿud's further campaign.[10] The group apparently was not present in al-Ta'if during or after its capture. Instead, al-Sulayman and Muhammad b. Shilhub were generally with the *sultan* handling the flow of money and supplies. However, on Ibn Saʿud's orders, the group (comprised of Wahbah, al-Damluji, al-Sulayman, and possibly Muhammad b. Shilhub) were amongst the first to enter Makkah after its capture—five days before Ibn Saʿud entered it[11]—in large part to reassure the population and to provide a check on the Ikhwan.

In Makkah, the members of the committee were assigned different tasks in connection with the governing of al-Hijaz. Wahbah was given responsibility for cultural and educational affairs (later becoming the first director of education), Damluji handled political affairs and relations with Western countries (and was later to become an under-secretary for foreign affairs), while ʿAbdullah al-Sulayman was put in charge of economic and social affairs, and daily activities inside Makkah. His role was also to once again inventory the property in the city, as he had done in Ha'il. At the same time, he was given many other tasks, such as collecting information, arranging for propaganda, and supervising conveyancing and transportation.[12]

Arranging for the supply of water and food from Makkah to the Najd army besieging Jiddah was another priority.[13] Ibn Saʿud repeatedly ordered al-Sulayman to send more supplies and the latter hit upon the idea of purchasing an entire caravan on its way to Makkah, paying full value for the caravan and for its expected profits, sending it to the Ikhwan at al-Raghamah outside Jiddah. He also instructed his men to spread the word around about the caravan and to say that more caravans were on the way.[14] Later, as Ibn Saʿud called for his son Prince Faysal to bring reinforcements from Riyadh, al-Sulayman found it necessary to purchase additional supplies from merchants he knew, agreeing to a reasonable profit.[15]

The surrender of Jiddah was peacefully achieved with the help of the British consul in the city. King ʿAli was permitted to leave with his possessions aboard a British warship on 22 December. The following afternoon, Sultan ʿAbd al-ʿAziz rode into the town at the head of his forces and was introduced to his new subjects at a reception.[16]

The situation in the newly added domains in the early months, however, was still not secure. The acting British consul for Jiddah reported in April that complaints were on the rise in al-Hijaz. The *hajj* was expected to be small because Persia had forbidden its pilgrims from attending and there were rumors that Egypt would not be sending the *mahmal* (the ornamental litter that the Egyptian delegation used to carry the *kiswah*—the covering for the Ka'bah inside the Great Mosque of Makkah, which was replaced annually—to each *hajj*). The complaints, he went on to say, "would appear to be admission of incapability to deal with circumstances. Whole trouble is undoubtedly lack of capable administrators to assist Sultan ...".[17]

The *hajj* in June and July 1926—the first under the new administration—took place with only one major hitch, even though the Saudi government, preoccupied with preparations for the Muslim Conference at Makkah, took no new steps for the management of the pilgrims, and many practices were prevented by zealots. In an unfortunate accident, a number of pilgrims were trampled by bedouin camels and donkeys at Mina and 'Arafat, however. A positive development, though, was the absence of any attacks on the caravan routes or the roads between Jiddah, Makkah, and al-Madinah, for the first time in living memory.[18]

At the same time, however, the *hajj* was marred by an incident involving the *mahmal*. As it was being carried from Makkah to 'Arafat, a group of Wahhabis intercepted it and began shouting that it was idolatrous and throwing stones. The accompanying escort opened fire and killed about 25 Wahhabis. Fortunately, Ibn Sa'ud was nearby and he sent Prince Faysal to calm the people, and later appeared himself. But this was followed by a second incident on the *mahmal*'s return to Makkah. A number of Wahhabis objected to its usual placement inside the Great Mosque and, as a result, upon the *mahmal*'s return to Jiddah, it was taken directly back to Egypt and not to al-Madinah. As a result, most of the funds that had been brought with it for distribution among the poor and for charitable works went back to Egypt with it.[19] In protest, Ibn Sa'ud refused to accept the *mahmal* during the 1346/1927 *hajj*, presumably because the Egyptians insisted on retaining their own armed guard for it amid fears that fanatical Wahhabis might attack it again.[20] The alienation caused by this incident continued to mar official relations between Egypt and Saudi Arabia until the latter half of the 1930s.[21]

As a consequence of the *mahmal* incident, it was announced in mid-1927 (Muharram 1346H) that al-Sulayman had been directed to establish a weaving factory and school in Makkah. Indian weavers would be used to create the *kiswah*, which would no longer be furnished by Egypt.[22] The *kiswah* factory was noted as in operation by 1929,[23] but the first *kiswah*, using materials imported from India, was produced at the end of 1346H (early 1928).[24]

The factory was not without controversy. The cost of the *kiswah* in 1928 was unexpectedly high and the scheme advanced to make *dhurri*s (Indian carpets) at the factory was unprofitable. In addition, the manager for it alienated all the Indian workers who left en masse.[25] The *kiswah* for the 1933 *hajj* was made by Indian weavers in Makkah after having been imported from Germany the previous year.[26] One result of the 1936 Egyptian–Saudi treaty was an agreement that Egypt would resume providing the *kiswah* and the *mahmal*.[27]

After the fall of Jiddah and ʿAbd al-ʿAziz had become the new king of al-Hijaz, an arrangement was reached whereby he took over responsibility for the military control and security of al-Hijaz, for which the people of al-Hijaz were to subscribe £160,000 per annum for his use in this regard. This amount was in addition to the £60,000 he was to receive as king of al-Hijaz and commander-in-chief of the Armed Forces.[28] Gradually, the Najdi troops were withdrawn from al-Hijaz and a new standing army of Hijazis, intended to reach 5000, was in the process of formation by September 1926.[29]

Ibn Saʿud's financial problems did not abate, however. Despite his official income as ruler of al-Hijaz, his expenses continued to escalate. It was estimated that additional costs of hosting delegates to the international Islamic Conference, held in Makkah during the 1926 *hajj*, cost him £20,000. Another £40,000 went to pay for a new water condenser for Jiddah, coal, motor cars, and new coinage. This was in addition to his subsidies to the tribes. As a consequence, all the income from the *hajj* was expended by the end of that event. The king necessarily resorted to soliciting loans from prominent Jiddah merchants, hoping to raise £40,000 but being offered only £15,000 because the *hajj* had not been very profitable.[30] During a visit to Jiddah later in the year, he asked the Jiddah merchants for another loan of £25,000 but there was resistance as it seemed the previous loan of £13,000 had not been repaid.[31] The troubles with the Ikhwan in Najd constituted another drain on the king's resources. In early 1928, £40,000 was sent from al-Hijaz to Riyadh with the expectation that the sum would be covered by soon-to-be-received *hajj* revenues.[32]

Another development shortly after the takeover of al-Hijaz involved a new distribution of posts in the Hijazi government (which was relatively sophisticated compared to the rudimentary and tribally oriented administration in Najd). ʿAbdullah al-Sulayman was said to have been appointed head of the Diwan (*raʾis al-diwan*), and gradually enlarged the scope of his activities to include taking charge of all household, bedouin, and financial affairs. At first, there seemed to be a division of labor: al-Sulayman held the financial reins for al-Hijaz while Muhammad b. Shilhub served as something of a counterpart in Najd.[33] By 1929, the British head of mission in Jiddah reported that al-Sulayman's "financial control since last autumn has been absolute. He seizes every penny that enters revenue-earning departments, and his omnipotence in Hejaz is unchallenged except perhaps by Fuad Hamza. He travels with a larger retinue and in greater state than Ibn Saud himself."[34]

Al-Sulayman's response to these charges that he was ostentatious for keeping such a large retinue was clear and forthright.

> I know that people say that I have an armed force and army of slaves. This is true. Everyone knows it. And everyone who knows me knows for what end did I create and put this army and slaves and what they do; they take care of things that no one else is able to do it. Some time they work as carriers, other times they work as water fetchers, or a mobile unit of guards, or correspondents coming and going. This matter is well known. At any given time you see some of them traveling to Najd, al-Madinah, Ha'il, al-Jawf, Yemen, and sometime they will all be on a trip at one time to one or all of these directions on urgent and important missions. All these matters are under my responsibility, and I am liable for any shortcoming or mistakes they make. I should be the one to be blamed for that. If you would like to relieve me of these responsibilities, then I would be happy starting from today to take only one servant to help me. I can actually take care of myself without him. I do not even need one. As for slaves, those who say I have slaves are delusional. If you ask the slaves I have about the way in which they became my slaves, you will find that all of them came from his excellency the king, save one or two who came from the family of the king. They are all property of the king and at the same time at his service, and serving his interest—none of them is serving my personal interest. I have nothing to put them to use for. You will find that some of them are drivers of cars that go back and forth carrying government's duties. Those who can't carry such duties, do other missions for the government.[35]

Al-Sulayman's center of operations shifted to al-Hijaz from the beginning of Saudi rule. The scope of his duties included financial tasks but were not limited to that arena, even in early years. Ibn Saʿud replaced Sharif Sharaf Rida, who had handled the *sultan*'s financial affairs after incorporation of al-Hijaz, with al-Sulayman in 1346/1927.[36] A few years later, in 1349/1930–1, al-Sulayman had been entrusted with the financial revenues of al-Hijaz and established an office to administer the province's finances. His success in this endeavor led Ibn Saʿud to entrust him with control of the entire country's finances.[37] In addition, his scope of control included defense and the *hajj* besides finance and he was regarded by the British as the most important man in the administration.

Part of the reason for the expansion of al-Sulayman's duties was the greater complexity of al-Hijaz. In Najd, military campaigns were organized more on a tribal level: when the ruler called for assistance, the tribes responded. In al-Hijaz, there was a standing army that required garrisons and armaments. In addition, the urban environment required policing amongst different segments of the population, including minorities that did not exist in Najd. Because the situation was more complicated, al-Sulayman was entrusted with additional responsibilities beyond finance.[38] Some of these involved the Saudi–Yemeni War of 1934 when al-Sulayman acted as the intermediary in Jiddah between the British and the king and subsequently organized the administration of al-Hudaydah in Yemen after Saudi forces occupied it temporarily.

PART I

FINANCES AND OIL BEFORE WORLD WAR II

CHAPTER 2

The Organization of State Finances

CONTROL OF THE TREASURY IN THE EARLY 1920s

One of the primary priorities of Ibn Saʿud in his first years of rule was to expand his financial base in order to pay for his military campaigns. As his political affairs grew more complex, so did his requirements for a financial administration, even though it was necessarily primitive in the early years. His assumption of responsibility for al-Hijaz in the mid-1920s brought him no financial relief. The region's finances depended on revenues from the *hajj* and these had been meager. Although he promised to keep the existing administration intact, he was forced at the end of 1926 to cut the salaries of customs and mechanical workshop employees by 50 percent.[1]

He instituted a blockade of Kuwait in 1920 and in May of that year he registered his objections to the ruler of Bahrain in regard to jurisdiction over his subjects.[2] These not only constituted efforts to make himself an independent sovereign but were also aimed at the establishment of a financial base for the emerging state. Prior to the al-ʿUqayr agreement—which established boundaries between Najd, Kuwait, and Iraq—Ibn Saʿud had few substantial sources of regular revenue and was dependent on the goodwill of Kuwait and Bahrain, both of which exacted a toll on both imports to and exports from his territories. The blockade imposed on Kuwait by the Najdi ruler appears to have originated in his attempt to tap into these revenues on the one hand and, on the other hand, to fashion a tool that he could use to make his own subjects more dependent on him. Though there had always been comparatively wealthy merchants operating on the mainland, these had tended to make their bases in the Gulf shaykhdoms or farther afield in India. Apart from exports of dates and animals, their trade consisted of importing the basic stuffs of life—such as rice, oil, and coffee—onto the mainland. It was difficult for Ibn Saʿud's treasury to lean too heavily on these sources of revenue without provoking hostility and evasion. He thus continued to depend on the British subsidy first paid during the war.

Thus, from the very beginning of his reign, Ibn Sa'ud found that finances were very thin. As a consequence of his penury, he placed considerable reliance on Britain to help him out. His and British interests coincided at the 1921 al-'Uqayr Conference. The agreement between Ibn Sa'ud and Sir Percy Cox gave the Al Sa'ud leader British recognition, established his boundaries with Iraq and Kuwait, and provided him with a subsidy. Cox wrote to 'Abd al-'Aziz detailing the provisions of the 'Uqayr Agreement and informing him that the subsidy of £5000 per month would be continued but that in view of Ibn Sa'ud's special hardship, an additional gift of £20,000 would be made in addition to the subsidy. By November, however, the subsidy was three months in arrears and the cash gift still had not been paid. Ibn Sa'ud had borrowed money on the basis of the British promise, which enabled him to embark on the very expensive siege of Ha'il. He was pressing Cox hard for the money and had sent Dr. Thomas Mann, his personal physician, to Baghdad as his emissary. Cox was startled to learn that the Government of India intended to pay the subsidy at the sovereign equivalent of £5000 and £20,000, a sum considerably below the customary 5000 sovereigns. This, Cox thought, was unexpected and unfair. It was also the first example of the currency confusion that was to plague so many of Saudi Arabia's financial transactions.[3]

CONTROL OF FINANCES IN AL-HIJAZ AND THE DIRECTORATE FROM 1927

It was during the period of expansion across Arabia in the first half of the 1920s that 'Abdullah al-Sulayman began to assume an increasing role in the control and administration of Ibn Sa'ud's finances. At some point after the absorption of al-Hijaz, Ibn Sa'ud gave him the portfolio for financial affairs as successor to Sharif Sharaf Rida.[4] When the traditional *bayt al-mal* or treasury in Makkah was reorganized in 1346/1927 as the Directorate of Finance (*mudiriyat al-maliyah*), al-Sulayman was named general deputy for finance (*mudir 'amm li-maliyah*).[5] From a modest start in administering the treasury in Najd to being the focus of administration in al-Hijaz, 'Abdullah al-Sulayman gradually expanded his authority over all financial matters in the kingdom. A British biographical sketch in 1933 noted that he "Continues to be supreme in the financial administration and has his finger in many other pies, being in effect Comptroller of the Privy Purse, Grand Master of Ordnance, Quarter-Master-General on occasion, general manager of the King's establishment of slaves and pilgrimage-organiser."[6] The report went on to add that he was "Probably entirely faithful to the King, whose needs he supplies at the expense of others having demands on the Treasury. A man of rather mean appearance, but emphatically a 'live wire.' Ready and energetic in conversation and full of ideas about development."[7]

The new General Directorate of Finance (*mudiriyat al-maliyah al-ʿammah*) was established in Makkah on 17 Rabiʿ al-Akhir 1346/12 October 1927 with al-Sulayman as its head. The equivalent directorate in Riyadh was transferred to his control sometime after that.[8] The British legation in Jiddah recognized that al-Sulayman was the director-general of finance in mid-1928, and it reported that he "has now full power, subject to the Council's sanction, in all matters of finance. No expenditure may now be incurred without his sanction; even municipal disbursements are previously submitted to him."[9]

The dire financial straits of the new kingdom had begun at least in 1923 when the British subsidy (paid since 1917) ceased. Upon Ibn Saʿud's acclamation as king of al-Hijaz in 1926, he was to receive £140,000 gold annually from al-Hijaz for providing the military forces of the country and assuring the security of the roads. In addition, as king, he was granted an annual revenue of £60,000, roughly the same amount as the British subsidy had been.[10] Al-Hijaz's ability to pay this depended on sufficient *hajj* income. This went well for 1927 and 1928 but the war in Najd against the rebellious Ikhwan ate up income and Ibn Saʿud was forced to resort to raising new taxes and paying bills by drafts on customs revenues. A report at the end of 1928 remarked that every penny raised by the government in al-Hijaz went to Riyadh and "Government bills are either left unpaid or met in unwelcome rials."[11]

As the global financial situation worsened in the 1930s, *hajj* traffic and receipts fell precipitously. In al-Hijaz, financial arrangements included responsibility for customs and the taxes on pilgrims, as well as other sources of revenue such as postal services.[12] As noted above, the British recognized that al-Sulayman had secured full financial control by 1928[13] and it was noted that "Finance, such as it is, is completely in hands of Sheikh Abdullah Suleiman."[14] The more developed administrative structure in al-Hijaz had included a Department of Finance in Makkah and a Secretariat of Finance in Jiddah, which al-Sulayman inherited. The arrangement was formally organized into the General Finance Department in 1346/1927.[15]

Amongst the department's requirements was wrangling loans to the state from various merchants. These were principally from al-Hijaz, although there were a few from Najd and al-Ahsaʾ Province. In addition, the government procured loans from the long-standing British commercial firm in Jiddah, Gellatly, Hankey (more commonly known as Gellatly's). The company was also prevailed upon to provide condenser plants for the water supplies, motor cars and trucks, silver coinage, clothing, and furnishings for the royal palace.[16]

The dire straits continued for years. In July 1929, the continuation of trouble with the Ikhwan required the King to maintain a large armed force, which resulted in a constant drain on the treasury. The head of finance in Jiddah was under instructions to remit daily the receipts of various government offices in Jiddah to 'Abdullah al-Sulayman in Makkah. The government owed money widely, had difficulty in paying its outstanding debts, and collected customs duties well in advance. In an effort to increase revenues, duties were raised on tobacco, motor cars and spare parts, benzine, and Persian carpets and rugs.[17] In October, the tribes around al-Ta'if and elsewhere in al-Hijaz were encouraged to produce £60,000 to help tide the government over before the *hajj*.[18]

CONTROLLER OF NATIONAL FINANCES AND THE FINANCIAL AUTHORITY (AL-WIKALAH) (1927–9)

Some of the fundamental duties of the financial administrator in the early years of the Third Saudi State revolved around such tasks as collecting *zakat* in the form of livestock, crops, and commercial offerings and administering the *awqaf*. Even more important was the securing of the fifth of the spoils of war, as well as related tributes. On the expense side of the ledger, the officer would have to buy gifts and keep them ready for the ruler to award, acquire supplies and weapons, and keep track of subsidies. He would be responsible for the upkeep of government buildings and property. In addition, he would be in charge of distributing the *zakat* to the poor, disabled, widows, mosque *imams* (prayer leaders and caretakers), and *mu'adhdhin* (prayer-callers).[19] After the unification of al-Hijaz, these tasks fell to 'Abdullah al-Sulayman.

The growing complexity of financial requirements and administration in the confederation of al-Hijaz and Najd led to the reorganization of finances into a *wikalah* or authority or agency in 1348/1928 and al-Sulayman was retitled the *wakil*, a term normally translated in more recent years as under-secretary or deputy (to a minister). To help organize the agency, the king brought in a Dutch expert, M. Van Leeuwen, as a financial consultant. The latter, however, was in ill health during his sojourn and therefore could contribute little help to the *wakil*.[20]

The year 1348 (1929–30) also witnessed the first attempt to produce a state budget, although it was not completed until 1349. Revenue and expenditure were estimated to be in balance at 10 million *riyal*s, although there was no breakdown of sources of revenue. Principal items of expenditure in the budget included (all figures in *qurush*, 10 of which were equal to one *riyal*): allowances to royal family (6.6 million); debt service (16.5 million); the princes, royal *diwan* (court), palaces, and treasury employees (12.65 million); border guards (3.85 million), al-Hijaz share of defense budget (22 million); communications, transportation, and equipment (11 million); the presidency of the judiciary and the courts (1.13 million), the office of the viceroy and local administration (3.15 million); the Majlis al-Shura and administrative council (578,000); the Ministry of Foreign Affairs (1.5 million); public health and quarantine (2.7 million); water purification (1.4 million); public education (1.7 million); tax administration (1.3 million); finance offices (2.3 million); public security (10.4 million); government press (161,000), religious guidance groups (165,000), diverse salaries (988,000), post, telephone, and telegraph (4.2 million); and the Grand Mosque and *awqaf* (religious endowments) (2 million). However, the lack of a cadre of competent officials to carry out the planned expenditures meant that the budget was little more than an abstract exercise.[21]

The original Directorate of Finance initially consisted of the *bayt al-mal* treasuries of Makkah, al-Madinah, and the other major centers of al-Hijaz. It presided over finance agents (trustees) of small towns and villages in al-Hijaz, as well as the accountants or controllers for the diverse finance and tax collection divisions. Originally, the financial office in Jiddah, responsible for the collection of customs duties and the *hajj* tax, did not fall under the General Directorate of Finance. In 1348/1929–30, Jiddah was combined with the General Directorate and the new entity was named the General Finance Authority (*wikalat al-maliyah al-'ammah*); the finance directorate of al-Ahsa' was incorporated soon afterwards.

In the initial stage, the directorate consisted of three divisions (*idarat*): ① the general office, which was in charge of all the areas in al-Hijaz; ② a special office in Makkah; and ③ the public accounting office. One of the first tasks of the new directorate was to establish a committee to formulate regulations for public finance.[22] Another contemporary source contends that the three divisions of the authority consisted of: the general directorate (which was in charge of the policy section), the accounts section, and a finance and capital section.[23] The Ottomans had organized customs collection in various ports of the Red Sea under a central Supervisory Office of Fees (*nadhirat 'ummum al-rusum*) based in Jiddah. This was included in the new Finance Authority in 1346/1927 and a royal decree in 1347 instituted a sweeping organization of specific duties. This was later modified but the system remained in use until the mid-1380s/2000s.[24]

The burden of making sense of the nascent system lay squarely on 'Abdullah al-Sulayman. He clearly found it frustrating as he wrote to his brother (and deputy) Hamad, while outlining his thoughts on how his office should be conducted:

> Things have been worsening year after year. The formations and arrangements, and changing of posts, and every act we do bring no benefit since people have gotten used to this and no longer care about it or even draws their attention. The reason for this is because all the changes and formation or reorganizations were not based on the foundations that other world governments follow. It seems that we have brought a new invention as if no one has thought of the excellent ideas we arrived at! This is indeed the source of error. There is no doubt that others and those who come before us have experienced administrative requirements and have done what we have done. And every time they did something and found it useless, they abandoned it and replaced it with new procedures until they finally arrived at the present way of managing their affairs in all countries. This has become the norm of all countries; where governance issues are running in normal order, proceeding in such exactitude as does a clock.... In every country, administrative procedures are followed where positions and their duties are clarified; where there are clear compensation and retribution procedures. There are ministries, where each is headed by a minister, appointed by the ruler. A competent minister is given the position with the power to carry out his mission. Consequently, he will be responsible for everything that happens with regard to that position.... All the matters pertaining to his ministry should be connected to him. He should have complete freedom of action to appoint or dismiss subordinates, carry out investigations, and promote or demote according to internal regulations.... He should be held accountable to the law under which he can be judged or penalized if necessary. Ministries should be run with the full knowledge of their ministers and under their direct command.[25]

Part of the growing complexity of management of the country's finances derived from the difficulties entailed by the use of several currencies in the country that constantly varied in their exchange rates. The government sought to concentrate on silver *riyal*s, evolved from the older Ottoman *riyal* or *majidiyah*. Shortly after the unification of al-Hijaz in the kingdom in late 1926, Gellatly's shipped an order of 140 boxes of currency to Saudi Arabia. The shipment included one million half piaster coins and one-half million quarter piaster coins.[26] However, the supply of silver coins was not enough and Gellatly's and Philby were invited in June to tender for the supply by the Royal Mint of a further 200,000 *majidiyah*s, 50,000 half *majidiyah*s, and 100,000 quarter *majidiyah*s.[27]

A few months later, it became known that a new silver coinage, to complement the gold sovereign, was to be introduced to replace the old Ottoman *majidiyah*.[28] The first new coins to be introduced into al-Hijaz by the king were the nickel coins struck at the (British) Royal Mint in 1926. The profit from the sale of these coins to the public, through the money changers, was sufficient to redeem the older Ottoman nickel coins at half their face value. Still, Turkish dollars and silver piasters remained in circulation while Maria Theresa dollars were not legal tender at the time of Ibn Saʿud's occupation.[29] The new "Najdi–Hijazi Currency System" was approved by royal decree on

4 January 1928. The new Arab *riyal* was to have the same value as the previous Ottoman *riyal*, as well as the same size, weight, and silver gauge. Currency exchange firms were envisioned to distribute the new *riyal*s in Makkah, Jiddah, al-Madinah, Yanbuʿ, al-Wajh, al-Lith, and Rabigh, and they were required to make it known that they would exchange the *riyal*s for gold, silver, or nickel currency according to the official exchange rates.[30]

By early 1928, the new coins struck by the Mint in Birmingham were put into circulation. Known at first as "Arab" or "Saudi" dollars, they were available in dollar, half-dollar, quarter-dollar, and piaster denominations, and their exchange rate was fixed at 10 dollars or 220 piasters to the pound sterling (110 piasters in the original decree). It was hoped that they would prove adequate during the *hajj* and thus eliminate exchange-rate pressure on silver currency.[31]

The difficulties in maintaining the envisaged exchange rate were exposed not long after the initial issue and the Netherlands Trading Society (in effect the only bank in the country), at the request of the government, spent £5000 in gold in an ineffective attempt to bolster confidence in the new currency.[32] The government's answer was to establish a number of government "banks"—in actuality, money changers—to buy silver and nickel coins, thus making the exchange rate stable and rendering the practice of hoarding for profit pointless.[33] This was only a temporary palliative and the worldwide increase in the value of gold in 1931, compounded by British abandonment of the gold standard, made any attempt to tie the *riyal* to gold impractical. Over the next few years, the *riyal*'s value fluctuated between 18 and 24 to the gold pound.[34]

The mixture of currencies was further muddled in 1935 when the government imported about two million Indian rupees for use in Najd. The idea apparently was to replace the Maria Theresa dollars with rupees, which had a fixed exchange rate vis-à-vis sterling. At the same time, the Saudi *riyal* continued to be used mostly in al-Hijaz.[35] Najdi resistance to the *riyal* derived from the fact that it was not accepted in Iraq, Kuwait, or Bahrain, the places with which Najd traded, whereas the rupee was widely used.[36]

Another government expense was incurred in 1929 when the kingdom purchased a number of airplanes and the services of pilots and mechanics to be used against the Ikhwan.[37] These airplanes were delivered in 1929 and the kingdom, although strapped for cash, promptly paid off the entire cost of about £15,000.[38]

Gradually during this early period, administrative improvements were introduced, at least on paper. In early 1931, a royal decree announced the formation of an initial "council of ministers." The Majlis al-Wukalaʾ was composed of the president of the council (*raʾis al-majlis*), the under-secretary for foreign affairs (*wakil al-kharijiyah*), the head of the Finance Department (*wakil al-maliyah*), and the vice president of the Legislative Assembly (*wakil al-shuri*). The decree also mentioned that the president of the council was to direct the viceroy's office (*niyabat al-'ammah*) as well as the Ministries of Interior (*wizarat al-dakhiliyah*) and Foreign Affairs (*wizarat al-kharijiyah*), and also the Military Department (*al-'askariyah*). This was the first mention of a Ministry of the Interior, which the decree declared would be the new name of the viceroy's office and that it would be charged with supervising the departments of health, education, posts and telegraphs, quarantine, central police, *shari'ah* (Islamic law) courts, and the municipalities.[39]

As was noted much later, with the unification of al-Hijaz, "three assistants of King 'Abd al-'Aziz ran the country in its beginnings. These three intelligent men who had special leadership skills were ① the heir apparent, Prince Sa'ud; ② Prince Faysal, who was the representative of King 'Abd al-'Aziz; and ③ Shaykh 'Abdullah al-Sulayman, who was the minister of finance in addition to public works, the *hajj*, defense, and royal affairs. And I swear that these multiple responsibilities are equal to six ministries in our current day, which is a strong piece of evidence for the regard that the king held for 'Abdullah al-Sulayman."[40]

ESTABLISHMENT OF THE MINISTRY OF FINANCE (1932)

The central importance of the growing country's financial administration put the authority of 'Abdullah al-Sulayman in a position of key importance. This was recognized in the 1931 announcement that he would serve as *wakil* (under-secretary) for finance, as one of four *wakil*s in a Majlis al-Wukala'. The other *wakil*s were of foreign affairs, interior, and legislation, all under the presidency of the viceroy, Prince Faysal. This announcement was made in the context of a larger description of the accomplishments of the ruler, Ibn Sa'ud, and the measures he had taken to reform his government. He also announced the creation of a budget (although no details were forthcoming), more concerted action to collect claims and to pay off liabilities, and the trimming of the allowances of various organs of government. In particular, he announced that revenues would be concentrated in a single administration, to be called the General Treasury (*al-sanduq al-'umumi*).[41] Just before that, an announcement was made that a Reorganization Committee had studied the various departments of government and reduced their budgets. Furthermore, the office of chief treasurer was created and his department established in Jiddah.[42]

The financial apparatus of the state was reorganized as the Ministry of Finance in 1351/1932 and 'Abdullah al-Sulayman was named as minister of finance, with his brother Hamad as deputy minister. Although officially declared the Ministry of Finance, its terms of reference went far beyond just finance. Responsibility was held for supply, *hajj*, agriculture, public works, transportation, and minerals, amongst other duties.[43] The decree establishing the ministry and the general treasury sought to regulate public spending by dividing it into four categories: salaries of government employees, the ruler's *diwan* (court), current expenses, and extraordinary expenses. It also divided the ministry into three divisions of administration, public accounts, and financial audit.[44] In addition, the writ of the ministry was extended to the entire country.[45] In 1931, it was said that, in addition to the viceroy, Prince Faysal, the two most important officials in al-Hijaz were "Sheikh Abdullah Suleiman, who is strong, and Fuad Bey Hamza, who is active and industrious."[46] Yet even in 1934, a visitor reported that "The Minister of Finance, 'Abdullah Sulaiman, in a land without banks or safes, kept the cash, mostly in English and Turkish gold pieces, in person with his guards."[47]

By the time the ministry was established in 1932–3, the work of the earlier authority had been further subdivided into 13 offices, including: the Minister's Office; the Office of the Under-Secretary of State for Financial Affairs; Directorate-General; Finance Office; Correspondence Office; General Accounts; Local Accounts; General Fund; Transport (motor and animal); Postal Affairs; Directorate of Postage and Currency Printing; Accommodation and Associated Accounting; and Inspectorate.[48] While the fledgling ministry was one of the most important institutions in the country, "A small wooden house served as the office and headquarters of the Finance Minister" in Nazlah, outside Jiddah, where the Khazam Palace was later built.[49] Ministry of Finance offices and customs houses were also established at al-Ahsa' in the east and at Jazan in the south.[50]

Although comprehensive budgets were long in coming, *Umm al-Qura* published on 12 June 1931 a number of small budgets for jurisdictions in Makkah and Jiddah and some provincial governorates. Their publication was among a list of decisions taken by the Legislative Council and Philby reported that there had been tension between the council and ʿAbdullah al-Sulayman over his responsibility directly to the king.[51] A similar debate emerged at the "National Conference" convened during 2–11 June 1931, consisting of elected town notables and representatives of the *ʿulama'*.[52]

When Ibn Saʿud moved back to Riyadh after a long stay in al-Hijaz in 1930–1, al-Sulayman assumed more responsibility for operations in al-Hijaz, which apparently encompassed managing government income and expenditure autonomously. His position in the administration of al-Hijaz was dominant. He even went so far as to appropriate private supplies of benzine when required for operations against the *imam* of Yemen. But increased responsibilities meant increased headaches. Given the shortage of funds throughout the country, the government was pressed to present small payments in goods rather than cash.[53] The only major payment was £500 presented to the Eastern Telegraph Company, even though that left more than £2500 unpaid.[54] Philby vouchsafed that he had staked all his economic future on King ʿAbd al-ʿAziz and that he was owed some £50,000 in total.[55] The Post and Telegraph Department was starved of funds and mail between Jiddah, Makkah, and al-Taʾif was being carried by donkeys.[56]

The dismal state of the economy, combined with the failure to pay the Najdi garrison in Jiddah and the decline of the *riyal* vis-à-vis the pound, increased tensions. Al-Sulayman had no choice but to continue pressing for loans and cutting corners everywhere. He made his way to Riyadh to make his case for further stringent measures before the king.[57] Several weeks later, there was still no word on a decision by the king and al-Sulayman issued orders from Riyadh to all finance officials in al-Hijaz to stop all payments.[58] In the midst of this, a contract was arranged with the Soviet Union to supply £30,000 worth of benzine at a very low price and then sell it on behalf of the government in al-Hijaz at the regular market price, resulting in a 200 percent profit that helped sustain government accounts.[59]

To recapitulate, a royal decree on 22 August 1932 had elevated the Wikalat al-Maliyah to a full ministry. In this connection ʿAbdullah al-Sulayman had been raised to minister (*wazir*) and his brother Hamad was named *wakil* (under-secretary or deputy minister).[60] In the following year, the British minister in Jiddah reported that "The attack made on his position in 1931 was so unsuccessful that the King not only reinstated him but conferred on him last year the title of Wazir, which had previously been held only by the Amir. Sheikh 'Abdullah ... is ... very useful to Ibn Sa'ud. . . ."[61] The Ministry of Finance, along with the Ministry of Foreign Affairs, transferred its headquarters from Jiddah to Makkah in early October 1937.[62]

Overall, al-Sulayman seemed to be more of a field manager than he was a desk-bound administrator. In addition to his frequent commutes between Makkah, Jiddah, and al-Taʾif, he was frequently called upon to travel to Riyadh when the king was in residence there. Furthermore, as his responsibilities covered the entire country, he traveled to al-Ahsaʾ region frequently, mostly for work unconnected with the oil concession. For example, in November 1936, he visited al-ʿUqayr, al-Khubar, and al-Qatif, where he removed the duties on dates and fruits and exempted al-Ahsaʾ from the *jihad* tax.[63] By the mid-1930s, he was assisted in his duties by ʿAbdullah al-Najawi, in charge of the Riyadh office, Salim al-Tawil in al-Ahsaʾ, Muhammad Surur al-Sabban in Makkah, ʿAbdullah al-Saʿd Ibrahim al-Juffali, and others.[64]

A chart of Saudi Arabian government organization in 1939 produced by the California Arabian Standard Oil Company (which held the oil concession in al-Ahsaʾ; see Chapter 3) diagramed the Ministry of Finance as in Table 2.1.

TABLE 2.1 ORGANIZATION OF THE MINISTRY OF FINANCE (1939).

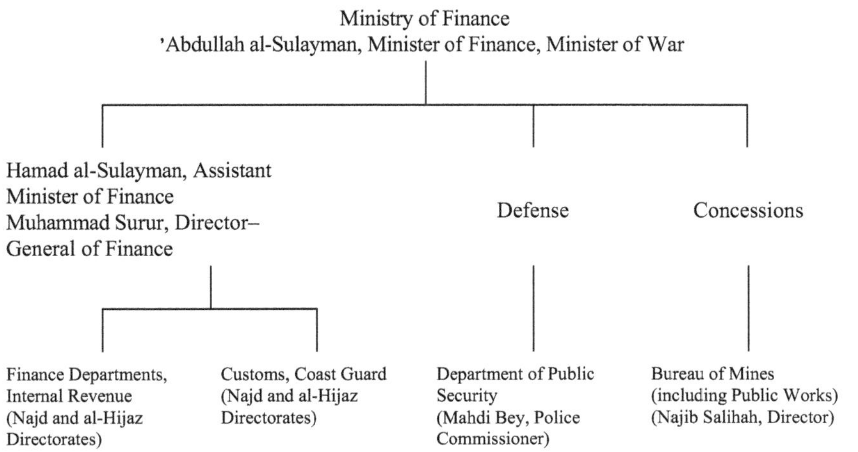

Notably, the chart showed that the Ministry of Finance reported directly to the king while the Ministry of Foreign Affairs reported to the Council of Ministers. That council was believed to be comprised of ʿAbdullah al-Sulayman, Yusuf Yasin, Head of the Political Bureau, Khalid Bey Gargani, Adviser, and Khalid al-Hakim, Adviser.[65]

ADMINISTERING FINANCES DURING THE GREAT DEPRESSION

The Great Depression of the 1930s produced as many serious financial difficulties for the fledgling state as it did for the world in general. The country's principal source of income had been the *hajj* and the numbers of pilgrims shrank as the depression took hold, as Table 2.2 shows. The subsequent outbreak of World War II served to prolong the dire situation and it took until the late 1940s for the number of overseas pilgrims recover to the levels of the 1920s.

A poor year for the *hajj* in 1929 was repeated in 1930, thus extending the precariousness of government finances. Jiddah merchants were pressured to provide loans through drafts issued on future customs revenues. In addition, the governor of Jiddah was ordered to hand over £5000 and the Jiddah representative of the Ministry of Finance was put on notice that a sum of £80,000 would be required immediately after the *hajj*.[66] By the end of November, Ibn Saʿud's cash reserve, estimated at £100,000 at the beginning of the year, had evaporated, the government owed over £30,000 to the Government of India for arms used against the Ikhwan rebellion, £4000 to the

TABLE 2.2 OVERSEAS PARTICIPANTS IN THE *HAJJ* (1926–51).

Year	*Number of Overseas Pilgrims*	*Source*
1926	100,000 +	FO/371/11442
1927	c.240,000 total; 132,109 overseas	FO/371/12250
		FO/371/20063
1928	c.200,000 total	FO/371/13010
1929	82,000 by sea +20 percent of previous year from the interior	FO/371/14456
1930	84,821 overseas	FO/371/20063
1931	c.42,000 overseas	FO/371/20063
1932	29,065 overseas	FO/371/16857
1933	20,705 overseas	FO/371/17932
1934	25,291 overseas	FO/371/17932;
		FO/371/19001
1935	33,898 overseas	FO/371/19002
1936	33,752 overseas; 34,252 foreign arrivals	FO/371/20843
		FO/371/20055
1937	c.80,000 total; 49,957 overseas	FO/371/21908
1938	63,788 overseas	FO/371/23267
1939	57,602 overseas	FO/371/23267
1940	32,152 overseas	FO/371/24585
1941	9,664 overseas	FO/371/27259
1942	c.25,000 overseas	FO/371/35155
1943	c.42,000 total; 34,668 overseas	FO/371/40283;
		FO/371/52799
1944	c.42,000 total; 37,857 overseas	FO/371/45546;
		FO/371/52799
1945	c.200,000 total; 41,000 overseas; 44,000 foreign arrivals	FO/371/52799
1946	c.150,000 total; c.55,000 overseas	FO/371/68779
1947	c.150,000 total; c.55,000 overseas (judged similar to previous year)	FO/371/68779
1948	93,000 overseas	FO/371/75505
1949	c.100,000 overseas	FO/371/82638
1950	108,500 overseas	FO/371/91767
1951	97,757 overseas	FO/371/91767

Eastern Telegraph Company, and some £22,000 to Gellatly's. Even private companies were in difficulty and the coming *hajj* was expected to be poorer than the previous year.[67] The financial administration was criticized, in particular because of the lack of a budget.[68]

By December 1930, the financial situation was so bad that salaries were said to be in arrears as much as eleven months and Ibn Saʿud's return to the Najd was delayed allegedly because of a lack of funds to pay for the trip. Expectations of another lean *hajj* provoked the government to prepare to tax the pilgrims as much as it could.[69]

When all else failed, al-Sulayman was forced to acquire stocks of vital goods using IOUs. For example, when receipts plummeted in 1931, he took over the petroleum stocks of the long-time British merchants, Gellatly Hankey, in Jiddah, worth about £12,000, and those of St. John Philby's Sharqieh Company, worth about £4,000. Both firms were eventually reimbursed, although it took some time.[70]

At the same time, however, Ibn Sa'ud, relying on his finance minister's help, approached Philby for help in attracting foreign capital. Philby's plan of attack was to make connection with Standard Oil of California (SOCAL), which expressed an interest in procuring an oil concession. How much Philby actually did in bringing SOCAL together with Ibn Sa'ud is debatable, but he did receive a retainer from the company—and kept it secret from the ruler.[71]

Dire financial straits also marked 1931. The early part of the year saw an increase in customs duty on most staple imports while the silver *riyal* slipped in value relative to the pound. A group of merchants in al-Madinah prevailed upon 'Abdullah al-Sulayman to pass on their complaint to the king about the poor economic situation and the rise in the cost of imported goods because of the rise in value of the pound.[72] At least Gellatly's received partial satisfaction with regard to the payment of debts. It was also said that the government owed the al-Qusaybi family £80,000 and the governor of Jiddah £4000.[73] The government's gold reserves were said to be exhausted by April and an arrangement with the Dutch Bank (formally, the Netherlands Trading Society) to exchange silver for gold at the official rate collapsed.[74] However, the money owed to Eastern Telegraph up to the end of 1930 was paid off and part of the debt to Gellatly's was also paid, while Ibn Sa'ud requested another year to repay the Government of India.[75]

Ibn Sa'ud turned to the idea of inviting a foreign concern to take up the duties of a state bank, which it was conjectured might provide £200,000 in return for a monopoly on banking operations and the right to issue notes.[76] There was also contemplation by the Dutch Bank of extending a £500,000 loan to the government, of which £200,000 would be used to support the silver *riyal*, another £200,000 for economic development such as mining that would provide a profit, and the remaining £100,000 to pay off debts and put the state back in working order.[77] Another financial complication seemed to be preparations for a military campaign, for which the Ministry of Finance was expected to produce the necessary funds.[78]

By the end of the year, the value of the *riyal* vis-à-vis the gold sovereign had dropped markedly below 17 to the gold sovereign and matters were made worse by the British abandonment of the gold standard in September 1931. Protests over the benzine affair prompted Ibn Saʿud to issue a proclamation on 13 November 1931 promising budgetary reform for al-Hijaz.[79] The resultant "budget", announced on 15 January 1932, amounted to little more than an estimate of expenditure in four areas to which revenues would be apportioned: 35 percent on official salaries; 25 percent on indebtedness, including arrears of salaries and the government's internal and external debt; 15 percent reserve; and 25 percent for extraordinary expenses, including the needs of pilgrims and the cost of developing the country's resources. Expenditures and revenues were given at the same amount of 106,442,544 piasters. The largest budgetary items were royal allowances (6,000,000 piasters), debt instalments (16,500,000), the equivalent of a privy purse and the officials of the Treasury Department (12,650,000), the share of al-Hijaz in Defense Departments (22,000,000), and public security (10,441,196). There was also some talk of employing a European financial adviser and it seemed clear that the country's financial capital would be Jiddah instead of Makkah.[80]

A closer look at the budget for al-Hijaz (Najd was not included) early in the following year, 1932, revealed a number of anomalies. About half of the total Hijazi income, or about £410,000, was to be devoted to royal and military needs, in addition to about £100,000 for communications and transport. Should there be less income than anticipated, it was conjectured that public indebtedness would be the last to see relief.[81] At the same time, M. van Leeuwen, the Dutch financial adviser, was engaged on a one-year contract.[82] On 17 June 1932, a government decree announced that arrears in salaries would be paid by supplies in kind and that all other debts would be met by drafts on customs where it had not been done already. The decree specified that 25 percent of customs revenue would be allocated for this purpose.[83] At the same time, Ibn Saʿud appealed unsuccessfully to the British for a loan of £500,000 while publicly denying it.[84] An internal intelligence report of the time noted that there were not enough funds to pay all debts because the government was unable to secure a loan—the British, French, and Dutch banks had all refused requests.[85] None of these measures seemed to bear much fruit and the budget experiment was not repeated.

A few months later it was reported that drafts on customs were being passed at only 34 percent of face value. This combined with a drooping market rate of $18\frac{1}{4}$ *riyals* to the gold sovereign, compared to the official rate of 10 to 1. The consequence was that the original holders of customs drafts had seen their loss grow to 80 percent. The country continued to be weighed down by external debt, estimated at nearly £200,000 in gold.[86] Schemes to raise more money ended in failure, including the attempt to create a national bank and a concession for a Jiddah-to-al-Madinah railway.[87] Only the al-Ahsa' oil concession provided any income.

It was perhaps not surprising that the acute financial predicament should weigh heavily on Ibn Sa'ud. By the end of 1932, the state's indebtedness was estimated at a minimum, of £219,200 in gold. The holders of debt ranged from Poles for arms purchased in 1930, to the Soviets for the oil bought in 1931, German and British firms that had supplied goods and services, the Dutch Bank for loans, and to St. John Philby and al-Qusaybi family.[88]

Given that the *hajj* was the government's main source of revenues, it is not surprising that the government vigorously sought to increase the number of pilgrims in 1933, using pamphlets and sending representatives to many Muslim countries. At the same time, the government made various improvements to facilities in Makkah, Jiddah, and al-Madinah, such as hotels and rest houses.[89] Only 20,000 pilgrims arrived from overseas, the worst figures since Ibn Sa'ud took over al-Hijaz and those who did make the *hajj* seemed to be from the poorer ranks. Customs receipts also suffered and in any case the government had mortgaged its revenue from that source by several years of issuing drafts on receipts to holders of its debt. The financial situation was made even more perilous at the end of the year by the expenditures made in preparation for war with Yemen; the government needed funding to provide for equipment, food, and transport of the thousands of tribesmen being mobilized from all over the country.[90]

Customs duties were significantly increased in May, including a range of specific duties per unit on many commodities. At the same time, however, payment for the telegraph service was paid promptly and government employees received partial salaries.[91] These somewhat surprising developments, as well as the war preparations, appeared to be financed by the money received from Standard Oil of California.[92] There were even rumors of negotiations with Dr. Grobba of the German government for a loan to Saudi Arabia secured by the port of Jiddah, or even of a £100,000 unsecured loan by German financiers—although there seemed to be little or no truth behind the rumors.[93]

Some relief was offered by a drop in the exchange value of the *riyal*. This perversely worked to the advantage of the government, which was able to collect customs duties at the gold rate and make *riyal* payments at the official rate.[94] However, the state's indebtedness continued, with £30,000 still owed to the Government of India and £50,000 owed to Philby's Sharqieh Ltd., broken down as £15,000 for oil, £15,000 for wireless construction, and £20,000 in own account. By November, government employees were receiving no pay, debts remained unpaid, and trade was at a standstill, thus adversely affecting customs receipts.[95] Publication of a "budget" in 1931 was not repeated and the government seemed unaware of the damage it had caused by ignoring, let alone repaying, its various debts. Furthermore, the *hajj* was the smallest in years, with only slightly more than 20,000 overseas pilgrims compared to 29,000 in the previous year. By the end of the year, the Saudi *riyal* had fallen to about 24 *riyal*s to the pound sterling.[96]

The situation became precarious in 1934 as income fell but expenditure rose, in large part because of the war with the *imam* of Yemen. The government was kept going only by tightening belts further, imposing new taxes, and benefitting from a slightly improved pilgrimage.[97] On the other hand, the Saudi government had received the second installment of the SOCAL concession loan, an amount of £20,000. Furthermore, there was a small loan in November from Egyptian politician and financier Tal'at Harb Pasha, thought to be secured by Egyptian pilgrim dues. One consequence was the payment to Philby of some £2000–£3000, half in cash, to be applied against the import of new motor vehicles and not to pay off the outstanding debt to him. Official salaries remained unpaid but, on the other hand, trade in al-Hijaz improved slightly and the Saudi currency had not depreciated significantly.[98]

Part of the reason for the steadiness of the financial picture at this juncture lay with the resourcefulness of the king's financial wizard. One of 'Abdullah al-Sulayman's tactics was simply to delay payment. It had become a frequent practice of the government to only make partial payments on its obligations and to leave accounts several months in arrears. This was illustrated by an example in 1930 when the Eastern Telegraph Company became increasingly disturbed over its Saudi government account on the Jiddah–Port Sudan telegraph cable. By late 1930, the government owed the company nearly 3000 Egyptian pounds and was more than three months behind in its payments. The British legation wrote on the company's behalf to the acting minister of foreign affairs, asking him "to persuade your colleague, the Minister of Finance, to meet his obligations towards the Eastern Telegraph Company more promptly." When Fu'ad Hamza raised the question of a reduction of the cable rates, the legation replied that that would be difficult because outstanding payments had not been received.[99]

By the end of 1934, Saudi finances were again in a precarious state. Al-Sulayman paid close attention to finances from Makkah and Jiddah and reportedly postponed pay to officials until after Ramadan ended in January, as well as ordered that drafts on customs could no longer be used in part payment of duty on newly imported goods.[100] The *hajj* of 1934 was scarcely better than that of 1933. Somehow, though, the government was able to meet the costs of the Yemen war and still pay part of its officials' salaries.[101]

The treasury was again forced to live from hand to mouth in the following year and a drastic cut to all official salaries was announced in June, despite an end to the Saudi–Yemeni War and a marked increase in pilgrims.[102] This was despite SOCAL's payment to the government of £20,000 in gold, which, combined with the previous payment in August 1933 of £35,000 in gold, represented a loan to the Saudi government (apart from £5,000 in gold assumed to be an annual rent).[103] The government did, however, manage to repay in May a small debt to the British government and 10 percent of a larger debt to the British government and the Government of India.[104] This may have been due in part to the fortuitous sale of 1000 camels to the Italians for service in their campaign in Eritrea.[105]

The first official and proper Saudi Arabian budget in 1934–5 estimated expenses at 14 million *riyal*s (about US$4.5 million).[106] The crucial importance of finding income to match expenditure was of course the preserve of ʿAbdullah al-Sulayman and it gave him a greater degree of independence in action than any of the king's other servants. While King ʿAbd al-ʿAziz managed all political affairs himself, he gave al-Sulayman a free hand in the Ministry of Finance as long as he was able to produce funds whenever commanded to do so. Much of this was raised from heavy taxation, balanced by irregular payments of the salaries of small officials and the police.[107]

Nevertheless, some progress in improvements to the country's meager infrastructure was made in small increments. In August 1934, tenders were invited for a mail concession by motor vehicle between Makkah, Riyadh, and al-Ahsaʾ, and between Makkah, al-Qasim, Ha'il, and al-Jawf. Related tenders were invited for the transport of pilgrims from the Gulf to Makkah and from "neighboring frontiers."[108] It was announced in *Umm al-Qura* on 20 October that a fortnightly mail and passenger service by car had been established between Makkah and Riyadh.[109] The Egyptian newspaper *al-Muqattam* estimated government revenue at £600,000 gold in 1354/1935–6. Of this £300,000 gold came from the *hajj*, £200,000 gold from customs, and £100,000 gold from other sources. The British estimated that half the revenue went to military purposes, including subsidies to the tribes, while the other half was spent on administration and some repayment of debt.[110] Desperate, the king appealed to the oil company in March 1936 for an advance of £25,000 out of the £50,000 that had been agreed as a credit in the original concession agreement.[111]

Little improvement in the economic situation was visible in 1937. Attempts were made to improve government revenues through other sources than taxation. This primarily meant a continued reliance on the *hajj* but also an appeal was made to pilgrims to subscribe to schemes dealing with aviation, local industry, water supplies, and orphans. The country's major problem was that it relied principally on the *hajj* as its main source of income and the *hajj* had become notoriously unreliable. No Saudi government figures on income from the *hajj* during this period are available. However, the British Legation's Indian Vice-Consul estimated that on a *hajj* of 45,000 pilgrims, more than £700,000 gold would be spent on dues, transport, customs, and living expenses in country. Government revenues would probably consist of more than 50 percent of this total.[112]

Furthermore, although al-Hijaz was the economically productive part of the kingdom, it had been subsidized by the Ottoman government in the past. Payments from the oil and mineral concessions had become of immense importance for the king even though they were only temporary palliatives. As a consequence, the government continued to fail to pay for the 1929 receipt of arms from the Government of India, the debt to Eastern Telegraph was more than £2000, and the salaries of government employees were months in arrears.[113] By 1937, Saudi debts to the British government totaled nearly £19,000 and to the Government of India more than £9,000. There was discussion within Whitehall about writing off the debt since there was little likelihood that it would be repaid, but no decision had been reached by the end of the year.[114] Desperate, the government resorted to the tactic of buying commodities at high price in the market, paying in customs exemptions for future imports, and then selling the commodities for a lower price in gold.[115]

Several developments gave cause for some hope in 1938. First, it seemed likely that production would begin shortly at the Mahd al-Dhahab gold mine. Second, CASOC had discovered oil in commercial quantities in al-Ahsaʾ and work was underway on a pipeline to the sea. The increased income for the state would mean it would not be almost entirely reliant on revenue from al-Hijaz, either from pilgrims or customs duties. Arrears in salaries for officials could be paid off, customs dues might be reduced, and high charges to pilgrims could be ameliorated. At the same time, however, plans for a regular army had been announced and it was expected that arming and maintaining it would absorb a large proportion of the increased revenue, as would consumer demand among the country's elite. Still, despite CASOC's payment of £50,000 upon the discovery of oil as obligated under its concession agreement, the government remained in serious economic trouble. Foreign debts were not paid off and government employees still had not received all their salaries.[116]

In December 1938, Lenahan of CASOC reported from Jiddah that the kingdom required an immediate CASOC loan of $500,000, to be turned over along with the current royalties of $250,000 by January 1939 or the state would be in serious financial disorder. This was prompted in large part by far lower than anticipated *hajj* revenues and he noted that ʿAbdullah al-Sulayman was trying to persuade the king to reduce his budget to essential requirements. Lenahan went on to say that the company should be prepared to loan $3 million to the government during 1940, which would equal about three-quarters of the kingdom's budget. He estimated that ARAMCO's loans could be repaid out of royalties by 1943.[117]

Despite the payments by CASOC, including advances on future oil revenues, and the Saudi Arabian Mining Syndicate, the Saudi Arabian government continued to find itself in dire straits financially. In 1939, the government owed Gellatly's £25,000, Zaynal Alireza, £40,000, Eastern Telegraph £7000, and as much as £80,000 to Sharqieh. In return for providing credit to the government, Gellatly's retained the quarantine fees of about £2 per pilgrim paid on vessels for which they served as the Jiddah agents. But the *hajj* in 1939 was smaller than expected and government orders heavier than usual. The specter of war threatened to reduce the *hajj* revenues even more.[118] It was believed that CASOC had advanced $1 million to the government against future royalties and ʿAbdullah al-Sulayman claimed to have advised the king not to go to Makkah in order to economize on the costs of transport and hospitality.[119] The king went anyway.

The outbreak and multiplication of combat arenas during World War II had a direct impact on Saudi finances, particularly as normal commerce was disrupted. Elementary materials such as tires and foodstuffs could not be found in markets. Fortunately, Saudi Arabia was able to secure subsidies from the United Kingdom and the United States. In 1943, for example, the British government subsidized King ʿAbd al-ʿAziz with £225,000 a month (or £2,700,000 for the year), plus an additional five million *riyal*s and 400,000 sovereigns in grant. The US provided eight million *riyal*s under the Lend-Lease program and was scheduled to add another seven million *riyal*s early in 1944. The Saudi government was also the recipient of a $1 million advance from CASOC (equating approximately to the rental and oil subsidies accruing to the government from the company's operations in Saudi territory). Despite these subventions and because of a reduced *hajj* of 30,000 at the end of 1942, the Saudi Arabian government budget for 1943 showed a deficit of 30 million *riyal*s (approximately £2,250,000 sterling).[120]

The British subsidy had been introduced to offset falling *hajj* revenues during the war. But as the size of the subsidy increased relative to such requirements, London informed Riyadh that the subsidy would have to be restricted to the actual requirements of the country. Furthermore, this would be affected as well as by the requirements of Britain's postwar economy. It was suggested that the Saudi government should reorganize their finances and economy in order to offset the loss of subsidy without hardship. In March 1944, the British government announced that their assistance would henceforth consist of a gift of 200,000 sovereigns and the cancellation of Riyadh's debt of 20 million *riyal*s to the UK Commercial Corporation against revenue derived from *hajj* tariff items. The loss of revenue to Saudi Arabia that this represented, however, was soon erased by an American offer to make up any reduction.[121]

In the eyes of the British minister to Saudi Arabia, S.R. Jordan, a group of the king's advisers had opposed the imposition of financial reforms. While Jordan's objectivity is a matter of debate (as discussed in later chapters), the question of how much assistance should be provided prompted intense discussion between US and British authorities in Washington and London, as well as at the Middle East Supply Center in Cairo. Eventually, it was agreed that any financial assistance should be negotiated jointly and shared equally.[122] The war certainly had a devastating impact on Saudi Arabian finances, even as it was responsible for creating the mutually dependent relationship between the kingdom and the United States, as shown in Chapter 5.

CHAPTER 3

The 1933 Oil Concession and Oil Affairs to World War II

EARLY OIL EXPLORATION IN ARABIA

There are two background factors in the early stages of the search for oil in Saudi Arabia that helped lay the groundwork for the 1933 concession. The first of these was the result of complex efforts to secure concessions in various localities along the Gulf while the second derived from the philanthropic interests of an American industrialist.

The history of oil exploration in the Gulf began with an eccentric Australian–British entrepreneur, William Knox D'Arcy, who undertook prospecting in Persia (now known as Iran) at the turn of the twentieth century.[1] His failure to discover oil despite investing several years of exploration at various sites forced him to join with Burmah Oil in the Concession Syndicate. New drilling began at Masjid-i Suleiman in the Khuzestan region of Iran and oil was discovered there in 1908. The operation, with Burmah Oil in the majority, was reformed as the Anglo-Persian Oil Company (APOC; later known as the Anglo-Iranian Oil Company, and eventually as British Petroleum or BP) to exploit the discovery. The British government obtained 55 percent of APOC's shares in 1914 to secure oil supplies for the Royal Navy during World War I. Throughout the ensuing years, APOC expanded its interests in exploration to other areas of the Gulf.

Meanwhile, the possibility of oil in Mesopotamia fueled interest there at about the same time. After the dissolution of the Ottoman Empire and the creation of the British Mandate for Iraq, the Iraq concession of the Turkish Petroleum Company (TPC) was finally confirmed in May 1925 and oil was discovered near Kirkuk in October 1927. Final settlement of ownership of the concession was concluded in July 1928 with Royal Dutch/Shell, Anglo-Persian, French interests, and the Near East Development Company (representing American interests) each receiving 23.75 percent of the oil. The remainder of 5 percent went to Calouste Gulbenkian, who had established the original TPC and was thereafter known as "Mr. Five Percent." To protect their interests, all the parties agreed to the "Red Line" Agreement, signed on 1 July 1928, which bound them to work jointly in all oil operations throughout the Middle East, from Turkey through to Yemen. Only Persia (Iran) and Kuwait were excluded from the agreed-upon territory.

Along the shore of the Arab side of the Gulf, the primary mover was an enterprising New Zealander named Frank Holmes.[2] A mining engineer and a quartermaster in the British Army during World War I, Holmes became convinced that there was oil along the Arab littoral. But he was virtually alone in his belief. Minerals in Abyssinia attracted more attention and Holmes had put together a group of investors to exploit these. But keeping his eye on the Gulf, he sought to interest his investors in the lapsed oil concession for the Farasan Islands in the Red Sea and for salt-mining on al-Salif Peninsula of Yemen. A new venture, the Eastern and General Syndicate (E&GS), was created in August 1920 to exploit these endeavors, but Holmes managed to extend the firm's area of interests to the entire Arabian Peninsula.[3]

The year 1921 marked the beginning of oil interest in al-Ahsa' (now the Eastern Province of Saudi Arabia). This interest was intricately tied up with similar developments in Bahrain. The APOC applied to Ibn Sa'ud for prospecting rights in 1921 but the ruler was reluctant to deal with a British oil company, a factor that influenced later negotiations as well. Meanwhile, Holmes also had designs on the area and managed to convince the E&GS board to allow him to pursue the chase for oil along the Arab littoral. About the same time, he made the acquaintance of Dr. Thomas Mann, a physician who had previously served on Sir Percy Cox's staff in Mesopotamia. Cox had promoted Mann to Ibn Sa'ud as his personal physician and this led to a four-year contract. Mann was also charged with representing Ibn Sa'ud's interests in Britain.[4]

In October 1922, the (British) Political Resident in the Persian Gulf (PRPG) received a report that Mann and Holmes were in al-Ahsa' and asked the (British) Political Agent in Bahrain to explain. In reply, the Political Agent said that Mann was attempting to sort out his employment as agent to Ibn Sa'ud and that he had brought Holmes along in the hope that Ibn Sa'ud could be interested in development schemes. Two weeks later, after Holmes had met the Najdi ruler, it was reported that Holmes had attempted to get a concession for exploration for oil for the E&GS, with the help of the Arab–American writer Amin Rihani, but that Ibn Sa'ud had delayed with an explanation that he wished to have an Arabic translation and to consult with Sir Percy Cox (formerly the PRPG and in 1922 the high commissioner for Iraq) first.[5]

Holmes had submitted a draft concession to Cox in early 1923 and, in March of that year, Cox suggested to Ibn Sa'ud that he should not make a decision until he had considered an APOC offer. There appeared to be some collusion between the two companies with an intention to share interests. This resulted in E&GS acquiring a concession on 6 May 1923 after Holmes had agreed with Ibn Sa'ud not to sell any part of the concession to APOC. Although the final terms of the concession were not available to the British, it was thought to include an initial payment of £6,000 and payments of £3,000 per annum for "special protection," as well as stipulations that the concession would be cancelled if there was no activity for more than 20 months. Holmes telegraphed the news to E&GS on 14 May 1923:

> Sultan Ibn Saud signed delivered to me the Hasa Concession fullstop The Neutral Zone Concession it is not yet signed Sultan Ibn Saud arranging with Koweit expect joint signatures on an early date fullstop Have given undertaking Sultan Ibn Saud not to sell the whole or part of any concession to The Anglo-Persian Oil Co. Ltd., fullstop Referring to your telegram of 8th in respect of The Territory of Nejd other than the Hasa Concession Area under The Hasa Concession total amount £7,000 £500 due after 60 days from the 6th of May fullstop If you could credit Sultan Ibn Saud this amount with the Eastern Bank Ltd. Baghdad without waiting until expiration of 60 days it would assist me materially to secure very strong hold over not only The Territory of Nejd other than the Hasa Concession Area but also over the Koweit territory(ies) and of Bahrein fullstop[6]

The concession ran into difficulties from the beginning. Ibn Sa'ud was unwilling to alter a clerical error regarding a date and the syndicate refused to advance any more money, at least partly because of concern by London financiers about the absence of British diplomatic representation in Najd, as well as a lack of promising geological reports. The concession effectively died soon after when Ibn Sa'ud's claim for a payment was refused by the syndicate.[7] In fact, the terms apparently were £7,500 for the concession with a yearly rental of another £3,000. In addition, presents of more than £2,500 in total value were made to various Saudi individuals and later the company provided an electric light plant and elevator for Ibn Sa'ud's palace in Riyadh at a cost of £3,000. E&GS sent a Swiss geologist named Heim to the area to report on the possibility of oil but Heim's report was regarded as vague and inconclusive. E&GS thereupon attempted to interest APOC in the concession but Heim's negative report apparently caused APOC to decline.[8]

Holmes had also devoted considerable attention to Bahrain where he had been engaged by the ruler to search for water. E&GS secured a concession for Bahrain in December 1925 and commenced exploration. However, when oil prospects seemed nonexistent, E&GS sought to sell its concessions to APOC. The latter firm refused, however, persisting in its belief that there was no oil in

Arabia. Beset by financial difficulties and unable to raise any additional British capital, E&GS sought to enlist the assistance of an American oilman, Thomas E. Ward, in interesting American companies. A desperate Holmes traveled to New York to meet him in August 1926.

Holmes described the situation to Ward as involving five actual or potential concessions. The Bahrain concession was fully in hand; al-Ahsa' concession had been signed but annual payments to Ibn Sa'ud were two years in arrears; the Saudi-Kuwait Neutral Zone concession had been jointly granted but payments for it too were in arrears; the Kuwait concession was being negotiated; and the Farasan Islands concession had been granted but several points required renegotiating with the ruler of 'Asir, in whose territory the islands lay. Holmes added that assistance for the Bahrain concession was the top priority, followed by options on the other areas.[9] Negotiations were in progress when the Farasan concession was taken over by the Shell Group.[10] E&GS suggested a price of $250,000 for all properties, with provision for a royalty to be paid to E&GS in the event of Bahrain production.[11]

Initially, the American companies, however, were no more interested than APOC had been. But Ward had connections with the Gulf Oil Company and on 30 November 1927 Gulf Oil formed Eastern Gulf Oil Company as a subsidiary to participate in the Bahrain and "Mainland" concessions. Ward (and his associates) received a 10 percent commission from E&GS, plus an additional 10 percent commission on any Bahrain royalties paid to E&GS.[12] Gulf sent a geologist, Ralph Rhoades, to the Gulf to do a survey. He reported that Bahrain was a perfect dome but there was no way of knowing whether oil was present without drilling. This could not be done until political complications were settled.[13]

The ruler of Bahrain granted a one-year extension to the exploration license on 2 December 1927. When the syndicate raised the question in October 1928 of another extension, the British Colonial Office maintained that it could be granted only if the syndicate agreed that the concession remained under British control. As an American company, Eastern Gulf Oil was prevented from operating in Bahrain by terms of the Turkish Petroleum Company agreement of 31 July 1928 (the "Red Line" agreement), which had accepted American participation (including by Gulf Oil) in that company. This contravened the arrangements between E&GS on the one hand and Gulf Oil on the other. Thus, because of the Red Line Agreement, Gulf Oil was bound to surrender its concession for Bahrain although it could continue to pursue the Kuwait concession.

Consequently, Gulf Oil assigned its rights to Standard Oil Company of California (SOCAL). SOCAL sought to get around the restriction on American companies operating in the Gulf by creating a Canadian subsidiary, the

Bahrain Petroleum Company (BAPCO), to control the concession. When E&GS sought a one-year renewal of its concession (i.e. from 2 December 1928) from the Colonial Office, the latter demanded as a condition of its assent that the original concession agreement should include provisions for the operating company to be British registered, its managing director and majority of its board be British subjects, and that no foreigner should control the concession.

As a result of US government involvement, the question was discussed at an interdepartmental meeting in London on 7 May 1929 and it was concluded that the British government was not on strong enough ground to deny American participation in the concession.[14] The matter essentially was settled when the companies involved (E&GS, Gulf Oil, and SOCAL) all stated that they would not engage in political activity in foreign countries and agreed that Frank Holmes should be their representative in exchange for British acquiescence to American participation in the concession.[15] The complications and efforts paid off when oil was struck in Bahrain in 1932.

The struggle for the concession in al-Ahsa' was even more complicated. The British government and APOC continued to oppose American interest in al-Ahsa' with an eye more to keeping the territory within the British sphere than in the expectation of any oil discoveries there. In early 1933, APOC wrote to the PRPG, Col. Trevor Fowle, and announced that they had been instructed to approach King ʿAbd al-ʿAziz (Ibn Saʿud) for an option over al-Ahsa' territory similar in terms to that acquired the previous year in Qatar.[16] There was also indication that the Iraq Petroleum Company (IPC; successor to the TPC) was interested in al-Ahsa'.[17]

The E&GS had not given up on resurrecting its original al-Ahsa' concession either, as evidenced by Holmes' letter to Ibn Saʿud on 23 December 1927 in which he explained the payment arrears had been caused by financial difficulties resulting from discouraging geological surveys. However, he continued, American backing had been secured and "I have been authorized by the American financiers and my Company to request an audience with Your Majesty with a view of arranging fresh terms and to make a liberal payment either in cash or in kind, such as water-well boring, to Your Majesty for such new agreement."[18]

The SOCAL geologists in Bahrain had a hunch that the Arabian mainland across from Bahrain would be a fruitful place to explore for oil, but getting access was a major problem. At the direction of Francis B. Loomis, a former under-secretary of state in the Theodore Roosevelt administration and an adviser to SOCAL on foreign affairs, geologist Fred A. Davies and William F. Taylor, general superintendent of SOCAL's foreign division, arrived in Bahrain in May 1930 and Davies determined the site for the first drilling. They pushed Holmes to arrange permission to explore the mainland but both men left in July without any success since Holmes was unable to secure permission. Davies went to Iraq and then Iran while hoping that permission might be granted but he eventually returned to the US. His communication back to SOCAL headquarters of 5 June was the "first official indication by any responsible Socal person that the Saudi Arabian development looked good."[19]

SOCAL was moderately interested but problems loomed. M.E. (Maurice) Lombardi apparently authored a memorandum that outlined the avenue by which SOCAL could use E&GS and Holmes to secure a concession.

> In view of the present uncertainty and lack of precise information regarding the policy and action of the Iraq Petroleum Company respecting its selection of areas and the turning back to the Iraq Government of the ones it does not desire, and the disposition of to be made of these areas, it may be advantageous to make a prompt and vigorous effort to acquire concessions covering all of Ibn Saud's territory supposed to contain petroleum . . . .
>
> As Holmes will be in London soon, and as it is doubtless advisable to deal in this matter, if we should desire to deal at all, through him and the Eastern and General Syndicate, I think it would be well to take up negotiations with the two of them in London; ascertaining at the same time for ourselves, for our information, the probable attitude of the Colonial Office and what we might expect in the way of protection at the hands of the British naval air forces, in or near Arabia, in case of trouble with some of the natives whom Ibn Saud could not control.
>
> It ought not to take more than ten days or a fortnight to arrive at some understanding and definite agreement with Holmes and the Syndicate.
>
> In this connection, it will be of great importance for us to have a personal, heart-to-heart talk with Major Holmes, for the purpose of ascertaining just what he is willing to do for us, now and in the future, and what his obligations to the Gulf are and where they may be expected to end. I think this is essential for the purpose of avoiding misunderstandings in the future.[20]

Nevertheless, doubt remained within SOCAL that Holmes was actively assisting SOCAL's efforts to enter Ibn Sa'ud's territory and there were suspicions that E&GS was negotiating with Gulf Oil for options on any concessions that E&GS might receive.[21] SOCAL's interest thereupon cooled for over a year.

H. St. John B. Philby, the former British official who had become a businessman in Jiddah and a confidant of Ibn Sa'ud, described Ibn Sa'ud's interest in any concession as being limited solely to "some ready money to enable him to ride out the economic storm until the re-establishment of the pilgrimage on a more profitable basis. He certainly did not look further than that; nor was he fired by any spark of optimism as regards the probable outcome of any such enterprise. His more imaginative Finance Minister took a rosier view of the prospects; and in a mood of more than ordinary depression the king agreed to take the first step in the desired direction."[22] That step was to accept the offer of American businessman Charles Crane to send an

American mining engineer to Saudi Arabia. This development, however, was to put E&GS in competition with its partner SOCAL and SOCAL eventually turned to other sources of assistance in getting into al-Ahsa'.

THE ROLE OF CHARLES CRANE AND KARL TWITCHELL

The name of Karl Twitchell evokes many parallels with Frank Holmes. Like Holmes, Twitchell was a mining engineer with a wide variety of experiences around the world. Holmes was a New Zealander while Twitchell was American. Both were involved in early efforts to discover water and oil resources in Arabia. Both spent considerable amounts of time in what was to become Saudi Arabia, but Twitchell's relationship with Ibn Sa'ud, 'Abdullah al-Sulayman, and the Saudi government was deeper, longer-lasting, and more comprehensive than that of Holmes.

The genesis of Twitchell's involvement in Arabia was a consequence of the philanthropic interests of Charles R. Crane. Crane, born in 1858, was the wealthy heir to the Crane and Camp plumbing-equipment company. Involved in humanitarian issues from a young age, he also backed Wisconsin's Robert M. Lafollette and his Progressive Republican Movement and later President William Howard Taft. As a consequence, the latter appointed him in 1909 as minister to China—the appointment, however was cancelled before Crane set sail across the Pacific. Crane's politics then turned to the Democratic Party and he was a major donor to Woodrow Wilson's presidential campaign. Sent on a mission to the Kerensky government in Russia in 1917, Crane was later rewarded in 1920 with the post of, yes, once again, minister to China.

Crane had long been interested in Oriental affairs and was a major backer of the American Armenian–Syrian Relief Committee during World War I. This led to his appointment by President Wilson to the Paris Peace Conference and his role in the Commission of Inquiry in Palestine and Syria, better known as "The King–Crane Commission." This served as his introduction to the Arab world.[23]

Crane subsequently traveled through Arabian Peninsula. His first visit to Jiddah appears to have been made early in 1923 as a guest of King Husayn al-Hashimi. He passed through Jiddah again in December 1926 on his way to Yemen and was met by Amir Faysal b. 'Abd al-'Aziz Al Sa'ud, Ibn Sa'ud's son.[24] The visit to Yemen during 1926–7 included a trip to Sanaa to meet with Imam Yahya. In another of Crane's philanthropic gestures, he offered to provide mining engineers to help identify possible sources of minerals. The outcome was Crane's engagement of Karl Twitchell to carry out this survey of Yemen.[25]

Karl S. Twitchell was employed by Crane in both Yemen and Saudi Arabia for some years to help institute the latter's benevolent projects. The initial connection was made by Twitchell in 1927. In April, he stopped in Aden on his way from Abyssinia to London. The American consul there told him about Crane's visit to Imam Yahya in Sanaa and how Crane had offered to help find American engineers to search for minerals in Yemen. Twitchell wrote to Crane from London offering his services and the two men met in New York and reached an understanding. As a consequence, Twitchell found himself arriving in al-Hudaydah in early November 1927 and then made his way to Sanaa to meet the *imam* and to carry out an initial exploration of the country. He then returned the following year to build a bridge in the mountains.[26] In late 1928, Twitchell was occupied in Yemen building a road from al-Hudaydah to al-Durayhimi and al-Ta'if in al-Zaraniq country, as well as making a garden for Sayf al-Islam Muhammad, the *imam*'s son and governor of al-Hudaydah.[27]

Word of Crane's munificence spread to Ibn Sa'ud in Riyadh and Crane visited Jiddah in February 1931 at the monarch's invitation. But Crane apparently had also stimulated some attention during his 1926 visit as well, since Twitchell wrote to Ibn Sa'ud from Yemen in late 1927 to say that Crane thought that wells along the pilgrim routes to Makkah would be beneficial and, given the king's approval, had instructed Twitchell to inspect the route from Jiddah and make arrangements for the wells. Twitchell expected to be able to arrive in late winter or early spring of 1928.[28]

Ibn Sa'ud journeyed to Jiddah on 25 February 1931 to receive Crane, who had come from the United States for this purpose.[29] As a result of this meeting, Crane summoned Twitchell to come from Yemen to investigate for water, which he did in April 1931. Ibn Sa'ud's principal interest at this time was finding new sources of water and Crane offered the services of his American engineer in a search for water resources in al-Hijaz. After receiving a cable from Crane on 31 March 1931, Twitchell wrote to Ibn Sa'ud asking for maps and details about locations of possible wells and dams, as well as vegetation and weather patterns. He added that it would not require much more effort to scout for minerals at the same time (even though Crane had not mentioned the possibility).[30]

Twitchell arrived in Jiddah in April, accompanied by his English wife. His explorations covered the vicinity of Jiddah and Wadi Fatimah during 22–24 April, followed by a second and longer trip of 1306 miles during 26 April–13 May.[31] On this trip, he first examined possibilities around Jiddah and then moved off towards Yanbu' and al-Wijh.[32] He announced on his return to Jiddah that he had found petroleum, a gold mine, and traces of lead. Information regarding Twitchell's initial survey in 1931 was published in

Umm al-Qura (essentially the official gazette for Saudi Arabia), together with suggestions for raising the water supply, building dams, importing windmills, and getting water to Jiddah. The British minister reported that Twitchell claimed to have found ample supplies of water, both between Jiddah and Wadi Fatimah but also at various sites to the north. Twitchell also said he had discovered petroleum deposits north of Jiddah and gold near al-Wijh. He then returned to duties in Yemen.[33] Philby regarded all these discoveries as 'rediscoveries' of deposits already known.[34] During this time, 'Abdullah al-Sulayman also asked Twitchell to examine the old water tunnel supplying Jiddah from the Waziriyah wells, which he did and recommended that it would be suitable for reuse in combination with a windmill.[35]

Twitchell's initial meetings were with 'Abdullah al-Sulayman (with Najib Salihah serving as translator), who queried Twitchell about the possibilities of water and other natural resources.[36] A month later, Twitchell again wrote to the monarch, saying that he had met with his representatives al-Sulayman and Yusuf Yasin. "Please do not think me presumptious [sic] if I congratulate you upon having such very able, competent men in your cabinet," he wrote.[37] Twitchell later wrote that Shaykh 'Abdullah had expressed considerable disappointment at the water results and, mentioning that the government relied almost entirely upon the uncertain revenues from the *hajj*, had asked Twitchell to recommend other possible sources of income. Twitchell was ready and advanced his positive impression of ancient mining sites that he had encountered during his search for water. Al-Sulayman presented Twitchell's ideas to Ibn Sa'ud who summoned Twitchell to meet him at Shumaysi along the Jiddah–Makkah road on 25 May to discuss the possibilities.[38] Shortly afterwards, Twitchell sent Ibn Sa'ud a note summarizing what had been agreed. Twitchell would write for quotations and terms on suitable equipment. After the monarch's decision on what elements of the proposed program were to be carried out, Twitchell would engage American assistants for 18 months' work. His salary would be partly paid by Crane and partly by the Saudi government.[39]

Al-Sulayman wrote to Crane in July 1931 with regard to his early interactions with Twitchell. In his letter, al-Sulayman expressed "my feelings of gratitude and thanks for the intensive interest you have shown in this country and for your kindness in sending Mr. Twitchell to enlighten us with his knowledge and rare talents." The finance minister went on to say that "I have had the opportunity of discussing with Mr. Twitchell all matters relative to his work in the Hedjaz dealing with his examinations and investigations for minerals, water and oils. I have agreed with him on all points about which he advised. I have requested him to take Your Excellency's personal opinion and to act according to what you deem best.... [W]e have mutually agreed to leave Mr. Twitchell's personal salary for your decision by which both will abide."[40]

Al-Sulayman also wrote to Twitchell at the same time that the government felt that the search for minerals and oil should have precedence over Twitchell's preferences of searching for minerals and water first. He also informed Twitchell that the government had approved the engineer's suggestion for the employment of four officials for mining and two for oil drilling and wished him to engage them, as well as to arrange for necessary equipment. The amount of Twitchell's salary was to be left up to Crane.[41]

Presumably as a result of Twitchell's favorable report on his exploration, ʿAbdullah al-Sulayman signed a contract with Twitchell in July 1931. By its terms, Twitchell would serve as the head of a concern to explore for minerals and oil with six experts answering to him.[42]

Twitchell returned to Jiddah on 19 October 1931, accompanied by his wife (and secretary) and an American prospector, but none of the six engineers according to the agreement were to be seen. One of the first actions he took was to set up wells and restore an old Turkish conduit to supply Jiddah with water.[43] The new mining engineer was H.R. Mosley, on his first trip to Arabia. Al-Sulayman was tasked with making accommodation arrangements for the trio and Twitchell explained his plans to Ibn Saʿud and the minister.[44] Furthermore, al-Sulayman provided Twitchell with samples of minerals he had extracted from various ancient mines and which Twitchell felt showed promise.[45]

Twitchell returned to Jiddah from his second exploration tour on 18 January 1932, advocating the sinking of wells along the Jiddah–Riyadh–al-Hufuf road, as well as the construction of a harbor at Ra's Tanurah on the Gulf coast. In the latter half of February, he examined the works at the old gold mine of Mahd al-Dhahab near al-Madinah. He then departed for Yemen in March, having left voluminous reports with the king and his advisers.[46] Indeed, the king wrote to Crane confirming that Twitchell had visited al-Ahsaʾ (where they met) to study water conditions and investigate possible oil deposits, before returning to Jiddah to look for gold.[47]

At about the same time, Ibn Saʿud informed Twitchell that he could not afford to carry out the development program the latter had advocated but added that he wished Twitchell to find capital in America for it. Stressing that he was only an engineer, Twitchell promised to help but only if Crane's approval were obtained.[48] Accordingly, Ibn Saʿud wrote to Crane:

> We received with pleasure the translation of your letter dated the 1st of September 1931 and express to you our deepest gratitude for the kindness, zeal and love you have shown for our country in particular and for the East in general. We are very sure of your absolute sincerity, noble intentions, high ideals and

perfect integrity. We accept with great pleasure your contribution of the services of Mr. Twitchell which have been highly appreciated. We are also pleased with your having sent the second engineer who is assistant to Twitchell. Furthermore, we are sincerely grateful for the two drills which you have so generously sent. We are thoroughly convinced that your sending this expedition is solely and entirely for the benefit of our country. Our nation shall always remember with greatest thankfulness and appreciation the assistance you are rendering us.[49]

Twitchell's own notes about this period dealt with his informing the finance minister about plants and grape cuttings received from the US, a notice that payment for the road equipment approved by the king amounted to $950 or £194 pounds gold, and details about domestic servants during Twitchell's trip to Yemen. In addition, Twitchell emphasized that al-Sulayman should read his No. 4 Report and wondered whether the finance minister had authority to make decisions. Twitchell also proposed an alternative whereby he would be given the money that the Saudi government budgeted for development for him to spend as best as possible.[50]

Twitchell was again in Jiddah in May 1932, apparently in the pay of Ibn Sa'ud this time and not Crane. But he seemed to have accomplished little, despite his explorations on the Gulf coast. The engineer Mosley, who had accompanied him in January, continued to prospect for gold.[51]

After Twitchell's involvement in the negotiation of the first oil concession in 1933, he kept his hand in Saudi Arabia in subsequent years searching for minerals and water in al-Hijaz, the north of the country, and al-Ahsa' province in the east. At the urging of 'Abdullah al-Sulayman, Twitchell formed the Saudi Arabian Mining Syndicate (SAMS) with both American and British backers, as well as the Saudi government as a shareholder.[52] Thus, Twitchell returned to Jiddah again on 27 June 1934 as the representative of the SAMS, which the press reported was registered in the UK as a private company with a capital of £20,000 in £1 shares. The controlling interest was the Anglo-Oriental and General Investment Trust but other investors were a Mr. McDermott and Gellatly, Hankey and Co., the merchant house with a long presence in Saudi Arabia. Twitchell seemed to have no connection with either SOCAL or Philby's Sharqieh in this venture.[53] Negotiations with the British government for its approval were completed on 23 December with the company reported to have achieved exclusive rights over al-Hijaz and much of 'Asir.[54] The syndicate's goal was to secure prospecting rights for gold. But it was not until October that he appeared to have secured the gold-mining concession.[55]

Twitchell's later activities in the kingdom were principally focused on the SAMS. In this connection he had an audience with the king on 17 August 1940 in Riyadh. At this meeting, Twitchell agreed to seek an engineer from the US government for road building in ʿAsir and Najran, sought to dissuade the king from enacting labor laws that would affect SAMS operations, gained permission for prospecting at a number of ancient mining sites (which would become the property of SAMS if successful), discussed the possibility of American archaeological excavations in Najran, al-Ahsaʾ, and other areas, and discussed the king's wish for an American firm to drill Artesian and other wells in Najd.[56]

Twitchell's interest in Saudi matters continued into the 1950s. In 1953, for example, he wrote to ʿAbdullah al-Sulayman with suggestions about improvements that should be made to navigation aids at the entrance of Jiddah harbor.[57]

THE ORIGINAL 1933 CONCESSION

The roots of the competitive negotiations for the oil concession in al-Ahsaʾ are complicated and not completely explainable. The principal competitors were: the Eastern and General Syndicate (E&GS), which had held and lost the original al-Ahsaʾ concession; Standard Oil of California (SOCAL), which had assumed the Bahrain concession from E&GS but had been looking hungrily across the water to the Saudi mainland; and the Iraq Petroleum Company (IPC; successor to the TPC), which seemed more concerned about freezing out American interests than in discovering oil in al-Ahsaʾ. Not surprisingly, these companies relied upon Western individuals long acquainted with the politics of the region. Frank Holmes was representing E&GS and Stephen Longrigg was sent by IPC while Twitchell had made a connection with SOCAL and the latter company had also engaged Philby as an advisor.

All the prospective concessionaires had begun their pursuit of Ibn Saʿud's decision by the beginning of 1933. The status of talks and the mindset of the monarch were vague, perhaps deliberately so on the part of Ibn Saʿud. It is clear, however, that ʿAbdullah al-Sulayman was at the heart of the deliberations.

In December 1931, al-Sulayman asked Twitchell to go to al-Ahsaʾ to search for water and oil possibilities. By his own account, Twitchell stopped in Najd on his way to meet Ibn Saʿud (where he also made the acquaintance of Philby) and then proceeded to Bahrain and al-Hufuf. There he met with Ibn Saʿud again, at which time he advised the monarch to wait for the results of Bahrain drilling before making expensive arrangements for oil. Twitchell counseled that if Bahrain was commercially successful, it might be possible to enlist American capital in the search in al-Ahsaʾ. Ibn Saʿud responded that he had been disappointed by the inability of E&GS to live up to the previous al-Ahsaʾ agreement and decided to follow Twitchell's advice. Thereupon, al-Sulayman, who had been present during these meetings and knew that Twitchell would be available for only six months at Crane's expense, pressed the American to return to Jiddah to look at ancient mines.[58]

Following up on Ibn Saʿud's request that Twitchell find American backers to explore for oil, Twitchell spent some time in the US during the summer of 1932 making the rounds of oil companies. An initial meeting with the Texas Company (TEXACO) proved fruitless and Twitchell pressed his case before the Near East Development Company (a subsidiary of IPC) and the Gulf Oil Company. Gulf Oil, after consultation with the IPC legal department, informed Twitchell that their IPC obligations prevented them from working in Saudi Arabia. By Twitchell's account, he was thereupon contacted by SOCAL.

As shown above, SOCAL had been interested in exploring in al-Ahsaʾ since 1930. By 1932, the company had concluded that E&GS was being obstructive and that Holmes was pursuing his own interests. Francis Loomis must have been in contact with St. John Philby already as he wrote to Maurice Lombardi, a director of SOCAL, on 13 July 1932 about Philby and the latter's views about the possibility of an American concession. Loomis also told Lombardi about Twitchell's report. Loomis contacted Philby in October and a week later Twitchell sent A.S. Coriell, the manager of SOCAL's New York office, his report on his Arabian tours together with letters from Ibn Saʿud and al-Sulayman. Shortly after SOCAL's legal counsel concluded in November that SOCAL no longer needed to communicate its plans with E&GS, SOCAL contacted Philby about working for them and the US State Department recommended that the company engage the services of Twitchell. After presenting his geological data to a SOCAL geologist, Twitchell met with Lombardi. Eventually, Lombardi informed Twitchell that SOCAL was interested in pursuing a concession and authorized Twitchell to act on behalf of the company. At the same time that Twitchell was preparing to travel to Jiddah, Philby spoke to the minister of finance about the possibility of an American concession.[59]

Twitchell met with Lombardi and Lloyd Hamilton, also of SOCAL, in London on 13 January 1933 where it was agreed that Hamilton would deal with the terms of the oil agreement and the legal technicalities while Twitchell's role would be to provide advice on Saudi Arabia and define the concession's boundaries.[60] SOCAL had signed him to a retainer of $1000 a month at the beginning of 1933, as well as some $2000 for expenses. Furthermore, a successful conclusion to the negotiations leading to drilling would result in a bonus of $15,000 and, in the event of commercial production of oil, then Twitchell would be paid an additional amount per ton of oil until the total sum he received reached $50,000.[61] Twitchell later insisted that SOCAL had offered Crane participation in the oil concession but that the latter had refused because "he did not wish it ever said that his expeditions had any commercial taint or carried any financial benefit to himself—he wished his unusual gifts to benefit only the recipients of his philanthropy."[62] At the same time, Philby had been retained to provide similar services as of 1 January 1933 at the rate of $1000 a month for at least six months, plus a cash payment of $10,000 if a concession was granted.[63]

In February 1933, the British minister in Jiddah reported that he was confident that no American oil concession had been granted, despite the expectations raised by Twitchell during his surveys. No longer in the employ of Charles Crane or the Saudi government, Twitchell returned to Jiddah in February 1933 with Hamilton and their respective spouses.[64] Reviewing the British minister's report on the matter, George W. Rendel, a principal in the Foreign Office, remarked "Now that oil has been found in Bahrein and in Koweit, the Hasa area is likely to prove equally important, and if the Americans succeed in getting a firm footing there, the whole political situation in the Gulf may be diabolically affected."[65] Hamilton and Twitchell opened negotiations with ʿAbdullah al-Sulayman on 19 February and Hamilton reported to W.F. Vane of SOCAL's Land and Lease Division that he thought SOCAL would have to offer $250,000 in either payment or a loan to secure the profession. It was Lombardi's opinion that the initial cash payment should be held to $100,000 while another $144,000 could be paid after a year or the company could abandon the effort. He felt that the amount was high but regarded it as a legitimate cost of obtaining the concession.[66]

In March 1933, the British minister in Jiddah reported that ʿAbdullah al-Sulayman had been negotiating with Twitchell and Standard Oil, as well as with IPC. His feeling was that Standard Oil had a better chance of reaching agreement than IPC.[67] "So the stage is set, the dramatics personae being an avid Abdullah Suleyman, who thinks of oil in Ahsa' as already a marketable commodity; Twitchell and Hamilton featuring Standard Oil of California; Longrigg and Mudarris, representing the 'Iraq Petroleum Company."[68] Holmes and the E&GS were clearly outsiders in the race but then their interest seemed to be primarily in the Saudi–Kuwait Neutral Zone. E&GS and SOCAL found themselves in hot competition throughout the Arab littoral of the Gulf, and there was some suspicion by SOCAL that E&GS had broken their telegram code.[69] For its part, E&GS felt betrayed when SOCAL negotiated and received the al-Ahsaʾ concession independently of their original partners.[70] Hamilton handed Holmes a note in Jiddah on 11 April 1933 referring to the "gentleman's understanding" between them and recapitulating the understanding that Holmes would leave Jiddah, ostensibly to consult with his principals in Cairo about a concession but actually would immediately wire al-Sulayman from Cairo that Holmes was not interested in obtaining a concession in the Neutral Zone or elsewhere in Saudi Arabia.[71] That left two competitors.

March saw ʿAbdullah al-Sulayman carrying out serious simultaneous negotiations with both SOCAL, represented by Hamilton and Twitchell, and IPC, represented by Longrigg. He and his Saudi associates proved to be shrewd and hard negotiators. "They played Longrigg's presence against Hamilton's, and vice versa, and played offer against offer. No sooner had Hamilton got what he thought were outrageous demands down to something reasonable and got San Francisco's approval of an offer, than the ministers made new demands as extravagant as the old ones."[72] Al-Sulayman apparently told William Burleigh of SOCAL at some point that "during the concession negotiations [al-Sulayman and the other Saudi negotiators] talked to the English in the morning and the Americans in the afternoon and then sat up all night comparing them, generally to the disadvantage of the British."[73]

The minister of finance was said to be holding out for a very large sum down and substantial royalties. This suited SOCAL but they sought to reduce the amount required. IPC, on the other hand, was prepared to offer only a rental for prospecting rights during a limited period. Furthermore, they insisted on paying in Indian rupees despite the Saudis' demand for gold.[74] Philby, in close contact with all parties, told Hamilton that he had emphasized to al-Sulayman that Longrigg had insisted that IPC's interest was only in keeping out competitors, since it had no need for more oil. Furthermore, Longrigg sought to persuade Philby to take over IPC negotiations since he was impatient to get back to other work and felt that SOCAL would be no more likely to meet the government's demands than IPC.[75]

According to Philby several weeks after these reports surfaced, the Saudis were insisting on a lump sum of £100,000 down and a substantial annual payment. But using the Iraqi concession as a guide, al-Sulayman also insisted on a minimum royalty of £200,000 once commercial exploitation began. This was unacceptable to Hamilton and it was deemed highly unlikely that IPC would agree.[76] Hamilton's negotiating strength was compromised by the fact that he had no idea whether oil would actually be found and he was approaching Ibn Saʿud on the same basis that he had for numerous other concessions around the world.[77] By April, the Saudi government had reduced its demand to £50,000 gold, an annual rent of £5000 gold, and a royalty of 4s per ton upon production.[78]

On 18 April, Hamilton cabled Vane that negotiations had very nearly broken down because of an inability to agree on the royalty guarantee.[79] Two days later, on 20 April, Hamilton conveyed what he considered to be the company's final offer to al-Sulayman, an offer that he expected to be accepted, in part because he was invited to meet Ibn Saʿud who had just arrived in Jiddah. The terms consisted of a £30,000 initial payment, £20,000 in 18 months, £50,000 within 60 days after commercial production (defined as 2000 tons daily), and £50,000 two years later (both of the latter sums to be advanced against royalty).[80] But the US government's announcement on that day of an embargo on gold threw the calculations into disarray since Ibn Saʿud clearly expected payments to be made in gold sovereigns. The Saudi team asked for a revised offer and Hamilton prevaricated in order to determine how high the IPC would go. By 5 May, however, the IPC had decided to quit the competition. Nevertheless, negotiations on the precise terms dragged on until both sides were exhausted and final compromises were reached.[81]

In the end, however, Ibn Saʿud agreed finally to grant the concession to the Standard Oil Company of California. He told ʿAbdullah al-Sulayman to "Put your trust in God and sign!"[82] The concession agreement was signed in Jiddah on 29 May 1933 and Hamilton left for London two days later. On 5 July 1933, it was ratified by the Board of Directors of SOCAL, and two days later a royal decree was issued by the king ratifying the agreement of 33 articles and making it effective from 14 July 1933. In December, a special subsidiary known as California Arabian Standard Oil Company (CASOC) was formed to operate the concession.[83] The amount of royalty was agreed at 4s gold per ton net weight of crude oil, or one US dollar per ton plus any difference in the exchange value between the two currencies.[84] The company provided an initial payment of £35,000 in gold: £5000 consisted of rent and £30,000 as a loan. Another £20,000 gold payment was promised in a few months and, upon discovery of oil, SOCAL was to make a further loan of £50,000. According to Philby, another payment of £50,000 gold was to be made at the end of two years, although this was not spelled out in the agreement.[85] Payment was made in pounds gold instead of US dollars, which would have been more favorable to the company, because the US went off the gold standard during negotiations.[86]

ʿAbdullah al-Sulayman not only negotiated the concession and presented his advice to the king but read out the royal decree on the agreement. When Karl Twitchell, as the initial SOCAL representative in Jiddah, delivered the 35,000 gold sovereigns agreed to as an initial payment, he handed them over to al-Sulayman and then watched him count them out at the Netherlands Trading Society in Jiddah.[87] The 35,000 gold sovereigns (the equivalent of £50,000 at the time) apparently were to be given as a loan secured against future royalties. They arrived in Jiddah on 20 August 1933 by a Khedivial steamer but, due to a mistake in the shipping documents, could not be unloaded and were taken on to the ship's next stop at Port Sudan. Twitchell, who had been inspecting old gold mines in al-Hijaz for the Saudi government, returned to Jiddah to take possession of the consignment.[88] He then proceeded to Bahrain to bring SOCAL's geologists to the concession area, with the help of the al-Qusaybi brothers who acted as agents for the company.[89]

Philby's role in the concession negotiations was complicated. He had made contact with SOCAL in 1931 and Francis Loomis, the former US under-secretary of state, wrote to Philby in July. On Loomis' instructions, Philby conferred with the king and al-Sulayman in Makkah in December, when they decided to ask the competing companies for a down-payment of £100,000.[90] However, unbeknownst to both the king and al-Sulayman, Philby was not an impartial adviser on the competing offers for the concession, as Lloyd Hamilton, SOCAL's chief negotiator, had Philby on retainer, and he had earlier offered his services to IPC. Two decades later, Yusuf Yasin told Philby that if he had known this fact, he would have blocked the transaction.[91] Philby continued to be a paid adviser to the oil company on Saudi Arabian politics at least through 1940.[92] Apparently Twitchell also received regular payments from oil royalties.[93] SOCAL was quick to take advantage of its new concession. William J. Lenahan, arrived in Jiddah on 18 October 1933 to take up duties as the company's Jiddah representative while five geologists were at work already in al-Ahsaʾ under Twitchell's direction, with more expected momentarily.[94] As activity picked up there, ʿAbdullah al-Sulayman announced the appointment of Sayyid Hashim Sultan as the first representative of the Ministry of Finance in al-Ahsa' on 29 June 1935.[95]

There remains some debate over the reasons why Ibn Saʿud preferred the American offer of a concession over a British offer. ʿAbdullah al-Sulayman later told an interviewer that "the indecision of the IPC and its inability to pay 30,000 gold sovereigns, an offer that SOCAL was prepared to make, were the overriding considerations upon which the concession was granted in SOCAL's favour."[96]

As drilling continued through the mid-1930s, the Texas Company (TEXACO) bought into the concession in 1936 with a half interest for $21 million.[97] The going was hard, however, as six wells proved unsuccessful. Due to the diligence and determination of the chief geologist, Max Steineke, work continued on the seventh well—despite the home office's doubts—and the hard work finally paid off on 4 March 1938 when oil was discovered at Dammam No. 7 in commercial quantities and production eventually commenced.[98] King ʿAbd al-ʿAziz was invited to Dhahran in April to turn on the tap. Company representatives Floyd Ohliger and Bill Lenahan were said to have presented him with a Cadillac, and also to have handed over a Chrysler to al-Sulayman.[99]

Ownership of the concession-exploiting company, renamed from CASOC to the Arabian American Oil Company (ARAMCO) in 1944, was further expanded in 1948 when Standard Oil of New Jersey (ESSO, later Exxon) and Socony Vacuum (later Mobil) became partners. The length of the concession's validity was also adjusted three times during World War II until its duration was pegged at 66 years from 1933.[100]

FURTHER DEVELOPMENTS IN THE ARAMCO CONCESSION

A number of supplementary and new agreements were concluded between the Saudi Arabian government and ARAMCO and other oil interests in following years. Most of these were negotiated by the finance minister, ʿAbdullah al-Sulayman. The agreements in which he had a hand (and affixed a signature) constitute a long and impressive list:

1. the original concession contract and agreement with Standard Oil Company of California, 29 May 1933;
2. the supplemental agreement with California Arabian Standard Oil Company, 31 May 1939;
3. the convention on the creation of the Trans-Arabian Pipeline (TAPline), 11 July 1947;
4. the offshore agreement with the Arabian American Oil Company, 10 October 1948;
5. the concession agreement with Pacific Western Oil Corporation, 20 February 1949;
6. the agreement on amendments to the concession held by the Arabian American Oil company, 30 December 1950;
7. the statement relating to outstanding matters with the Trans-Arabian Pipe Line Company, 6 March 1951.[101]

These agreements deserve outlining in greater detail. In 1938, negotiations began on a supplementary agreement for the 1933 concession. While CASOC's concession covered the eastern part of the kingdom, Stephen Longrigg, representing an IPC subsidiary, Petroleum Concessions Limited, won a concession for much of al-Hijaz and ʿAsir in 1936. Petroleum Development (Western Arabia) Limited was formed to exploit the new concession. But in 1938, the company sought to renegotiate its concession and add the two Neutral Zones to it. It faced resistance from the Saudi government from the beginning, which was wary of any extension of British influence in the country. By terms of its original concession agreement, CASOC was forced to present a competing offer. But ʿAbdullah al-Sulayman sought to interest CASOC in taking over a concession for the Saudi interests in the Kuwait Neutral Zone, in return for which the Saudi government would endeavor to persuade the ruler of Kuwait to give CASOC the same rights for its share of the zone. Thus, the Saudis reasoned, British influence in Kuwait would also be lessened. Although Lenahan, CASOC's local representative and its negotiator, expressed his doubts about the viability of this idea, eventually CASOC and al-Sulayman reached an understanding that the supplementary agreement should include both Neutral Zones as well as other areas of Saudi territory.[102]

CASOC's bid was also opposed by Japanese companies and the concession holder pressed Twitchell to complain to al-Sulayman and for Lenahan, the company representative in the kingdom, to complain directly to the king that the Japanese interest was motivated by political factors and not commercial ones.[103] After another long and arduous series of negotiations with al-Sulayman, CASOC won its case. The supplementary agreement negotiated and signed by al-Sulayman was concluded on 31 May 1939 and extended the size of the concession area to 440,000 square miles, including both the Saudi–Kuwaiti and Saudi–Iraqi Neutral Zones. It also extended the concession duration by six years.[104] CASOC made the agreed-upon bonus payment of £140,000 gold on 12 August.[105] The other sets of negotiations are covered in Chapter 8.

It should be noted in addition that there was serious interest in an oil concession for the Farasan Islands in the Red Sea, even before King ʿAbd al-ʿAziz had secured sovereignty over the islands.[106] This may have been one reason for the king's interest in exerting his sovereignty over the region. However, the political complications arising from the Saudi assumption of a protectorate over the Idrisi realm meant that the king insisted on an entirely new concession contract: the Red Sea Petroleum Company thereupon withdrew from its operations.[107] In 1933, however, the Saudi government told the British that an Italian company was interested in prospecting for oil in ʿAsir and the Farasan islands. The king let it be known that he preferred British interests and the Petroleum Department of the British Foreign Office managed to stir up some interest by IPC in ʿAsir and both APOC and Shell in the Farasans, but the interest was short-lived and all the companies declined to investigate further.[108]

Still, several individuals, ʿAbd al-Ghani Ydlibi and a Col. E.T. Etherton (originally brought to Jiddah by Philby for a motor transport monopoly scheme), continued to negotiate with Ibn Saʿud about a Red Sea concession to cover the regions to the north and to the south of the central al-Hijaz, which both men intended to sell to IPC subsidiary Petroleum Concessions Ltd. Furthermore, Stephen Longrigg of IPC seemed to be ready to enter in direct negotiations about this concession.[109] Etherton subsequently told the Foreign Office that he had been negotiating with al-Sulayman, that Philby's participation in the oil negotiations was not necessary, and that Ibn Sa'ud preferred to deal with a British company.[110]

In the end, Longrigg arrived in Jiddah at the end of June 1936 and negotiations with al-Sulayman (assisted by Khalid Abu al-Walid and, latterly, Yusuf Yasin) were carried out jointly by Longrigg, the CFP representative, Ydlibi, and Etherton.[111] The talks dragged on for two weeks but were concluded successfully and Longrigg and the others were al-Sulayman's guests in Jiddah for several days. The concession was for the entire Red Sea coast, up to 100 kilometers deep, including the Farasan Islands but excluding the central area of al-Hijaz (between Rabigh and Lith). Financial terms consisted of £30,000 gold to be paid initially, followed by an annual rent of £7500 gold and then £150,000 gold per year in royalties two years after the discovery of oil in commercial quantities.[112]

After four years of fruitless drilling and exploration, and faced with difficulties caused by World War II—not least of which was the Saudi government's refusal to delay contractual obligations until after the war—the company announced its intention in 1940 to abandon the concession. This alarmed the Saudi government and al-Sulayman claimed that the loss of the concession would make it difficult to deny a concession to the Italians. As a consequence, the Saudi government agreed to suspend the concession for the duration of the war on the grounds of *force majeure* and to accept a reduced annual rental.[113]

As a footnote, the career of 'Abdullah al-Turayqi – subsequently the country's first minister of petroleum – in the oil company ARAMCO began during this period. In 1357/1938, the king wrote to 'Abdullah al-Sulayman recommending several young men for employment. One of them was Turayqi, whom the king said "studies in Egypt on a scholarship. He has been praised for his good work and therefore we think he is qualified to the same thing. And since the government is in need of its own people to do this work, we would like you to check with the California Company and let us know if it is possible to find him work there."[114] Al-Turayqi did indeed do well.

CHAPTER 4

Early Administrative Arrangements

It always bears emphasizing that the Ministry of Finance was by far the most important government department during the 1930s and 1940s. When an attempt was made in 1936 to create a supervisory organ to oversee the organization and transactions of various government agencies, ʿAbdullah al-Sulayman declared that such an audit bureau would play a valuable role in ensuring an efficient government and he made various suggestions about how it could perform its duties beneficially. However, he also noted that "if the aim behind the aforementioned administration for auditing the transactions of the different bodies is to have a higher authority than that of the ministry itself, this is not consistent with the confidence that the government has put in the ministry" and suggested the formation of ad hoc committees to examine any problems that might occur.[1] In the end, the minister of finance and his ministry exercised authority over many different functions of government and controlled the effective workings of a wide range of agencies through control of the purse strings. An examination of some of these seemingly tangential roles serves well to illustrate the fashion in which the rudimentary bureaucracy of the kingdom developed in its formative years.

MILITARY AND DEFENSE

On the face of it, it may seem surprising that the minister of finance, and a non-military man at that, should have been entrusted with responsibilities in the field of defense. But given the extent of the king's trust in him and his vast role in the administration of the country, it was in fact logical. Additionally, ʿAbdullah al-Sulayman's role in this respect essentially centered on military procurement and logistics. He did not serve as a commander-in-chief since that was reserved to the king and his sons. The royal decree establishing the "council of ministers" in late 1931 also confirmed that he held the positions of quartermaster-general and master of ordnance in the Military Departments, in addition to director-general of finance and the king's comptroller.[2] Then in September 1934, he was appointed deputy minister of defense. "As you are aware," the British minister in Jiddah reported to London, "the Minister of Finance has for some time, and notably during the recent conflict with the Yemen, effectively performed the functions of Minister of War."[3] There was no ministry but only an agency or authority (*wikalah*), which al-Sulayman headed.[4]

One of the consequences of the war with Yemen in 1934 was the exhibiting of more interest by the kingdom in a mercantile marine for immediate use in operations and perhaps later for transporting pilgrims. In the autumn of 1933, a motor-launch was reconditioned and two others were purchased. The Arabian Steam Navigation Company was formed in 1934 with two small steamers brought from Beirut and put into service between the Red Sea and the Gulf.[5] This initiative, like the Arabian Export Company formed about the same time, appeared to have been the creation of ʿAbdullah al-Sulayman, whose original idea to use the two ships for military transport had been transformed into a scheme for making commercial advantage with them and perhaps even to transport pilgrims in the future. The manager of both companies was Muhammad Surur al-Sabban, one of the minister's deputies who rose in the ranks over the years and eventually succeeded al-Sulayman as minister of finance. Although ostensibly a private company, the Arabian Steam Navigation Company was in fact a government entity, which seemed to incorporate a guarantee against any loss.[6]

Two official announcements in late 1934 regarding a recruiting call for the standing army as well as establishment of a military school in Makkah seemed to provide evidence of the intention to strengthen the country's "regular" army, provoked perhaps in part by the just-ended Saudi–Yemeni War.[7] There was a division of responsibility in this area between al-Sulayman, who controlled the army, and Prince Faysal, who controlled the police in his capacity as prime minister and minister of the interior.[8] Then, in 1937, al-Sulayman, in his capacity as deputy minister of defense also negotiated with a firm in the United Kingdom to purchase equipment for a cartridge-making factory in Riyadh.[9] As an illustration of his prominent role in this capacity, al-Sulayman was often referred to by British diplomats and even St. John Philby during World War II as minister of defense.[10]

AIR AND TRANSPORT

The emerging ministry of defense also was involved in early efforts in aviation, both in the creation of a small air force and in the establishment of air routes.[11] Somehow, funds were found to put together a fledgling air force in the 1930s, initially using White Russian pilots and mechanics. It was not an auspicious beginning since its minuscule budget made even obtaining petrol for flying difficult. As a British observer explained, "As you are aware, in Saudi Arabia finance and defence are in the hands of the same official, Shaikh Abdullah Sulaiman, and this arrangement which might lead to extravagance in defence in another country, leads to parsimony here, where the treasury is always short of funds."[12] He continued to be interested in the development of the flailing air force, over which he could exert control, but funds were scarce and the air force was low on the list of priorities.

Amongst the many other personal interests that al-Sulayman pursued officially was civil aviation. Along with other high Saudi officials, it was noted that he seemed to have become more interested in the potential of aerial services for both political reasons and internal communication. The initial meeting of the Arab Aeronautical Society was held in his house on 13 November 1930, with the intention of encouraging aviation in the kingdom. Its petition for recognition was approved by the king.[13] Al-Sulayman subsequently spoke about an air-mail service between Jiddah and Riyadh, together with the purchase of new airplanes for it, and mentioned he had an aerial survey map from Standard Oil of California that would be useful for the service.[14] A few years later in 1938, he opened the air route between Jiddah and al-Madinah by taking the initial flight to al-Madinah and back.[15] He also played a key role in the establishment of the first airport at Jiddah before World War II, particularly in terms of providing graded land for the runways, wireless communications, and meteorological facilities, as well then for Riyadh airport.[16]

Various other aspects of transportation in the kingdom also fell within the purview of the Ministry of Finance. In June 1929, Ibn Sa'ud's return from Makkah to Riyadh was delayed by the lack of sufficient drivers for the cars and lorries that had been commandeered in Jiddah and Makkah for his retinue and accompanying troops (these had been thought necessary because of rumors of trouble from the 'Utaybah tribe). When the ruler lost patience and railed at his advisers and ordered the punishment of other members of his entourage, al-Sulayman quickly hurried to Jiddah to round up anyone who could be pressed into service as a driver.[17]

Because of the ministry's responsibilities regarding the *hajj*, it also intervened in the carriage of pilgrims. When a backlash against the requisitioning of private motor cars by the government broke out, al-Sulayman was ordered in November 1929 to reach an agreement with the car companies by which a guarantee would be issued against the risk of requisition in return for a fixed sum on each pilgrim carried. In addition, he was reported to be building a large garage at Makkah and purchasing a large number of cars to cover government use.[18] Then on 19 June 1934, al-Sulayman signed a revised agreement with Sharqieh Ltd., Philby's firm, regarding motor vehicles. It reconfirmed Sharqieh's monopoly on the provision of cars (all Fords) to the government and set new terms for the Saudi government to settle part of their debt with the Ford company, as well as stipulating that Sharqieh was to set up service stations at various locations.[19]

The minister of finance was also involved in the operations of the Motor Transport Company and he presided over a meeting of the company in Makkah on 10 July 1937. He announced to the meeting that a major garage would be opened at Makkah and that 400 new buses would be ordered. He also opposed a motion by directors to increase the bus fares between al-Madinah and Makkah so that pilgrims would not be burdened by the extra cost.[20] The responsibility brought him into conflict with Philby once again, who complained to the king about onerous conditions presented to Sharquieh, which had a monopoly on the supply of parts for the motor transport company.[21]

By 1938, the only actual road in the country stretched from Jiddah to the mine at Mahd al-Dhahab and had been constructed by the Saudi Arabian Mining Syndicate. Work on other roads between major cities had been held up by disagreements by the governments of Saudi Arabia and Egypt, which was to undertake the work.[22]

FOREIGN AFFAIRS

It should not be surprising that the Ministry of Finance's prominent role as perhaps the most an indispensable office available to Ibn Sa'ud meant that its tasks sometimes strayed into the realm of foreign affairs, even though this was more properly the realm of Prince Faysal b. 'Abd al-'Aziz and his deputies Yusuf Yasin and Fu'ad Hamza. For example, during the summer of 1933, 'Abdullah al-Sulayman served as the intermediary between the king and the British Legation due to the absence abroad of Fu'ad Bey Hamza, who normally acted for the Ministry of Foreign Affairs. When a commercial agreement was reached with the Soviet Union in early 1933, the British minister in Jiddah surmised that there was some reason to think that the minister of finance might attempt to "hamper the Russian trade by devious methods, but this can only be a matter of speculation." This view was primarily based on the fact that negotiations with the Soviets had been conducted by al-Sulayman during the previous year, while the 1933 agreement had been reached with Prince Faysal and Fu'ad Hamza.[23] This fear, however, appears to have been groundless.

Later again, when Prince Faysal spent a month in Najd in 1940, al-Sulayman filled in as acting minister for foreign affairs. The British representative remarked that "From the point of view of the Legation this is a satisfactory arrangement as he is always prepared to come down to Jedda for discussions with His Majesty's Minister. He has shown himself to be helpful and understanding, whilst his views on the European situation are sound and he realizes the imperative need in Arab interests for an Allied victory over the aggressors 'who know no God.'"[24]

Furthermore, the involvement in tasks related to foreign affairs of the minister of finance and his subordinates seemed to occur whenever necessary, such as receiving the credentials of the new Turkish chargé d'affaires in 1936 or sometimes signing the official communications of the Ministery of Foreign Affairs.[25] Indeed, according to Philby, who spent the summer of 1938 in Riyadh, an enervated King ʿAbd al-ʿAziz did little over the summer apart from building al-Murabbaʿ palace and "left the rule of the country, except Beduin affairs, to Shaikh Abdullah Sulaiman, the Minister of Finance."[26] A few years later in 1939, both Prince Faysal, the minister of foreign affairs, and Fuʿad Bey Hamza, the prince's deputy in that department, left the kingdom to participate in international discussions on Palestine in London. That left only clerks in the ministry and prompted the king to appoint al-Sulayman as acting minister of foreign affairs.[27]

Al-Sulayman's relations with British diplomats generally were fulsome from the late 1920s throughout his tenure as minister of finance. In part, this was due to the fact that much of the Anglo-Saudi relationship revolved around financial and commercial matters, thus necessitating close British contact with the minister of finance. In part, it was also due to the minister's frequent presence in Jiddah where the British mission was located while most other luminaries kept to prohibited Makkah or Riyadh. But the principal reason undoubtedly was Ibn Saʿud's reliance on one of his most trusted assistants whom he frequently turned to regarding tasks big and small. While al-Sulayman's relations with most British representatives were productive and cordial, there were moments of tension with some. This was particularly true of S.R. Jordan, who served as British minister in the mid-1940s. Jordan seemed to irritate almost everyone, his diplomatic and Whitehall colleagues included. Al-Sulayman's response to Jordan was to deal directly with HMG through the Saudi ambassador in London, Hafiz Wahbah.[28]

Al-Sulayman's official relations with Egypt were also close. In part, this was due to a personal relationship with several prominent Egyptians. In the early 1930s, he journeyed to Jerusalem and Beirut and met on board the ship the writer Hasanayn Haykal. Later, perhaps through Haykal, he met in Egypt Muhammad Talʿat Harb Pasha, an Egyptian senator and chairman of the board of directors of Banque Misr.[29] Talʿat Harb was Egypt's leading banker. In December 1933, he made a high-profile visit to Jiddah, gathering attention not least by his arrival by air. His visit was thought to be prompted by questions of shipping for Egyptian pilgrims during the *hajj*, finding markets for Egyptian cotton goods, discussing the possibility of Banque Misr opening a branch in Jiddah to assume the functions of a state bank, and demonstrating one of Misr-Airwork's airplanes to the king.[30] A tangible impact of Talʿat Harb's visit was the subsequent construction of a road from Jiddah to Makkah by the Egyptians.[31]

Talʿat Harb led an even bigger Egyptian mission to al-Hijaz in December 1934, the principal interests of which were thought to be arrangements for the Egyptians partaking in *hajj* and trade prospects, as well as the distribution of charitable donations. The delegation was housed in new premises in Jiddah, originally intended for the Soviet Legation but taken over during 1934 by Banque Misr, apparently as an investment.[32] Talʿat Harb also extended a loan through the Ministry of Finance, enabling the Saudis to build the somewhat misleadingly named Banque Misr Hotel in Makkah.[33] Talʿat Harb made at least one subsequent visit to Jiddah in 1937.[34] While al-Sulayman may have played no part in the negotiations leading to the Egyptian–Saudi Treaty of Friendship of 1936, the official Egyptian publication of the treaty included an exchange of congratulatory telegrams between him and the Egyptian Prime Minister.[35]

A mission was sent to Egypt in December 1936 to discuss *waqf* (endowment) payments with the Egyptian government as well as other pilgrim matters. A point of discussion, according to the Egyptian press, was that *waqf* money left over from the repair of the Makkah and al-Madinah mosques should be used for paving the Makkah–Jiddah–al-Madinah road, creating a water supply and an electrical lighting scheme for Makkah, instead of being distributed to the poor and bedouins.[36] After considerable discussion, an agreement was finally signed in October 1939 for the construction of roads between Jiddah and Makkah, Makkah and al-Madinah, and partway between Jiddah and al-Madinah. The understanding also included water and electricity schemes for Makkah. The importance and controversy (since it required Egyptian involvement in domestic Saudi affairs) meant that the final document was signed by the king.[37]

In addition, there was at least incidental contact with Axis Powers prior to World War II. Diplomatic relations between Italy and Saudi Arabia began with the signing of a treaty in 1932 and were strained, but not interrupted, by Italy's conquest of Ethiopia. In 1938–9, the minister of finance was entrusted with purchasing some small arms from Italy and then was hard pushed to find the £15,000 to pay for them. At least part of the debt seems to have remained after the war.[38] Saudi inquiries about the purchase of German arms in 1938–9 may have been at the direct instigation of the king.[39] At the same time, Germany's ambassador to Iraq, who was also accredited to Saudi Arabia, Dr. Fritz Grobba, was seeking to establish closer relations between Riyadh and Berlin.[40] It was left to al-Sulayman to inform the Italian envoy in Saudi Arabia on 22 January 1940 that a German envoy would not be welcome in Jiddah at that time.[41]

The Ministry of Finance also played a role in informal relations with other countries. Perhaps because of his connection with the *hajj* rather than his residence as a young man in India, ʿAbdullah al-Sulayman was a point of contact between Ibn Saʿud and Indian groups (not necessarily the British Government of India). This connection may have begun as early as the Muslim Congress in the 1920s on the Holy Places in Arabia.[42] He also served as chairman of the Saudi Arabian committee collecting aid for victims of floods in Syria in 1937, a role that included hosting meetings to organize the aid in his own house.[43]

HAJJ ADMINISTRATION

In an administrative system where the largest income came from the *hajj* (the annual pilgrimage to Makkah), it should not be surprising that dealing with various matters related to the annual *hajj* constituted another responsibility of the Ministry of Finance. Administratively, the organization of the *hajj* in the twentieth century began with the "supervision of pilgrims' affairs" (*muraqabat al-shuʾun al-hajj*) during the Hashimi period but was reorganized by Ibn Saʿud who appointed Shaykh Muhammad Saʿid Abu al-Khayr as the director of *awqaf* (religious endowments) with *hajj* arrangements under him. With the issuance of the kingdom's general laws in 1345/1926, *hajj* affairs were delegated to a Committee of Hajj Administration (*lajnat idarat al-hajj*). Subsequent regulations regarding the *hajj* specified the obligations of the *mutawwafin* (guides), *al-zamazimah* (those providing pilgrims with Zamzam water), the *mukhrij* (those who provide pilgrims with transportation by camels), and the employees of the health directorate. The committee, apparently under the minister of finance's direction, continued to supervise the *hajj* until 1365/1948 when the Directorate of the General Affairs of the Hajj was created as part of the Ministry of Finance and was supervised by Muhammad Surur al-Sabban.[44]

MINING ACTIVITIES

The country's parlous financial state led to considerable interest in the possibility of minerals other than crude oil. With this in mind, Karl Twitchell had been either directed—or was encouraged by his existing inclination—to expand his searches for water and oil to mining. Twitchell later wrote that the search for minerals resulted from a conversation held with ʿAbdullah al-Sulayman in 1931 following Twitchell's fruitless search for water deposits. The minister asked if Twitchell could recommend other sources of income to supplement the *hajj* revenues. Twitchell had anticipated the question and said that he thought the ancient mines he had come across in his earlier survey might be worth bringing back into production. Al-Sulayman, after conferring with Ibn Saʿud, presented the engineer with a check for £700 to cover the initial expenses.[45] This task Twitchell, a mining engineer and geologist by background (as detailed in Chapter 3), took to heart with enthusiasm. The first survey was discouraging, however, and Twitchell did not return to the task until after the al-Ahsaʾ oil concession was concluded.

Twitchell identified the ancient mine of Mahd al-Dhahab (about 400 kilometers north-east of Jiddah and 50 miles south of al-Madinah) as the most promising site for renewed mining and he accordingly played a key role in the formation of the Saudi Arabian Mining Syndicate Limited (SAMS) in May 1934, which signed a concession agreement for al-Hijaz with the Saudi government on 24 December 1934. Negotiations with ʿAbdullah al-Sulayman, accompanied by Yusuf Yasin and Khalid al-Qarqani, were again difficult until Twitchell managed to persuade him that the mining venture would not be able to pay cash or any loan as the oil company had done.[46]

SAMS thereupon set to work to exploit Mahd al-Dhahab. By the beginning of 1936, there were some 25 Europeans and 700 laborers employed at the mine site and work was well in hand for the construction of a road from Jiddah to Mahd al-Dhahab.[47] SAMS shareholders were both British and American, as well as a few Saudis, and 15 percent of the shares were allocated to the Saudi government. It later became a subsidiary of American Smelting and Refining Company (ASARCO). The first gold extracts from the mine, consisting of 150 special barrels and worth some $100,000, were sent to Jiddah in 1939, where they were loaded onto a ship bound for Colombo and then the US.[48] At the end of 1953, the largest shareholders were ASARCO with 833,068 shares and the Saudi Arabian Government with 585,680. No other shareholder held more than 141,920. Sixteen Saudi individuals and companies also owned shares, mostly numbering between 1200 and 4000.[49]

For the second half of 1939, the SAMS reported that it had milled 43,060 tons to produce 15,985 ounces of fine gold, 17,876 ounces of fine silver, and 8,837 pounds of copper. This was all from the Mahd al-Dhahab mine.[50] World War II, however, had a particularly adverse impact on mining operations. The scarcity of shipping space and needed supplies because of the priority given to the war effort forced the company to scale back operations in 1943, although there was hope that it would be able to resume in 1944.[51] Twitchell had done all he could to maintain operations, overemphasizing the importance of the company to the Saudi Arabian economy, misrepresenting the situation in Cairo to obtain 50 tons of explosives, and persuading the Ministry of Finance to provide a certified statement that SAMS' continued operation was essential to the Saudi economy. When the king was told in 1943 that the company would have to be shut down, his reaction was muted.[52]

Despite war restrictions, production at Mahd al-Dhahab mine had increased through the 1939–43 period, with production of gold and silver rising by about one-third.[53] Fortunately, the company was able to continue operations with greater access to shipping in early 1944 before being forced to close down. By March 1945, however, SAMS was able to recommence gold mining operations after a lapse of more than a year. Furthermore, the king, Amir Mansur, and ʿAbdullah al-Sulayman visited the operations at Mahd al-Dhahab and voiced their satisfaction.[54] SAMA was not out of the woods by far, however. In practice, the company was obliged to sell its refined product in the US at the US Treasury price despite sharply increased operating costs in the kingdom. As a consequence, no dividend was paid to shareholders in 1946. Production in 1946 totaled $1.7 million in gold concentrates and over $800,000 of by-products, chiefly silver and zinc.[55]

Still, the mines were steadily being played out. By 1950, annual production was down to 1,057 ounces of gold and profit before depreciation totaled £289,348.[56] SAMS operations lasted only into the early 1950s when it had exhausted all the commercially viable ore. The company was dissolved in November 1954 and its staff left the kingdom.[57] Another factor in the company's dissolution may have been the Saudi government's refusal to heed the company's contention that it was not subject to the new income tax law because of the terms of its concession.[58] Over the enterprise's entire life (from June 1939 through October 1953 and including estimates through closing), it was calculated that more than 720,563 ounces of gold had been recovered with a gross value of more than $30 million. The total of silver production was more than 908,000 ounces with a gross value of over $725,000.[59]

Gold was not the only mineral that attracted the Saudi Arabian government's attention. In 1938, for example, a bauxite concession was discussed with St. John Philby and the latter's associate, Joseph Dudler, although nothing seems to have come of it.[60]

ELECTRICITY AND WATER SUPPLY

In addition to the above concerns, the Ministry of Finance found itself involved in a variety of other financial and development projects during the 1930s. One of these was the electrification of Makkah and Jiddah. Action was taken in early 1930 to establish a new electricity power plant to supply the two cities, since the existing plant was too small for increasing demand and furthermore was dependent on a single condenser. The effort to expand electricity supply apparently was an initiative of al-Sulayman. A committee was created to examine the problem and, after deliberation, a general meeting was held on 27 January at the Ministry of Finance in Jiddah with Prince Faysal and other notables in attendance. It was proposed that a company be formed to administer the scheme with two-thirds of its shares to be held by the Makkah Municipality and the Ministry of Finance; the remaining third was to be open to public subscription. This was followed by a similar meeting in Jiddah. There was, however, considerable skepticism by the public about the scheme's success, partly because capitalization was deemed insufficient but especially since the government would be the principal consumer and quite possibly might not pay for its electricity.[61] The ministry also had a hand in the establishment of the Saudi Electric Company, a private concern, which initiated electricity in al-Ta'if, Jiddah, al-Madinah, and al-Hufuf in al-Ahsa', as well as Riyadh, al-Dammam, and al-Khubar.[62]

Simultaneously, attempts to improve the water supply of Jiddah were evident from nearly the beginning of Ibn Sa'ud's control over al-Hijaz. The installation of the water condenser in Jiddah was executed in late 1927 and early 1928 by two Scottish engineers from Merrilees Watson, in addition to their supervision of the construction of a new road from Jiddah to Makkah.[63] The provision of fresh water to Jiddah by means of an old Turkish conduit from the foothills gained new life in the early 1930s as additional sources of water were joined to the conduit. However, the old age and uncleaned nature of the conduit made potable water impossible and the Waziriyah Committee (named after the location seven miles inland where the conduit began) in charge of the water supply seemed unable to secure an estimated £5000 that would repair and renew the conduit. 'Abdullah al-Sulayman was believed to be hostile to the scheme because it would shut down the condensers from which the government derived some income. It was reported that "The local merchants on the committee are far too much in awe of him to act effectively. Whilst, therefore, the yield of certain municipal taxes has been voted for furthering the scheme and there is some talk of a future levy on pilgrims, no efforts are being made to raise an adequate sum for the purpose ...."[64]

Karl Twitchell was intimately involved with this water project as well in 1931, following which Ibn Sa'ud requested that he carry out a water survey in al-Ahsa' province.[65] Using wells and existing tunnels, the new water supply line of more than seven miles length, from al-Waziriyah to Jiddah, was put into operation on 26 August 1933. The delivered water was held in the reservoir of Idarus near the poorer quarters of Jiddah, which was of considerable benefit to the poor who could take their water from the reservoir without charge.[66] More improvements were made in late 1934, particularly in the pipeline, resulting in better quality and quantity of water. Operations were underway to extend piped water to various quarters of the town.[67] Reliance on the condenser continued through the years, though. The death of the Indian condenser manager in 1937 forced ʿAbdullah al-Sulayman, in yet another example of his myriad responsibilities, to ask the British Legation for assistance in providing someone to run it.[68] The search continued into 1938 when a visiting California Arabian Standard Oil Company (CASOC) team reported that Shaykh ʿAbdullah had asked the company to investigate the possibility of bringing water by pipeline from Wadi Fatimah.[69]

OTHER MINISTRY OF FINANCE RESPONSIBILITIES

Short mention only can be made of a wide variety of miscellaneous duties and connections associated with the Ministry of Finance and ʿAbdullah al-Sulayman. Despite the early efforts of Karl Twitchell, abundant supplies of water were not discovered. The government turned to the oil company for help in 1938 and CASOC drilled near Jiddah without success before turning to Riyadh.[70] However, artesian wells were drilled by CASOC at al-Qatif and elsewhere in the east. Al-Sulayman outlined his hopes for agriculture in al-Kharj to CASOC and whisked CASOC personnel visiting Riyadh in September 1938 to al-Kharj for a look at the sites.[71] The wheat grown with the water provided by runoff from winter rains was said to have relieved hunger in Najd during the late 1930s and early 1940s.[72] But as part of his effort to find water for more extensive irrigation, al-Sulayman directed that a pump should be installed in al-Kharj.[73] Iraqi engineers were engaged to put in pumps and the minister visited the oasis to check on developments in December 1939.[74] These activities were to provide the genesis of al-Sulayman's involvement with the al-Kharj agricultural project, detailed in following chapters.

The Ministry of Finance also found itself dealing with the nascent civil service. The Al Saʿud state retained the Kingdom of al-Hijaz system of administration of government employees' affairs upon the latter kingdom's absorption in 1926 and a more thorough administrative structure was promulgated in 1929. Responsibility for civil service affairs was taken over by the ministry in 1939 when it created an Office of Employees and Expected Revenues. Al-Sulayman continued to supervise civil service affairs until his retirement in 1954.[75]

Not surprisingly, given the ministry's financial responsibilities, it was also involved in schemes to develop banking in the country. The first effective bank establishment in the country belonged to the Netherlands Trading

Society (Nederlandische Handel Maatschappij, commonly called the Dutch Bank), which opened a branch office in Jiddah at the end of 1926. Its primary purpose was to facilitate letters of credit and provide foreign exchange for pilgrims from Java and elsewhere. The company was said to have imported £20,000 in gold from the Bank of England for this purpose. Although not functioning as a bank, the company later provided nearly the only banking facilities in Saudi Arabia for some years.[76] Some banking facilities were available also through Gellatly, Hankey (Gellatly's), and, occasionally, International Agencies (Limited) and Haji Abdullah Alireza and Company.[77]

Two other schemes were the proposed Khedivial Bank and then another to be established through the Hedjaz Development Corporation. ʿAbd al-Hamid Bey Shadid was involved in both schemes and he hinted that Westminster Bank were interested in the latter. In both cases, relevant proposals were received but nothing came of either.[78]

But consideration of prospects continued and it was reported in 1939 that approval for the Netherlands Trading Society to open a branch in Dhahran (to handle oil company business) was being delayed in hopes of establishing a Saudi National Bank. Such an institution would handle financing of government operations (including both exports and imports) as well as stabilize the currency. Nothing came of the scheme at that time because, as the British Treasury observed, the function of managing government payments was being handled already by the Dutch Bank, the attempt to regulate foreign exchange would likely exacerbate financial difficulties and stifle trade, and efforts to stabilize the currency would not be achieved simply by the creation of a central bank in the absence of adequate government management of its currency. Additional problems existed in the unbalanced seasonal demand for currency because of pilgrim traffic.[79]

As another example of the breadth and detail of his duties, the minister of finance was called upon in 1938 to enact arrangements for the merchants Gray Mackenzie to operate from the new terminal at Raʾs Tanurah on the Gulf.[80] At about the same time, he was instrumental in negotiations for bulk petrol purchases by the government with CASOC and Gellatly's, the Jiddah agent for Shell. Gellatly's feared losing the monopoly they had hitherto enjoyed but Shell was not interested and so the field was left to CASOC, which also declined. The minister was left without a partner but managed to persuade SAMS to build an extra storage tank adjacent to its own outside Jiddah. He then placed a bulk order with CASOC, pointedly ignoring Gellatly's.[81]

It is well worth noting in addition that, in reflection of the personal nature of administration, King ʿAbd al-ʿAziz called upon ʿAbdullah al-Sulayman to either carry out a multitude of small and often personal tasks, or to supervise or keep an eye on the execution of these tasks. It is impossible to distinguish the tasks between part of his duties as minister of finance in an environment where there was virtually no bureaucratic structure, and the king's reliance on him as a particularly trusted adviser. A selection of telegrams written from the king to al-Sulayman in the 1930s or copied to him instruct the recipient to, *inter alia*, make suitable arrangements to pick up the son of a foreign dignitary arriving before the *hajj* and have him driven to al-Madinah; distribute specified amounts of *zakat* to certain religious leaders and shaykhs; provide advice on what aid could be provided for martyrs and families in Palestine; standardize weights for Riyadh, Makkah, and Ra's Tanurah; order parts for radio broadcasting equipment; arrange for religious schoolteachers to be sent to Riyadh to instruct younger members of the king's family; stop the exporting of all products from sheep and goats since they were scarce and needed in the kingdom; and send smallpox vaccine and medical aides to administer the vaccine to Riyadh.[82]

Some idea of al-Sulayman's workload can be discerned by a look at a collection of his correspondence during the year 1350/1931–2. Most of the more than 200 messages received consisted of greetings and acknowledgments, minor administrative matters, *zakat* collection, purchases for the royal household, and requests from apparently ordinary people for money, clothing, or employment.[83]

PART II

THE IMPACT OF WORLD WAR II

CHAPTER 5

British Wartime Assistance and the Emergence of Anglo-American Rivalry

As the twentieth century wore on, the new state of Saudi Arabia found itself increasingly bound up with events beyond its borders. The debut of oil payments and loans brought only partial relief to the kingdom's endemic financial problems. It also brought into high relief the country's weakness in relying on multiple currencies and the dangers inherent in the lack of effective currency and banking control. World War II brought additional problems and hardships but, at the same time, it also produced the beginnings of a new alliance with the United States. Finally, the war years demonstrated the requirements for administrative changes necessary to administer an increasingly complex government.

The outbreak and multiplication of combat arenas during World War II had a direct impact on Saudi finances, particularly through the disruption of normal commerce. The Italian air strike on the California Arabian Standard Oil Company (CASOC) facilities in Dhahran shut down most oil operations for the duration of the war (more details are given in Chapter 8). Increased risks and obstacles to shipping reduced *hajj* traffic and disrupted trade crossing the Red Sea. Elementary materials could not be found in markets. Fortunately, Saudi Arabia was able to secure subsidies from the United Kingdom and the United States. The outbreak of the war itself caused a brief commotion in the financial situation in al-Hijaz, as the merchants withdrew all their gold from the Netherlands Trading Society, making it difficult for foreign pilgrims to cash drafts in foreign currency and causing prices to rise in the *suq* (market) [1]

Wartime exigencies required subsidies and other provisions for countries friendly to the Allies. This was certainly true in the case of Saudi Arabia. Beyond arrangements for arms, problems in supply had a major impact on the kingdom as difficulties grew in procuring tires and other items made of materials required for the war. A related problem involved acquiring essential foodstuffs. In addition, the difficulty of transport and increased regulations meant that the *hajj* (pilgrimage) grew smaller, striking a significant blow to the Saudi economy which remained heavily dependent on *hajj* revenues. The Government of India even forbade its citizens from making the *hajj* for safety reasons in 1943 and 1944, leading to a 20 percent decrease in the number of anticipated pilgrims. In addition, the Saudi Arabian government had difficulties in maintaining adequate numbers of vehicles and supplies for transportation of pilgrims, and orders of necessary drugs from abroad were either unobtainable or lost en route.[2]

Even before war broke out, the British government agreed in May 1939 to provide Saudi Arabia with more than £66,000 in credit to purchase arms and construct an arms factory. In this connection, the British government authorized the Saudi issuance of Treasury notes, signed by the Saudi minister to London on behalf of the Ministry of Finance, for purchases in the UK and backed by the Export Credits Guarantee Department of the Board of Trade.[3] The outbreak of the war caused London to withdraw the export credit but apparently it had been decided already to postpone the arms factory.[4] Nevertheless, it was clear from the beginning that Saudi Arabia would need substantial financial assistance throughout the duration of the war.

THE INCEPTION OF BRITISH WARTIME SUBSIDIES

The British government, cognizant of the looming impact of the war on Saudi Arabia, offered a credit of £100,000 to the kingdom in early 1940. The king's first reaction was one of dismay that the amount was so small—he had hoped for £800,000. However, he was mollified when the British minister pointed out that the ready extension of the offer in only a few days after the request was made was a good sign of British support in itself.[5] In the end, the British offered £200,000 in credit in addition to £85,000 already offered for the purchase of arms. In addition, London offered to provide part of the credit in *riyal*s, to be manufactured in Britain, up to a maximum of one million *riyal*s at an approximate cost of £33,500. With this credit, it was suggested, Saudi Arabia would be able to purchase foodstuffs in India or in British African colonies within the sterling area.[6] Eventually, the British government decided to make the credit a subsidy, feeling that the chance of it ever being repaid was remote.[7] The Saudi government also received CASOC loans of $3.25 million during 1940.[8] Barely six months later, London decided to add another £600,000 to their subsidy—to be paid in installments of £200,000 every two months. In this manner, the king would receive the entire £800,000 that he had originally asked for. His stated intention for use of the first installment was to pay salaries and buy foodstuffs.[9]

The country's dependence on the *hajj* for revenue threw the government into despair when the 1941 *hajj* produced the fewest number of pilgrims since the mid-1920s strife in al-Hijaz: fewer than 10,000 from overseas compared with more than 30,000 in the previous year (see Table 2.2). The king's appeals for assistance resulted in a CASOC advance of $3 million and £900,000 from Britain, as well as the gift of ten million Saudi *riyals* minted in India at a cost of about £450,000. The United States government declined to proffer any aid because it felt that Saudi Arabia lay within the British orbit, even though the British believed at one point that President Roosevelt had authorized $6 million in credits for American goods despite the fact that Saudi Arabia did not qualify for the Lend–Lease Act. At the same time, however, the State Department suggested that an agricultural expert newly assigned to the Cairo embassy would be available to study irrigation possibilities in the kingdom.[10] Nevertheless, and despite the British assistance, the Saudi government faced a deficit by the end of 1941 of more than £1 million due to unpaid bills and unpaid salaries.[11] The grave situation prompted the minister of finance to approach the British during the summer of 1941 about the possibility that an installment of the loan could be paid early due to pressing circumstances.[12]

Meanwhile, J.A. Moffett of CASOC sought to persuade the US government to provide the $10 million in aid required, or at least to prevail upon Britain to maintain its aid to Saudi Arabia at that level. His other idea was for the US to advance $6 million per annum for the next five years by purchasing $6 million worth of petroleum products from CASOC, using what it needed and selling the remainder. The king would receive the proceeds of this sale and in return would forego royalties on it. Moffett's motive of course was to relieve CASOC of its frequent burden of providing large advances. The State Department considered the idea but concluded that it raised legal difficulties. Instead, it proposed that the US Navy should purchase $3 million worth of petroleum products and the balance of $3 million could then be provided in commodities through Lend–Lease. This idea was subsequently shot down by the Navy, which informed the President that the type of petroleum products produced in Saudi Arabia were not suitable for Navy use.[13]

With the kingdom's financial situation deteriorating as the year progressed, Prince Faysal b. ʿAbd al-ʿAziz, the foreign minister, wrote to US ambassador Alexander C. Kirk in Cairo in June requesting a credit of $10 million, citing the decline in pilgrim numbers, the curtailment of oil production, and the onslaught of drought. The State Department delayed in answering but internally supported the request. Eventually, State received word that the President had turned down the request through a note to an aide saying "Will you tell the British I hope they can take care of the King of Saudi Arabia. This is a little far afield for us."[14] As the State Department and CASOC had both expected, the result was King ʿAbd al-ʿAziz's feeling that the refusal to provide aid was a slight to his honor.[15] Nevertheless, the US government acted positively on the suggestion of an agricultural mission to the kingdom as a way of softening the blow (the mission is discussed in more detail below).

ʿAbdullah al-Sulayman provided the British with details of the country's financial situation in November 1941. For three years before the war, the kingdom's annual expenditure was approximately £3 million. This was paid for by about £2 million from customs, pilgrim dues, and internal taxation and £1 million in payments by oil and concessionary companies. Expenditure in 1941 increased by about £750,000 while revenue fell by nearly £1,800,000. The decrease in revenue was argued because of the diminished number of pilgrims, reduced customs revenues (partly because of fewer pilgrims entering the country but also due to a reduction in customs to allow impoverished residents to buy essentials), and the emergence of a serious drought in Najd, requiring additional assistance to tribes there. Even after total British disbursements of £1,400,000, Saudi Arabia's debt in 1941 would total about £1,150,000 from supplies obtained on credit and government officials' salaries in arrears.

Furthermore, al-Sulayman calculated expected expenditures for 1942 would be the same as 1941, i.e. £3,700,000 while revenue was expected to be only £1,000,000, including payments from oil companies. This would leave the government's coffers short by £2,700,000. Adding in the deficit from 1941, the total requirements through the end of 1942 would be £3,850,000, of which at least £250,000 was needed urgently. He had appealed to Washington for $10,000,000 but gathered that they had declined to help because they expected London to provide some aid out of the funds provided to Britain under the Lend–Lease Act.[16]

Stonehewer Bird, in evaluating the information provided to him by al-Sulayman, reported that he had confirmed the kingdom's immediate need for £250,000 with CASOC and added that "I would stress the point that any help given to Ibn Saud must now be regarded ... as a war measure. . . ."[17] Whitehall, although skeptical of the minister of finance's figures and after asking Jiddah to provide more details, rather grudgingly agreed to an immediate payment of another £250,000.[18]

A further problem arose in relations with CASOC and the kingdom's insistence on an increase in payments. There were two arguments. First, the minister of finance complained that the net amount received in royalties had been decreased because of changes in exchange rates while at the same time the world price of oil had been increasing. Second, he argued that royalties should be calculated on productive capacity rather than exports since exports had been greatly reduced because of the war—or at least the principle of a minimum royalty should be established with the company making up for it in years of high exports. After serious arguments and an implied threat to cancel the concession, CASOC agreed to advance up to $6 million for the year.[19] In the end, CASOC does not seem to have provided more than $3 million.

In addition, the war itself touched the kingdom directly again in 1941, as it had with the bombing of Dhahran in 1940. Three Italian destroyers made for Jiddah in April but British naval and air action drove them ashore some 10–15 miles south of Jiddah, where they were scuttled by their crews.[20]

Saudi Arabia's precarious finances during the war revolved around two fundamental difficulties: securing sufficient supplies, particularly foodstuffs, and maintaining an adequate cover of local currency. The extension of a British subsidy necessarily had to address both problems. Arrangements for supplies were handled through the United Kingdom Commercial Corporation (UKCC) and the Middle East Supply Center (MESC). Purchases were paid for in sterling from the Ministry of Finance's account and the Saudi government would then resell the imports within Saudi Arabia for local currency. The kingdom also sought to minimize the effects on currency of smuggling and hoarding by purchasing *riyal*s with sterling from local banks and indirectly by issuing import licenses for the purchase of rupees or sterling to merchants, which would be redeemed by Gellatly, Hankey and charged to the Ministry of Finance's sterling account. These measures were not sufficient, however, for Saudi Arabia to meet its expenditures on goods, salaries, and tribal subsidies. As a consequence, Britain also found itself supplying silver *riyal*s to the kingdom as part of its subsidy.

THE KINGDOM'S DIRE INTERNAL SITUATION IN 1942–3

Hardly had the contentions over aid provisions for 1941 been settled than the process began again for 1942. In November 1941, CASOC officials met with State Department officials to provide background on 1942 requests. They informed State that King ʿAbd al-ʿAziz had requested $4.5 million for the last quarter of 1941 from the British but was to receive only $1 million. Furthermore, the British reduced the request for $21 million for 1942 to $15 million. They added that CASOC intended to advance $3 million for the year but they were reluctant to leave the king so reliant on British assistance for fear that the British would insist on oil rights.[21]

A particular aspect of the problem of *hajj* revenues was the absence during the war of Javanese and Malay pilgrims, who were considerably more prosperous than other pilgrims and tended to stay much longer and spend more money. Because of the increasing poverty of the kingdom's people, tax revenues were down and taxes were necessarily reduced. Figures produced by the Ministry of Finance showed that government revenues had declined in nearly all fields compared to the previous three years. Customs, for example, fell by 70 percent (duties were reduced by 20 percent for the duration of the war); quarantine dues collapsed by 93 percent, impacted both by a decrease in pilgrims and a 25 percent reduction of pilgrims' dues; *zakat* fell by 79 percent in large part due to the drought; *jihad* tax was suspended for the duration of the war. The two biggest items, the car tax and professional licenses, fell away to nearly nothing because they depended on the transport of pilgrims and the licensing of the *mutawwif*s (the *hajj* guides).[22]

A detailed CASOC memorandum in early 1942 reiterated many of the same reasons for the desperate economic straits that the kingdom faced. Its author, Roy Lebkicher, doubted that *hajj* revenues even before the war were sufficient to keep the government afloat but the war and problems of internal currency compounded the problem. Nevertheless, he noted that the 1942 budget was the largest ever despite a decline in locally generated income. He ascribed the big problems of a currency muddle and supply problems to poor economic management. The government, he said, was simply incapable of planning and thus could not anticipate real needs of supplies accurately. Furthermore, the shortage of gold sovereigns meant that the government could not rely on its traditional solution to the problem of a shortage of *riyal*s: sell sovereigns to the merchants for *riyal*s that had been hoarded. With the war, sovereigns increasingly were either being smuggled out of the country for profits on foreign exchange or simply hoarded. Lebkicher argued that the US government should shoulder part of the aid burden.[23]

Not surprisingly, Saudi Arabia pressed the British in January 1942 for early payment of the first tranche of £250,000 in expected aid.[24] Shortly afterward, the king's intention of sending ʿAbdullah al-Sulayman on a mission to India, presumably connected with currency questions and the purchase of foodstuffs, was shelved after the British minister convinced the king that he thought the minister of finance's presence was required at home while the supply of coinage was under consideration.[25] With regard to foodstuffs, al-Sulayman made the suggestion in late 1941 that it would be cheaper and more satisfactory if a British government organization purchased supplies for the kingdom directly and the amount could be deducted from the British subsidy. This proposal received approval in London and King ʿAbd al-ʿAziz gave his approval. However, only 500 tons of wheat and 200 tons of sugar were supplied by the UKCC through the end of March 1942.[26]

The situation grew worse during the year. When the British minister, F.H.W. Stonehewer Bird, made his way to Riyadh at the end of 1942, King ʿAbd al-ʿAziz expressed his understanding that the needs of war had an abiding claim on Britain's expenditures. But he also voiced his frustration at the country's poverty:

> But the hungry man doesn't always understand. "We are hungry and there are hungrier folk behind us," as they say. This is a wide country. In our faroff parts, by the borders of Iraq and Transjordan, there are people starving. Then there is the question of money. Both here in the Hejaz and on the eastern side nothing comes in. With the new arrangements that we have made for getting supplies of foodstuffs, customs receipts have dwindled away. The demands on me increase. I have to give great sums in charity. All day and every day beggars are at my door and petitions pour in from great and small, all saying the same thing: 'I'm hungry, I want, I want....' On this visit to the Hejaz I have found the money I brought with me for charity not enough. I have purposely left Ibn Suleiman [the minister of finance] behind in Nejd for a time so that I can stave off the clamorous by telling them to wait until Ibn Suleiman comes. I have insisted on the strictest economy in my own family and have not allowed any of them to come with me to Mecca this time unless they could pay their own way.[27]

In April, the Najdi tribes started to converge on Riyadh for their overdue subsidies while no government salaries had been paid for four months. In addition, five million rupees (Rs.) were needed immediately.[28] A British financial expert, Sir F. Rugman (financial secretary to the Sudan Government), visited the kingdom in April and discussed affairs with the minister of finance. His report concluded that "It is on a gold standard but its government has no gold and no subsidiary silver currency.... There is no adequate system of state accounts, financial control or war-time supply." Filling the wide gap between the state's reduced income and the minimum expenditures needed to feed the people and maintain the government, the report concluded, would require Saudi Arabia to be brought within the sphere of the MESC in Cairo with all essential supplies imported through the UKCC. Finally, the report recognized that Saudi Arabia would need an additional amount of currency to cover subsidies to tribes and government salaries and recommended the provision of Rs. 5 million or, as a last resort, 100,000 sovereigns.[29] Due to Indian objections to the circulation of so many rupees outside the country, London agreed to provide the sovereigns, which were delivered to the minister of finance in Jiddah in April 1942.[30] The rupees were provided later.

Although Saudi Arabia agreed to the plan, opposition from the Government of India and the inability of the MESC to provide all the required goods eventually led to a modification of the plan to a system of import controls.[31] All the main imports were to be ordered through Gellatly's, which would issue rupee drafts on behalf of the government. The minister of finance realized that this would not provide enough *riyal*s and asked for a further five million *riyal*s to be minted in India. The additional *riyal*s were shipped to the kingdom in September. Naturally, it was difficult for the

Ministry of Finance to know how much the country could import if it did not know how much in the way of funds it would have to pay for the goods. Therefore al-Sulayman pressed the British government for a more definite answer as to the amount of subsidy that Saudi Arabia would be receiving. London was reluctant to provide this information on the grounds that the kingdom would not adhere to strict economies if it knew. In the end, however, the Foreign Office agreed to let al-Sulayman know the precise amount and it promised to make monthly payments of £150,000 through the Saudi government's account with Gellatly's.[32]

Britain provided about £3 million in aid to the kingdom in 1942, part of which was presented in the form of Saudi *riyal*s to help ease the currency shortage. This assistance went a considerable way to paying officials' salaries, alleviating the effects of drought in Najd, and enabling food and other goods to be purchased from abroad. But even greater difficulties were seen for 1943, both in terms of transport of supplies and in the likelihood that all available foodstuffs in India would be required for domestic use there. A representative of the MESC was posted to Jiddah to help work through the problems and Britain also provided the services of a transport adviser and a few mechanics to help improve maintenance of Saudi vehicles and to organize better regional transportation. An increase in the number of pilgrims for the 1942 *hajj* was one of few welcome improvements.[33] At the same time, however, the operations of both CASOC and the Saudi Arabian Mining Syndicate (SAMS) were hampered by their inability to get equipment and supplies.

A perusal of the Saudi government account with Gellatly's showed £1,200,000 in receipts and £1,195,178 in payments for the year 1942. The largest payments were to National Provincial Bank in London, the National Bank of India, and the National Bank of Egypt, while other payments went to Saudi legations abroad.[34] At year's end, it was estimated that the final Saudi budget deficit would be only £20,000.[35]

During this period, the British advanced various schemes for efficient provision of needed imports into the kingdom. Because of the obstacles created by the war in purchasing and shipping, it was originally thought best that the Ministry of Finance should control the import and sale of all goods. A modified plan reduced the ministry's role to control of essential rationed goods such as foodstuffs, combined with issuing import licenses for non-essential goods. As a result, the ministry found itself exercising considerable power and making all the merchants dependent on government permission to trade.[36]

The king repeated his pressing requirements for foodstuffs and transportation to Lord Moyne, the British minister resident in the Middle East, who visited at the end of 1942. As there were no available supplies from surrounding countries, the kingdom was entirely dependent on British help for its supplies and suitable transportation was needed to get food to areas devastated by the drought (which had also laid waste to pastures for camels who therefore could not be used for transport). Even though the king had purchased £72,000 worth of needed cars, he had given permission to the British Army to make use of them in Egypt. When Lord Moyne introduced Major Smith of the MESC to answer the king's questions on supply, the king pointed to ʿAbdullah al-Sulayman and said "Let the experts get together." To further show British determination to help Saudi Arabia, a MESC representative and a British transport adviser were assigned to the kingdom late in 1942 to assist in the formation of supply plans for the country. Their Saudi counterpart was to be Najib Salihah of the Ministry of Finance.[37]

As the year 1943 neared, the familiar process of determining the amount of the British subsidy started anew. The Americans estimated that only £250,000 of the government's budget of £4 million was generated locally—and the budget was expected to increase to £5 million for 1943, far more than the £3 million in anticipated British subsidy.[38] After discussion with the minister of finance and Rugman, the British financial expert, the British minister in Jiddah reported that £4,080,000 would be required to balance the Saudi budget in 1943. About two-thirds of the amount would be required in sterling and the rest in newly minted *riyals*. The increase in aid required was attributed to a reduction in CASOC advances by nearly 70 percent, as well as increased expenditures because of higher food prices and stepped-up distribution to the needy (which had reached nearly one-third of the total government expenditure).[39]

The Saudi government's simple budget figures produced in mid-1943 showed an increase of 500,000 *riyals* in revenues to three million *riyals*, a drop in loans from CASOC from 10 million *riyals* to two million *riyals*, and a growth in subsidies and advances by Britain from 56.4 million *riyals* to 66.7 million. Expenditure was stated to be equal to receipts with the increase mainly carried under the heading of salaries, subsidies and reliefs (nine million *riyals*).[40]

In 1943, the British government subsidized King ʿAbd al-ʿAziz's state with £225,000 a month (or £2,700,000 for the year), plus an additional five million *riyals* and 400,000 sovereigns in grant. The US provided eight million *riyals* under the Lend–Lease program and was scheduled to add another seven million *riyals* early in 1944. The Saudi government was also the recipient of a $1 million advance from CASOC (equating approximately to the rental and oil subsidies accruing to the government from the company's operations in Saudi territory). Despite these subventions and hurt by a reduced *hajj* of 30,000 at the end of 1942, the Saudi Arabian government budget for 1943 showed a deficit of 30 million *riyals* (approximately £2,250,000 sterling).[41]

In part, this deficit was due to a major increase in salaries, subsidies, and reliefs. When Najib Salihah of the Ministry of Finance was queried on this point, he explained it as being partly due to a 25 percent increase in the salary of government officials (given the high cost of living) and partly to the increasing impoverishment of the people requiring more food and supplies to be distributed by the government.[42]

The process of determining the level of subsidy began again with planning in late 1943 for the 1944 subsidy. A revised Saudi budget for 1943 and estimates for 1944 were presented at the end of the year. Revenue for 1943 was calculated at 76 million *riyal*s, derived from the British subsidy, Lend–Lease aid, CASOC loan, and local income in that order. Expenditures, however, totaled 106 million *riyal*s, thus producing a deficit of 30 million *riyal*s. Estimates for 1944 were only slightly larger. Expenditure was estimated at nearly 109 million *riyal*s while local revenue would contribute only 36 and a half million *riyal*s. As a consequence, a subsidy of 72 million *riyal*s was required.[43]

ISSUES WITH THE BRITISH SUBSIDY FOR 1944

The British subsidy had been introduced to offset falling *hajj* revenues during the war. But as the size of the subsidy increased relative to such requirements, London informed Riyadh that the subsidy would have to be restricted to the actual requirements of the country. Furthermore, this would also be affected by the requirements of Britain's postwar economy. It was suggested that the Saudi government should reorganize their finances and economy in order to offset the loss of subsidy without hardship. King ʿAbd al-ʿAziz's reaction to this advice was to admit the need for financial reform to the British and to dismiss Najib Salihah, the director of mines and public works, and to replace him with ʿIzz al-Din Shawa, a Palestinian. In March 1944, the British government announced that their assistance would henceforth consist of a gift of 200,000 sovereigns and the cancellation of Riyadh's debt of 20 million *riyal*s to the UKCC against revenue derived from *hajj* tariff items. The loss of revenue to Saudi Arabia that this represented, however, was soon made up by an American offer to make up any reduction.[44] Washington also agreed to provide silver on Lend–Lease for use in minting Saudi *riyal*s.[45]

In the eyes of the British minister to Saudi Arabia, S.R. Jordan, a group of the king's advisers had opposed the imposition of such financial reforms, principally on the grounds of opposing change and the threat that it implied to their entrenched positions. Indeed, he wrote that they believed that the replacement of British aid by American aid was "the easy and profitable way out and played on the king's natural anxiety for his country in order to get the best deal."[46]

While Jordan's objectivity is a matter of debate (as discussed below), the question of how much assistance should be provided prompted intense discussion between US and British authorities in Washington and London, as well as at the MESC in Cairo. Eventually, it was agreed that any financial assistance should be negotiated jointly and shared equally.[47] After agreement, a joint supply program for 1944 totaling some $15,184,000 was presented to the king in early August 1944 and consisted of supplies allocated to the kingdom through the MESC, supplied through commercial channels and paid for by importing merchants, as well as a joint subsidy for essential commodities. Furthermore, Britain would provide £10,000 a month to cover the cost of Saudi missions abroad while the US would provide ten million *riyals* under Lend–Lease.[48] In addition, the Saudi Arabian government received a loan for £100,000 from Gellatly's in October as an advance on pilgrimage dues collected abroad.[49]

A contributing factor to the dispute over the size of the subsidy was the attitude of S.R. Jordan. While Stonehewer Bird had gotten along well with his Saudi counterparts and the king, Jordan was more confrontational. His antagonistic attitude brought him into conflict with ʿAbdullah al-Sulayman and the Ministry of Finance, as well as his American colleagues. His revision of Saudi budget estimates, scaling down expenditures and pushing up revenues, was a principal reason why Britain sought to reduce the subsidy for 1944. In Jordan's opinion, the Saudi budget for 1944 should balance at about 100 million *riyals* and the subsidy should be only 47 million *riyals*. In addition, his claims of extravagance at the royal court and pervasive corruption throughout the government alarmed the Foreign Office in London and strengthened the British Treasury's call for a reduction, particularly since it became clear that Saudi government payments to the UKCC had fallen behind the value of the goods delivered.[50]

In early 1944, Jordan pointed out to ʿAbdullah al-Sulayman, Yusuf Yasin, and Hafiz Wahbah (minister to London but in the kingdom at the time) that while the British subsidy four years previously amounted to £400,000, they were now asking for £8,000,000 during 1944 to cover their estimated budgetary deficit and the carry-over from 1943. He warned that while the British and American subsidies could be justified under the unusual war conditions, there could be little hope for them after the end of the war, particularly if both donor countries experienced another wave of economy as had happened after World War I. Because the sudden cessation of assistance might bring difficulties and even unrest to the kingdom, Jordan advised that the Saudi government should "endeavour to put their house in order now to mitigate as far as possible the ill effects of a considerably reduced revenue after the war. I realized that the revenue from oil royalties would increase but the

Saudi government already owed the company considerable sums and it was unlikely that any large revenue from this source would materialize for some three or four years to come."[51]

Jordan added that the country's principal source of income in the past had been the *hajj* and this would amount to only a quarter of what the Saudis were asking for in 1944. The three Saudis all offered their comments in return. Al-Sulayman admitted that some control of Saudi finances was badly needed and suggested the formation of a bank with an adequate capital which would act as controller of Government expenditure. But he also blamed the rising prices of commodities as a major reason for increased expenditure.[52]

Jordan and al-Sulayman had a lengthy conversation on the same subject shortly afterwards, when the latter informed Jordan that he had spoken with the king, who asked his minister of finance to speak frankly about the subject with Jordan. After a long preamble, al-Sulayman asked Jordan for his views on how to achieve financial stability. The diplomat responded that the essential point was reduction of the government's expenditure and he asked the minister of finance how he could achieve this reduction. Al-Sulayman replied that at the present time it was impossible to economize on the largest item of expenditure, that is, the distribution of charity for the poor. This included maintaining the livelihood of the bedouin who had been hard hit by the continued drought, which had killed off much of their livestock.

To Jordan's rejoinder that the 20-fold increase in the request for a British subsidy in only four years seemed unreasonable, al-Sulayman cited the rise in cost of a coffee cup from a quarter *riyal* to three *riyal*s. This was in large part because of transport problems and he pointed out that a sack of wheat cost 30 *riyal*s in Jiddah but 90 *riyal*s in Riyadh. Jordan then said that prices should be controlled, to which the minister of finance reminded him that the Saudi government had been forced to monopolize trade and take it out of the hands of merchants, thus creating a new class of paupers.

Jordan thereupon changed tack to assert that there was no shortage of *riyal*s in the country; hoarding simply had to be stopped. The import of more *riyal*s could only drive prices up. When al-Sulayman inquired as to how the government could acquire more *riyal*s, Jordan replied that the government should increase the sale of goods as well as foreign exchange to merchants wishing to import goods; this would also raise customs revenues. He then returned to the attack, advocating government control of prices to keep price rises down to a reasonable profit. Al-Sulayman replied that the king disliked the idea of control but he had ordered the establishment of government centers for the sale of commodities at a fixed price. This had brought prices down but applied only to "old" stocks and the merchants were unable to import more.

When the minister of finance protested that the MESC had been responsible for creating the Saudi government monopoly, Jordan brushed the point aside by remarking that it was only to be expected that a new and inexperienced agency would not be infallible and, in any case, the MESC was now advocating that trade should be restored to the merchants. Jordan also informed the minister of finance that a MESC Coordinating Committee was to be established in Jiddah and would be composed of British, American, and Saudi representatives.[53]

Some justification for ʿAbdullah al-Sulayman's contentions about government and merchants' stocks appeared shortly afterwards in a report by Jordan's stand-in in Jiddah. Discussions with the American minister in Jiddah, the MESC representative, and Gellatly's had produced the conclusion that while there was no general shortage of food in the country, there were probably local shortages produced mainly by transport difficulties. At the same time, government stocks were nearly exhausted and it was being forced to buy supplies in Jiddah from merchants at considerably higher prices than what they had been sold to the same merchants, in order to transport them to Riyadh. "This has played into the hands of merchants who have been holding on to the stocks in the hope of higher prices."[54]

In order to free the ability of merchants to buy commodities from abroad, it was necessary to free up restrictions on the export of gold. In July 1944, King ʿAbd al-ʿAziz issued an announcement that the export of gold would henceforth be permitted. However, any merchant doing so would be required to guarantee that he would import goods to the value of the gold exported within a stated time frame. The process would be supervised by the Ministry of Finance.[55] Finally, after discussions with al-Sulayman by the American and British ministers in Jiddah, the latter two proposed to solve the supply problem by establishing a MESC storage center for cereals in Jiddah; the Saudi government would provide the facilities and MESC would pay for the cereals and their shipping, as well as accept any loss through deterioration.[56]

In the end, as a consequence of Jordan's alarms, the Foreign Office decided to reduce the 1944 subsidy, handing over a slightly reduced amount for six months and then cutting it substantially thereafter. While London would continue to cover outstanding payments to the UKCC and fund necessary imports and the kingdom's foreign missions, it would not cover internal currency requirements. Those it expected would need to be met by American contributions and the sale of supplies, while the free distribution of goods would have to be cut.[57]

Jordan's insistence on the justification of cutting back on the free distribution of food and other supplies is contradicted by the widespread conditions of famine in the interior of Saudi Arabia. The hardships were detailed by the newly appointed American minister in Jiddah, William Eddy, on a visit to the SAMS operations at Mahd al-Dhahab in April. The SAMS doctor there confirmed that the Mutayr tribe was subject to slow starvation and reduced resistance to disease. They could no longer afford rice and sugar because of rampant inflation and unscrupulous merchants who had conspired to prevent the government from providing free transport to the interior.[58]

Eddy's findings were backed by a report by the US Office of Strategic Services that noted that the king had apparently stated that "if the situation were not promptly relieved, food riots would break out in a month or two which he would be unable and unwilling to control since he could not shoot starving people." Underlying reasons for this state of affairs were identified as the disruption of imports because of the war and a deterioration of motor transport because the government was unable to keep vehicles in good repair. Belying Jordan's contention, the report contended that the warehouses on the east and west coasts of the country were not even large enough to hold a stock of sufficient food. Furthermore, the food shortage existed in the interior where the greater majority of consumers resided. Since most of these lived at a bare subsistence level, any reduction in the amount of their food resulted in starvation.[59]

More evidence of dire conditions emerged in the following months. The king asked both the British and the Americans in June for assistance and instructed al-Sulayman to provide details of the situation. In essence, the latter reported that imports had declined precipitously because of unfavorable exchange rates, government salaries were in arrears, free distribution of food had ceased causing shortages, the British subsidy was insufficient, and two months of discussions with the Americans had produced no results.[60]

The government pleaded that people were dying of starvation in southern al-Hijaz and there was no food left to hand out. Asked for further details, the government provided figures on receipt, distribution, and the sale of food around the country supporting its contention that there was a serious shortage of food.[61] The king, accompanied by his minister of finance, even presented his case to ARAMCO. The company, convinced that the shortage was genuine, agreed to give $500,000 for the purchase of food in Cairo and another $1 million credit in the US to allow Saudi Arabia to buy gold with which to purchase additional supplies.[62] However, the MESC questioned the extent of shortages and challenged the Saudi government's figures.[63] Even as the British and American ministers in Jiddah met the king, backed by al-Sulayman, in Riyadh in August to present the joint supply program (see below), the king continued to argue that the aid was not sufficient and the country would not be able to cover the costs for the next few years.[64] Despite these pleas, Jordan remained unshaken in his convictions and claimed that a confidential source had informed him that a substantial amount of cereals had entered the country on dhows outside of MESC controls.[65]

After receiving Jordan's further comments on cutting the budget, the Foreign Office informed him that it had been decided to assume tighter control over the subsidy by addressing the problem for only the first half of the year. Payments would be made only for amounts actually shipped by the UKCC and henceforth, instead of Gellatly's receiving a regular amount, the company would have to apply to the British government for the necessary funds once it had received Saudi government's instructions to pay on the basis of invoices it had received from the UKCC. The situation would be reviewed at the end of June and another decision made for the remainder of the year.[66]

Jordan and the Saudi Arabian government finally reached agreement on the terms of financial aid in April. Among the main points were the free gift of 200,000 gold sovereigns to Saudi Arabia and the cancellation of the approximately 20 million *riyal* debt owed to the UKCC in 1943. In addition, the monthly instalment of £225,000 was canceled in favor of the free supply of cereals, tea, sugar, dates, and cotton goods equal to the amounts shipped in 1943. Additional provision was made for lorries to transport supplies into the interior.[67] The minister of finance subsequently attended the Middle East financial conference in Cairo in April, accompanied by Jordan and 'Izz al-Din Shawa, although he did not appear to take an active role in the proceedings.[68]

Al-Sulayman did use his trip to Cairo as an opportunity to plead Saudi Arabia's case with Lord Moyne, the minister resident in the Middle East. After the two men met on 28 April, al-Sulayman provided Lord Moyne with a long letter setting out his explanation of Saudi Arabia's economic plight. He argued that the figures upon which the new budget was based were the same as in the previous year except that new expenditure was required to provide food and clothing for the destitute. He pointed out that the Saudi government "distributes not less than 1,600 tons of grain every month to the people. Moreover the Government distributes not less than 1,000 tons of grain per month to its employees. The Government finds it necessary to continue rendering such assistance to that class of people, so long as there are no industrial or agricultural enterprises in the country."[69]

The minister of finance contested the allegation that the government had been hoarding foodstuffs (as Jordan had charged) and asserted only his government could possess the correct figures of available quantities in the country. The accumulation of goods at customs for days and weeks did not, he said, mean that stocks were more than required but simply that Saudi Arabia had only two ports and poor transport throughout the country. In addition, he complained that the pilgrim dues, collected in various countries on Saudi Arabia's behalf had not been turned over. It was not the government's money, he said, but money owed to guides and the owners of dhows, camels, vehicles, and guides; the government had been forced to borrow money in order to pay these people.[70] Lord Moyne's reply is not recorded but his views on the kingdom's financial situation and the difficulties over it that he had encountered with the US government were outlined to the secretary of state for foreign affairs (as discussed below). To bolster his case, al-Sulayman also communicated information on the country's finances to the US Legation in Jiddah.[71]

Determining Saudi Arabia's financial requirements was made especially difficult by the lack of adequate budgetary information. As a consequence, both the British and American authorities prepared a number of budgetary estimates on which to base their subsidy calculations. These were extremely rudimentary by necessity since there was still no proper budget prepared by the Saudi Arabian government. Jordan reworked the figures in May 1944 and calculated a figure of 20,500,000 *riyal*s for "probable normal revenues." These consisted of *hajj* (12.5 million), royalties and rents from the oil and gold concessions (4 million), and customs dues (4 million). He noted that although at the time of writing the Saudi government received only 1 million *riyal*s from the oil company, that was likely to increase as exports picked up. At the same time, the kingdom had received £6.6 million/87.4 million *riyal*s from the UK and £15 million/102 million *riyal*s from the US.

On the other side of the ledger, Jordan pointed out that the Saudi government's estimate of expenditures for 1944 totaled 108 million *riyal*s. If supplies passed through merchant channels, received as Lend–Lease, or deriving from British donations were removed, then expenditures could be split into salaries and subsidies, and both figures, Jordan averred, could be reduced substantially. Jordan felt that expenditures should be reduced to 20 million *riyal*s, which he regarded as the "normal" amount available after the war and the end of the subsidies. Against this long-term goal, he set an immediate reduction of expenditures from 65 million to 50 million, which would require 29.5 million to be derived from the sale of supplies received from Britain and the US. Jordan noted that many of these supplies were distributed free but had no specific suggestions of how the government could raise all of the 29.5 million in revenues. In conclusion, Jordan suggested a British subsidy for 1944 of about £3 million rather than the £6 million for 1943.[72]

An American working of the budgetary figures followed a few days after Jordan's efforts. That appraisal of the kingdom's budget compared expenditures according to the 1943 actuals (106.46 million), the kingdom's estimates for 1944 (108.77 million), and Jordan's estimates (100.15), and came up with a revised figure of 87.07 million *riyals*. Regarding income, the 1943 actuals of 108.16 million, kingdom's estimate of 108.77 million, and Jordan's estimate of 87.75 million, were recalculated at 88.50 million. This included British gifts of currency and American Lend–Lease silver but separated Lend–Lease goods as well as both the British and American subsidies. The value of these items was 93.66 million in 1943 (including a 78.66 million British subsidy and a 15 million American subsidy) while the American estimate placed the 1944 value at 47.57 million (including equal 23.50 million British and American subsidies). The American appraisal differed from Jordan's particularly in their view that a greater percentage of imports should be moved through commercial channels rather than through the government, which they regarded as lacking the necessary facilities. Government imports should account only for goods to be distributed for free.[73]

London and Washington did agree, however, on a 50/50 split of the subsidy.[74] However, it was soon recognized that the agreed subsidy and budget would not provide a basis for the future because of the increasing problem of inflation. Despite Jordan's assurances that prices were essentially unchanged, information provided to Cairo by Jordan's number two, Ellison, showed that, *inter alia*, prices for staple foodstuffs in 1944 were between four and six times their prices in 1939. This caused the Foreign Office to conclude that, first, Jordan's estimates for cutting the figures for Saudi salaries and food subsidies from 45 million *riyal*s to 32 million were clearly unreasonable. Second, it would be impossible to end the subsidy in 1945; instead some assistance would probably be required for another four or five years. Consequently, British insistence on drastically reducing Saudi Arabian expenditures began to soften.[75]

Jordan's attitude and his twisting of the figures, resulting in the drastic reduction of the 1944 subsidy, created immediate problems in his relations with the Ministry of Finance. But it also had a longer-term impact by constituting a supporting factor in the shifting of influence in the kingdom from Britain to the United States. In a telegram to King ʿAbd al-ʿAziz, ʿAbdullah al-Sulayman noted that Jordan had spoken of the need to reduce expenditure but "gave no indication as to what reductions should be made or where." Furthermore, the minister of finance added that he felt that delays in providing transport were Jordan's doing and that the British government in London was not being kept informed about the issue.[76]

For his part, Jordan, in transmitting Najib Salihah's intercepted telegrams to London, argued that he "and a group of associates have been systematically robbing the Saudi government." Since it was not surprising that the group should resist any reform of the government, Jordan asserted that at least one of these officials opposed Jordan's proposals for closer supervision of expenditure in an attempt to create discord between Jordan and King ʿAbd al-ʿAziz. Jordan also alleged that the group's strategy included advocating closer ties with the US, "no doubt prompted by recent United States activities in Saudi Arabia which have been characterized by an enthusiasm which carried them beyond the limit of discretion."[77]

Much of the dispute settled around personal animosity between Jordan and Najib Salihah, and Jordan pressed the king to dismiss Salihah and the British minister reported home that the king mentioned he might send him to Dhahran as representative to the oil company and then dismiss him after six months. In his letter to the secretary of state for foreign affairs, Jordan also turned his attack on al-Sulayman and sought unsuccessfully to persuade the king that al-Sulayman had been overly extravagant during his India trip.[78] This was not Jordan's only accusation against the minister of finance. The Foreign Office, however, counseled Jordan against opposing al-Sulayman since it was feared that the king might resent any intervention against "so powerful an official, who has held Ibn Saud's confidence for so many years."[79] The matter did not rest there. Apparently al-Sulayman had communicated two requests from the king for Jordan's removal in mid-1944.[80] Some weeks later, Jordan responded to the Foreign Office letter claiming that he had no intention of raising the matter of the minister with the king, unless the king asked for a personal opinion.[81]

Relations were also tense between Moose and Jordan. In May 1944, the State Department informed the British embassy in Washington that the American chargé d'affaires, James Moose, was being replaced with a higher ranking officer and suggested that the British replace Jordan.[82] A month later, William Eddy, on a visit to Saudi Arabia, where he would later replace Moose, wrote to the State Department with his decidedly negative impression of Jordan that alleged "emotional instability" and a pattern of hurling "vile epithets" at colleagues.[83] Shortly afterwards, Cordell Hull, the US secretary of state, called in the British ambassador in Washington, Lord Halifax, to tell him that the American officials in the Middle East were convinced that Jordan "was doing his level best to injure the American Government's relations with the King and, in other ways, endeavoring to undermine the American situation, and that we just could not put up with this without constant and louder complaint."[84]

The British response was frank and defensive of Jordan, contending that much of the American complaint was based on a "mischievous report" to Foggy Bottom from Moose. In addition to refuting some specific points, the Foreign Office expressed surprise at the allegation of Jordan's anti-American attitude and noted that Jordan had complained that "his efforts to establish cordial personal relations with his United States colleague have not been reciprocated." Furthermore, London denied that Jordan had made any suggestion regarding Najib Salihah's dismissal but claimed that "We have little doubt that Najib Salihah is one of the men at the bottom of the present mischief-making that is disturbing Anglo-American relations in and over Saudi Arabia."[85]

But Moose was not the only American official critical of Jordan and his methods. The American representative to MESC reported that Jordan had withheld information regarding MESC support for the use of anti-locust mission lorries to transport food on behalf of the Saudi government.[86] Jordan's efforts to remove Najib Salihah and ʿAbdullah al-Sulayman were interpreted as attempts to promote British interests at the expense of American interests, particularly since both individuals were thought to be sympathetic to the US and Salihah's replacement in the Bureau of Mines and Public Works, ʿIzz al-Din Shawa, was regarded as being close to Jordan.[87] After Salihah's dismissal, Jordan confided to Moose that al-Sulayman was out of favor with the king and that he "would have to go. I am afraid the job has got too big for him."[88]

When Eddy replaced Moose in Jiddah, he soon arrived at a similar opinion of Jordan, describing him as devious and disliked.[89] Jordan was also regarded as obstructive during the attempts to forge a joint subsidy program. In September, he apparently told al-Sulayman that the US had over-committed themselves in their supply promises, a remark that the latter apparently passed off but that the American Legation found unacceptable.[90] In addition, Eddy reported that Jordan's insistence that the Saudi budget return to the level of 1939 was foolish since it denied all efforts at development.[91] This suspicion of Jordan led to American efforts to have the Foreign Office recall him, followed by the Foreign Office's reaction described above.

At the beginning of 1945, Eddy reported to the State Department on the king's words about Jordan. "King stated bluntly, 'I have always found goodness and honor in my American friends, as usually in my British friends ... but Jordan is our enemy and an enemy of the USA too. To the extent of his power he has sought to prevent our good relations and to injure my country. Except for his evil influence, I am sure the mutual interests of Saudi Arabia and the USA would have developed more rapidly months ago. I have confirmed that his more malicious acts were his own without knowledge of the British Government.'"[92]

THE US SUPPLANTS BRITISH INFLUENCE WITH THE 1945 SUBSIDY

Despite the Anglo-American differences and the question of Jordan's competency, it was necessary to lay the groundwork for the 1945 subsidy.

While the size of the subsidy was a matter of strong debate, it was recognized that subsidization provided an intangible benefit alongside the immediate requirements: King ʿAbd al-ʿAziz "gets good value for his money—or, more precisely, for ours—in terms of internal peace and public security. Present conditions in his dominions are without precedent in this respect; and British and other pilgrims benefit hardly less obviously than the frontier tribes of Iraq and Transjordan."[93]

A.W. France of the Foreign Office laid out the subsidy requirements in late November 1944, noting that, as the MESC had made its recommendations for 1945 already, it only remained necessary to link the subsidy to that program. Subsidies should be restricted to those items directly under the Saudi government's control, i.e., MESC supplies and Lend–Lease goods. Britain and the US were agreed that free distribution should be continued and therefore there could be no reduction in salaries and cash subsidies.[94] But at the end of the year, the British government was uncertain about American contributions. Whitehall was concerned that either the US might be intending to make a unilateral agreement with King ʿAbd al-ʿAziz or that it was considering abandoning the Lend–Lease system (which eventually was terminated in any case with the surrender of Japan in August 1945).[95]

In British eyes, the differences between London and Washington boiled down to British suspicion that Saudi Arabia had enough funds to pay for its 1945 imports—and thus the British taxpayer should not have to pay more unnecessary subsidy—while the US was content to regard Saudi budgetary presentations as suitable in order to retain the king's goodwill. The British attitude moderated somewhat after the replacement of Jordan but there was still concern that British standing with the king might be jeopardized if the Americans passed out British Treasury denunciations of the Saudi financial projections.[96] Thus, it was clear that British aid to the kingdom was diminishing while that of the US was rising. At the same time, however, it was also clear that Britain was loathe to lose influence to the US.

The budget for 1945, prepared by the Saudi Ministry of Finance in February 1945, claimed that expenditure would remain the same as in 1944 for a total of 108,768,220 *riyal*s, from which 43,616,020 *riyal*s were deducted for the cost of the commodities which the UK and the US would provide. This left a balance of 65,152,200 *riyal*s. But income was estimated at only 37,885,219 *riyal*s, thus leaving a deficit of 27,266,981 *riyal*s. When adding the remaining deficit from 1944, the total deficit in 1945 was estimated at 32,832,409 *riyal*s. A British review of the budget, however, put government income at 75 million *riyal*s and, when adding the subsidy as envisaged in the Saudi calculations, at a total of 105 million *riyal*s.[97]

The wrangling over the joint subsidy continued well into 1945 and it was decided by the two Western governments that the 1945 subsidy be continued on the basis of the 1944 subsidy for the first six months of the year and then the remainder adjusted on the basis of the final agreement. This meant that the king was not informed about the subsidy level for 1945 until 29 July 1945. The British contribution to the subsidy was fixed at £1,250,000, a figure one-half that of 1944, while London sought to persuade the US to reduce its contribution so that the joint total would be £2,500,000 or $10 million. The US, however, refused to accept British conclusions about Saudi Arabia's financial strength and pushed for a joint subsidy consisting of £1,650,000 contributions by each country. London refused to reconsider and thus the 50:50 basis of the subsidy was abandoned.[98]

As a consequence of the tardiness in resolving the 1945 budget, al-Sulayman unsuccessfully approached Gellatly's for a loan of £500,000 to be secured by 1945 *hajj* duties.[99] At the same time, the British minister in Jiddah managed to acquire a presumed reliable list of sums owed by the Saudi Ministry of Finance as of mid-March. These amounted to 12 million *riyals* with the major creditors being Muhammad Surur (5 million), Sadaq and Siraj Ka'ki (moneychangers; 3,750,000), and Bin Salim (livestock; 2 million). A number of other merchants were owed smaller sums.[100] Desperate for cash, the minister of finance tried again in August to secure a E£200,000 loan from Gellatly's.[101]

The Anglo-American note presented to the king on 29 July outlined a joint program of supply of cereals, US textiles, tires and tubes, sugar, tea, replacement parts for US-manufactured cars in service with the Saudi government, and a continuation of the £10,000 monthly contribution to the maintenance of Saudi missions abroad. The total cost of this would be £2,500,000 while the US offered additional credits for *riyal*s and commodities. In addition, Britain informed the king that they would not contribute to any 1946 subsidy while the US earmarked $25 million in credit from the Export-Import Bank during 1946–8. Another indication of the shift in influence came with the dissolution of the MESC in November, which resulted in the transfer of MESC administration in Jiddah to the US legation.[102] The British minister, L.B. Grafftey Smith, personally informed al-Sulayman in November that there was little likelihood of a renewed British subsidy in 1946. The minister seemed to express no surprise and indicated that the government would be able to contract for first-quarter 1946 supplies independently.[103]

The shift in influence was now in full swing. As early as January 1944, a State Department research paper had concluded that American economic interests in the kingdom had reached a point such that US policy should no longer be subordinate to the British. The paper also noted that the American refusal to lend money to Saudi Arabia in 1941 was in deference to British interests, as well as a more general lack of American involvement in the Middle East at the time.[104] Subsequent US government deliberations were characterized by the War Department's positive view of increased assistance, as long as Saudi Arabia did not end up playing Britain off against the US. Thus, there should be an understanding between Washington and London that their interests would be mutually respected.[105]

CHAPTER 6

The Beginnings of the US–Saudi Partnership

The origins of ties between the US and Saudi Arabia go back decades before World War II. The subject of American recognition of King ʿAbd al-ʿAziz's state had been raised several times in the 1920s and 1930s. In 1931, an American diplomat in London wrote to the Foreign Office, informing him that the US government was considering recognizing al-Hijaz and Najd but that further information regarding the administration of justice was required.[1] Not long after that, the American embassy informed the Foreign Office that the US had recognized the country on 2 May 1931.[2]

The first American diplomat accredited to the kingdom was Alexander C. Kirk, also serving as US ambassador to Egypt. Kirk made his first trip to Jiddah in May 1942 when he had audiences with the king, Prince Saʿud, and Prince Faysal. He also met three times with ʿAbdullah al-Sulayman, who had made all the arrangements for Kirk's stay. Al-Sulayman praised the work of Americans in the kingdom, singling out Charles Crane, Karl Twitchell, and the Saudi Arabian Mining Syndicate (SAMS) and California Arabian Standard Oil Company (CASOC) operations. Kirk also introduced the newly arrived US Agricultural Mission to the king.[3] Kirk had been preceded by a few days by James S. Moose, the new chargé d'affaires, who arrived in Jiddah on 22 April 1942 and opened the American Legation on 1 May. He had made a courtesy call on al-Sulayman on the day of his arrival and, on 27 April, received a note assenting to the establishment of the legation from Hamad al-Sulayman in his capacity as acting minister of foreign affairs.[4]

For the next several years, American aid contributions, especially in the shipment of silver *riyal*s under Lend–Lease, increased regularly until by 1944 they surpassed those of the UK, as detailed in the previous chapter in the context of Anglo-American jousting over the kingdom. It can be debated whether Saudi Arabia saw the United States as a welcome source of new aid or more as a counter to Britain and its increasingly critical attitude toward government expenditure, as expressed by its minister in Jiddah, S.R. Jordan. In any case, the kingdom was becoming increasingly desperate to meet its expenses and the US seemed willing to protect its growing interests in Saudi Arabia by providing aid. On 13 April 1944, the minister of finance met with Moose to tell him of the king's request for additional aid.[5] Ironically, President Roosevelt had agreed to an increase in American participation in the allied subsidy to the kingdom on the same day.[6] As a result, Moose ostensibly traveled to Riyadh to present a telephone system for one of the king's palaces but actually to discuss finances with the king and further assess the kingdom's situation.[7]

By July, a joint supply program had been agreed between the US and the UK. Both Moose and Jordan were to go to Riyadh to explain the 1944 subsidy to the king and to press on him the need for economic reforms.[8] As was made clear in an internal US policy paper though, the primary American concern was to protect US interests in Saudi oil, which entailed preventing excessive British control over the economy.[9]

This concern led to contingency planning for long-term economic aid for Saudi Arabia after the war as a way to assure the Saudis of American commitment to the country and to maintain a balance with British interests. Thus, in September 1944, William Eddy, the new minister in Jiddah, outlined potential measures that included a $55 million loan, a concession for military and civil airlines, a road system, and a financial adviser.[10] At roughly the same time, the State Department's Petroleum Division was realizing that Lend–Lease would not be available after the war and so direct loans were necessary. These would assist in the purchase of a 500-million-barrel oil reserve and in the improvement of US measures to protect oil interests. In addition, a development plan was envisaged, to be built around US official loans, private US and Saudi capital, and the provision of a wide range of American advisers.[11]

American intentions to provide more aid to the kingdom began to coincide with a British reluctance to contribute. But the funding for US government aid was a matter of proposal and counter-proposal throughout 1944 with the War and Navy Departments and the Export-Import Bank all mooted as possible sources. The American role in funding the Saudi government grew more pronounced after the British government informed the king that their 1945 contribution to the Anglo-American joint subsidy would be one-half the amount of the 1944 contribution and that they would not offer any financial contribution at all in 1946.

While the Anglo-American rivalry over Saudi Arabia ebbed with growing American dominance, it did not die. When the US extended an invitation to

King ʿAbd al-ʿAziz to meet with President Roosevelt on the latter's return from the Yalta Conference in early 1945, the king immediately told the British government of the invitation and of his intention of refusing it unless he were also able to meet Prime Minister Churchill in Egypt at the same time. A meeting was arranged and the king traveled to Fayyum in the Egyptian desert from his rendezvous with Roosevelt in the Suez Canal. The US even relented in accepting the king's journey back to Jiddah on a British destroyer, after he had left the kingdom on an American one. British face suffered a minor blow, however, when the car promised to the king by Churchill as a gift still had not arrived by the end of the year, while the king was able to make good use of the 17-seat Douglas aircraft presented to him in April by Roosevelt.[12]

THE HISTORIC MEETING BETWEEN KING ʿABD AL-ʿAZIZ AND PRESIDENT ROOSEVELT

By the beginning of World War II, Saudi Arabia had become a country of considerable interest to the United States. Although the Arabian American Oil Company (ARAMCO) concession had just begun to see its promise fulfilled with the initial production of oil (the first commercial shipment from Saudi Arabia took place in May 1939), most production was shut down because of the war. Nevertheless, oil was a valuable commodity—at all times but particularly in wartime—and the US considered Saudi Arabia's oil deposits as a strategic asset that it could not permit to be threatened. While the kingdom was late in declaring war on Germany and thus becoming a formal ally, relations between the two countries—as well as between Riyadh and London—were warm and close. Furthermore, Washington took pains to make sure that the relationship continued to remain strong.

This attitude also served the American oil company's interests as well, both at the time and in future years. At this stage, there still was some fear of British oil interests infringing on the American concession, a fear that the US government seemed to share to some extent despite Britain being its principal ally in the war. Later of course, ARAMCO actively pursued its political links in Washington to acquire favorable treatment and interpretation on such matters as taxes.

In the meantime, however, King ʿAbd al-ʿAziz's main concern was getting financial assistance to help manage his vast and undeveloped country while making sure that Saudi Arabia's stocks of foodstuffs remained adequate. Thus the oil company served as an efficient and welcome interlocutor with the Roosevelt administration.[13]

The war spurred more direct contacts between Saudi Arabia and the United States. American diplomatic representation became resident in the kingdom for the first time in 1942 and the US inquired about the possibility of overflight rights and the use of airfields. King ʿAbd al-ʿAziz still regarded Britain as his closest Western ally but circumstances were pushing him towards the US. As the newly arrived British minister reported rather smugly at the beginning of 1944, "The United States Government is still rather an unknown quantity for [the king], and he is anxious concerning the possible repercussions of extensive American activities in the Near East. He expressed his fears in at least one message to His Majesty's Government in which he said bluntly that he preferred Britain to guide the destinies of the Arab States rather than America. He considers Britain, with her long record of co-operation with and friendship for the Arabs, can manage the Near East quite well by herself and that there is no need for America to butt in."[14] But as a sign of the kingdom's increasing importance to the United States, the American representative in Jiddah was upgraded to the status of minister resident in 1943 and the country began to receive a flow of American officials.

President Roosevelt extended an invitation in July 1943 to King ʿAbd al-ʿAziz to visit the United States or, if he was unable to do so, to send a member of his family.[15] It was never likely that the king would accept this offer for himself and he steadfastly maintained that Prince Saʿud, as his successor, should not leave the kingdom either. Thus his second son, Prince Faysal, accompanied by Prince Khalid and Hafiz Wahbah, journeyed to the United States in September–November 1943. Prince Faysal met with Edward Stettinius, the acting secretary of state, and other State Department officials in Washington on 1 November, where the topics discussed in the meetings included the provision of silver and other items under Lend–Lease, the establishment of a US consulate in Dhahran, and possible US government participation in CASOC.[16]

The growing American interest in Saudi Arabia was reflected in 1944 by the growing size of its legation in Jiddah and by the appointment of a full minister in the person of Col. William A. Eddy. Another step in the US–Saudi relationship took place when Parker Hart opened the US Consulate in Dhahran on 2 September 1944. The consulate not only catered to the needs of American employees in ARAMCO but provided an observation post beyond the Eastern Province to Bahrain and the other smaller states of the Gulf as well. Hart wrote a long despatch in December praising the cooperation he had received from Saudi officials in the province and describing the situation of ARAMCO.[17]

The year 1945 was a particularly significant one for Saudi Arabia in its relations with the outside world. The kingdom joined the Arab League, it declared war on the Axis Powers and thus joined the Allies, and it became a charter member of the United Nations.[18] Just as importantly, the

American–Saudi relationship came into full fruition with the meeting between King ʿAbd al-ʿAziz and President Roosevelt at Great Bitter Lake. Even so, the tête-à-tête essentially was the most visible symbol of the growing economic interactions. As a consequence, American–Saudi relations were shortly to become at least as important as the Anglo–Saudi relationship had been, if in fact it had not supplanted it to a large degree.

The impending meeting between the American president and the Saudi monarch was a closely held secret until a few days before because of war conditions.[19] The USS *Murphy* made a courtesy call in Jiddah in February 1945, the first ever visit by a US naval vessel, but actually intended to pick up the king and his entourage. The king, in announcing to his court his intention of striking camp at Makkah, left his sons Princes Saʿud and Faysal in charge of Najd and al-Hijaz respectively, and traveled directly to the pier at Jiddah to embark on the *Murphy*. His arrival on board was preceded a few hours before a briefing to the ship's captain that a large amount of provisions, including 100 live sheep, would need to be taken aboard as well. This was contrary to the captain's orders and the American minister, Eddy, finally negotiated a compromise by which seven sheep were brought aboard and the remainder sent back. The king's party of 48 were given accommodation wherever possible and another cabin was shared by ʿAbdullah al-Sulayman, Yusuf Yasin, and Hafiz Wahbah.

The voyage marked the first time in more than 20 years that King ʿAbd al-ʿAziz had left his country. The *Murphy* arrived at Great Bitter Lake in the Suez Canal on the morning of 14 February and tied up next to the USS *Quincy*, which was carrying President Roosevelt. The king, accompanied by the three princes with him and ʿAbdullah al-Sulayman and Yusuf Yasin, made his way over to the *Quincy* at 10 a.m. Promptly at 3:30 p.m., the king returned to the *Murphy* and the *Quincy* departed for the US.

The opening topic of conversation was Palestine and the US role. The President said that he wished to assure His Majesty that he would do nothing to assist the Jews against the Arabs and would make no move hostile to the Arab people. The king responded that it might be a good idea to send an Arab mission to Europe and the US to present the Arab and Palestinian case, to which the president added his assent. King ʿAbd al-ʿAziz also brought up the situation of Syria and Lebanon, to which the president assured him that the French had guaranteed the two countries' independence. President Roosevelt then turned the conversation to agriculture, telling the king that he himself was a farmer. The president encouraged the king to develop water resources and irrigation and to increase the land under cultivation.

Despite Saudi Arabia's obvious financial problems, King ʿAbd al-ʿAziz regarded his meeting as an opportunity for friendship and not to plead for assistance. As the US minister in Jiddah later said, "at no time did Ibn Saud even hint at economic or financial aid for Saudi Arabia. He traveled to the meeting seeking friends and not funds, in spite of the fact that, at that date, he had no reason to expect that Arabian oil would be produced in quantity to multiply his national income but, on the contrary, ruled in 1945 over a pastoral land which could not produce enough to feed its population, and a land cut off by war from importing the necessities of life."[20]

It was a significant indication of the relatively suppressed Anglo-American rivalry in the Middle East that Prime Minister Churchill was perturbed to discover very late that Roosevelt had arranged to meet King ʿAbd al-ʿAziz. Churchill insisted on a hastily arranged meeting for himself with the Saudi monarch at Fayyum Oasis in Egypt three days after the US–Saudi meeting. The king traveled back to Jiddah aboard British destroyer HMS *Aurora*.[21]

WARTIME SUBSIDIES AND LEND–LEASE ASSISTANCE

The possibility of extending Lend–Lease assistance to Saudi Arabia had been discussed in Washington as early as 1941—and rejected because the kingdom did not fit the requirements (for one thing, it remained officially neutral in the war). But the topic gained steam in 1942 as it seemed to offer a way to increase Saudi prestige and build goodwill. This would be necessary when it came time to request air routes and airfields. Furthermore, plans for a high-octane refinery in Bahrain would increase demand for Saudi oil and the Saudi oilfields would only be of increasing value after the war.[22] In January 1943, Assistant Secretary of State Dean Acheson proposed Saudi eligibility on the grounds that it was the only large country in the region not eligible, the king had shown himself loyal to the allied cause, the country was strategically located for both shipping and air routes, and plans to obtain air facilities were unlikely to be granted without material aid. The Lend–Lease Administrator, E.R. Stettinius, also sent a memorandum to the president along similar lines.[23] Accordingly, President Roosevelt approved Lend–Lease for Saudi Arabia on 18 February 1943.[24]

No announcement of this action was to be made public until after the king was officially informed and that did not happen until Ambassador Kirk visited Jiddah in April 1943. To show American goodwill, Kirk had proposed that the US offer the kingdom badly needed trucks and irrigation equipment as the initial transactions under Lend–Lease. Kirk met with ʿAbdullah al-Sulayman who was very keen on both asking for 80 trucks and the possibility of receiving irrigation equipment.[25] Al-Sulayman was present at all of Kirk's meetings in Jiddah and he reached agreement with the ambassador that the Ministry of Finance would be responsible for Lend–Lease matters and that either the minister or his secretary would sign requisition orders. The first supplies under the agreement arrived by the end of the year.[26] The State Department also mooted a proposal to send a "young financial expert" to Jiddah to assist in gathering information on the Saudi Arabian economy—it was thought that he could also be made available for advice to the Saudi government if desired.[27]

The extension of Lend–Lease to Saudi Arabia marked a second key turning point in the kingdom's relations with Britain and the US. After the American oil concession, Lend–Lease introduced the beginning of a close official relationship between the Saudi and American governments. The turning to the United States provoked considerable friction with ally Britain, as outlined above, with responsibilities of subsidies to Saudi Arabia constituting a major area of contention. Lord Moyne, the British minister resident in the Middle East, wrote a lengthy letter to Anthony Eden, the secretary of state for foreign affairs, in September 1944 outlining his view of the problem. Voicing concern that the US was undermining British attempts at curtailing the size of the subsidies, Lord Moyne recommended that London limit its assistance to the supply program and leave development and welfare entirely to the US. He added a final caveat that Britain should impress on Washington its concern that nothing should be done to endanger King ʿAbd al-ʿAziz, drawing attention to "astonishing blunders" by the US and warning that "If the results of misguided American benevolence should be to undermine the independence of the country and make it a satellite of the U.S.A., it would have serious reactions throughout the Moslem world and gravely prejudice British interests."[28]

By the end of 1944, the United States was convinced that Saudi Arabia required long-term assistance and that it was better for it to come from Washington than from London. Therefore, the State Department searched for legitimate methods of extending long-term aid after the wind-up of Lend–Lease. The department was of the opinion that the kingdom would require financial underwriting for five to ten years until oil revenues increased sufficiently. Direct aid, an Export-Import Bank loan, and War Department expenditures were suggested as possible means but Congress was seen as unlikely to approve aid requests.[29] Stettinius telegraphed the US Legation in Jiddah that "you should inform the king that a comprehensive plan has been worked out for the extension by the American government of substantial financial and economic assistance to Saudi Arabia on a long range basis" but to also explain to the king that the plan still required Congressional approval.[30]

Other schemes advanced by the Petroleum Division of the State Department involved getting the US Navy to have the oil companies set aside reserves for which advance payments could be forwarded to the Saudi government. Alternatively, ARAMCO could guarantee a minimum yearly royalty to the Saudi government, recovering the amount of the loan against future royalties. A third idea was for a direct government loan that would not be repayable. But the division also stressed that the political and economic situation in the kingdom should be stressed to leading senators, along with a warning about Saudi Arabia again falling into the British sphere of influence.[31]

By 1945, the US had determined even more strongly that its economic interests required the provision of long-term economic development assistance to Saudi Arabia and proposals for various projects were presented to the king. The State Department argued that Saudi Arabia's budgetary deficits were the consequence of war and no relief would be forthcoming until oil production was significantly increased and the pre-war volume of trade restored. The provision of direct financial assistance was necessary to secure "the welfare of Saudi Arabia and ... the national interest of the United States." This was defined as ① the need for a stable Saudi state in the region, both politically and economically; ② the oil reserves in Saudi Arabia, both because they were in the hands of an American company and because they formed part of the West's reserves of world supply; and ③ military facilities in Saudi Arabia were required for aircraft staging on the way to the Far East.[32]

Because of the difficulty of acquiring Congressional approval for each civilian development project, the US government attempted to package development schemes with military assistance to the kingdom and the quest for a military airfield at Dhahran. Thus the emerging bilateral military relationship was characterized by two factors: the American desire for an airfield and overflight rights, as well as military training missions; and as a cover for a wide-ranging spectrum of assistance schemes that were actually non-military in nature. Various schemes for funding mechanisms were discussed, including Army and Navy advance purchase of oil from ARAMCO that could be used for advance royalty payments. Another idea was to appropriate $50 million for dispensing to the kingdom over about five years, in return for appointment of an American financial adviser and repayment beginning in 1955.[33]

After the war, a State Department paper on relations between the two countries summarized American aid contributions to the kingdom as shown in Table 6.1. Between 1940 and 1947, grants and loans of more than $100 million had been arranged to ensure the kingdom's continued stability and development. Of this, only the bullion was regarded as recoverable aid.[34]

MILITARY PROVISIONS AND THE DHAHRAN AIR BASE AGREEMENT

At the beginning of World War II, Saudi Arabia had very little in the way of organized armed forces. The outbreak of the war had put an end to the prospect of a large consignment of rifles and ammunition being extended

TABLE 6.1 UNITED STATES AID CONTRIBUTIONS TO SAUDI ARABIA (1944–6).

① 1944–5 Joint US-UK Aid Program, US share	$11,000,000
② 1945 Supplemental US Aid Program	$3,000,000
③ 1945 US-UK Military Aid Program, US share	$3,000,000
④ Transport cost of silver (approximately) (Saudi Arabian government paid for minting costs of $280,000)	$136,000
⑤ 1,031,250 ounces of silver lost at sea	$733,000
⑥ Total Lend–Lease Aid (approximately)	$17,869,000
⑦ Silver to be repaid in kind within five years, 21,323,250 ounces @ 71 cents per ounce	$15,139,507
⑧ Al-Kharj Agricultural Project commencing in 1942 and continuing through 1946; the value of supplies under Lend–Lease were included in previous calculations	ca. $1,000,000

In addition, dates and amounts of Lend–Lease advances of silver were given as:

3 October 1943	5,167,000 ounces for 15,000,000 *riyal*s
24 April 1944	3,437,500 ounces for 10,000,000 *riyal*s (for sale to ARAMCO, foreign diplomats and businesses, 60 percent of proceeds deposited with the Federal Reserve Bank)
21 September 1944	3,437,500 ounces for 10,000,000 *riyal*s
23 June 1945	5,843,750 ounces for 17,000,000 *riyal*s (for sale to ARAMCO, etc.)
18 August 1945	3,437,500 ounces for 10,000,000 *riyal*s

Source: RG59, 711.90f/4–1147, State Department, 11 April 1947.

partly as a gift by Germany. Plans announced in 1938 to create a large standing army and an air force did not proceed very far: the majority of recruits were ex-Ottoman soldiers, there were no capable Saudi officers, leadership at the top was not reliably effective or respected; equipment remained rudimentary; the few Saudi pilots had poor flying skills; there were few mechanics; and there was little comprehension by the government of the technical requirements necessary to put such a force into operation.[35] The US legation in Jiddah estimated that the formal army consisted of about 2,000 soldiers, stationed primarily in urban areas, but that the king could call upon between 40,000 and 100,000 bedouin as irregulars.[36]

The war had an immediate impact on the kingdom in a variety of negative ways. But it also hastened cooperation with the United States and created the beginnings of a military-security relationship that endures today. One of the first foundations of this was the king's reported willingness in 1942 to accept around 100 American troops in Dhahran to protect the oil installations until Saudi troops could be trained.[37] At the same time, the United States initiated informal inquiries regarding possible use of Saudi airfields and overflight rights to ferry aircraft to the Far East. The response generally was encouraging on the possibility.[38]

More serious negotiations between James Moose, the newly appointed American minister in Jiddah, and ʿAbdullah al-Sulayman began in July and the British minister, F.H.W. Stonehewer Bird, agreed to join Moose in the discussions. When they asked al-Sulayman for his opinion on the king's likely response to a request for airfields and flight paths, the minister of finance replied that the king would be likely to agree to non-stop flights over the northern part of the kingdom. He added that it would be better if the questions of overflights and airfields were separated and he agreed to approach the king on this basis.

He returned shortly with a favorable but informal answer from the king: he was prepared to grant "to his friends the British" non-stop air routes from Khartoum to Basra but stipulated that it should be kept secret. American flights would have to be made through the British, a turn that Moose attributed to the fact that the US government had not created goodwill in the kingdom by providing material aid. Al-Sulayman also counseled that a joint approach should be made in formal negotiations. These negotiations were handled with Yusuf Yasin who was seen as less helpful than al-Sulayman. The latter also requested that Yasin not be informed of Shaykh ʿAbdullah's earlier involvement in the question.[39] Nevertheless, the Americans decided that they would make their approaches about airfields through the minister of finance rather than Yasin and would offer some form of aid as an inducement.[40] In fact, Ambassador Kirk suggested to the State Department that the US pay part or all of the kingdom's anticipated budget deficit, about £750,000, in return for the rights.[41]

An initial US military mission arrived in Jiddah in December 1943 to ascertain requirements for arms and ammunition for the Saudi Arabian army.[42] The king appointed a small commission to discuss details with the mission. The group consisted of ʿAbdullah al-Sulayman, in his capacity as minister of defense (sic), Yusuf Yasin as acting minister of foreign affairs, and Khalid al-Qarqani, one of the king's counsellors. The mission asked questions regarding the size, arms, and equipment of the Saudi army, and Saudi plans for increasing the size of the armed forces. The commission averred that the king had 8,000 regulars, 15,000 as his special guards and the guards of the district governors, and 80,000 militia. Furthermore, he wished to increase the size of the regular forces from 8,000 to 15,000, including police, to be stationed in Riyadh (6,000), Makkah (4,000), and other posts (5,000). The mission also ascertained Saudi wishes regarding the Jiddah water supply (with water to be brought from Wadi Fatimah).[43] In addition, the team was accompanied by an oculist who treated the king and members of his entourage.[44]

The team concluded from its whirlwind visit that military equipment should be provided by a joint Anglo-American effort, requests for airplanes and a munitions factory should be deflected, and further study should be given to requests for road repairs and the development of water supplies. Furthermore, a regular army of about 11,000 men was necessary for internal security and requirements for this should be supplied.[45] The first arms were delivered on 6 March 1944 and a team of 12 men was sent to provide instruction in the care and maintenance of equipment supplied through Lend–Lease.[46]

A few months later in July, a small group of dignitaries were invited to the opening ceremony of the US training mission at their new camp in al-Ta'if.[47] Although the mission was intended to serve only until the first batch of 50 officers had completed the course, its presence was extended to at least the end of the year. In addition, the US proposed that there should be a small air mission in the kingdom in lieu of training Saudi pilots in the US.[48] The mission was regarded as a great success when Princes Faysal and ʿAbdullah were fêted as the guests of honor at the graduation exercise of the first class.[49] A secondary success seemed to be the apparent failure of a rival British military mission, at least as perceived by the Americans.

The Americans returned to the quest for an airfield at Dhahran in May 1945. The British government endorsed the idea and a note was presented to the Saudi government. As it turned out, however, the note asked not just for a military airfield but also a 60-year concession for its use by US civil aircraft. In addition, an American Military Mission of 50 officers and 110 other ranks was offered for providing staff and operational training, medical services, air training, road construction, and petroleum exploitation and development. The king agreed to the military airfield but, following discussions through the summer, he declined the military mission while at the same time pressing for initiation of the development assistance. The latter, he insisted, should be via a civilian agency rather than the US military. In the end, the US government dropped all the proposals, although they were to appear again later.[50]

The combining under the aegis of military relations of development assistance with the requests for the military airfield and civilian air rights was an attempt by the US government to execute its intended long-range aid program for Saudi Arabia in an environment that would see the termination of Lend–Lease and deflect potential Congressional objections to direct civilian aid. A first step had been to win British agreement for the American scheme, which was achieved in April 1945.[51] A small development in the emergent Saudi–American military relationship was Saudi approval of the stationing of two to three US Navy officers at Dhahran or Ra's Tanurah to inspect oil cargoes for their ships.[52] In an indication of gathering movement, the Ministry of Defense was established in April, a few months after Prince Mansur (one of the king's sons) was named minister of defense.[53]

British approval of the Dhahran military airfield was received in May 1945 and negotiations were opened by the chief of the US Military Mission with the king on 9 May.[54] By June, however, the War Department was having second thoughts on both the utility of the Dhahran base and on military provision of aid, while King ʿAbd al-ʿAziz continued to reject the idea of a military mission.[55] The Saudi government agreed in August to the establishment of the Dhahran military airfield. The terms included the provision that the base would revert to Saudi property three years after the end of hostilities with Japan and that US personnel would not be subject to Saudi law as long as they were actually on the base. Questions of air routes, civilian air flights, the military mission, and repairs to the road between Dhahran and Riyadh were left for later.[56] With the end of the war with Japan, it was necessary to change provisions of the agreement. This was effected in late December, which also permitted the use of the base for commercial traffic.[57]

The Dhahran runway was opened on 1 January 1946 and the same month saw a number of Congressional junkets to the base.[58] Construction on the airbase continued through 1946 and the site received the personnel and stores from Payne Field in Egypt, which had been acquired by the Egyptian government.[59] No agreement on a renewal of the air base agreement had occurred by the time of the expiry of the original date in 1949. Nevertheless a one-year extension to June 1950 was granted while negotiations continued. King ʿAbd al-ʿAziz's position was to suggest a mutual security pact that would allow continued American use of the air base while the kingdom would receive military equipment and a guarantee of support against external aggression. The most that the State Department could offer at the time was a survey of Saudi military needs until legislation could be passed to allow arms sales to Saudi Arabia. Although the US government budged little on the negotiations, the Saudis extended the agreement again to 1 February 1951.[60]

The American position in the negotiations relied on the massive "O'Keefe Report," carried out by a Joint US Survey Group of US and Saudi officers and completed in early 1950. This report sought to quantify both American requirements at Dhahran and the military equipment and training needs of the Saudi armed forces. A program over five years costing $107 million was proposed, although this amount was whittled down to $75 million later in the year.[61] In this manner, the groundwork for an extensive record of US–Saudi cooperation in military matters was laid in the aftermath of World War II, a cooperation that soon grew to considerably greater importance than Anglo-Saudi ties in this arena.

CHAPTER 7

Administrative Developments

The importance of the Ministry of Finance and ʿAbdullah al-Sulayman to the administration of Saudi Arabia was recognized by the United States government even during its initial contacts with the kingdom. In 1940, Bert Fish, the US ambassador to Cairo and newly accredited minister to Jiddah, described al-Sulayman as "Minister of Finance and Defense. Next to the king is regarded as the most powerful figure in the present government. He has under his jurisdiction all matters of finance, taxation, national defense, mining, customs, telegraphs, radio communications, post office and road building."[1] His role in defense was further attested to in an American military report on the Saudi armed forces: Shaykh ʿAbdullah was described as "Active head of the army" and "Minister of War and Minister of Finance."[2]

The British annual report on Saudi Arabia for 1945 was even more explicit about the position and role of the minister of finance:

> The Government of Saudi Arabia is a benevolent but complete personal autocracy; and the so-called Ministry of Finance and its occasional budgetary manifestations are merely an attempt to provide a Western alias for the Arabian Nights system by which one man, Sheikh Abdullah Sulaiman ..., is personally responsible to Ibn Saud for the provision of: (i) the king's own and his family's needs; (ii) the wherewithal to subsidise tribes and individuals; (iii) other Government expenses, official salaries, &c .... Ibn Saud's reliance on Sheikh Abdullah Sulaiman is absolute, and His Majesty is not really interested in changing or in controlling this man's methods.[3]

Circumstances and the lack of a developed administration forced the Ministry of Finance gradually to adopt a variety of roles, many only tangentially related to finance, in the 1930s. These ancillary roles continued into the 1940s. The British explorer and businessman based in Jiddah, St. John Philby, described al-Sulayman's role in detail in August 1945:

> the Ministry of Finance, has for more than 15 years been under the virtually independent control of Sheikh Abdullah Sulaiman, a Najdi of outstanding ability, who is also Minister of Defence and who in respect of both departments is directly responsible to the king alone. He also exercises a wide measure of control over such other departments of State—e.g. Medical, Education, Public Works, Posts Telegraphs and Wireless, Mines, etc.—as are administered not by Ministers but by Directors-General. The Minister of Finance, by reason of these multifarious activities, is by far the most important officer of State and maintains at all provincial and district centres a stall of officials responsible to himself and independent of the local governors. He alone enjoys the privilege of a body-guard and maintains a semi-regal state comparable with that of the king and the royal princes. And he alone, by reason of his close understanding with the king, enjoys a measure of administrative independence which even the viceroys do not aspire to. His regime is in every way comparable with that of the Barmecide Ministers of the time of Harun al Rashid; and the explanation of his power and independence is probably to be sought in the fact that he is entrusted with the administration of a department with whose intricacies and ramifications the king is not familiar.[4]

The following pages explain some of the ancillary roles that the Ministry of Finance and its minister assumed during the period of the 1940s.

ENDEAVORS IN AGRICULTURE

The principal agricultural project established during King ʿAbd al-ʿAziz's reign was that at al-Kharj, south of Riyadh. In large part this was the result of ʿAbdullah al-Sulayman's abiding interest in agriculture, which he exhibited from early in his career until well after he retired. The king's interest in the scheme was said to have derived from his goals of increasing Saudi Arabia's food supplies, thus lessening the need for imports, and in settling the nomadic population of the country.[5]

The efforts to have wells drilled at al-Kharj in 1938 and 1939 have been detailed in Chapter 4. Always anxious to expand the effort of developing the oasis, al-Sulayman invited the engineer Karl Twitchell to visit al-Kharj in 1940. Shortly afterward, Twitchell had an audience with the king in which the questions of drilling for water and interesting an American company in doing the drilling was raised by the king. Twitchell thereupon asked for the Ministry of Finance's assistance in collecting data on agricultural produce in the kingdom at that time.[6] A major factor behind efforts to expand agriculture in al-Kharj was the fact that the king was responsible for feeding 30,000 people in Riyadh, for which staples needed to be imported. Establishment of a large agricultural development at al-Kharj would reduce the amount of imports required.[7]

Since the inauguration of an irrigation project at al-Kharj in the late 1930s, approximately 2,500 acres had been put under irrigation by 1941. Of this, about 700 acres were being cultivated intensively with vegetables, maize, and forage crops. The other 1,800 acres were cultivated only in the winter months to provide grain, mostly wheat and barley, but further cultivation through the summer season was prevented by a lack of water.[8] At the same time, al-Kharj also served a staging post for cattle drives during the war from Yemen to Dhahran to feed CASOC employees.[9]

To find adequate water sources for agriculture at al-Kharj, al-Sulayman approached the oil company CASOC in 1941 for assistance in determining the viability of an irrigation project there. The initial CASOC report on the possibilities of irrigation at al-Kharj concluded that "the great pits at Kharj do provide a source of additional supply of considerable magnitude." The authors recommended installing pumping units in the pits and constructing the necessary canals and drainage channels, as well as leveling additional land for cultivation. If all the recommended steps were taken, the authors predicted a several-fold increase in land irrigated and crops grown.[10] The plans submitted by CASOC to the home office carried an estimated cost of $219,000 for drilling, pumping equipment, and the use of CASOC employees.[11]

In 1941, Saudi Arabia appealed to the United States to provide it with financial assistance. The request was turned down but, to soften the blow, Washington agreed to send an agricultural mission. The genesis of this idea appeared to lay in King ʿAbd al-ʿAziz's entreaties to Karl Twitchell to seek out American help in the endeavor. Twitchell approached American companies about investment but could attract no interest. Consequently, he approached departments of the US government where he had more success in gaining cooperation. An agricultural mission team was assembled by February 1941 with Twitchell as its head. The three-man team arrived in Jiddah in May and was quickly presented to the king.[12]

The mission dealt directly with the minister of finance, sending its recommendations to him, visiting a number of his farms, and benefitting from the arrangements he made for their travel and work. Al-Sulayman accompanied the team to al-Kharj just a few days after their arrival where they inspected the 1800-acre wheat cultivation project at Khafs Dagharah that the minister had initiated. The mission then made its way to al-Ahsa' where it surveyed the minister's gardens.

Later, al-Sulayman's Khamasiyah gardens in al-Qatif were inspected and the mission returned to al-Kharj to meet with him again in August. Twitchell presented the minister with the proposed organizational structures of a department of agriculture and of the management of al-Kharj. Pleased with the result, the minister asked Twitchell to help find the necessary experts in the US to execute both plans. He also asked the mission to use its influence to clear the export from the US of irrigation pumps destined for al-Kharj.

The mission then journeyed to ʿUnayzah to look at the gardens there. Twitchell also discussed personnel for the project with the Egyptian chargé d'affaires in Jiddah, a follow-up on the Saudi government's arrangements with the Egyptian government for assistance. The mission's final trip was to ʿAsir, stopping in al-Taʾif to examine the gardens of Prince Faysal and then in Shubrah to examine government gardens there. In addition, the gardens of the deputy minister of finance were also visited.

The mission returned to Jiddah in early December after having covered 10,000 miles of terrain. There it presented proposals for a department of agriculture and al-Kharj to the king. The proposed department would comprise sections for animal husbandry, agriculture, and arts and crafts. Both the department and al-Kharj project would fall under the jurisdiction of the Ministry of Finance and Twitchell envisioned an American expert attached to each of the department's sections.[13]

While in the US, Twitchell investigated the feasibility of carrying through the mission's recommendation of a wool and camel hair industry. He telegraphed al-Sulayman with the information that there was a market for white wool and asked for further samples of wool. Unfortunately, the latter was in India at the time and the Ministry of Foreign Affairs, to whom the message was passed, apparently did nothing. A further letter from Twitchell to the king prompted a reply thanking the engineer for his efforts and promising an answer from al-Sulayman. Twitchell wrote again to the king to recommend establishing an irrigation scheme at al-Aflaj, felt to be the third most important target after al-Kharj and al-Ahsaʾ, as well as relaying the information that an agricultural consultant was being sent to the kingdom by the US-based Near East Foundation.[14] Twitchell had more luck pressing the State Department to provide pumps for the irrigation project, and these were sent off under Lend–Lease in October.[15]

CASOC already had been employing three American advisors at al-Kharj since 1941 and an agreement was reached between CASOC and the king in 1943 for CASOC to supply more men and machinery.[16] CASOC also championed a recommendation in the Agricultural Mission's final report that it might be possible to grow the country's wheat requirements inside the kingdom. The oil company asked the State Department to find a suitable agricultural adviser for this purpose and offered to pay his salary. The US government, however, thought it better to appoint an adviser itself and appointed J.G. Koogler in October.[17] Clearly, the king and ʿAbdullah al-Sulayman placed great emphasis on al-Kharj project. In an *Umm al-Qura* interview on 12 March 1943, the minister of finance was quoted as saying that "it was imperative to grow the maximum quantity of food inside Saudi Arabia... [and that al-Kharj] area had been chosen because of the existence of deep and copious wells and because of the good quality of the soil."[18]

In addition, an Egyptian agricultural mission was dispatched on a two-year mission to al-Kharj. But the team found numerous problems on their arrival and it seemed unlikely that the members of the team would fulfill their full contracts.[19] Nevertheless, al-Sulayman remained positive on the project, as he portrayed it in an interview with *Umm al-Qura*. He described the extent of cultivation and the types of crops being introduced while noting difficulties with the irrigation. In his opinion, the irrigation project would have been completed if the US had not joined the war.[20] In another interview with the Arab News Agency in Cairo, al-Sulayman praised the work of the Egyptian agricultural mission and described the government's attempts to encourage local agriculture, including a government regulation promising farmers corn, seed, money, and camels to assist in cultivation, some of which had already been distributed.[21]

More attention was paid to agriculture in 1944, including by the Allies' Middle East Supply Center (MESC) in Cairo. The center sent a mission to Saudi Arabia in March and its report resulted in improvements to the administration of al-Kharj.[22] The US Agricultural Mission had already made efforts to obtain irrigation equipment for al-Kharj in late 1943. The question of pumps and other equipment was tied up with postwar plans for the development of al-Aflaj to the south. Confusion between the two projects created administrative problems for the US Legation and Lend–Lease. Karl Twitchell was said to have ordered some equipment earmarked for al-Aflaj in his capacity as head of the agricultural mission. But equipment for al-Kharj had not been authorized and al-Sulayman seemed content to leave the development of al-Aflaj until after the war.[23] At some point, other agricultural projects were also initiated in and around al-Ahsa' in the east and at al-Madinah in the west.[24] A group of four team members was sent from the US under the auspices of the Foreign Economic Administration in late 1943 or early 1944, and plans were underway to send another four specialists.[25]

A necessary concern was whether water was available to continue or expand the project, and this depended on geological mapping. Consequently, Glen Brown of the US Geological Survey (USGS) was sent to Saudi Arabia in 1944 and made his way to the "Roosevelt Mission" headquarters in al-Kharj. The mission had been authorized by the king at the request of al-Sulayman, "who had earlier succeeded in growing winter wheat during a period of food shortage in central Arabia and had persuaded the king of the necessity of starting irrigation projects there, raising food, mostly legumes and other plants high in proteins."[26]

Efforts continued as well to uncover water sources elsewhere in the kingdom. Al-Sulayman asked the American team to investigate Wadi Khulays, north of Jiddah. Although there was no agriculture at the site, water did come down a *wadi* (watercourse) on the western slope of the mountains. Drilling produced evidence of water, which was soon utilized by some Hijazi merchants to grow vegetables and citrus fruits. It later served as a water source for Jiddah as well.[27]

Another immediate requirement for water derived from the drought affecting the country and especially Najd. The bedouin begged the king for assistance as their camels, sheep, and goats died from lack of water. This led to drilling beneath Riyadh in the Hanifah limestone, which turned out to be dry. Another attempt at al-Hayr, about 30 kilometers south of Riyadh, was more successful, and a well and pipeline produced supplies for the watering of animals. French attempts to drill deep wells, as had been done in the Sahara, resulted in the discovery of salty and corrosive water. As a consequence, it became necessary to bring saltwater to Riyadh from the Gulf for distillation.[28]

A negative report on progress by the MESC in March 1944 did not seem to raise concern, since an American proposal to send eight more US agricultural and engineering advisers to al-Kharj was mooted in Washington in August, with the intention of increasing local food production and thereby reducing import requirements. King ʿAbd al-ʿAziz apparently was not satisfied with the proposal, complaining that the assistance was not enough and that some shipments were of poor quality. As a consequence, ʿAbdullah al-Sulayman requested additional assistance from the Arabian American Oil Company (ARAMCO, as CASOC had been renamed) and the king sought more cereal shipments.[29] In September, however, the US proposed to send four US agricultural experts to al-Kharj to replace the ARAMCO engineers.[30] There also seems to have been some thinking about pressing nomadic tribes such as the Al Murrah around Jabrin and al-Aflaj to settle for farming, although this may have been purely Twitchell's idea.[31] The US Legation in Jiddah also investigated the possibility of reviving goat and sheep skin exports.[32] The project at al-Kharj suffered a setback in 1945, however, when its palm groves and crops were devastated by locusts.[33]

In contrast to the MESC conclusions, two US State Department reports on the operation of al-Kharj project praised the work of the US Agricultural Mission and recommended that it be kept on until May 1949, rather than it terminating in December 1945. It was noted that no more land could be included in the project, given the current strength of the team and, at the same time, the importation of food was suggested as a cost-effective choice due to the high cost of production in the kingdom.[34]

The agricultural experiment at al-Kharj seemed to lose its luster in the short run in 1946. The contracts of the American agricultural team ended and King 'Abd al-'Aziz, although enthusiastic about the project, was increasingly concerned with the high costs for small return. Al-Sulayman was the target of criticism for expending so much on agriculture in the years when the economy remained tight. Nevertheless, his interest never waned amid the realization that the development of agriculture necessarily was a long-term investment. His views were echoed by the American Harris Agricultural Mission, which visited the project during the year and concluded that it was a justified area of expenditure because it provided agricultural education.[35]

A report by the US Legation on a ten-year plan for the development of agriculture stressed that agriculture was important to the kingdom to help counter famine conditions, to encourage settled communities, to promote a stable government, and to provide a suitable avenue for American aid. The report suggested that additional missions be formed for the mountains of al-Hijaz and the Red Sea coastal areas while a renewed mission to al-Kharj should help establish a Ministry of Agriculture and train Saudi technicians.[36]

Al-Kharj continued to remain the largest agricultural development in Saudi Arabia after the war. Its significance was not lost on the US as President Truman wrote to the king that "Al-Kharj I am told stresses the production food crops. My understanding is that other projects in contemplation at Hofuf, Qatif, Taif and Jeddah will be devoted to such practical problems as increased crop production, livestock production, educational programs for farmers and the organization of 4–H clubs for Arabian boys."[37]

By late 1947, between 1100 and 3000 acres were under cultivation at al-Kharj with 1100 workers employed. All produce was delivered to Riyadh for the palace's use and for distribution within the city. Al-Sulayman continued to play a significant role in the project, handling many of its finances, arranging for the importation of required equipment from the US, and paying the salaries of the Saudi workers. But agriculture was not immune to the government's financial woes and adverse weather conditions and insects caused more problems. In addition, the costs of the project could not be offset by the sale of produce.[38] Its value as an experimental farm ironically was reduced by the popularity amongst the population of Riyadh of a very large type of watermelon grown there—the consumers kept the watermelon seeds for their own gardens instead of sending them back to al-Kharj for replanting.[39]

In the postwar years, the administration of agricultural efforts in the kingdom became more organized. The first directorate (*mudiriyah*) for agriculture was established in Rajab 1376/April 1948 with Muhammad Salih Qazzaz as its director under Ministry of Finance supervision. Gradually agricultural offices were established in Riyadh, al-Ahsa', al-Qasim, and al-Madinah, while concerns included establishing farms, digging Artesian wells, the planting of many trees, and providing loans to farmers. Eventually, the directorate expanded into a Ministry of Agriculture with Prince Sultan b. 'Abd al-'Aziz appointed as its first minister in 1373/1954.[40]

CONTINUING DEVELOPMENTS IN FOREIGN AFFAIRS AND DEFENSE

Although the king relied closely on his son Faysal and a selection of northern Arab officials for his conduct of foreign affairs, it was unavoidable that 'Abdullah al-Sulayman through the years had close contact with foreign emissaries in Saudi Arabia and undertook trips of an official nature to other lands. As many of the kingdom's needs were related to finances and financial assistance, naturally the Ministry of Finance maintained a vital role in the conduct of foreign affairs and al-Sulayman dealt directly with the British, the Americans, and other powers throughout the duration of the war.[41]

Even more pertinent, al-Sulayman's role in defense continued into the war period as well, although in an increasingly peripheral way by the end of the war as American and British military missions began training a modern army. He was described in February 1944 as "now Minister of Defense, in addition to retaining his old post at the head of the Saudi financial administration. His achievements as minister of finance have met with general approval. But, in the absence of any reliable information, one cannot credit him with the necessary qualifications for organizing an army."[42]

However, recourse to his authority seemed to be instrumental in 1944 when it was improbably thought that Prince Mansur b. 'Abd al-'Aziz, abetted by a Javanese officer and others, may have been planning a *coup d'état*. The commander of the British military mission mentioned his suspicions, albeit indirectly and discreetly, to al-Sulayman, and then let the officers in question know what he had done. The minister had been extremely angry upon hearing this and the mention of his name to the presumed plotters was said to be enough to make them back down.[43] The incident did not prevent the king from naming Prince Mansur as minister of defense and inspector-general of military affairs at the end of the year.[44]

In another instance of the minister of finance's defense role, Col. Eddy wrote to him in October 1944 proposing that the US establish an air training mission in Saudi Arabia for Saudi pilots. The king declined.[45] According to Philby, al-Sulayman controlled the *nizam* or regular army, although not the *jihad* or tribal forces, which were under the control of local viceroys. The police were under the control of a director-general based at Makkah but the minister of finance exercised authority for administrative purposes while either the crown prince (Prince Saʿud) or the viceroy-general (Prince Faysal) controlled them for operational purposes.[46]

Al-Sulayman continued to remain involved with military matters in an administrative and logistical capacity. He provided guidance in Makkah for the first batch of trainees in the military school run by the British, made arrangements for them in Riyadh, and guided their integration into the new Royal Guard.[47] He also arranged for them to carry out repairs to the Great Mosque in Makkah, to improve roads and bridges between Makkah and Riyadh and between Riyadh and al-Kharj, and to cement the walls of the king's palace in Riyadh. In 1941, after the revolution of Rashid ʿAli al-Gaylani in Iraq, the king ordered al-Sulayman to inspect the northern and eastern borders of the kingdom, a task which took him about six months to complete before returning to Riyadh and submitting his report.[48]

BANKING AND CURRENCY

Currency problems continued to plague the kingdom during the war years. No matter how many silver Saudi *riyal*s were pumped into the economy, there was always a need for more because of continuous hoarding. The lack of cover for the *riyal* meant that it had no exchange value. Prior to the war, the problem was solved by importing gold sovereigns from Europe for exchange but the war put an end to that practice and led to a depreciation in the value of the *riyal*. This in turn made the Saudi government more dependent on foreign assistance with which to buy sovereigns. ʿAbdullah al-Sulayman pushed again for the establishment of a state bank but British experts felt that it would not be feasible without a British guarantee, which was unlikely to be forthcoming.[49] The Foreign Office rejected all these ideas, including the establishment of a state bank, with the remark that there was "no real necessity for such an institution even if it were feasible."[50]

The (British) financial secretary of the Sudan government journeyed to Jiddah twice in 1942 to discuss the currency problem with the minister of finance and other Saudi officials but it proved intractable. Indian silver rupees were not allowed to circulate alongside *riyal*s because of the Prophet Muhammad's "injunction that objects of the same substance may not be exchanged unless they have the same intrinsic value." Furthermore, Maria Theresa dollars were unacceptable for reasons of policy. The only viable solution was seen in the issuance of paper notes but there were difficulties involved in taking this course of action as well.[51] When the minister of finance suggested to the king that paper rupees be imported, the latter allegedly upbraided him in front of others.[52] Nevertheless, the king gave his informal assent to the possibility of introducing banknotes at the beginning of 1943 while still foreseeing considerable difficulty in his people accepting them.[53]

More discussion on a proposed Saudi Arabian Currency Board took place in 1943, with preliminary work carried out by the accountant-general and currency officer of Palestine, A.L. Peters.[54] British thinking on the Currency Board centered on the issuance of banknotes (preferably denominated in Saudi *riyals*) at a fixed rate against the gold sovereign, which therefore meant that the notes could be exchanged only for sovereigns. The board would not bear any responsibility for coinage and it was thought best it be established in London, with agents in Saudi Arabia, in order to better supervise the ordering and printing of the notes and handling the sterling received against them. It was thought that the convertibility into sterling and the knowledge that Gellatly's would accept notes as payment would help install confidence in the notes.[55]

Furthermore, Peters emphasized in discussions in Jiddah with Yusuf Yasin and Najib Salihah that a supply of gold (estimated at approximately 600,000 sovereigns during 1944) would be needed through 1944.[56] If the difficulties in introducing paper currency were not enough, the exchange value between *riyals* and sterling dropped from 11 or $12\frac{1}{2}$ to nine and then $8\frac{1}{2}$ *riyals* by the end of May 1943, thus making silver *riyals* extremely scarce.[57] The absence of al-Sulayman in the currency discussions may well have been due to the fact that he was seriously ill and in June the king proposed sending his minister of finance to India for a possible operation as well as rest and recuperation, along with two of the king's sons. Consequently, al-Sulayman was in India during July.[58]

Another sign of growing American concern with and influence in Saudi Arabia was the US government's observation in 1943 that it would be better for Saudi currency to be linked to world currencies and not reliant on silver prices, as well as their insistence that part of the Saudi reserve should be held in US dollars to ensure easy dollar/*riyal* convertibility.[59] One reason for the American suggestion was a fear that Britain might try to include Saudi Arabia in the sterling bloc.[60] The State Department retained a retired adviser, Max Thornburg, to produce a report on the currency situation in Saudi Arabia in July 1943. He concluded that the *riyal* had doubled in value vis-à-vis the US dollar in three months. In his view, this phenomenal rise was the consequence of hoarding, the melting down of coins and their resale to industry in the region, increased government expenditure, and the unscrupulous activities of money-changers.[61]

To a certain extent, British fears that the United States sought to use the currency question to increase its influence in the kingdom were justified. Moose, the chargé d'affaires in Jiddah, described British aid efforts in an

April 1943 report on the Saudi economy and expressed concern over a British monopoly of aid that might be used after the war to make demands regarding oil concessions. In addition, he noted that British plans would put the proposed currency board under British control.[62] The question of acceptance of paper notes continued to be debated. Thornburg pointed out the acceptance of paper currency in Bahrain and noted that rupee notes were being circulated already in al-Ahsa' Province.[63]

Through the remainder of 1943, various agencies of the US government discussed the possibility and means of providing Saudi Arabia with sufficient silver to ease its *riyal* shortage. It was generally supposed that the silver could be provided and the kingdom could reasonably pay it back after the war from oil revenues. But at that point the US Treasury Department discovered that the government had other debts. At the current rate of repayment, the debt just to CASOC would take 40 years to pay off. Furthermore, the Treasury representative sent to Jiddah to discuss matters was unable to meet with 'Abdullah al-Sulayman, then in India for medical treatment. Although Treasury realized that there was no suitable alternative to providing Saudi Arabia with the required silver, al-Sulayman's absence meant that he would not be available to sign the contract. The American legation in Jiddah reluctantly agreed to an arrangement whereby the contract would be signed by another official and his signature confirmed by the king. In the end, Bashir Bey al-Sadawi signed the contract on 3 October and the royal decree authorizing the signature contained the explanation that al-Sadawi had signed on behalf of the government "because of the absence of our minister of finance—Abdallah As Sulaiman."[64]

Even more, Washington seemed to be considering the possibility of creating a national bank in Saudi Arabia with the capital derived from Lend-Lease funds. The Saudi Arabian government, it was envisaged, would hold 50 percent interest in the operation. The British were suspicions of American intentions. The new British minister in Jiddah, S.R. Jordan, commented pointedly that "Ibn Saud in a recent interview stated that his firm and lasting friends were Great Britain and he wished those relations to continue with him and his children after him. The United States he added were new friends and it remained to be seen whether their friendship was based on the same altruistic principles as that of His Majesty's Government. They were, he thought, primarily concerned with the exploitation of the rich oil areas which they had acquired in Saudi Arabia."[65]

Jordan went on to contend that "I gather from my informant that King fears that His Majesty's Government may surrender their predominant position in Saudi Arabia to United States and support United States economic aspirations." He added that the Saudi government was prepared to enter into immediate negotiations for the creation of a currency board in order to forestall US proposals for a bank.[66] Meanwhile, the American role increased towards the end of 1943 when it took over the minting of Saudi *riyals*.[67] Rivalry surfaced in a related matter: the question of a financial adviser.[68] The American position was that the US had become preponderant in Saudi economic matters and so it should provide economic advice while a joint mission could be formed for military affairs. London's contention was that King 'Abd al-'Aziz would wish a Muslim adviser since he would be expected to work in Makkah.[69] The British proposed an Indian candidate but the US continued to object.[70] British attempts to persuade Washington went for naught and the matter was dropped in December 1944.[71] It was seen in London as another sign of diminution of British influence.

But the war also struck a financial blow from another direction. A major reason for the continued presence of the Netherlands Trading Society in Jiddah, acting as the only real bank in the country, was its ability to obtain gold sovereigns in India and export them to Saudi Arabia. At the end of 1943, the Government of India announced that they would be forced to stop the supply of gold and it was uncertain whether the bank would continue operations.[72] In 1944, it was believed that the bank was receiving the necessary gold through the Netherlands Legation in Egypt.[73] The position of the Netherlands Trading Society was also threatened that year by negotiations by the National City Bank of New York for branches in the kingdom, as well as by the interest shown by Britain's Eastern Bank.[74] In September, the Saudi government apparently approved the opening of a National City Bank branch in Dhahran, provided that they would make advances to the government of up to £500,000 without interest every year and that a subordinate branch would be opened at Jiddah.[75] In addition, the Banque d'Indochine opened a branch in Jiddah on 27 March 1948.[76]

Saudi Arabia continued to suffer from a shortage of currency throughout 1944. In January of that year, Yusuf Yasin informed the US Legation that the Saudi government was "completely out of funds" and pleaded for a quick delivery of seven million *riyals* that had been promised and the possibility of shipment by air was raised.[77] The disagreement between London and Washington over subsidy questions and Jordan's unwillingness to approve the budget without reforms he felt were necessary were principally responsible for the continuing delays.[78]

The US government chose to publicize the delivery of the *riyals* when they eventually arrived, but it turned out to be more farcical than momentous: the *riyals* had been delivered already when a State Department delegation arrived from Cairo for the ceremony. The deputy minister of finance, Hamad al-Sulayman, was asked to count the *riyals* so he could be photographed to which he rejoined that the ministry had other employees for such jobs. Among the American group was Kermit Roosevelt, who described the American activities as clumsy and insulting and regarded the fact that many of the notables were absent in Riyadh as the only positive aspect.[79]

While this particular incident may not have had any impact on Anglo-American relations with regard to Saudi Arabia, the tussle over the supply of additional silver to the kingdom remained an area of debate. The British argument that the injection of more *riyal*s was inflationary was countered by the American counter that a large amount of silver was either hoarded or smuggled out of the country, thus the impact of new silver was neutralized. A continued supply was seen as necessary because of the tradition whereby the king provided the tribes with both food and currency subsidies, despite the fact that it was also unduly enriching a small number of people.[80]

In April, the kingdom agreed to a US plan whereby an additional 10 million *riyal*s would be supplied under Lend–Lease for resale to the US legation and US companies in Saudi Arabia. They would pay for the *riyal*s in US dollars, which would be credited to accounts held in the US by the Federal Reserve Bank. Sixty percent of the proceeds would be placed in a deposit account for the eventual repayment of silver after the war while the remaining 40 percent would be used to finance the minting and shipping of *riyal*s and purchase of gold from the US Treasury.[81] Instructions were issued that the 10 million *riyal*s be delivered to Ra's Tanurah. The first installment of two million was handed over to ARAMCO but the sinking of the ship *John Barry* in the Arabian Sea with three million *riyal*s aboard was an unexpected obstacle.[82] The Saudi government subsequently used these funds to purchase gold from the Federal Reserve Bank on several occasions in 1944.

Despite the US opinion vis-à-vis London on the number of *riyal*s to send to Saudi Arabia, the precise amount was not decided until July of 1944: only 10 million (in addition to the number assigned to American purchases in Saudi Arabia), which constituted just half of the Saudi request in January of that year.[83] In addition, the remaining amount of *riyal*s were inordinately late in arriving, well after the *hajj* (the annual pilgrimage to Makkah), which raised the value of the *riyal*, thus increasing foreign exchange costs for pilgrims, and causing another shortage throughout the country.[84]

The export of foreign bank notes, as well as gold, was prohibited in an attempt to put an end to smuggling. This step apparently was taken only as a last resort, since the kingdom obviously needed the trade in goods to continue. There was also some suspicion that it was taken in order to raise the price of gold, which could prove useful for the government in order to receive a greater return on gold recently imported from the US.[85]

The recurring dispute between London and Washington over subsidies and the provision of *riyals* not only provoked suspicion between the two allies but also forced the question of a central bank to be raised again. Anglo-American discussions on the nature of the bank took up most of 1944. For their part, the British were adamant that the Saudi government should not have a controlling position on the board while the Americans did not wish any Saudi currency to be linked to the sterling bloc. A compromise reached in August was for a currency board based in Cairo with a single representative each from Saudi Arabia, Britain, and the US. But disagreement remained over which currency the *riyal* should be tied to and the *riyal*'s foreign-exchange value. Consequently, Britain broke off talks in November.[86]

DEVELOPMENT PROJECTS

Another of the Ministry of Finance's responsibilities, and one of ʿAbdullah al-Sulayman's passions, lay in the field of socioeconomic development. Many of the schemes advanced in the 1930s and 1940s were either entrusted to al-Sulayman or instituted by him. Thus, it was not surprising, for example, that in the 1940s he undoubtedly had at least some involvement in another of Karl Twitchell's ideas. Twitchell had been employed by the American Eastern Corporation as a consultant and had interested the company in opening a branch in Jiddah and later in Dhahran. American Eastern's intention was to carry out a wide range of development activities with the hoping of becoming the Lend–Lease and Foreign Economic Administration (FEA) agent for Saudi Arabia. Prospective feasibility studies included trade, agriculture, roads, shipping, and water supply. The first scheme envisioned was the construction of a warning beacon in Jiddah harbor, incidentally a particular interest of Twitchell, and a later proposal involved the formation of a Saudi steamship company. With a recommendation from the US Legation, the Saudi government approved the Jiddah branch.[87]

In January 1945, Twitchell presented a proposal for a Saudi Arabian Shipping Company, to be financed by American Eastern and other American interests but with a 15 percent stock holding for the Saudi government. The proposal was frowned upon by the State Department, however, which had reservations regarding the scheme's financing and its proposed monopolistic status.[88] Amongst the other schemes advanced by Twitchell was one of a fish industry, involving drying, smoking, canning, extracting oil, and shark oil and leather.[89]

American Eastern's intention was to create the Saudi Arabian–American Development Corporation (SAADCO) and, in April, Twitchell reported that the king had approved the establishment of the company and had appointed

Khalid al-Qarqani to discuss details, even though it was obvious that al-Sulayman was keenly interested in the development proposals. Twitchell added that he hoped to meet with al-Sulayman about a concession to provide electrical power and lighting for Riyadh.[90] In July, Twitchell wrote to Marcel Wagner, the president of American Eastern, giving him details of the proposed SAADCO that he had been negotiating with al-Sulayman and Ibrahim Shakir. Initially, the company was to be 45 percent Saudi and 55 percent American-owned, with 20 percent of the American shares offered for sale to Saudis after 25 years. Al-Sulayman, Shakir, Wagner, and Twitchell were to be permanent directors of the company for the first ten years of its existence.[91]

But the State Department voiced objections to SAADCO just as it had to the shipping company. In its view, American Eastern was essentially interested in making a profit in regard to the expenditure of the Export-Import Bank loan without investing a large sum of money. The company had no experience in development projects, which the State Department felt were better served by subsidiaries of the government rather than private companies. It would be better, the department said, for the Saudi government to employ advisers recommended by the US government, to supervise the expenditure of the loan.[92] These views were communicated to the American Eastern president with the conclusion that "it would not look with favor on an arrangement between any company and a foreign government which would establish a monopoly."[93]

This attitude did not immediately prevent American Eastern's involvement in Saudi trade, though. Towards the end of 1945, pointing out that the quota of textiles from the US was too small to meet demand, the Saudi government proposed that it buy the piece goods in bulk and sell them equitably to all importers. The State Department agreed to this plan and also to the use of American Eastern as the intermediary with the Saudi government.[94]

Nevertheless, SAADCO's fate was sealed when King ʿAbd al-ʿAziz refused to sign the decree establishing the company. American Eastern protested to the State Department that the king had been influenced by Britain—in opposition to the entrance of American concerns into the kingdom—and Saudi commercial interests led by the Alireza family. Even ARAMCO's suggestion to the king that American Eastern should carry out the improvements to the Jiddah water supply was rebuffed. ʿAbdullah al-Sulayman's interest in SAADCO appeared to be driven by his search for foreign planning and construction assistance in carrying out development projects. With SAADCO's departure from the scene, that assistance came from Bechtel, as detailed in Chapter 9.[95]

MISCELLANEOUS ACTIVITIES

The range of the responsibilities of the minister of finance and his ministry was sometimes logical and sometimes surprising. In addition to his major roles in finance, development, and defense, the minister was often ordered to take on a variety of smaller tasks, some as small as procuring items for the king's palace in Riyadh, others more directly concerned with the country's incipient development.

One of the constituent departments of the Ministry of Finance was the Bureau of Mines and Public Works. As Chapter 3 has noted, 'Abdullah al-Sulayman took a keen interest in the development of minerals in the 1930s and had negotiated the Saudi Arabian Mining Syndicate (SAMS) concession. Thus the bureau fell directly under his supervision. 'Izz al-Din Shawa had taken Najib Salihah's place as director in 1944, but he was transferred to Riyadh in 1945 as a privy councillor to the king and the bureau was dissolved. A new Directorate of Companies, still within the Ministry of Finance, was established in its stead with Sayyid Sami Kutbi in charge.[96]

In 1944, King 'Abd al-'Aziz and Jordan discussed the "deplorable state" of the Jiddah–Riyadh road. The king said that he would give instructions for the organization of road gangs to repair the roads where they could but added that he would like British assistance in providing an expert and some foremen to supervise the repairs.[97] The MESC arranged for the provision of seven British personnel.[98]

Continued problems in the Saudi government's transport services were reported in 1945 when the British minister Jordan, not surprisingly given his animus, characterized it in a very hostile and irrational way. The 1945 *hajj* was able to function by the provision of some 200 trucks under Lend–Lease from US Army stocks in the Gulf. Nevertheless, the king's dissatisfaction with the poor state of his garages led to the dispatch of a British technician to reorganize the services.[99]

Another illustration of the Ministry of Finance's wide-ranging duties came in mid-1944 when the US military authorities in Egypt invited King 'Abd al-'Aziz to send 12 Saudis for training in transport and motor engineering to US workshops in Egypt. The king was pleased with the offer and instructed the American diplomat to work with the minister of finance in the selection of the 12 Saudis.[100] Another example arose when the US legation wrote to al-Sulayman later in 1944 to discuss the idea of a national radio corporation to supersede the Eastern Telegraph Company and Cable & Wireless's monopolies, since they did not allow direct communication with the US. After the minister of finance had reported this to the king, the latter instructed him to get British views on the matter.[101]

PART III

POSTWAR PROSPERITY AND ECONOMIC DEVELOPMENT

CHAPTER 8

Oil Emerges as the Financial Engine

The start of Saudi Arabia's oil age effectively dates from after the end of World War II. While the kingdom had benefitted before then from concession payments, in addition to loans and advances, it was not until production burgeoned in the postwar years that significant, and significantly expanding oil revenues began accruing for the government. In a sense, the war also marked a qualitative divide between the role of Saudi Arabia as a passive recipient of international oil company offers in the prewar period and its more sophisticated postwar role in regaining control over its most valuable natural resource in the context of and in conjunction with developments in the global oil industry. The common thread through all of this was the central role of 'Abdullah al-Sulayman. He negotiated with the oil company on the behalf of the king and kingdom throughout, from the relatively simple settling of the original concession to the more complex issues of income tax liabilities and 50/50 sharing, as well as the controversial "Onassis" tanker affair of the 1950s.

OIL COMPANY RELATIONS DURING THE WAR

The business operations of the Arabian American Oil Company (ARAMCO) in Saudi Arabia quickly became more than just pumping oil. The company was involved in a number of development projects, provided personal assistance to the king and his family, and contributed to the exploration and mapping of the country. It also managed the agricultural project at al-Kharj and later built the railway between al-Dammam and Riyadh.[1]

But a serious bone of contention soon arose between company and government over the method of payment for oil. The original 1933 concession agreement, confirmed in the 1939 agreement, specified that the company would pay royalties at the rate of four shillings of gold "or its equivalent" per ton of crude oil, after the annual rents prior to the discovery of oil. But supplies of gold became limited after the outbreak of World War II and the price of gold sovereigns more than doubled over the New York and London official rates. The government considered that it should be paid at the higher market price obtaining in the kingdom, since many of its expenses were payable in gold sovereigns. The company, naturally, insisted on the official exchange rate. The impasse created a lengthy period of tense relations between the company and the government's negotiator, ʿAbdullah al-Sulayman. Finally in 1948, the Saudi Arabian government proposed that dollar payments should be calculated at a rate of $12 for each gold pound. The company accepted this in a letter dated 10 March 1948. This meant a royalty rate of $2.50 per ton—or 32¢ per barrel—of crude oil and the matter was closed when ARAMCO made an adjustment payment of $20.3 million.[2]

Another source of friction with the oil company and with the Saudi Arabian Mining Syndicate (SAMS) had emerged in August 1942 when the government enacted new labor regulations that impacted only foreign companies. The regulations gave the Ministry of Finance the power to regulate conditions for Saudi employees, including a 48-hour week and one month's pay for redundancy. The ministry was also empowered through its Bureau of Mines and Public Works to inspect industrial facilities and control who worked for the companies. Both the California Arabian Standard Oil Company (CASOC, as ARAMCO was known at the time) and SAMS opposed the regulations and approached the king and al-Sulayman in efforts to change the law.[3]

An additional serious oil-related problem for Saudi finances took place in 1940. On the night of 18–19 October, three Italian aircraft dropped some two dozen bombs on the CASOC camp at Dhahran, fortunately causing only slight damage to the pipeline. Bombs were also dropped during the same night on the Bahrain Petroleum Company operations in Bahrain. The aircraft apparently took off from and returned to Asmara. The kingdom made an official protest to the Italian government, which apologized for the incident and asserted that there had never been any intention to bomb Saudi territory.[4] There was an immediate impact on CASOC's operations, which had been producing 15,000–18,000 barrels per day (b/d) and had expected to increase to 30,000 to 40,000 b/d in 1941.[5]

As a consequence of this raid (as well as other factors), CASOC's parents decided to curtail production for the duration of hostilities. This decision was discussed by CASOC officials with the Saudi government in al-Khubar in March and the beginning of April, which undoubtedly did not please the Saudis.[6] By late 1941, production had been reduced to only 7,000 b/d being sent to Bahrain and only 100 Americans were left at Dhahran. Even the small refinery at Ra's Tanurah, which provided refined products for the use of the company and the Saudi government, was not being fully utilized. As a result, superfluous wells were plugged with cement.[7] Although CASOC cut back on advances to the Saudi Arabian government due to its curtailment of production, its efforts to provide remaining assistance were stymied by its difficulty in obtaining foreign exchange because of tight British restrictions. Thus the company was unable to respond to the government's January 1942 appeal for an advance of $500,000 to pay for automobile parts already in transit and for the purchase of sovereigns in India.[8]

Throughout 1942, there was discussion between CASOC and the US government about the desirability of destroying the oil wells to deny them in case of an enemy advance. In addition, there was fear of damage to the fields in case of more enemy bombing raids. This was easily minimized in part by plugging non-producing wells. But CASOC balked at the US government suggestion that the company carry out full destruction of producing wells and useful equipment without informing the Saudi Arabian government. Quite naturally, it was felt that the king would never agree to full destruction. The only breakthrough in this area occurred in October when a Saudi agreement in principle was obtained for the positioning of anti-aircraft guns in the vicinity of oil installations with US military personnel manning the guns.[9] Nevertheless, the oil company reported in October that the oil installations at Ra'S Tanurah and Dhahran were protected by sand and concrete structures, the stationing of guards, and the plugging of non-essential wells.[10]

While CASOC's operations had slowed to near-dormancy during the war, they did not end completely. In part, this was due to Washington's war requirements, as in the US government's planning in 1943 for an oil refinery to be built by CASOC at al-Dammam. The refinery would have a capacity of 100,000 b/d and produce aviation and motor gasoline, diesel oil and naval fuel.[11] At the same time, however, Washington was considering purchasing CASOC through the Petroleum Reserves Corporation (PRC). While the purpose was to gain control of the kingdom's oil reserves, the US government intended to stress its devotion to Saudi Arabia's development, including the reserve of enough oil to satisfy the country's internal needs.[12]

The US government felt it optimal to link the ideas of the company's purchase and the construction of the oil refinery since the oil company would not be able to finance the refinery without government aid. CASOC's parent companies, Standard Oil of California (SOCAL) and the Texas Company (TEXACO), however, opposed the sale because they anticipated considerable postwar profits from the concession. A tug-of-war ensued between Harold Ickes, the chairman of the PRC, and the companies. A number of options were discussed, ranging from complete government ownership to minority participation to the earmarking of Saudi oil reserves for sale to the US government. By November, King ʿAbd al-ʿAziz had been informed of the negotiations and, by December, the discussions had progressed to a plan for full government ownership (through the PRC) of the refinery with CASOC building, running, and supplying oil to it.[13] However, the PRC cancelled its letter of intent, which caused Cordell Hull, the secretary of state, to write to Ickes, complaining about the cancellation of the project, particularly since the king had been told about it. Ickes defended his position by citing the opposition of CASOC's owners to US government ownership of the company.[14]

As an alternative, the idea of a pipeline found favor with Ickes, who felt that Saudi Arabia would benefit financially while British encroachments would be blocked. In his diary, he quoted J.D. Rockefeller as saying "If we build the pipeline in the North East and run it, it will mean the Government will have a larger measure of control than it has ever had of any private industry, because without transportation the oil is useless."[15]

In the end, CASOC informed the Saudi government in January 1944 that it was building a 50,000 b/d refinery at Ra's Tanurah solely on its own. The company also informed the king that it had changed its name from CASOC to the Arabian American Oil Company (ARAMCO) and that it would participate in a US government plan to build a pipeline across Arabia to the Mediterranean, with the king's approval.[16]

The pipeline appeared to be another effort by the PRC to secure control over Arabian oil, following on the unsuccessful attempt to take over CASOC a year earlier. In addition to the PRC and ARAMCO, SOCAL, TEXACO, and Gulf Oil had all reached preliminary agreement on the pipeline. The US government would finance the pipeline and build it with assistance from the companies; in return, the US government would receive access to one billion barrels of oil at a favorable rate and would be guaranteed the return of its investment plus interest within 25 years. Actual construction would hinge on the approval of all governments in whose territory the pipeline would cross.[17] However, as the war ended, the pipeline project became vaguer and its importance was regarded as a gambit that brought Britain to the negotiating table over postwar oil interests.[18]

Meanwhile, ARAMCO was experiencing persistent labor problems. The Saudi Arabian government's unilateral enactment of Labor Regulations in 1942 provoked ARAMCO protests that they were already providing adequate wages and benefits. In June 1943, ARAMCO representatives engaged in prolonged talks with ʿAbdullah al-Sulayman. The minister of finance appeared to be trying to mollify the company by assuring the representatives that the government was convinced that the company had the best interests of the country at heart and the company responded that it sought to assist the development of the country. Furthermore, al-Sulayman assured the company that "the Government had no intention whatever of imposing anything upon the Company which was going to add to the difficulties of our problems in Saudi Arabia." The discussions seemed to provide a valuable exchange of opinions and ideas and the ARAMCO summary of the talks noted that "There is no doubt that the Minister himself strongly feels the need for increased productivity in this country and most of his efforts are now devoted toward doing something constructive along this line. The work that he has done at Kharj has been under criticism as being expensive and useless, and I think that he wants to prove to the skeptics that things of this kind can be made a success."[19]

A visit to Dhahran by the minister of finance in April–May 1945 was intended to arrange a change in the local government but he also raised the question of suitable housing for Saudi workers with ARAMCO in an attempt to forestall the possibility of a strike.[20] In August 1945, a strike by Italian employees was followed by one by Arab workers, forcing the Saudi government to intervene.[21] Al-Sulayman became involved with the issue when he presented ARAMCO's Jiddah representative with a telegram from the king insisting that Saudi employees be treated the same as foreigners of the same rank.[22] Nevertheless, the company was hit by a strike by all Saudi employees, bringing drilling to a halt. Eventually, the Saudi government filled the role of arbiter and helped bring an end to the strike.[23]

Despite the return to work, relations of ARAMCO with its workers and the Saudi government continued to be problematic. The atmosphere required more involvement by al-Sulayman. In November, he urged the company to inaugurate a plan for regular incremental pay increases for semi-skilled, skilled, clerical, and technical workers. ARAMCO responded with a list of suggestions for approval.[24]

TAPLINE AND OTHER OIL CONCERNS (1946–9)

The US government's efforts to finance and construct a pipeline to the Mediterranean during the war may not have been successful but the idea remained alive. The creation of the postwar Trans Arabian Pipeline (TAPline) was a success, however. But, as the greater part of its course was through Saudi territory, it presented a major cause of protracted and difficult negotiations between the Saudi Arabian government and the oil company. It was also the opening salvo in a changing atmosphere of government–company relations.

TAPline Arrangements

The year 1946 saw changes in ARAMCO ownership. The existing owners, Standard Oil of California and Texas Oil Company, agreed to sell 40 percent of ARAMCO's stock to Standard Oil of New Jersey and Socony Vacuum. This would give ARAMCO access to marketing facilities of the older-established American companies as well as help in raising new capital for the TAPline project. The construction of the pipeline would relieve ARAMCO's dependence on sales to the US Navy in the Pacific as its primary market.[25]

As ARAMCO expanded and shifted its marketing focus from the Pacific to Europe and the United States, a more efficient way of delivering oil was required. Planning and negotiation for TAPline began in 1946 and deepened in 1947. In part, the pipeline needed settlement with the Saudi government regarding the route and transit fees, but similar negotiations were necessary for each of the countries through which the pipeline was to pass on its way to the Mediterranean. The originally proposed route was through Transjordan, Syria, and Lebanon, but frustrating negotiations with Syria throughout the year held up planning.

As regards TAPline's presence in Saudi Arabia, ARAMCO President F.W. Moore traveled to Saudi Arabia in July 1947 to discuss the pipeline with the king. This led to a signed agreement regarding TAPline's obligations to the kingdom. While the company escaped paying transit fees for 15 years, it agreed to responsibility for the defense of the pipeline and the establishment of pumping stations. In addition, it also agreed to provide hospitals, schools, and water wells around the pumping stations.[26]

Nevertheless, final negotiations on TAPline, which involved the governments of Syria and Lebanon, through whose territory the pipeline would also pass, were protracted through 1948. In part this was due to Arab sensitivities over Palestine and anti-American attitudes. But the Saudi government was in no hurry to conclude an agreement either, using the gold clause dispute, the railway, and outstanding requests for loans from ARAMCO to put additional pressure on the oil company.

In addition, Saudi Arabia's arrangements with TAPline were strained throughout the early part of 1951 on the question of payments for defense of the pipeline. ARAMCO was not willing to pay all the government charges for defense arrangements, believing that the government was seeking to have it pay for the entire defense of the northern part of the country. In response, the government increased the amount of the payment demands and threatened to suspend TAPline temporarily if ARAMCO did not agree. As in the case of royalty payments and loans from ARAMCO, ARAMCO decided to approach the king directly who commissioned a fact-finding mission. Although the mission did not reach an agreement, King ʿAbd al-ʿAziz subsequently ruled that TAPline was not responsible for funding the Saudi armed forces, but only to provide housing and for the well-being of government officials in the area. An agreement was reached soon afterwards on this basis.[27]

Offshore Concessions

In the meantime, the minister of finance was conducting talks about offshore concessions with both British and American companies. This gave rise to another dispute with ARAMCO, which claimed the area as part of its concession while al-Sulayman contended that ARAMCO's claim was limited to the three-mile limit of territorial waters and that the government still maintained full ownership of minerals under its continental shelf.[28]

After months of discussion and consultation between the various oil companies and the British and American governments, ARAMCO and the Saudi government reached an agreement in principle in September that confirmed ARAMCO's rights to the offshore area in return for ARAMCO relinquishment of rights in the Saudi–Kuwaiti Neutral Zone. The agreement was signed by ARAMCO and al-Sulayman on 14 October 1948 but took effect from 1 October. Further agreements, including claim to a six-mile limit were signed but not published in March 1949. It should be noted that these agreements predated international resolution of offshore boundaries between the Gulf states.[29]

FINANCIAL RELATIONS BETWEEN THE SAUDI ARABIAN GOVERNMENT AND ARAMCO (1946–9)

From the early days of the concession through the halcyon days of the war, ARAMCO had sought to balance the Saudi demands for additional revenue with the fiscal requirements of its owner companies and their shareholders. The war, with its official American and British subsidies, had benefitted ARAMCO indirectly in this respect. But the withdrawal of the subsidies after the war threatened to increase the pressure on the producing company. This led to increasing tension in the late 1940s and early 1950s between company and government.

The officers of ARAMCO who found themselves frequently jousting with ʿAbdullah al-Sulayman over financial matters regarded him as a persistent obstinate negotiator. "Gary Owen, for example, used to moan that as far as Shaykh ʿAbdullah was concerned he was Mr No, that is Gary Owen's job was saying no to everything that Shaykh ʿAbdullah wanted. Well, of course, as you can imagine, they had more than a few rounds; and yet, ʿAbdullah al-Sulaiman was respected by the people who had to fight with him, who had to negotiate with him. He was not only an admirable adversary, he was somebody, he had qualities."[30]

As the Saudi budget grew in the postwar years, it remained nearly impossible to meet expenditure by growing oil payments—despite the fact that oil revenue far outstripped the *hajj* (annual pilgrimage) as the state's main source of income. This led to more and more demands upon ARAMCO to provide advances and services, all of which were presented by al-Sulayman.

One of the most protracted issues of disagreement involved the "gold clause" of the original 1933 concession agreement.[31] By its terms, the company agreed to pay a royalty of 4 gold shillings per ton—or its equivalent in US dollars or sterling. The dispute arose over how the conversion rate from dollars into gold shillings should be calculated. The company's position was that the dollar/gold rate in New York should be the basis of calculation while the Saudi government insisted that the prevailing rate in Jiddah should be used for conversion. The difference in rates could be enormous, as at times the Jiddah rate yielded twice as many dollars as the New York rate.

Strapped for cash, the Saudi government raised the matter in 1947. The company claimed to have been always nervous about the calculation of royalties in gold since there was no way of telling how the value of gold might appreciate over time. Its solution was to replace references to gold pounds in the concession agreement by stipulating the sum of $5. Originally, and up to 1939, the company had made royalty payments in sovereigns because sovereigns were required by the Saudi government to pay its internal debts. The outbreak of war, however, produced a shortage of gold and the company switched to payment in dollars. This was, however, to the government's disadvantage because of costs associated with converting dollars into currencies used within the kingdom.

The two sides managed to reach agreement that while ARAMCO had loaned the government gold against future royalty payments, those payments would be credited against the government's gold debt and subsequent advances would be made in dollars, thus converting the government's debt from gold to dollars. As a result, two accounts were kept: royalty payments and advances were entered in dollars while a separate account was kept of the company's gold debt to the government. The wrangle over reconciliation of the two accounts led to an eruption of the dispute in 1947.

The company claimed that the exchange rate in Jiddah was contrived by the Netherlands Trading Society from the rupee/gold rate prevailing in Bombay and noted that its royalty rate compared favorably to other concessions in the region. The government's argument was that it needed to purchase sovereigns in Jiddah by converting dollars or sterling. The cost of doing so was continually rising because Britain had withdrawn the sovereign as legal tender. The company was convinced that the government was simply using the gold issue as a way of increasing royalties while the company was reconciling itself to increasing payments and hoping to offset the cost against US taxes. Another ARAMCO tack to forestall changes in royalty was an offer of a development fund of $1 million to $5 million per year as an outright gift, in addition to the loan of $32 million already in the works for the railway. A proposal to have Britain mint more sovereigns for use in Saudi Arabia was rejected by London.

In the midst of the negotiations, the king pressed the president of ARAMCO on a visit to Riyadh in October 1947 to extend a new 10 million *riyal* ($3.5 million) loan, to which the company acquiesced. No resolution was reached by the end of 1947 but agreement was made in 1948 on terms that were more beneficial to the Saudi government.

The "gold clause" dispute reached a head in 1948 with prolonged, intense, and even acrimonious negotiations spearheaded by President Moore from ARAMCO and al-Sulayman. Initially Moore and ARAMCO suggested that ARAMCO make a lump-sum payment to cover past obligations and offered a number of ways to settle future obligations, including payment in dollars at a 46 percent premium over the official New York or London rate. At the time, this would be about $12 per sovereign. Al-Sulayman reportedly agreed orally to the offer but negotiations continued for several months.[32]

Agreement apparently was reached on 13 March 1948 as indicated by Moore's letter to the king: "I am most happy to confirm my acceptance during the meeting of your offer to settle the gold pound controversy on the basis as stated by you, namely, that the Company when it does not pay in gold sovereigns and elects to pay in dollars, will compute the dollar amount payable at the rate of US$12 for each gold pound due under the concession agreement...."[33] Two days later, Moore also accepted that negotiations would be re-opened if the official US gold rate changed from $35 per ounce.[34]

ʿAbdullah al-Sulayman disclosed his understanding of the terms in an interview published in *al-Bilad al-Saʿudiyah* on 28 March. The controversy had been settled after the case had been presented to the king and it was thereupon agreed that "the Company will pay in British Sovereigns in Saudi Arabia in accordance with the agreement, and when it is unable to pay these, the Company will pay 12 dollars in lieu of each sovereign. As for the past accounts they will be settled in dollars at the rate agreed upon" He also disclosed that the Saudi government was receiving about 10,000 gold sovereigns per day in royalties and that production was estimated at 300,000 b/d.[35]

Indeed, the king was instrumental in reaching agreement. Impatient with the increasingly confrontational nature of the negotiations, he reportedly declared that the $12 formula should be accepted without any reference to compensation in changes in the price of gold. Al-Sulayman reportedly was horrified since the result was less than what ARAMCO had offered earlier. He managed to get negotiations re-opened but the final agreement was little changed.[36]

While the agreement put a stop to further souring of relations between government and company, the consequences proved to be nearly disastrous for the kingdom. First of all, the company had managed to purchase a trove of sovereigns from Argentina at a favorable price, with which it was able to pay the $4 million owed in back payment and royalties until the end of 1948. There was also a possibility of more sovereigns being made available. The effect on the Saudi government was great difficulty in securing foreign exchange for the dollars it required for both imports and to service the Export-Import Bank loan, not to mention depressing the exchange rate with so much gold. The government could acquire dollars only by selling gold in local and regional markets and by selling *riyals* to ARAMCO for its local operations. If the *riyal*/gold rate remained high, the government could make a profit by using ARAMCO's gold to purchase *riyals* and then re-sell the *riyals* back to ARAMCO.[37]

It seemed that the minister of finance held the mercantilist view that the highest aim of financial policy was to accumulate the largest possible volume of gold within the boundaries of Saudi Arabia. While that strategy seemed to bring a short-term success, it played havoc with internal exchange rates. The value of gold sovereigns in terms of dollars began to fall to as low as $11, i.e. below than the agreed upon $12 rate for converting royalties.[38] Thus, both the Saudi government's income and its ability to procure dollars had been reduced significantly. The mixture of currencies circulating in the kingdom and their variable exchange rates was seen increasingly as a financial handicap. Thus, talk in 1948 turned again to creating a paper currency, as well as a central bank, and consultation on the subject was held with a US Treasury representative, Judd Polk.[39]

Various agencies of the United States government were hoping to use the advice provided by Polk as a spur to getting the Saudi government to accept a financial adviser. Polk regarded Saudi Arabia's central bank plan as having three advantages: it would fix the value of the two major mediums of exchange, thus eliminating speculation and arbitrage; centralizing the government's place of sale for gold would improve accounting procedures; and a paper currency could be introduced. Success, according to the Treasury representative, depended on fixing a reasonable exchange rate between the *riyal* and the dollar.[40]

Gold and currency were two of the principal worries at the heart of Saudi Arabia's continuing financial difficulties. During most of 1949, the government received just over 365,000 sovereigns per month in royalties.

However, shortages in funds forced the government to seek partial payments of royalties earlier in the month than the official date of payment. These began at 50,000 in advance in April and by November had reached 325,000, which accounted for most of the royalties due for that month. Furthermore, the payment in sovereigns forced the government to seek buyers for its sovereigns in order to pay its dollar debts, including $100,000 per month in installments for the 1946 $10 million loan from the Export-Import Bank and about $400,000 a month for the al-Dammam–Riyadh railway. The government continued to insist on payment in sovereigns because it could achieve a profit in exchange rate transactions when it paid ARAMCO in dollars.[41]

However, three additional problems arose during the year. First, declining production meant that ARAMCO paid less in royalties to an already strapped Saudi government. Second, part of the reason that ARAMCO did not produce more was because it had difficulty marketing its oil in sterling areas.[42] Third, the agreement by which ARAMCO was obliged to buy *riyal*s from the government at a premium rate to meet its in-country expenses was threatened by ARAMCO's resistance to paying for over-valued *riyal*s and the government's growing inability to furnish the amount of *riyal*s required.[43]

All of these issues contributed to growing tension between government and company. In early 1949, the king ordered ‘Abdullah al-Sulayman to summon F.A. Davies of ARAMCO and insist on more money in order to relieve the cash-strapped treasury. Al-Sulayman also informed ARAMCO that oil revenues must be paid into the treasury and that any attempt to do otherwise would result in cancellation of the concession.[44]

The imprecision of the royalty arrangements in the original 1933 concession proved to be another bone of contention in 1949. Al-Sulayman, on behalf of the Saudi government, vigorously contested the arrangement throughout the year, spurred on because of the country's pressing financial difficulties and aided by the new arrangements with the Pacific Western Oil Company. He even hinted at taking a second trip to the US to discuss royalties with ARAMCO's parent companies.[45]

It was during this period that the idea of imposing a Saudi income tax on ARAMCO was first mooted, apparently suggested by the US Treasury representative G.A. Eddy during his 1948 visit to the kingdom. The prospect was appealing, not least because ARAMCO was paying more to the US government in taxes than it was to the Saudi Arabian government in royalties. ARAMCO opened discussions with the State Department about the possible income tax and voiced its intention to demand as a *quid pro quo* the elimination of certain practices such as the premium payment on the purchase of *riyal*s from the government and currency restrictions on royalty payments. The State Department, for its part, pointed out that ARAMCO's annual payment of $60 million in US income tax made for good American public relations and voiced its uncertainty whether the US Treasury would allow Saudi taxes to be offset against American taxes.[46] As it turned out, these were opening moves in the 50/50 agreement that came to fruition in the following year, as detailed in the following section.

The split of revenues from the TAPline formed another arena of dispute in the late 1940s and early 1950s. After considerable negotiation, as usual, an agreement was reached between al-Sulayman and W.J. Lenahan on 11 July 1949 and was confirmed by King ʿAbd al-ʿAziz on 24 October and published in *Umm al-Qura* on 25 November. At the same time, the minister of finance and Lenahan exchanged supplementary letters that detailed ARAMCO's obligations to the Saudi government. The pumping stations were also to serve as community centers for the surrounding area, providing health and education facilities. The road paralleling the pipeline would also be used to enhance the kingdom's communications. In return, the company would be exempted from transit dues for 15 years.[47]

OIL NEGOTIATIONS AND RELATED MATTERS (1950–4)

The failure of oil revenues to keep up with expenditures in the late 1940s and early 1950s increased the pressure put on the minister of finance to find the necessary funds. As a consequence, al-Sulayman continually drove hard bargains in numerous discussions regarding Saudi Arabia's share of income from the profitable concession.[48] The ever-expanding requirements for expenditure in the kingdom fueled the government's hard-nosed discussions with ARAMCO regarding Saudi Arabia's income from the profitable concession. While ARAMCO payments rose from $5 million in 1945 to $30 million in 1948, Saudi Arabia's financial requirements rose at an even greater rate.[49]

The increasing contention between ARAMCO and the Saudi government was also prompted by ARAMCO's problems with a shrinking oil market where oil was paid for in US dollars. Therefore, fewer sales meant lessened production and, in turn, that resulted in smaller revenue to the government. As a consequence, the company also attempted to impress on al-Sulayman, and his deputy negotiator, Najib Salihah, the desirability of the government accepting some of its royalties in sterling, since those payments could then be used to purchase British goods. ARAMCO made little headway, however. When ARAMCO ran out of sovereigns in August 1950, the government was forced to accept sterling and agreed to postpone determination of the precise exchange rate until later. This became a largely moot point with the adoption of the 50/50 agreement at the end of the year.[50]

The Fifty–Fifty Agreement of 1950

King ʿAbd al-ʿAziz's position vis-à-vis the company had been strengthened by two developments at the end of the 1940s. The first of these involved settlement of the conversion rate of British gold sovereigns (in which payment was originally denominated in the 1933 concession) into US dollars (in which the company began to pay during World War II and after). To resummarize, the company contended that the rate should be based on the official exchange rate of $8.24 to the sovereign, and was using that rate in its payments, while Saudi government insisted that it be based on the market rate in Jiddah, which fluctuated between $16 and $20. After protracted negotiations in early 1948, an agreement was reached in March that an exchange rate of $12 should be used.[51] ARAMCO made a lump-sum payment of $19.32 million to end the dispute.

The second development derived from ARAMCO's relinquishment of concession rights in the Saudi–Kuwaiti Neutral Zone in 1948 (in exchange for recognition of offshore rights). Thus, Saudi Arabia was able to sell its half-rights in the Neutral Zone. The highest bidder turned out to be J. Paul Getty's Pacific Western Oil Company and the concession agreement signed in January 1949 was regarded as the most beneficial concession in the Middle East.[52] In fact, Pacific Western's success in getting the concession was attributed to its offering better terms than competitor AMINOIL.[53]

Pacific Western offered a considerably higher royalty rate than ARAMCO, plus 12.5 percent of gross proceeds from sales of natural gas, 20 percent of the profits from a refinery built in the Neutral Zone, stipulated amounts of gasoline and kerosene from the refinery, the right to buy 25 percent of any subsidiary company formed to operate in the Neutral Zone, and significant contributions to Saudi education in and outside the country, amongst other items. The generous terms achieved by the Saudi government were expected to have repercussions on other Middle Eastern concessions.[54]

The Neutral Zone concession convinced the king that the terms of the 1933 ARAMCO concession were unfavorable to the kingdom. Consequently, pressure grew on the Saudi side to renegotiate the 1933 concession agreement.[55] Discussion began in July 1950 between the ARAMCO president and vice-president (F.W. Moore and Fred Davies) on the one side and ʿAbdullah al-Sulayman on the other. ARAMCO's goal was to reach agreement on a simple formula for payments, instead of the piecemeal demands that the Saudis pressed on it. Eventually, the negotiations revolved around the question of income tax, both American and Saudi Arabian. At this point, the United States government became involved because of the perception that Saudi oil was a vital and strategic resource that needed to be protected.

These talks were only the culmination of a number of disputes between the company and the king, as pursued on his behalf by al-Sulayman. "Throughout 1949 and into 1950 Al Sulaiman continued to press Aramco for payment of the cost of harbor piers and railroads then under construction, contributions to a Saudi 'welfare fund,' royalties on oil used in refinery operations, deferred repayment of money already advanced, and—in general—a larger share in Aramco's profits."[56]

Within ARAMCO, the fear arose that conceding additional payments to Riyadh would wipe out the company's profits and arouse the anger of its parent companies and their shareholders. One strategy was to point out to the Saudis that in 1949 ARAMCO had paid $40 million in income tax to the US government but only $38 million to the Saudi Arabian government. Naturally, the kingdom was more than a little perturbed at this.[57] ARAMCO's strategy seemed to be deflecting al-Sulayman's demands for a full-scale renegotiation of oil revenues by making small concessions, such as deferring the monthly deduction for expenses involved in the railway and the $6 million loan agreed at the beginning of the year. But the minister countered by putting greater pressure on ARAMCO when he added such demands as a welfare fund of about $10 million a year, royalties on refinery operations, ARAMCO's assumption of responsibility for the cost of both the railway and al-Dammam pier, and postponement of current invoices until January 1951 (estimated at more than half a million a month).[58]

ARAMCO continued to resist throughout the year but the Saudis would not revise their position. The Saudi government engaged an American tax lawyer to provide advice while ARAMCO arranged for the dispatch to Jiddah of a US Treasury official, George A. Eddy. When asked by "a Saudi official" (presumably al-Sulayman) about the possibility of raising more money from "foreign firms," Eddy suggested that either the government could demand an increase in royalties or to institute its own income tax. He further elaborated that while increasing royalties would impact the company's profits, the latter approach would simply divert income tax revenues from the US government to the Saudi Arabian government, since under US law tax paid to a foreign government could be deducted from US payments.[59]

By November, ARAMCO and the State Department, with whom the company had been discussing the issue, agreed that some sort of profit-sharing similar to what had been arranged in Venezuela was likely and negotiations between ARAMCO and the Saudi government began in earnest in November. The oil company proposed that there be "an equal participation (in) net profits after foreign taxes and withdrawal outstanding Saudi government demands" but al-Sulayman demurred, uncertain of what benefit would accrue to the government. His counter-offer was for an ARAMCO guarantee of an increase of at least 40 percent in government revenue per barrel. ARAMCO would not guarantee the figure but, on 12 December, the company provided the minister with estimates of what the government could expect to receive. Al-Sulayman then indicated that he was fully prepared to accept the proposal and would do his best to persuade Prince Faysal, the overall head of the Saudi negotiating team, to agree. The two men then traveled to Riyadh about 16 December to discuss the matter with the king.[60]

The king was persuaded as well and so the kingdom enacted an Income Tax Law by royal decree on 26 December 1950. The legislation called for a 50/50 split of profits from oil exploitation by introducing a 50 percent tax on all companies involved in the production of petroleum or hydrocarbons. The tax was calculated on profits after all other sums paid to the government, including royalties, rentals, and duties, had been deducted. The effect on Saudi Arabia was dramatic: the receipts from ARAMCO in 1950 totaled $56,700,000 while in 1951 these increased to $110,000,000. At the same time, ARAMCO suffered no additional cost as the company simply wrote off their Saudi Arabian taxes against their liabilities for US tax. In addition, the question of which currency payments were to be made in disappeared as ARAMCO was permitted to pay royalties in any currency for which it sold oil or in gold.[61]

The implementation of the income tax arrangement accounted for only part of the overall question of payments. After months of talks, the two sides also agreed in December 1950 that they should adopt the 50/50 arrangements, i.e. each side would receive 50 percent of the concession's income, along the lines that Venezuela had obtained just previously.[62] That more or less settled the question of Saudi income tax, since all existing royalties and taxes would be included in the 50 percent accruing to the Saudi government. The remaining question was whether American income tax should be deducted from operating income before or after calculation of the 50/50 sharing. ARAMCO was able to rest easier in 1955 when the US Internal Revenue Service finally ruled that the company would be permitted to deduct its Saudi taxes from its obligations for American income tax.[63]

Another aspect of the new agreement was that both company and government shared an interest in the maintenance of the posted-price system of crude oil since any reduction in posted prices would reduce both the company's net profit per barrel and the government's income.[64] Furthermore, although the 50/50 agreement was signed in December, ARAMCO agreed to apply the agreement retrospectively for all of 1950. Future payments were to be made on a quarterly basis, one year in arrears, but ARAMCO also agreed to break the first quarterly payment for 1951 into more frequent installments to help the government with its finances.[65]

Al-Sulayman served as the principal Saudi negotiator in this affair and ably demonstrated his skills in pressing ARAMCO to accept new terms that benefitted the kingdom. King ʿAbd al-ʿAziz had yet another reason to be satisfied by the trust he put it in his financial guru. At the same time, however, al-Sulayman earned the enmity of ARAMCO because of his tough bargaining. Gary Owen of ARAMCO, accompanied by Floyd Ohliger, even discussed with US embassy officials in Dhahran in 1951 the possibility of forcing al-Sulayman out as minister of finance.[66] ARAMCO adviser William Eddy wrote home that the minister was telling the king that ARAMCO was insulting and cheating him and so ARAMCO should leave the country.[67] ARAMCO Vice-President James Terry Duce, accompanied by Eddy, had earlier argued in the State Department itself that "Shaikh Abdallah Sulayman must necessarily leave the Ministry of Finance which might pave the way for a more orderly system of collecting and expending Saudi Arabian revenue to be inaugurated."[68] In subsequent meetings with Crown Prince Saʿud, Duce reported that the prince was planning to replace al-Sulayman with the head of the Ministry of Finance office at Dhahran, ʿAbdullah b. ʿAdwan, a figure that ARAMCO viewed much more favorably.[69] This tactic, of course, failed.

Tense relations between ARAMCO and the government persisted into 1952, centered principally on the government's chronic lack of funds and attempts to procure advances and loans from the oil company. Still, there were some bright spots in the relationship. For example, agreement was reached on the location of ARAMCO's headquarters and on Saudi participation on the board of directors.

TAPline Negotiations

Although ARAMCO and the Saudi government had signed the initial agreement for TAPline in 1947, many matters still remained to be settled. Indeed, construction of the pipeline was not completed until towards the end of 1950. Questions were still unanswered about how much TAPline should reimburse the Saudi government for the cost of defending and administering the pipeline. Government arrangements for a defensive force went far beyond ARAMCO's conception and the company refused to pay all the cost. It also resisted the demand of Prince Mansur, the minister of defense, that TAPline take over the burden of defending Saudi Arabia's northern borders, arguing that it was responsible for financing protection against "marauding bedouin" and not external attack. Even though the pipeline was scheduled for completion in September 1950, outstanding disagreements on financing defensive forces remained an additional source of rancor between ARAMCO and the Saudi government.[70]

Another TAPline dispute arose when the government announced its desire to have TAPline in Saudi Arabia transferred to ARAMCO, which would then bring it under the terms of ARAMCO's concession. ARAMCO countered with a suggestion that the government apply a tax on TAPline. The difficulty lay in fixing the price of oil for such a tax: ARAMCO sold oil from Ra's Tanurah at $1.43 a barrel but TAPline offered it at $1.73 at the Saudi–Jordanian border and the price at the Sidon (Lebanon) terminal was $2.41.[71]

Another point of contention concerned the amount of the payments that ARAMCO was obliged to make to the government. For the years October 1950 to September 1952, the Saudi government insisted on a payment of 6.5 million *riyals* while ARAMCO claimed the amount should be less than 1 million *riyals*. Saudi Arabia countered ARAMCO's obduracy by applying pressure through customs obstructions. ARAMCO finally agreed to the government's demands simply to get the obstructions removed.[72]

OTHER FINANCIAL RELATIONS BETWEEN THE SAUDI ARABIAN GOVERNMENT AND ARAMCO (1950–4)

ARAMCO's negotiating position with the government centered on the argument that its payments had been between only $3 million and $5 million during World War II but had ballooned to nearly $57 million in 1950. Any increase in payments would have be met by higher and thus uncompetitive prices charged for its oil. The government's response was that the company had recouped its investment in five years and so could afford to pay. Even the US government became involved, attempting to play a conciliatory role. But the Saudis pushed for the Venezuelan example of a 50/50 split of profits, to which ARAMCO eventually had no choice but to capitulate. As a consequence, government revenues nearly doubled during 1951.

That landmark agreement did not put an end to squabbling over finances between company and government, however. The government's chronic shortage of funds led the minister of finance to press ARAMCO continually for more advances. In January 1952, ARAMCO suggested to al-Sulayman that taxes for 1951, estimated at $99 million less $25 million already received by the Saudi government, be paid on a monthly basis. This was seen as a way for the government to better control its expenditures to the level of its income. However, the $5 million a month suggested was immediately questioned by the Ministry of Finance as not sufficient to meet current monthly needs.[73]

In addition, serious and prolonged negotiations were carried out in the early part of the year, primarily by ʿAbdullah al-Sulayman and Najib Salihah on the Saudi side. ARAMCO conceded the point that the division of profits should be made prior to the subtraction of foreign taxes, as well as the principle that tax payments should be made as current as possible. This would make $10 million available to the government each month instead of the previously proposed $5 million. In addition, ARAMCO agreed to move its headquarters to Dhahran (but refused to register the company in Saudi Arabia) as well as to accept two but not three Saudi members on its board. Some points of disagreement remained, such as terms for production of new fields and relinquishment of concession area. In addition, the two sides differed on payments for TAPline and the book price of crude oil.

With the talks in deadlock over these issues, the Saudi government engaged the firm of DeGoyler and MacNaughton, which had acted as adviser to the US Navy, to assist with negotiations. Lewis W. MacNaughton began discussions with ARAMCO in November and proposed a complicated pricing formula. The situation was further muddled as ARAMCO's production dropped towards the end of the year, which of course reduced the kingdom's tax revenues. The negotiations failed to produce any results by the end of the year.[74]

In 1953, one of the unresolved issues dealt with the price of oil for calculating tax payments to the government, a considerable sum especially when considering that the final settlement would be backdated to the signing of the 50/50 agreement in 1950. The situation was further complicated by differences over costs claimed by the Saudi government in relation to TAPline. MacNaughton continued to negotiate on the government's behalf. Although MacNaughton predicted an early resolution, there still was no end to the question by the end of the year. Interruptions were caused by prolonged absences by al-Sulayman, ARAMCO's labor difficulties, and the ill-health and then death of King ʿAbd al-ʿAziz. It seemed, however, that the accession of King Saʿud produced no changes in al-Sulayman's authority to negotiate with ARAMCO.[75]

Other, lesser, differences also marred relations between the Saudi government and ARAMCO. One of these was the new schedule of charges on the railway, which had been turned over to government control. ARAMCO also complained of import and export stoppages on instructions of the Ministry of Finance, as well as difficulties in obtaining visas, more stringent labor regulations (ARAMCO had experienced strikes in November and December), and demands that Arabic be adopted as the language for all records. In an attempt to mollify the minister of finance, the company made offers of settlement of TAPline expenses and customs duty refunds. This strategy, however, only angered al-Sulayman as he regarded it as an attempt to suborn the Saudi government. Relations improved somewhat with resolution of the TAPline dispute.[76]

ONASSIS AND THE SATCO AFFAIR OF 1954

The attempt by Aristotle Onassis to create a monopoly on the tanker carriage of Saudi crude oil created the first major test in Saudi–American relations of the King Saʿud era. It also involved ʿAbdullah al-Sulayman with the affair since he was responsible for negotiations with ARAMCO and because of its financial implications for the kingdom. There are conflicting accounts of the origins of the agreement, who was involved, and the reasons for its resolution. Al-Sulayman is portrayed in some accounts as a principal villain in the affair and his resignation from his long-held position as minister of finance took place in the heat of the dispute. Credible evidence of his secret involvement in helping to arrange the agreement has never been forthcoming, however, despite the considerable attention given to the matter in various publications.[77]

The origins of the scheme to capture the tanker market for Saudi oil is generally traced to Spyridon (or Spiros) Catapodis, a Greek shipowner based in southern France, who allegedly first interested Aristotle Onassis in the scheme. This was the version given by ARAMCO in July 1954 to the State Department.[78] Meetings on the scheme were alleged to have been held in Cannes and Paris. A draft agreement was drawn up in which Onassis was said to have promised to assign a tanker fleet to the Saudi Arabian flag and pay royalties for the initial privilege of carrying a guaranteed 10 percent—about 4 million tons—of the country's annual oil output. The real value to Onassis was in his ability to fix above-market transport rates. Furthermore, the agreement provided an escalation mechanism that meant that, as existing tankers were retired, they would have to be replaced by Onassis tankers. Onassis also promised to create a maritime training school for young Saudis for employment with the fleet.

Negotiations ended with an agreement on 20 January 1954 signed by ʿAbdullah al-Sulayman for the government and Muhammad ʿAlireza for Onassis.[79] The agreement established the Saudi Arabian Maritime Tanker Company (SATCO), a private firm chartered in Jiddah that was authorized to register a minimum of 500,000 tons of tankers under the Saudi Arabian flag. The Saudi Arabian government would receive a royalty of about 20 cents for every ton of oil carried by the company's fleet to any port in the world. The agreement would last for 30 years and was renewable. In addition, SATCO agreed to a school for training 15 Saudi students in navigation and mechanics.[80] Al-Sulayman sent a letter to ARAMCO on 23 January 1954, informing the company that an agreement between the Saudi government and Aristotle Onassis required the oil companies, with two exceptions, to transport oil and oil products on SATCO ships.[81] ARAMCO then exhorted the US government to help persuade the Saudi government to nullify the agreement. King Sa'ud was disinclined, however, because the agreement's advantages were that the tanker company would transport 50,000 tons of oil for the Saudi government at no cost, 50 Saudis would be trained every year by the company, and a fleet of some 30–5 tankers would fly the Saudi flag.[82]

But the first sign of the agreement's eventual collapse occurred in February 1954 when Onassis was arrested in the US for his role in a surplus ships scheme. Meanwhile, SOCAL and TEXACO lobbied Secretary of State John Foster Dulles against the agreement in early 1954. The oil companies' pressure had the desired effect. In April 1954, the embassy in Jiddah was instructed to tell King Sa'ud that the US government felt that the agreement was not in keeping with the oil concession and would harm both US and Saudi defense interests.[83] The king, however, was reported by ARAMCO disposed to support the agreement, believing that there was no contravention of the concession and that it was to the kingdom's benefit.[84] In fact, he issued a royal decree in April ratifying the agreement as signed by al-Sulayman on 20 January. ARAMCO's response was threaten to reduce production to a level that could be lifted by the company's own tankers.[85]

The vehemence of ARAMCO's objection to the decree provoked US Ambassador George Wadsworth to seek an audience with King Sa'ud on 30 April 1954. The king on this occasion seemed ambivalent about the contract. Although he did not cut off discussion, he considered the matter closed, perhaps because he found the subject distasteful. Nevertheless, he still had not ratified the agreement by this time, probably because of ARAMCO's heated opposition. Onassis steered well clear of the fracas, necessarily because of his legal difficulties.[86]

During the months from May to August 1954, the controversies surrounding the Onassis Agreement, as well as the GOVENCO affair (viz., the contract signed with a Germany company to carry out development in the kingdom; see Chapter 11 for details), came to a head. The agreement was not published until it appeared in *al-Bilad al-Sa'udiyah* on 7 June 1954 and *Umm al-Qura* on 14 June 1954, albeit with significant modifications. One provided SATCO with priority in the transportation of oil and its products, apart from ships owned by the oil company and its parent companies and regularly involved in the transport of oil from Saudi Arabia prior to 1954. A price floor was also specified for freight charges that appeared to be exceptionally favorable to Onassis. The agreement was to last 30 years.[87]

Meanwhile, Onassis sought to persuade the State Department of the merits of his scheme, offering to renegotiate its terms, and he even flew to Jiddah. ARAMCO, however, refused categorically to negotiate with him, threatening to turn SATCO ships away from Ra's Tanurah. Indeed, later in the year, the oil company issued a statement to the effect that "whatever the outcome of arbitration proceedings ARAMCO would not agree to do business with Onassis because of serious doubts cast on his integrity" and threatened to insist to the king that Onassis was an "unsavoury character."[88]

Nevertheless, Onassis pressed on with his plan and the first SATCO ship was launched in Hamburg. Onassis also approached Getty and secured a draft agreement for Getty's use of SATCO tankers at a lower rate. Getty held off implementation, however, on State Department advice to wait until the ARAMCO matter was settled.[89] The State Department raised the possibility in July 1954 that Onassis was beginning to tire of all the complications related to the agreement and was willing to make a deal with the oil companies. Speculation arose again that it had been Onassis's intention from the beginning to reach some agreement with the oil companies for the purchase of his ships.[90]

It may have been the intention of Onassis to name the first ship the *King Sa'ud I* to curry Saudi sentiment and thereby force ARAMCO to load the tanker. The seriousness with which the US government viewed the possibility of the agreement being implemented was indicated by the conclusion of US National Security Council (NSC) reports that baldly stated that "The United States should take all appropriate measures to bring about the cancellation of the agreement between the Saudi Arabian Government and Onassis" and "The Saudi Arab Agreement with the S.A. Onassis interests to form a maritime company for the shipment of Saudi Arabian oil directly threatens U.S. interests... The ultimate solution of this and similar problems is necessarily bound up with future developments in U.S.–Saudi Arab relations."[91]

By August 1954, it looked increasingly like the agreement was in trouble because of intense US government pressure on Riyadh, resistance from ARAMCO and other oil companies, and representations from a number of other governments and shipping companies. Ambassador Wadsworth's discussions with King Sa'ud seemed to indicate that the king was willing to back down but he needed a public pretext for doing so. A first step involved bringing Karl Twitchell, the American entrepreneur who had long held Saudi trust with his role in the search for water, oil, and minerals, back to Saudi Arabia to convince the king that it would not be in his best interests to pursue the Onassis agreement.[92]

By the end of August, a Saudi committee of enquiry was investigating the GOVENCO affair. On 31 August 1954, 'Abdullah al-Sulayman tendered his resignation as minister of finance and economy. At the same time, both 'Abd al-'Aziz 'Abdullah al-Sulayman and Ahmed Musli resigned from the Ministry of Finance. King Sa'ud appointed Muhammad Surur al-Sabban as Shaykh 'Abdullah's replacement, which was not surprising given the king's earlier patronage of Muhammad (al-Sulayman's resignation is treated in more detail in Chapter 11).

After many deliberations between ARAMCO, Onassis' rival Stavros Niarchos, and King Sa'ud and his advisers, the king summoned Onassis to the kingdom in October, Although Onassis gave a good account with himself as the victim of a conspiracy, the king would not be dissuaded. Accordingly, he informed ARAMCO and the American embassy that if Onassis could be shown to have refused a reasonable renegotiation of agreement, he would let it go to arbitration. At long last, ARAMCO began negotiations with Onassis and successfully backed him into a corner over the question of fixed rates for the carriage of oil. ARAMCO triumphantly reported Onassis' refusal to the Saudi government, which agreed to go to arbitration in 30 days. The agreement essentially was rendered moribund in December 1954 when *al-Bilad al-Sa'udiyah* published a statement by the new minister of finance, al-Sabban, indicating that if agreement between the Saudi Arabian government and ARAMCO could not be reached by 15 January 1955, the matter would be put to arbitration.[93]

What in fact was 'Abdullah al-Sulayman's connection to SATCO? As mentioned above, most accounts charge in passing that he was one of the instigators of the scheme for financial gain. The affair is not mentioned by Anthony Sampson in *The Seven Sisters* or Daniel Yergin in *The Prize*.[94] Other accounts are either hostile to King Sa'ud's role or seek to implicate al-Sulayman. An American historian contends that al-Sulayman's dismissal was actually part of a deal between ARAMCO and the Saudi Arabian government. By this account, King Sa'ud dismissed the so-called "architect of the Onassis tanker deal" as *quid pro quo* for ARAMCO's agreement to pay retroactive royalties back to December 1951, a step that would produce $70 million in additional Saudi revenue.[95] This view seems to argue that ARAMCO had finally found a suitable opportunity to rid itself of its long-time nemesis.

Many of the details surrounding the affair came to light after al-Sulayman's resignation. Catapodis gave his version of the negotiations leading to the agreement in a statement on 18 September and subsequently swore out an affidavit in front of the British vice-consul in Nice. Catapodis claimed that Muhammad 'Alireza had been given two bank drafts of £125,000 each for himself and £100,000 for the minister of finance. Catapodis made no contention that al-Sulayman had either received any payment or had asked for one. The British embassy in Jiddah reported that when al-Sulayman heard about the allegations (following Catapodis' statement in September), he went to the king and offered to submit to investigation to prove the allegations were false. The king accepted his offer and established a committee under the chairmanship of Muhammad Surur al-Sabban, the new minister of finance.[96]

There is no credible evidence that ʿAbdullah al-Sulayman received any money from the affair. The essential allegations of his complicity revolve around his necessary involvement as minister of finance. He was responsible for official negotiations with ARAMCO and his tough negotiating stance over the years had earned him considerable enmity from within the oil company. Accordingly, ARAMCO's vehement opposition to the tanker deal would not surprisingly implicate the company's old enemy, the minister of finance. It is undeniable that al-Sulayman signed the SATCO agreement in January 1954 but this was in his official capacity; he certainly could not have done so except at the direction of King Saʿud. His resignation in August 1954 as the deal was collapsing has been interpreted either as royal indignation at his greed or as his being made the scapegoat so that the regime could save face. The problem with this argument is that the allegations of bribery became public only after Catapodis made his statement in September, weeks after al-Sulayman had resigned and before the storm of negative publicity blew up. Furthermore, he asked for a board of enquiry to exonerate himself and the board found no fault with his actions. As is discussed in Chapter 11, there are many, often conflicting, reasons advanced for his resignation after so many years in royal service.

CHAPTER 9

Postwar Stringencies and the Push for Development (1945–9)

A NEW NORMALCY AFTER THE WAR

Although Saudi Arabia was not a participant in World War II (apart from its technical declaration of war on the Axis Powers at the end), the war had a profound impact on the kingdom, as it did on most corners of the world. It produced a financial crisis by drastically reducing the number of pilgrims on the *hajj* (annual pilgrimage)—which still provided the most important domestic source of revenue. Its finances were kept afloat only by the extension of massive subsidies by Britain and the United States. Famine in Najd proved to be a major problem because of the combination of drought and plagues of locusts while the lack of motor transport made the transfer of food supplies from the coasts to the interior problematic. Because of the threat of enemy action and the curtailment of civilian shipping, the potential of oil was not realized and Arabian American Oil Company (ARAMCO) advances in payments were the norm rather than income from actual sales of crude oil.

The Shift from Britain to the United States and the Effective Beginning of the Oil Era

While the old Anglo-Saudi alliance remained intact and relations between King ʿAbd al-ʿAziz and the British government were friendly and close, the war had brought a sea change. The United States had begun the process of supplanting Britain as Saudi Arabia's principal ally. There were a number of reasons for this. The oil company was American in ownership and this facilitated the opening of an American consulate in Dhahran, the only diplomatic representation outside Jiddah. The Saudi Arabian Mining Syndicate (SAMS) was also a largely American entity but its importance was rapidly diminishing. British eyes on postwar economies forced London to back away from continued subsidies. The US, however, took over the burden, recognizing that the Saudi oil reserves represented a major asset in American and world oil supplies. In addition, the US began a commitment to Saudi development that was to strengthen Saudi–American ties for decades to come.

Oil revenues began to rise after the war. Net oil revenues payable in 1946 were estimated at $8 million and $14 million in 1947. At the same time, however, the government owed ARAMCO $11 million for earlier advances and $2 million to the US government for surplus war material.[1] Nevertheless, and although revenue since 1939 had increased sixfold, the budget remained unbalanced. Part of the problem was that a great proportion of government revenue was received in the form of foreign exchange and the budgetary problem could not be resolved without a substantial increase in the volume of imports, which also had the effect of producing deflation. The reason why expenditures had increased so dramatically in six or seven years was difficult to ascertain, although increasing military expenditure played a significant role.[2]

Nevertheless, it was estimated that the Saudi Arabian government would spend $100 million on development in the five years following the war and ARAMCO was expected to spend $400 million on the exploitation of Saudi oil. While there was some hope that the government would be able to finance its development projects itself, the US government favored commercial loans as a bridge.[3]

While change was clearly on the horizon, many facets of life and administration in Saudi Arabia remained unchanged from before the war years. Nevertheless the foundations for enormous change had been laid and the postwar years began a boom without adequate infrastructure. For this reason, ʿAbdullah al-Sulayman continued to play perhaps the most important role outside the royal family in the development of the kingdom's finances and administrative structure. No mechanism for financing the short-term needs of the government existed, thus forcing the Ministry of Finance to engage in periodic struggles with the trading community.

The United States government and private American enterprise became increasingly involved in Saudi Arabia's development during these years. In the immediate postwar period, Saudi Arabia was regarded increasingly as an important target of US aid. In return for this aid, the kingdom was expected to protect American commercial interests (read ARAMCO) and to give strong consideration to US insistence on internal financial reform. As the State Department noted in March 1946, "If ... Middle East countries seek future financial assistance from the United States, we have every right to insist upon such reforms in both the internal and external financial and monetary practices of each applicant country as will insure that United States' assistance is utilized in the best interests of the people as a whole and results in some permanent improvement in the economic position of the country." In Saudi Arabia's case, vital improvements were seen in currency reform, financial advisers, and supervision of the expenditure of Export-Import Bank loans.[4]

At the beginning of 1946, international aid to Saudi Arabia, including American government assistance, was summarized as consisting of: the US Agricultural Mission for al-Kharj, British anti-locust assistance, and the American and British Military Missions training Saudi personnel in the use of small arms and mechanized equipment respectively. Furthermore, an Egyptian Road Mission had macademized the road from Jiddah to Makkah in 1942, the Middle East Supply Center provided transport advisers during the war to help reorganize Saudi transport, and the US Army in the Middle East Headquarters sent some experts during the war to help repair and improve the kingdom's telegraph system. In addition, an American engineer provided assistance supervising beacons and reef markers around Jiddah harbor, the US Legation in Jiddah set up a modern medical clinic while Britain was planning a full hospital, and assistance was sought from an American airline to help institute local aviation.[5] As can be seen much of this assistance originated from the US government. But the American private sector was also becoming involved about this time.

One American corporation that developed extensive interests from the late 1940s was Bechtel Corporation. Its entry into Saudi Arabia had been through the construction of the Trans-Arabian Pipeline (TAPline) but it had also become

> the principal public works contractor for the Government and was involved in building the Jeddah and Dammam harbours, the airports there and at Riyadh, the electrification schemes for the two cities, the resurfacing of the Mecca–Medina road, and other building programmes. Bechtel had negotiated what looked to by a very cozy arrangement whereby it was paid for costs plus a guaranteed profit. It was much resented and was referred to as *maktal*, "the place of killing". Towards the end of 1951, however, the company decided that its involvement was more trouble than it was worth. It was owed $1.8 million by the Saudi Exchequer when the arrangement was terminated .... The company continued, however, to carry out work on behalf of Aramco.[6]

After disappointments with several more American firms, the central American role in the kingdom's development efforts came to be assumed by the US Corps of Engineers following King Faysal's request that the US government become the "national manager of Saudi development contracts" in 1965.[7]

In the midst of this activity, ʿAbdullah al-Sulayman was intimately involved with the negotiations over the construction of premises for the US embassy in Jiddah and its consulate in Dhahran. The talks were prolonged because of al-Sulayman's insistence that foreigners were not allowed to own property in the kingdom. Thus, the Saudi government offered a 25-year lease on the land, after which the premises (constructed at US expense) could be rented by the US government at prevailing rental rates in Jiddah. This was unacceptable to American negotiators, who suggested that al-Sulayman's tough bargaining stance owed something to his dissatisfaction with the outcome of the agreement over Saudi purchase of US surplus property. The American consul-general in Dhahran, Parker Hart, wrote that the minister of finance "is a heavy real estate owner and while he may not live 25 years he seems intent on defending established real estate practices."[8] In the end, a compromise was reached by appealing to the king, who agreed to fix the future rent at 2 percent of the construction price.[9]

The US Air Force base at Dhahran was another indication of growing US–Saudi ties. The establishment of the base generated a certain amount of contention. There was some feeling that it was constructed as a tangible indication of serious US interest in the kingdom and its oil production, in particular to prove to the king the depth of American commitment to his regime. On the other hand, some in the US military and political establishment regarded the base as a white elephant.[10]

ʿAbdullah al-Sulayman remained involved in matters involving the base, particularly those of a financial nature. In October 1947, Prince Mansur, the minister of defense, and al-Sulayman approved a $686,000 construction program at the base, which included a hotel, residences for instructors, customs buildings, a post office, quarantine buildings, and warehouses.[11] As these items indicate, civilian traffic as well as military was foreseen for the Dhahran facility.

He was also involved as liaison for the technical advice provided through the US government's Point IV program in the 1950s.[12] Although the program was not as successful as it could have been, in large part because of a lack of coordination with relevant Saudi government departments, it did lay the groundwork for two significant accomplishments: the establishment of the Saudi Arabian Monetary Agency as Saudi Arabia's central bank and the revision of customs tariffs. The Ministry of Finance was responsible for signing agreements on the provision of financial advisers and looking after water survey teams for Riyadh and mining areas.

ʿAbdullah al-Sulayman's Trip to the US (1946)

The significance of ʿAbdullah al-Sulayman's continued role in Saudi Arabia's finances and development was perhaps best illustrated by his visit to the United States in 1946. Because of the minister's many responsibilities and interests, there probably could not have been anyone else, other than the king himself or his senior sons, better suited to open the new era of Saudi–American relations. Al-Sulayman departed Saudi Arabia for New York via Cairo on 29 July 1946 and returned on 29 October, exactly three months later. His accompanying delegation consisted of Husayn al-ʿUwayni (later the prime minister of Lebanon), Ahmad Mawsili (the director of the minister's office), Muhammad Ba Harith (a senior official in the minister's office), Maʿtuk Hasanayn (a financial expert in the ministry and later the first deputy governor of SAMA), ʿAli ʿAlireza (who was in school in the US at the time and served as translator), ʿAli al-Hamrani (the private secretary to ʿAbdullah al-Sulayman); Khalid al-Hamad (a nephew of al-Sulayman who also just happened to be studying in the US at the time), and ʿAbd al-Razzaq al-ʿAtiq al-Sulayman (another relative who also just happened to be studying in the US).[13]

Shortly after his arrival in the US, al-Sulayman called upon President Harry S. Truman on 14 August 1946. Besides exchanging courtesies, the two men briefly discussed the route and financing of the al-Dammam–Riyadh Railway and plans for irrigation in the kingdom. The president suggested that the Saudi minister visit lands in Arizona and California that had been successfully reclaimed from desert.[14] Following this courtesy meeting at the White House, al-Sulayman carried out a full schedule of meetings and visits to various parts of the country. He and his party—accompanied by several ARAMCO officials—flew to Phoenix on 26 August to examine the Salt River Project. Then the party traveled overland to Los Angeles via the Grand Canyon, Boulder Dam, and Palm Springs, returning to Washington on 2 September.[15]

ARAMCO played a supporting role throughout the trip. Al-Sulayman was the guest of honor at a tea party arranged in Washington on 14 August by James T. Duce of ARAMCO. Al-Sulayman also gave a dinner at Washington's Shoreham Hotel in honor of Edwin Locke, the Special Assistant to the President, on 5 October. In addition, Shaykh ʿAbdullah presented the President and Mrs. Truman with complete Arab costumes.[16]

While the Saudi minister had several objectives for his visit, he was concerned principally with arrangements for the promised Export-Import Bank loan. As explained in the previous chapter, the US had decided on a loan from the Export-Import Bank as the most suitable means of extending aid to Saudi Arabia in the postwar period. Although it took until late 1945 to arrange details, it was decided that Saudi Arabia would require a loan of $25 million to meet its budget deficits over the period 1945–9, with $5 million earmarked for loan during 1946. The $25 million loan of credit was approved by the newly constituted board of directors of the bank on 3 January 1946 and it was agreed that al-Sulayman would sign the agreement in Washington during his forthcoming trip.[17]

Even after the offer was extended, though, there were hiccups. King 'Abd al-'Aziz objected to the loan because all future oil revenue was to be mortgaged to a foreign bank and because repayment with interest contravened Islamic law. Apparently, the king was unaware that al-Sulayman had arranged for loans with interest payments to both Gellatly's and the Netherlands Trading Society. However, after the Saudi government's inability to negotiate a commercial loan, the minister of finance was instructed to recommence arrangements with the Export-Import Bank. This he carried out during his stay in Washington.[18]

'Abdullah al-Sulayman's first objective, in his role as effectively minister of trade and commerce, was to acquire the funds for the $10 million initially promised in the first Export-Import Bank loan. This sum was needed to purchase transport equipment, foodstuffs, textiles, and medicine. Long before his visit, he had been frustrated by his inability to purchase the quantities of sugar, rice, and fertilizer that were needed to put an end to the short supply in the kingdom, and the $10 million line of credit, which he successfully managed to acquire on 9 August, was meant to correct this.

In addition, he sought the remaining $15 million credit line with the Export-Import Bank for financing infrastructural development, roads, railways, harbors, and hospitals. In this regard, King 'Abd al-'Aziz was insistent on building a railway from al-Dammam to Riyadh. Washington regarded this as uneconomical. The Saudi insistence on a railway created problems for agreement on suitable projects for the loan. It was pointed out to the minister of finance that the railway would likely require all $15 million of the second loan, thus meaning that the Jiddah water supply project, the electrification of Riyadh and Makkah, and two hospital projects would have to be abandoned. Instead, the Export-Import Bank suggested to Shaykh 'Abdullah that $50,000 be used for a further feasibility report on the relative merits of a road versus a railway. This seemed to be a face-saving maneuver since the king was dead-set on the railway. At this point, ARAMCO informed the State Department confidentially that it was prepared to finance and construct the railway itself if the king insisted on going ahead.[19]

Apparently there were two camps among the king's advisers, one pushing for emphasis on railways and the other advocating expenditure on roads. Al-Sulayman was said to belong to the second camp. Nevertheless, he loyally supported the king's views and pressed for the railways option during his US trip.[20] When al-Sulayman reported that the American officials with whom he had met had advised that a highway would be more economic, the king cabled him in no uncertain terms, "I want you to get me a railroad, don't talk to me about a highway, get me a railroad."[21] The king also made his views known directly to President Truman, writing him that "If paved roads for cars are of benefit to other countries our country on the contrary will not reap any benefit except at considerable expense and great loss. The railroad is the only medium by God's willingness whose advantage will prevail and reduce the expenditure which are made for transportation, aid in the development of the country and serve other various uses."[22]

Many of the minister of finance's serious discussions, not surprisingly, were with the State Department. He met with Secretary of State Dean Acheson twice. The first was on 5 August, shortly after his arrival, and he saw Acheson again for a courtesy call on 10 October just before leaving the US.[23] In addition, al-Sulayman met with Paul F. McGuire, the department's assistant chief of the division of financial affairs, on 10 August, with whom he discussed currency matters. McGuire suggested that Saudi Arabia avoid the cost of purchasing silver abroad to mint *riyal*s by simply using gold to purchase *riyal*s in the kingdom. The minister expressed reservations about flooding the Saudi market with gold and pointed out that he was still making a profit on the resale of *riyal*s. He apparently did not respond to McGuire's suggestion that US banks be allowed to open branches in Saudi Arabia.[24]

Al-Sulayman also used his stay in the US to discuss participation in Saudi development projects with Bechtel (see below) and to visit various parts of the country, as mentioned above. Furthermore, he demonstrated his abiding interest in promoting Saudi agriculture by visiting farms in arid areas of the US and attempting to arrange for fertilizer exports to the kingdom. Because fertilizer was in short supply, there was difficulty in arranging exports, even after al-Sulayman stated that it was for use in government farms. J. Rives Childs, the US minister in Jiddah, added his strong support to al-Sulayman's efforts.[25]

While the visit was of great importance for the minister of finance and Saudi Arabia, it was also regarded as essential for US foreign policy. As a memorandum prepared for President Truman noted,

> The Department of State is interested in encouraging worthwhile development projects ... in order to guide the steadily rising Saudi Arabian national income into constructive channels. Furthermore, increased trade between the United States and Saudi Arabia will not only stimulate employment in America, but will encourage the growth of the middle class in Saudi Arabia and thus strengthen true democracy and the American position in that country.[26]

On his return to the kingdom, al-Sulayman was "met by a great throng of friends and officials," before reporting to the king and proceeding on the *hajj*. Shortly afterwards, he met with Childs, the US minister in Jiddah, and told him of his excellent reception in Washington, in particular that given by Paul McGuire. He also disclosed that he had reached agreement with Mackay Radio Company to establish a radio station in Jiddah. Furthermore, al-Sulayman had

had discussions regarding the leasing of quarters in Jiddah and Dhahran to the US legation and consulate and for Bechtel to construct the buildings as well.[27]

ESTABLISHING A CONTROLLED BUDGETARY PROCESS AND SPEARHEADING SOCIOECONOMIC DEVELOPMENT

World War II, not surprisingly, provoked an abnormal period in Saudi Arabian finances and the conclusion of the war had several momentous results. First, the restrictions on shipping and shortages of essential commodities disappeared. Second, economic assistance declined precipitously: the Lend–Lease program was wound up and the joint Anglo-American subsidies to Riyadh ended.[28] Third, on a positive note, though, economic opportunities presented themselves. The number of pilgrims on *hajj* grew. Oil production increased dramatically, thus adding to the kingdom's coffers. Furthermore, the US government, anxious to protect its economic interests in the country, began a long-term development assistance program. While the king was able to squeeze more money out of ARAMCO and welcomed American help, the depth and variety of demands on the treasury also expanded exponentially.

Finances and Currency Reform During 1945–9

In one of his rare recorded ruminations about his role, ʿAbdullah al-Sulayman told a visitor in the late 1940s that

> First, I am anxious as Minister of Finance, to increase the resources of this country. Secondly, I am eager, after the war, to reconstruct. The war stopped everything. We want to build the railways and airports and water in Jedda and we wonder what is the first, the most important, to begin. Three schemes are in hand. The railway from Ras Tannura to Riyadh will cost 20 million dollars, and take two years to build. The ground is flat. Americans are building the railway, an English company has a £250,000 contract for providing water in Jedda.

When asked about his long tenure as minister of finance, he replied, "What gives me the greatest pleasure as I look back on these 23 years? The last 10 years, because the resources of our country have been increased and we may be able to do something".[29]

Although wartime subsidies had been terminated, Saudi Arabia was still in economic dire straits. Foodstuffs and other necessary items were still in short supply worldwide and the government encountered considerable difficulties in procuring adequate supplies. Paying for these goods, as well as meeting recurring government expenses such as salaries, was made problematic because of the plethora of currencies in circulation in the country—and the volatility in exchange rates between them—as well as the requirement for sufficient funds in sterling to pay for imports from neighboring sterling-bloc countries.

Furthermore, the kingdom continued to require extensive direct external assistance. As previous chapters have shown, the burden of such assistance had shifted during the latter part of the war from Britain to the United States. British aid in 1946 was limited to establishing an eye hospital in Jiddah and providing a limited amount of military training. With the end of Lend–Lease, other mechanisms were created for providing the aid that the US government believed the kingdom required. This marked a qualitative change in the US–Saudi relationship, establishing the strong bonds that endured for well over 60 years in political relations and military support as well as fundamental and multifarious development assistance.

Even before World War II ended, the US State Department created a committee to study Saudi Arabia's financial needs. It concluded that, as late as 1949, more revenue would be received from the *hajj* than from oil revenues and that the cumulative budget deficit for 1945–9 would be about $50 million. Means discussed of providing the kingdom with assistance to meet the shortfall ranged from loans and grants to the purchase of oil reserves, either extracted or remaining in the ground. In addition, thought was given again to providing the kingdom with US financial advisers.[30]

In discussion of the possibility of aid to the kingdom, two schools of thought emerged in the US administration and Congress. One felt that the extension of aid would set dangerous precedents and was in the long run both unwise and unnecessary.[31] The other group believed that control of Saudi oil was essential to the US national interest, and it was even hoped that cheap oil from the Middle East to fuel European reconstruction would relieve demand on US domestic stocks. Another variant was to force ARAMCO to provide the needed financial assistance as an advance on future oil royalties.[32] In addition, advantages to using the Export-Import Bank were seen, including avoiding the need for new legislation.[33] The State Department presented a memorandum to President Harry S. Truman in May, indicating its support for an aid program to Saudi Arabia, and the president agreed in principle on 29 May.[34]

Internal US deliberations on the financial package continued through the year 1945, in a similar process as 1944. It must have been exceedingly difficult for the king and his government to plan expenditure without knowing how much money would be available even in the same year. Both British and American complaints were voiced at the time about the haphazard nature of financial management in the kingdom, but it should be recognized that at least part of the blame must fall on London and Washington and their haphazard approach to aid programs. In June 1945, Eddy relayed Washington's notice that plans for long-range aid were unlikely to be finalized before 1946 and the proposed Export-Import Bank loan would probably not be available until 1946 either. The minister of finance expressed understanding of the delay in the 1945 loan but he was dismayed at the news of the other delays. The plans that the Saudi government had formulated for improvements in irrigation, water supply to cities, transport services, and electric power had to be placed on indefinite hold while a locust plague made matters even worse.[35]

The US government's pressure on ARAMCO to provide dollar currency to enable the kingdom to repay the Export-Import Bank loan bore fruit only insofar as the company agreed with al-Sulayman to extend a $3 million advance to the Saudi government, a sum that was later revised to $3.6 million. The advance was paid in a combination of dollars and sterling.[36] Matters improved after the depressing news in June. During Prince Faysal's visit to the United States in July, he was informed that the joint Anglo-American aid program would consist of $10 million. In addition, the US government would provide another $3 million worth of goods, 10 million *riyals*, and 17 million resale *riyals*. Furthermore, the Export-Import Bank loan was definite and ARAMCO had agreed to provide the government with enough dollars to meet the debt repayments.[37]

The promise of *riyals* had arisen by a request made in March for 30 million *riyals*. Of these, 15 million were for resale to ARAMCO while the rest were to meet the kingdom's currency requirements. Al-Sulayman explained there were three reasons for the *riyal* shortage: the decline in the use of Maria Theresa dollars and of the Indian rupee, the practice of merchants hoarding their wealth in *riyals*, and the growing use of *riyals* in the manufacture of jewelry.[38] The resale *riyals* were intended for use by the US legation and American companies in Saudi Arabia, while 60 percent of the Saudi government's proceeds from the sale were to be deposited in the king's "special dollar account" held with the Federal Reserve Bank. While the amount in the accounts cannot be determined, credits of $900,000 and $600,000 by ARAMCO were made in January and March respectively.[39]

At the same time, Saudi Arabia found itself able to pursue a method of profitable currency transfer for some time. The Saudi government would use dollars received from ARAMCO to purchase gold in the US. The gold would then be exchanged for British gold sovereigns at the Reserve Bank of India. These sovereigns commanded a premium in the Saudi market, thus making the venture profitable both for the Saudi government and the Reserve Bank of India.[40]

On the development side, the Export-Import Bank loans enabled the kingdom to get started on essential projects throughout the kingdom. The American firm Bechtel served as the partner during this early period. Bechtel was a far more suitable choice than the Saudi Arabian American Development

Company (see Chapter 7) could have been and it enjoyed the initial advantage of being favored by ARAMCO. As government demands on ARAMCO increased, the oil company had become increasingly uneasy at shouldering the burden of construction and providing other services to the Saudi government.

In an effort to relieve the oil company of responsibility for government construction projects, James Terry Duce of ARAMCO suggested to the king that negotiations with the Export-Import Bank be reopened and to consider Bechtel for assistance with a broad development program. At the same time, ARAMCO called upon Bechtel to provide work at the Ra'̓s Tanurah oil terminal while encouraging the company to consider providing services directly for the Saudi government.

In this connection, a Bechtel vice-president, E.F. English, visited the kingdom in July 1946 and discussed a railway project and the rehabilitation of US Army surplus equipment left in Dhahran. English felt it necessary to point out to the king that the railway would be uneconomic but the king was of the firm belief that highways would weaken the kingdom's defenses and that reliance on motor transport was too unreliable (as the experience during the war had demonstrated). It was agreed that the minister of finance would be tasked with getting a US government loan for the railway during his impending visit to the US and that the contract for construction would go to Bechtel if the loan were secured.[41] The king's determination to have his railway seems to have influenced Bechtel, as its experts estimated the cost of the Dhahran–Riyadh railway at under $20 million in late 1946, a figure less than half of the $50 million cost they had estimated earlier in the year.[42]

Indeed, al-Sulayman did discuss the railway and other matters with Bechtel during his trip. He first approached Bechtel to handle the purchase of goods that Saudi Arabia would procure under the $10 million Export-Import Bank loan. Bechtel did not seem very enthusiastic about this idea but finally agreed under the pressure of both the Saudi government and ARAMCO. Al-Sulayman also persuaded Bechtel to handle the construction of housing facilities at the US air base at Dhahran, with an idea that Bechtel could be utilized for other projects once the airfield construction personnel had left.[43]

The Saudi government continued to press Bechtel for work on the railway, despite Bechtel's agreement with the State Department and the Export-Import Bank that the idea was uneconomic. But Bechtel also recognized that the king would not be dissuaded, given his belief that the railway would be the center of his communications system. Furthermore, the king stressed that it would for the first time provide true unity for the country and ensure the effectiveness of central government authority over the old regime of inter-tribal strife. Consequently, Bechtel selected engineers for a transportation survey party, which arrived in Dhahran in November.[44] (Bechtel's further involvement is discussed below.)

At the same time as the negotiations for the Export-Import Bank loans were taking place, the US government remained concerned with financial management in the kingdom. Childs, the US minister in Jiddah, once again brought up the idea of a financial adviser in discussions with his British counterpart, L.B. Grafftey-Smith. They agreed that reform was necessary within the Ministry of Finance and felt that ʿAbdullah al-Sulayman needed assistance in carrying it out. At the same time, however, they recognized that al-Sulayman's relationship with the king was unbreakable. In Childs' words, "it was unlikely in the extreme that anything could be done which would in the slightest way prejudice Sheikh Abdallah es Sulaiman's position so long as the king lived."[45] While the pair sparred over whether an adviser should be Muslim, American, or neutral, they concluded that it would be fruitless to press any adviser on the king.[46]

Despite the postwar increase in oil revenues and the Export-Import Bank loan, Saudi Arabia's finances continued in all-too-familiar dire condition with the government finding itself faced with the persistent necessity of finding enough funds to meet both ordinary expenses and an emerging development process. ʿAbdullah al-Sulayman's 1946 trip to the US was followed in 1947 by a visit by the heir apparent, Prince Saʿud. He approached the Export-Import Bank for a $40 million loan, $20 million of which was for the railway project and $20 million for infrastructure and utility projects. The secretary of state, Dean Acheson, counseled Prince Saʿud against expecting a further loan from the bank and instead suggested that the railway be funded by ARAMCO and private US interests.

At the same time, Childs in Jiddah advised the secretary of state that the Export-Import Bank loan be used as a lever to get US economic advisers accepted by the kingdom where they could bring order to the country's financial crisis and stop the Ministry of Finance's currency speculation. For his part, al-Sulayman went so far as to tell Childs that he was planning a second visit to the US to lobby for the additional loan after Prince Saʿud's return. As a final compromise, Prince Saʿud was told that if the Saudi government could find commercial sources for the railway funding, the bank might be persuaded to increase the remaining allocation from $15 million to $20 million. No doubt even this small increase was motivated at least in part by the inability of the Saudi government to pay for food orders it had made in the US.[47] Al-Sulayman only changed his mind about his contemplated second trip to the US after the US Legation in Jiddah firmly explained that any idea of additional funds was purely speculative.[48]

The government's financial difficulties were highlighted by its problems in meeting installments for the repayment of funds owed to the US government. Al-Sulayman instructed ARAMCO to pay one installment to the State Department but late in the year the minister of finance informed Childs that the Saudi government was in fact unable to pay the first of five loan installments for a line of credit negotiated in May 1946 for the purchase of surplus US property goods in Saudi Arabia, Egypt, and elsewhere. This line of credit had been used to purchase aircraft for the new Saudi airline, construction equipment for the public works program, motor vehicles, and equipment for a hospital.[49]

Faced with the admission that the Saudis could not pay the installment, Childs reported that "There is no indication that the strained financial position of the King and his Government is easing, either with reference to dollars or riyals .... Wily, but aging, Shaikh Abdullah had managed to keep the Saudi ship of state afloat by virtue of foreign loans, domestic loans from commercial 'partners' of the Finance Ministry, and by non-payment of Government payrolls for months at a time."[50] If financing recurring government expenditures and development programs were not enough, continued drought conditions added to expenses and to increased demand for food imports.

December 1947 also witnessed the withdrawal of Fuʿad Hamza from responsibility as minister of state for development projects and his return to Riyadh as adviser to the king. As Childs reported from Jiddah, "The lesson to be drawn, it is believed, is that so long as Sheikh Abdallah remains in good health he is likely to maintain undiminished control both of the Ministry of Finance and of the Public Works program."[51] His control, despite health problems, was reinforced by the promotion of Muhammad Surur al-Sabban as his adviser. The supporting positions of ʿAbdullah's brother Hamad as deputy minister of finance and his nephew, Sulayman al-Hamad, as assistant deputy minister of finance remained intact, although Hamad al-Sulayman was regularly indisposed due to illness and Muhammad Surur had gained seniority over Sulayman al-Hamad. Sami Kutbi and Bashir Nuʿman were nominated as director-general and administrative officer respectively of the Bureau of the Ministry of State for Development Projects.[52] In 1948, Muhammad Surur was promoted to the position of minister of state without portfolio, a promotion that was regarded as well deserved because of his assumption of an increasing burden of work within the Ministry of Finance.[53] Indeed, it was reported that the minister was leaving an increasing share of routine work to Muhammad Surur.[54]

When the Saudi government managed in 1947 to get ARAMCO to fund the railway as a loan against future royalties, in effect it mortgaged another sizeable sum of its future revenues to current expenditures. The railway and al-Dammam pier would result in a $42 million loan (see below for details). This project represented the lion's share of the Saudi government's efforts to secure a total of $52 million in loans for all development projects.[55] At the same time, the "extreme disorderliness of the Saudi Arabian Government's fiscal, monetary and exchange policy ..." was seen as a major impediment to development. This judgment derived directly from the country's currency muddle and from its inefficient over-control of imports. In addition, the public works program was seen to focus too heavily on consumer projects, such as health and education, rather than productive projects.[56]

The acquiescence of ARAMCO in paying for the construction of the railway was used as a lever by the minister of finance in early 1948 to not only press for the payment of the second Export-Import Bank tranche of $15 million but for another $5 million as well. Undoubtedly the kingdom's acute dollar shortage was a principal factor in the finance minister's request. The minister pointed out that Prince Saʿud had been assured on his 1947 trip to the US that extra funds would be available from the bank if the railway was funded privately. American officials, however, were doubtful that the bank would extend the extra $5 million because its loans were meant for development and al-Sulayman was asking for money to pay outstanding debts to American companies for foodstuffs, textiles, and similar goods.[57]

A few months after the additional $5 million in aid was requested, it was indeed turned down because it was for consumption goods. Childs, the US minister in Jiddah, relayed the bad news and pointed out that it was difficult for the US government to justify providing aid to Saudi Arabia while its income was obviously increasing in leaps and bounds. His advice was to prioritize the development program and pursue it more deliberately. Al-Sulayman also faced criticism internally for the demands of the development program and he promised Childs that his budget would be made public. Accordingly, the 1947–8 budget was published in *Umm al-Qura* and indicated a balance in income and expenditures at 214,586,500 *riyal*s. Childs reported that al-Sulayman "had determined to take the people into his confidence over certain opposition in the Legislative council," presumably to gain public support for development.[58]

A contemporary analysis of the budget revealed that it was already outdated since total revenues from ARAMCO were estimated at about 240 million *riyal*s rather than the 140 million given in the budget. It was notable that use of the budget's figures showed that concessionary companies provided some 90 percent of the country's revenues.[59]

A further blow to development programs came with the announcement to Childs that the king had decided that Saudi Arabia would take up no more of the Export-Import Bank loan, including the $15 million already promised. His action apparently was in protest against US policy in Palestine.[60] This may have been a purely symbolic gesture, however, since the British Legation in Jiddah reported in early 1948 that Bechtel had used up the $25 million line of credit supplied by the bank. In July, Bechtel was reported to have overspent the line of credit by $1,174,000, forcing the Saudi government to find other means to pay the additional amount, and by October, Bechtel had virtually ceased work on the Jiddah pier.[61]

At long last, the issuance of a royal decree, published in *Umm al-Qura* (No. 1209, 7 May 1948), was a welcome step in currency reform. The decree announced reorganization within the Ministry of Finance with the creation of a Bureau of Currency Control. The office's purpose was to supervise exchange deals and to control the use of foreign exchange through licensing. Although al-Sulayman's former interpreter, Sayyid Ma'tuk Hasanayn, was named head of the bureau, it was expected that Muhammad Surur would be responsible for granting the actual licenses.[62] The bureau's creation was seen as the nucleus for a nascent National Bank of Saudi Arabia.[63]

Still, there was a long way to go. George Eddy and Raymond Mikesell were sent to the kingdom by the American government in October–November 1948 to offer advice on monetary reform. While the pair easily convinced the finance minister to link the *riyal* to the dollar (at one *riyal* equal to 25 cents), as he was said to have been well disposed to the idea already, it was more difficult to convince him to discard any link between the *riyal* and gold. There was an inescapable problem in that the *riyal* could not be linked to both the dollar and the sovereign because dollar/sovereign rates were subject to fluctuation. Eventually though, al-Sulayman agreed and a decree to that effect was prepared on 22 November. The decree, however, was not published, possibly because of the minister's desire to conclude negotiations on profit-sharing with ARAMCO. At the same time, fewer *riyal*s were exchanged for dollars than expected and the government was forced to borrow 20,000 sovereigns from the Banque de l'Indochine to cover the latter's purchases on the government's behalf. More sovereigns were needed to meet the government's expenditure requirements above the number of available riyals. In the end, the fixed rate of 25 cents to the *riyal* failed to alleviate the *riyal* shortage and merchants resorted to buying dollars with gold, leading to gold exports from the kingdom. By the end of the year, it was clear that more substantial measures had to be taken.[64]

The situation grew acute during the first few months of 1949 as *riyal*s continued to be scarce, the *riyal* rose in value vis-à-vis the sovereign, and the government was forced to dip into *riyal* reserves to meet its payroll.[65] Furthermore, the effect of the Egyptian government ban on the repatriation of

Egyptian pound notes greater than E£10 rendered the use of Egyptian pounds as an intermediary between currencies—e.g. gold and convertible sterling—more difficult. Saudi Arabia's alternatives seemed to be introducing dollars and cents into circulation (which was occurring already on a minor scale in the Eastern Province) or minting more *riyal*s. The US government was in favor of short-term use of dollars but the Saudi government backed away from its earlier contemplation. The situation was further complicated by the falling value of the sovereign and the reluctance of banks to convert sovereigns into dollars.

Consequently, the minister of finance announced in March that 60 million new *riyal*s would be introduced (although he subsequently revised the figure downward). This had the effect of reversing the situation and making *riyal*s more available. At the same time, he seemed to be considering a return to a *riyal*–sovereign link, prompted perhaps by a belief that ARAMCO's falling production was related to its inability to sell oil for sterling as well as an attempt to bolster the sovereign market in Egypt. American concern was aroused by his visit to Egypt during April–June and subsequent indications that he was attempting to maintain simultaneously a *riyal*–dollar rate at 4:1 and a *riyal*–sovereign rate at 55:1. On the return of the minister and Muhammad Surur to Jiddah in June, they found the sovereign had appreciated significantly against the *riyal* but they were unable to rectify the situation throughout the rest of the year.

Saudi Arabia's financial situation steadily worsened throughout the year as the government was constantly short of funds.[66] By July, work on Jiddah Pier was threatened and merchants were owed large sums for goods sequestered by the government upon arrival in Jiddah, particularly cars. Government salaries were in arrears and ARAMCO was pressed for increasingly larger advances on monthly royalties. Both al-Kharj agricultural project and Saudi Arabian Airlines were reported to be suffering from a shortage of funds. A US embassy analysis of the Ministry of Finance's estimate at the beginning of the year that there would be a surplus of $19,500,000 by the end of 1949, not counting the $9,500,000 received from the Pacific Western oil concession, revealed that the estimate had drastically under-estimated the cost of various development projects. Rumors of debts owed to merchants varied between $26 million and $40 million. The provision of a $6 million loan to Syria drew criticism.[67] By December, the king had ordered that government salaries be paid immediately and the level of debt be reduced.

Restructuring within the vastly important Ministry of Finance was one response. Najib Salihah was brought back from Egypt to become assistant deputy minister of finance and to take charge of public works and concessionary companies, a move that effectively demoted Muhammad

Surur. Al-Sulayman also entrusted him with control of expenditures. The government payroll totaled 8–9 million *riyal*s a month and was between three and eight months in arrears depending on the part of the country. The government sought to remedy the situation by seeking further loans, although ARAMCO pushed it toward borrowing from banks. Nevertheless, the government's debt at the end of 1949 equaled about one-third of its annual income.[68]

Development Projects During 1945–9

Bechtel had taken over many of the services previously provided by ARAMCO and thus entered into a direct relationship with the Saudi government and the Ministry of Finance. While this enabled the company to avoid some of the problems that foreign firms faced in doing business in the kingdom, it did not solve them all. Bechtel's first contract with the Saudi Arabian government was signed on 25 July 1946 and was for the reconditioning of US surplus property bought by the government. Gradually the company's responsibilities grew. In October, it was commissioned to improve Riyadh airport and, in November, it began survey of the al-Dammam–Riyadh railway. Additional work in 1946 was for building a camp at the Dhahran air base and in 1947 Bechtel continued reconditioning the surplus property and building facilities for TWA, Bechtel, and the US Army at Dhahran. In Jiddah, Bechtel surveyed the airport and made preliminary reports on road and railway construction. Jiddah's wall was demolished for a base for the Jiddah pier, as well as for paving stones. In Riyadh, work was begun on the airport, an electrification survey made, and various tasks were undertaken for the royal family.[69]

The expiry date of Bechtel's original contract was extended from 30 June 1947 to 31 December 1948, when it was superseded by another contract for work beyond 1948.[70] In November 1947, despite receiving a contract extension, Bechtel had growing concerns about an outstanding invoice for $500,000. When the US minister raised the matter with the minister of finance, he was told that ARAMCO was examining Bechtel's accounts for the government and any answer would have to await ARAMCO's comments.

Al-Sulayman subsequently informed Bechtel that arrangements were being made to pay the amount owed but he also brought up the 1948 development program for discussion. This was intended to include a pier for Jiddah, the electrification of Riyadh, the modernization of the airports in Jiddah and Riyadh, and the construction of housing at Dhahran airport. The total cost was estimated at $6 million but Bechtel advised the government to slow down developments efforts in order to spread the costs over a period of time.[71]

Bechtel International Corporation was contracted to carry out much of the government's construction requirements through a syndicate named Bechtel

Morrison Svedrup. In 1947, its activities included the reconditioning of surplus property, maintaining the government's motor vehicles, constructing housing for its own employees, building facilities for US representatives in the kingdom, and improving the airports in Jiddah and Riyadh. Other potential projects being mooted with the government included electricity for Riyadh, telephone systems for Jiddah and Makkah, road improvements in al-Hijaz, and a Jiddah–al-Madinah railway.[72] By 1948, Bechtel had completed a new runway at Jiddah airport and built a number of homes between the airport and the town. In addition, construction of the railway had reached Abqayq from Riyadh (but there were problems keeping it free of sand).[73] A year later, the railway had reached al-Ahsa' and non-scheduled trains were running between al-Dammam and Abqayq. ARAMCO's costs were subtracted from its royalty payments to the government.[74]

Another Bechtel project was the Jiddah harbor improvement, consisting of a long pier for deep-water anchorage, for which the walls of Jiddah were demolished to be used as fill. Already by 1928, it had been recognized that there was no room for expansion within Jiddah's city walls and new residential quarters outside the walls were deemed necessary.[75] The sequence of events leading to the dramatic end to the walls were described by an American State Department official as follows:

> One day in the late spring of 1947, Mr. English, an American vice-president of the International Bechtel Corporation, ... was driving around Jidda with Sheikh Abdullah Suleiman, Minister of Finance for Saudi Arabia. They were discussing a project long dear to Sheikh Abdullah's heart, the construction of a pier in the harbor of Jidda which would enable ocean-going steamers to come alongside. "Where can we obtain fill?" the Finance Minister asked as the car passed through a gate in the wall of Jidda. The engineer considered a moment. Then he gestured toward the wall. "There is the sort of material we need." "Then take the wall down and use it," ordered the Finance Minister. It remained standing for some time longer, however, and the rumor spread that it was too much for Bechtel. But one day, within twenty-four hours, dynamite charges were set off all along the base, and the whole structure went down like the walls of Jericho, to be flattened by a battery of bulldozers and hauled away in giant trucks. The dirt and rocks that kept Arab, Egyptian, and Portuguese invaders out of Jidda now help travelers to come ashore.[76]

Still, the financial problems arising from the depletion of the Export-Import Bank loans hit Bechtel hard and, by the end of October, work on the Jiddah pier was reported to be at a virtual standstill.[77]

The envisaged development program to which the $15 million Export-Import Bank loan would have contributed was published in *al-Bilad al-Sa'udiyah* in January 1948, the first time that development plans were published in the kingdom. The program consisted of:

1. Jiddah pier and harbor ($3.3 million)
2. Jiddah airport ($850,000)
3. Jiddah–Makkah road ($11.3 million)
4. electrification of Jiddah, Makkah, and al-Madinah ($3.5 million)
5. telephones for Jiddah, Makkah, al-Madinah, and al-Ta'if, plus connecting long distance lines ($2 million)
6. two dams near al-Ta'if ($1.25 million)
7. Makkah–al-Ta'if road ($900,000)
8. Jiddah Hotel (no estimate)
9. harbor beacons (no estimate)
10. Riyadh airdrome ($1.3 million)
11. projects in Dhahran including the construction of buildings at the airport ($1.3 million).

These projects were estimated to total a cost of $24 million.[78] Another projected scheme was a cement factory in Dhahran, to be a joint Saudi government–ARAMCO venture; eventually it would be 51 percent Saudi-financed.[79] Moreover, Bechtel constructed the US Consulate in Dhahran and erected warehouses and barracks for the US Army, in addition to its work for ARAMCO and the TAPline.

The process for selecting development projects involved the agreement of ʿAbdullah al-Sulayman with a committee comprised of members of the Legislative Council and an adviser to the Ministry of Finance. Once a project had been selected, it would be presented to the Legislative Council for approval, although this was likely to be simply *pro forma*. The projects envisaged concentrated on Jiddah, al-Madinah, Makkah, and Riyadh, while ARAMCO assumed *de facto* responsibility for work in the Eastern Province. Bechtel was contracted to handle the lion's share of implementation the projects.[80]

Bechtel continued to serve as the government's main contractor for public works in 1949, at least those paid for in dollars. The power plant in Riyadh was completed during the year while work progressed on both the Jiddah pier and the railway.[81] At the same time, however, the company suffered from the government's chronic financial difficulties. This severe constraint reduced the scope of the development program and forced a slower pace on projects already under way. Bechtel's proposals for the 1949 public works program were approved by the government on 17 March. Although some $9 million in expenditures was forecast for the program, the government's budget for this heading was less than $8 million and the difference would have to be carried over to the next year. Bechtel's response was that fluctuations in the completion dates of individual projects meant that would not be a problem.[82]

By July, it was necessary to revise the 1949–50 program and budget and Bechtel sought to cancel pending purchases in the US. Both sides still remained committed to completing the Jiddah pier despite the lagging payments to Bechtel. Part of the problem was that there was little control over expenditure and various individuals had the capability of ordering goods and services from Bechtel directly.[83]

The budgets for Bechtel's work steadily increased in value from $339,415 for 1946 up to February 1947, to $2,830,000 for February–December 1947, $7,888,000 for 1948, and $7,757,000 for 1949. Actual costs often outstripped the budget, however, running at $3,060,000 for the 11 months in 1947, $7,122,650 in 1948, and $9,600,000 estimated for 1949. Although Bechtel had contracted with the Saudi government in September 1946 for the disbursement of the $10 million Export-Import Bank loan, it continued its role after the loan was exhausted and spent more than $20 million on the government's behalf between September 1946 and 31 December 1948. For this service, Bechtel charged the government 0.8 percent of the total amount.[84]

While some progress was being made, however slowly, in development, the British ambassador judged that "In general it cannot, however, be said that the country's real needs in regard to development had been properly considered; money would usually have been better spent on foreign advisers, public health, education and agricultural development, and sound technical advice from engineering specialists than on some of the undertakings, often of doubtful value and managed by incompetent individuals, on which it was lavished, not to mention the building of palaces at Riyadh, Mecca and elsewhere for the king's enormous family."[85]

CHAPTER 10

The Broad Remit of the Postwar Ministry of Finance

Even though the kingdom of Saudi Arabia was changing in the postwar years and its rudimentary bureaucracy was expanding, the Ministry of Finance continued to be the locus of a large share of government activities. Because of Abdullah Sulayman's prominent position for nearly two decades, as well as the lack of infrastructure throughout the government, the Ministry of Finance assumed many roles that would later devolve to individual ministries after the death of King ʿAbd al-ʿAziz. These roles covered both older functions, such as administration of the *hajj* (annual pilgrimage) and health, and newer emerging ones. Other chapters deal with currency and finances, the principal function of the ministry, and with oil, the primary source of the government's income. This chapter explores some of the other functions that the ministry continued to exercise.

Despite the ministry's expanded role, its administration and personnel remained limited. A list of its top officials as of 1947 is given in Table 10.1. All of these officials were situated in Makkah, apart from the last one. In addition, Sami Kutbi, secretary-general to the Bureau of Development and Construction operated under the auspices of the ministry.[1]

A major part of the ministry's responsibilities involved dealing with a wide variety of socioeconomic development projects. The minister of finance outlined many of these in a 1948 interview, citing the ministry's role in agriculture, transport, seaports and airlines, radio, hospitals, schools, mosques, and assistance for house-building.[2] He provided more details on "reform projects" in a December 1947 interview. These included:

1. creation of a government department for *hajj* (annual pilgrimage) affairs personally supervised by ʿAbdullah al-Sulayman
2. provision of transportation for pilgrims by the Arabian Car Company

3. erection of mobile umbrellas in the Ka'bah by the Public Waqf Administration
4. erection of al-Mash'ar umbrella
5. opening al-Hujun Road
6. paving of internal streets in Riyadh
7. installation of water pipes and taps in pilgrim areas, along with a decrease in the price of the water (and the intention to make it free in the future)
8. repair of al-Madinah road with the intention of paving it in the near future to the same standard as the Makkah–Jiddah road
9. beginning construction on al-Haramayn Port in Jiddah
10. improving access to 'Arafat by opening new roads and expanding existing ones
11. continuing work underway on improving Jiddah streets and completing a project to bring fresh water to Jiddah from Namir, 65 kilometers away

Projects shortly to begin included:

1. the provision of electrical lighting in Makkah, al-Madinah, and Jiddah
2. the construction of hotels in Jiddah and Dhahran
3. the institution of electrical lighting in Riyadh
4. paving of the road to al-Ta'if.[3]

In 1946, sewage systems had also been planned for Makkah and Jiddah, along with a new customs house and hotel at Jiddah, a hospital at Makkah, and an opthalmic hospital at Jiddah, although none of these was actually under way. Only the Jiddah water scheme was in a state of play with a contract let to Gellatly's.[4] But a crucial element in all these plans was getting the country's currency morass under control.

THE ESTABLISHMENT OF THE SAUDI ARABIAN MONETARY AGENCY

The roots of the Saudi Arabian Monetary Agency (SAMA) can be said to lay in a proposal to establish a Saudi Arabian Currency Board in London in 1943. The accountant-general of Palestine, A.L. Peters, visited Jiddah in March where he had lengthy discussion with both British and Saudi officials, as did Captain France of the staff of the (British) minister of state resident in the Middle East. These discussions took place at the same time that the kingdom was receiving war subsidies from both the UK and the US.[5]

Certainly the question of the management of the various currencies that the Saudi Arabian government held, particularly in light of Riyadh's rapidly increasing revenues, was a matter of grave concern for the minister of

TABLE 10.1 PERSONNEL OF THE MINISTRY OF FINANCE (1947).

ʿAbdullah al-Sulayman al-Hamdan, Minister of Finance
Hamad al-Sulayman al-Hamdan, Deputy Minister of Finance
Sulayman al-Hamad, Assistant Deputy Minister of Finance
Ibrahim Islam, Director–General of the Ministry of Finance
ʿAbdullah al-Saʿd, Assistant Director–General of the Ministry of Finance
Ahmad Bey Lari, Assistant Director–General of the Ministry of Finance
ʿAbd al-Razzaq Hindawi, Director of the Department of Inspection
Nuri ʿAbbas, Director of the Department of Accounts
ʿAli Amir, Director of the Department of Personnel Records
Muhammad Salih Kashmiri, Director of the Department of Current Accounts
Salih Qazzaz, Director General of Pilgrimage Affairs
Yahya Raffa, Acting Director
Muhammad Sulayman al-Turki, Director General

finance and he was open to advice on the matter. In April–May 1948, Judd Polk, a US Treasury representative attached to the Cairo embassy, visited Jiddah and held discussions with al-Sulayman and his assistant, Muhammad Surur al-Sabban. Among other things, Polk suggested that a paper currency should be introduced and that foreign consultants should be hired to advise the government on its monetary problems. The finance minister said that the government intended to establish a central bank with a deposit of 214 million paper *riyal*s (equivalent to the amount of budgetary expenditure), which would be tied to the gold sovereign (i.e. 100 percent backed by gold)—although he was open to alternative suggestions. While the possibility of Egyptian experts was discussed, al-Sulayman made a point of wishing to continue the advice of the "friendly American government."[6]

The following years saw both Britain and the United States offer repeated suggestions about the provision of financial advisers, as well as needed currency reforms. Finally, desperate finances prompted al-Sulayman in April 1951 to accept the appointment of Arthur N. Young as a currency affairs adviser. Anxious to receive Young's services, al-Sulayman signed an agreement in October for a team of financial advisers—including a financial expert, a budget expert, an accounting officer, a customs administrator, a tariffs expert, and a secretary—to be made available under the US aid program, Point IV.[7] Because US legislation required that everyone connected with Point IV be investigated by the US Federal Bureau of Investigation (FBI), Young's departure for Saudi Arabia seemed delayed until it was agreed that he would act temporarily as an employee of the Saudi Arabian government instead of the Technical Cooperation Administration.[8]

While al-Sulayman and the Saudi government were anxious to establish a central bank, Young was told before leaving Washington that he was not engaged on a technical assistance project so much as one with very important political implications. A major objective of his work would be to persuade the Saudi government to rein in expenditures and to put an end to advance ARAMCO payments. In addition, he was encouraged to steer the government away from its idea for a bimetallic currency system.[9]

Young wrote a memorandum on the existing financial system some time after his arrival. He determined the system was inadequate because the government had no adequate fiscal agent or institution capable of handling receipts and payments, a task made more difficult by the fact that the vast majority of the revenue was in foreign exchange. Furthermore, proper machinery was needed to handle monetary affairs, such as introduction of the new gold coin, to regulate banking, money changing, and various other functions. Amongst his other concerns, he noted there were no facilities for intermediate or long-term credit for development schemes, nor was there any provision for economic research. He suggested the name of Saudi Arabian National Bank but not central bank, since conditions were not suitable for the creation of a central bank.[10]

Young presented a preliminary report on the establishment of a government bank in November, which he saw as carrying out three primary activities: ① serving as fiscal agent of the Saudi Arabian government; ② providing monetary and banking services to the government; and ③ conducting economic research. He proposed that al-Sulayman should be the chairman of the bank but that the governor should be a foreigner since there were no Saudis with the necessary expertise. The bank would take over the responsibility of making budgetary payments to government departments and to contract holders. It would be responsible for currency stabilization and the introduction of new coinage; and it would receive its income from a commission on exchange dealings that it would take over, in part, from the Netherlands Trading Society and Salih ʿAbd al-ʿAziz al-Kaʿki and Salim b. Mahfuz Company. The report also determined that the bank should not issue currency, deal with private customers, or make loans to the government.[11]

The finance minister was very pleased with the report but, when it was presented to the king, he objected that it should not be called a bank, since that implied that interest was involved. Young suggested that it be called a "fiscal agency," later amended to "monetary agency," to which the king agreed. On Young's return to Jiddah, he was asked to draw up a charter so that the decree establishing the agency could be established that day. Young had made drafts already so it was relatively simple to write out a charter of 12 articles, which were accepted and issued. It was, he thought, the shortest time ever taken to create a central bank. A building was assigned in Jiddah to the new institution. Young, however, declined the Saudi government's request for him to be the agency's first governor and arranged for George Blowers from the International Monetary Fund to take up the appointment.[12]

SAMA was formally established on 20 April 1952 with Blowers as its first governor. ʿAbdullah al-Sulayman was proclaimed the agency's president in September and it opened for business towards the end of the year, with its first concern being the issue of the Saudi gold sovereign. The board of directors consisted of: al-Sulayman, president; Najib Salihah, vice-president; George A. Blowers, ex officio; Sayyid al-ʿAttas (of the Netherlands Trading Society), member; and Salim b. Mahfuz (of Kaʿki and Company, member). The agency's authorized capital was the equivalent of 500,000 gold sovereigns, calculated at a value of $6 million, and a building was under preparation in Jiddah to serve as its headquarters and vault.[13]

An early innovation of SAMA was the issuance of "pilgrim receipts," which were paper notes fully backed by silver *riyal*s held by SAMA. SAMA assured al-Sulayman, however, that they were not the basis of a permanent paper currency.[14] The receipts were a great success and approximately 25 million *riyal*s worth of receipts were issued. Only 15 million had been redeemed by the end of the *hajj*, thus leaving 10 million still in circulation.[15] By November, only 2 million receipts remained outstanding as SAMA had ceased issuing them in August. The agency was actively seeking to recall all the receipts solely because they were too easy to counterfeit and thought had been given to producing a more complex design for 1954.[16]

MINING ACTIVITIES AND TRANSPORT

Early interest in the development of mining has been discussed already in Chapters 4 and 7. Given that the Saudi Arabian Mining Syndicate (SAMS) was responsible for constructing one of the first durable roads in the kingdom and also made improvements to Jiddah harbor, it is not surprising that the Ministry of Finance also found itself overseeing activities related to transportation as well. These interests were of course supplemented by a variety of other concerns.

Mining. Even as World War II ended, al-Sulayman continued to take an interest in the possibility of exploiting minerals in new locations. He asked St. John Philby, just back after having been detained in England during the war, to lead a mining survey of Midyan in the north and "offered to hire an Egyptian mining engineer if [Philby's commercial partner] Mitchell Cotts would finance the investigation."[17] The minister's interest may well have been prompted by concern in finding a replacement for the SAMS, which eventually ceased production in 1953. Thus, he was looking elsewhere for opportunities. In 1951, the Ministry of Finance's Bureau of Mines made a preliminary exploration of mining at Muwayli–Dhulm in Najd and the mine was opened officially in March 1953.[18]

Al-Dammam to Riyadh Railway. By early 1947, Bechtel's negative attitude to the railway was beginning to change, probably because of the company's presumed desire to protect its increasing business in Saudi Arabia. Bechtel Vice-President E.F. English informed J. Rives Childs, the US minister in Jiddah, of his new belief that the railway would cost less than his original estimate, and Childs, in view of this information, gave his opinion to Washington that the railway should be supported rather than to continue to antagonize the king. Bechtel subsequently provided new estimates of the cost at around $18.5 million and Childs reported that "Report concludes railway not only economically feasible but likewise economically justifiable."[19]

Payment for the railway continued to be a major obstacle, particularly as it became increasingly clear that the Export-Import Bank would not pay for it. The king seemed reluctant to pressure ARAMCO, as suggested by the State Department, in part because he feared that ARAMCO financing of the railway might give it a claim to ownership.[20] Nevertheless, al-Sulayman approached the oil company for help in acquiring commercial loans for the project and suggested that the government might repay the company from future oil royalties. ARAMCO had informed the State Department in January 1947 of its willingness to finance the scheme and in June it agreed to loan the Saudi government $32 million—which the company felt was a more accurate estimate than that of Bechtel—for the construction of the railroad and the al-Dammam pier, in addition to a further $10 million for the development of al-Dammam. The government would receive ownership of both the railroad and the pier.[21]

The railway was completed at the end of 1951 with an inauguration ceremony held on 27 October. A railway committee, established as a precursor to eventual Saudi control, held its first meeting at al-Sulayman's house where he took charge of the proceedings. Nevertheless, the Saudi government remained heavily in debt to ARAMCO for the railway's construction. At the time of the opening, the oil company estimated its cost at more than $37 million and calculated that the government still owed $24 million in payment for it. ARAMCO was deducting $1 million per month for reimbursement from its royalties payments but costs were still running at $500,000 a month, meaning that it would be years before the government could pay off its debt.[22] ARAMCO was reported also to be reluctant to relinquish control over the railway since there remained unresolved contractual matters and the company would henceforth be required to pay for use of the line. Nevertheless, repeated requests from the government resulted in the changeover at the beginning of 1953.[23]

In the mind of the king, the railway from al-Dammam to Riyadh was little more than the first step in a broader network of railways in the kingdom, including repair of the old Ottoman al-Hijaz Railway and an extension of the new railway from Riyadh to Jiddah. Consequently in 1952, a survey of the Riyadh–Jiddah route under the Point IV program was requested. The State Department approved the survey although with misgivings over suspicion that the US might be eventually asked to construct the railway. The survey agreement was signed in November. By its terms, the US government was to finance it to the sum of $330,000 while the Saudi government provided housing for the personnel and the equivalent of $27,000 for local expenditure.[24]

Roads. The emerging prosperity after World War II enabled the Saudi government to begin constructing a national road network. New roads were built and existing ones—such as Makkah–Jiddah, Makkah–ʿArafat, and internal streets in Jiddah, al-Madinah, and al-Taʾif—were paved.[25]

More progress in transport-related development projects was made in the next few years. At the end of 1950, al-Sulayman gave a magazine interview in which he outlined development projects in transport and communications that were current at that time. The two most important of these, he said, were the paving of the Makkah–Jiddah road and the construction of Jiddah port. The road was being done by the British company Braithwaite whose Saudi Arabian agent was Mitchell Cotts. Work began in late 1950 and was expected to take four years to complete at a cost of nearly £5,400 per kilometer. Another £3 million was earmarked for improvements in villages along the road. In addition, other roads had been paved, including Makkah–al-Taʾif and between Dhahran, Khubar, and al-Dammam. Furthermore, the railway between Dhahran and Riyadh was underway and airports were being built in Jiddah, Dhahran, Riyadh, and al-Taʾif.[26] An agreement was reached in January 1950 with Braithwaite for a paved road between Jiddah and al-Madinah. Al-Sulayman initially refused to sign the agreement because the government had no money to pay for it but Philby, acting on behalf of Mitchell Cotts, appealed to the king who instructed his finance minister to sign the actual contract in May.[27]

Work on the Jiddah to al-Madinah road continued in 1953 with the Directorate of Public Works reportedly taking over the completion of the project from the British contractor, Thomas W. Ward. A company owned by Muhammad b. Ladin, the director of public works, was to do the work, with some assistance from ARAMCO. This would be the first project undertaken without foreign participation and both al-Sulayman and Prince Saʿud supported it.[28]

Airline. The year 1946 also saw the establishment of government-owned Saudi Arabian Airlines, created and maintained with the assistance of TWA. Eight Douglas C-47-B aircraft were purchased in Cairo and used to carry Saudi officials and mail, although fare-paying passengers were accepted as well and peripatetic flights were made to Cairo.[29] In addition to the construction of the railroad and the purchase of maritime vessels, the number of Saudi commercial airplanes was increased from 12 to 18. International routes were supplemented by *hajj* flights from countries such as South Africa, India, Turkey, Egypt, Syria, Lebanon, and the UK.[30]

Harbor. Plans were also made to improve Jiddah harbor. The port was congested and there often were not enough lighters to unload cargo from ships in the harbor, resulting in long delays of up to a week. In addition, congestion on the Customs quay sometimes prevented lighters from unloading.[31] Thus there was considerable interest in improving both the north and the south ports of Jiddah.[32]

SAUDI EMPLOYEES IN ARAMCO

The Ministry of Finance's relations with ARAMCO not only dealt with concession and finance matters but also with ARAMCO's role in the kingdom's development, especially through its employees. In 1947, for example, the minister discussed an educational survey with the company. ARAMCO informed him that it was organizing an educational system for both its American and Arab students. Al-Sulayman responded that it would set an example for the rest of the country to follow.[33]

In May 1948, al-Sulayman in a visit to Dhahran, followed a month later by Foreign Ministry official Yusuf Yasin, insisted to ARAMCO officials that Arab employees must receive living conditions approaching those of Americans and that eventually Arab and American housing should merge together.[34] These activities were not surprising as the Ministry of Finance was made responsible for labor matters following the promulgation of the labor law in 1948. Furthermore, the ministry had established a labor office in al-Dammam even earlier in 1945 to deal with ARAMCO employee affairs.[35]

AGRICULTURE

Saudi Arabian interest in agriculture continued in the postwar period, despite the fact that there had been no money available for agricultural projects during the war. However, by 1948, 7 million *riyal*s had been allocated in fact for the purpose and a directorate of agriculture established. In addition, American experts had been engaged and new machines and water pumps purchased, and sold to farmers for a subsidized price. Five experimental farms had been created throughout the kingdom and agricultural programs had been extended from crops to include poultry and livestock.[36] ARAMCO continued to supervise the hiring and work of American personnel at al-Kharj, and arranged for spare parts and experts in electricity and mechanics when required. The shortage of funds hit the agricultural project as well as everywhere else and morale suffered in late 1947/early 1948 when salaries and food supplies were interrupted for some months. Nevertheless, production levels increased and the project received the support of local officials and praise from visitors.[37]

The minister of finance continued to take a close interest in agricultural and closely supervised the government directorate. Nevertheless, the government's financial woes exacted a toll and in fact limited agriculture's budget to 3 million *riyal*s. In spite of this, the budget permitted the purchase of more than a thousand water pumps for distribution to small farmers on soft loan terms. A study was made of dams in al-Ta'if and plans for new ones initiated. Similarly, a study was commissioned on the cementing of irrigation canals to reduce water loss and several drilling rigs were put into operation to dig Artesian wells. An item in *Umm al-Qura* in April announced that the government would make grants of "waste land" to citizens to cultivate. Tractors were made available for nominal rent and fruit trees and seeds were distributed for free.[38]

Al-Kharj continued in operation despite problems in keeping pumps operating, differences between the project's director and ARAMCO, and a freeze that killed off winter crops and was followed by a shortage of rainfall.[39] Nevertheless, an expert from the US Department of Agriculture, sent to al-Kharj to evaluate the project, concluded that "Taking everything into consideration, it appears that the program of agricultural development in Saudi Arabia is progressing in as satisfactory manner as can reasonably be expected."[40]

Still, ARAMCO persuaded the government to accept a new plan for the administration of the government's agricultural program in 1950. The plan would include the administrative division of agriculture into: ① producing farms, such as al-Kharj; ② experimental, demonstration, and research projects; and ③ long-range development of agricultural resources, such as dams and well drilling. ARAMCO offered to take over the first category and run the farms on a commercial basis. The latter two sections were to be under the Director of Agriculture, with ARAMCO's involvement being restricted to supply and maintenance.[41]

ʿAbdullah al-Sulayman also took a close personal interest in the Hadda Agricultural Project, located in Wadi Fatimah between Jiddah and Makkah, and received weekly reports on progress. Hadda, like al-Kharj, did experimental work in crops and equipment and sold its produce, especially dates as well as vegetables, livestock, and dairy items, in the markets of Jiddah and Makkah.[42]

In 1950, the Saudi government asked ARAMCO to take over the administration of al-Kharj and to run it on commercial lines, dropping the roles of demonstration and research. Although Crown Prince Sa'ud was designated the official owner of the farm, al-Sulayman continued to manage its budget and supervise much of its operation. American employees at the project were being gradually phased out in favor of Palestinian refugees in accordance with government policy. Al-Kharj constituted one part of a larger Department of Agriculture (contained within the Ministry of Finance) that was also charged with establishing a number of extension centers to demonstrate modern farming techniques and experiment with new crops.[43]

At the Saudi government's request, a mission from the Food and Agricultural Organization (FAO) of the United Nations toured throughout Saudi Arabia in March and April 1950 to study agricultural requirements. The mission's final report suggested the improvement of existing irrigation schemes and the development of new and better sources of water supplies, as well as other recommendations. In August, an agreement was signed with the FAO on technical assistance while the provision of FAO experts in agriculture, with costs shared between the FAO and the Saudi government, was mooted at the same time. In addition, the use of a half-dozen American agricultural experts under the US government's Point IV program for technical assistance was requested. The US Geological Survey (USGS), with the assistance of Dr. Glen Brown (who had worked in the kingdom before), also carried out a water survey of western Saudi Arabia. Other well-drilling projects were scheduled for Jazan and Yanbu', as well as improvement of the water supply for Makkah. The USGS also carried out aerial mapping of parts of al-Hijaz, 'Asir, and the Tihamah.[44]

The USGS team found water sources for nearly all inhabited places along the Red Sea coast from Jazan to the Gulf of 'Aqabah. It recommended that pipelines be constructed to bring water into Makkah from transverse wadis south of the city, to supplement existing sources at 'Ayn Zubaydah and later a pipeline from Wadi Fatimah. Water found at Hadat al-Sham, north of Wadi Fatimah, permitted the establishment of an experimental farm. While the water found in wadis in the mountains was fresh, it tended to collect salts as it ran downstream towards the Red Sea. For this reason, the team recommended that seaside settlements be provided with flash-distillation plants.[45]

OTHER RESPONSIBILITIES

Over the years, the official activities of the Ministry of Finance continued to grow and not only in terms of its main responsibilities in finance, currency, oil, mining, and agriculture. There were also a multitude of lesser responsibilities that took up the time of the ministry and its minister as well. Some of these should be noted, even if briefly.

Water Supplies. New improvements in the water supply for Jiddah was a top postwar priority (see Chapter 7 for earlier activity) due to the growth in the city's population and increasing numbers of pilgrims on *hajj* passing through Jiddah. There was considerable competition between local businessmen for the project's contract and one of the competing groups was in league with the American Eastern Corporation. This, as explained earlier, had become a serious disadvantage. In the end, after further complications, King ʿAbd al-ʿAziz asked ARAMCO to construct pipelines to Jiddah from Wadi Fatimah or Wadi Asfan, perhaps as a way of circumventing the competition.[46]

While suggestions for the use of Wadi Asfan for the water pipeline continued to be made, the Wadi Fatimah pipeline was approved and construction began in early 1947. Some Wadi Fatimah farmers protested that they suffered water losses and the pipeline suffered instances of sabotage. The first piped water from Wadi Fatimah arrived in Jiddah on 8 November 1947, marking completion of the first phase of the improvements. The official opening of the pipeline took place on 18 November and a celebration was organized at Jiddah's north gate with Crown Prince Saʿud as the guest of honor. A crowd of 30,000 was reported to have turned out for the festivities and the Saudi Airlines and Royal Saudi Air Force put on an aerial display. The pipeline was named ʿAziziyah in honor of the king.[47] In December 1950, the Jiddah Water Commission, which had been charged by the king with supplying water to the poor for free, took over administration of the system from the Ministry of Finance.[48]

Radio Broadcasting and Publication. ʿAbdullah al-Sulayman played a key role in the inauguration of Saudi radio broadcasting in the kingdom. He was quoted in 1948 as saying that the radio station would enable Muslims to hear the call for prayer from the land of the Prophet Muhammad and it would broadcast the Qurʾan, religious speeches, Islamic songs, news, and historical and scientific programs. Additional religious programs would be broadcast during the *hajj*. Its establishment and operation would require help from Egyptian engineers.[49]

In May 1949, al-Sulayman represented Saudi Arabia in negotiations with the International Standard Electronic Company at the Saudi embassy in Cairo. With him was ʿAbd al-Hamid Ghunaym, the president of the Egyptian directorate of telephone and radio who was serving as a consultant for the Saudi government. Agreement was reached for the company to establish the station with costs to the government put at $250,000 for general costs, $15,000 for yearly maintenance, and $60,000 per annum in salaries for the engineers and miscellaneous costs. The station began broadcasting on 1 October 1949 with religious and educational programming. Programs of 15 minutes or less were aired on poetry, health, selected stories, Arabic literature, Arab history, sports, and presentations for children and students. Al-Sulayman served as supervisor of the station during the early years. It was not until 1955 that broadcasting became independent and answerable directly to the council of ministers.[50]

In a related area, the finance minister had long been interested in communications and publication. He became a partner in the Printing and Publication Establishment Company, Ltd., established in 1953, along with Prince ʿAbdullah al-Faysal, Hamad al-Sulayman, Sulayman al-Hamad, Muhammad Surur, Ibrahim Shakir, Ibrahim Islam, and ʿAbd al-ʿAziz Jamil.[51]

Hajj and Hajj Transportation. In 1947, it was noted that organization of the *hajj* and transportation of pilgrims was much improved and that this reflected considerable credit on Muhammad Surur, the director of *Hajj* Affairs and adviser to the minister of finance.[52] The Ministry of Finance continued to exercise supervision of the annual *hajj* and a *hajj* directorate was created within the ministry about 1948 to cater for pilgrims' requirements by hiring hundreds of employees, building new hotels, and improving roads.[53]

Public Works in Makkah and Jiddah. In a 1948 interview, al-Sulayman noted that Saudi Arabia and Egypt had made an agreement before World War II for the provision of electricity, water, and sewage in Makkah. The war, however, had made it impossible to carry out these plans. With an end to the war, the minister of finance expressed his hope that the project could be resumed.[54] When Jiddah's electricity supply suffered from excessive demand, the Ministry of Finance was closely involved in approving and acquiring new generators for the city.[55]

Karl Twitchell's Postwar Role. Twitchell, who had played numerous roles in Saudi Arabia over several decades, returned to center stage in 1948 when al-Sulayman appointed him as technical adviser to the Ministry of Finance. His duties were to include periodic trips to the kingdom at the ministry's request and the formation at some point of a technical company in Saudi Arabia, as well as providing liaison and inspection of American factories.[56] Twitchell later played a role in the Onassis tanker affair, as described in Chapter 8.

Health Care. Another concern of the Ministry of Finance involved health care. In February 1949, the ministry sanctioned a 2.5 million *riyal* budget for a health program in central al-Hijaz to care for both pilgrims and residents. Then in April, the purchase of £60,000 worth of medical supplies in the UK was arranged. But health concerns were also subjected to budgetary constraints and the ministry was forced to conclude that the rest of the anticipated health program—including a general hospital, an eye hospital, and a storage building for medical supplies—would have to be postponed to the following year.[57]

Industry. ʿAbdullah al-Sulayman signed a contract on 24 February 1949 with Edwin Locke, representing the Saudi Arabian Industries Corporation (SARINCO; formed in November 1947) for the creation of al-Hasa Cement Company. The Saudi government and individuals were to hold up to 45 percent of the shares, rising to a majority after 12–15 years. The cement company was given a monopoly on cement production in al-Ahsa' and given mineral exploration rights throughout the country. In lieu of tax, the Saudi government was to receive 3 percent of the cement produced or its cash equivalent in *riyal*s over a period of 25 years.[58] In the end, the cement factory never materialized.[59]

It can even be said that ʿAbdullah al-Sulayman possessed a prescient vision to what was to become a major Saudi industrial strategy: petrochemicals. In 1953, he raised the subject of a fertilizer factory with the US Technical Cooperation Administration (TCA). Such a factory would make use of the kingdom's natural gas resources, further agriculture in the kingdom (always one of al-Sulayman's particular interests), and perhaps even provide exports. While the TCA and the US Embassy sought to discourage the idea, arguing that the cost was too high and markets were unsure, the FAO backed the project and the Ministry of Finance sought to secure bids for the factory from foreign companies. However, nothing had been decided by the end of the year.[60]

CHAPTER 11

The Emergence of Prosperity (1950–4)

The 1950–4 period was a key transitional period in modern Saudi Arabian history. The 50/50 profit agreement with ARAMCO and the crisis over Iran's nationalization of its oil concession saw oil production—and thus revenue—increase substantially in 1951. The growth in government revenues and expenditures and the general expansion of the country's economy in the early 1950s meant that establishing a controlled budgetary process could be put off no longer. Furthermore, it was necessary for the government to take a positive role in spearheading socioeconomic development in a systematic fashion, rather than the piecemeal approach of previous years. Despite the growing bureaucratic complexity and his long years of government service, ʿAbdullah al-Sulayman still carried the burden of the superministry's work. Sometime after he left his position as US ambassador to Saudi Arabia, J. Rives Childs remarked on "Sheikh Abdullah Sulaiman, titular Minister for Finance but who was in reality the grand vizier of the kingdom and the most influential personality in it outside the king."[1]

FINANCES AND CURRENCY REFORM

Currency confusion marked the beginning of the new decade of the 1950s as it had for decades in the past. The balancing act between Saudi *riyal*s and gold sovereigns could never improve, for if the value of one increased, then necessarily the other must decrease, thus constituting a negative impact on the government's income. Discussion of a reform of the monetary system had been raised for years but the repetition of short-term crises virtually dictated that a major reform of the monetary system had to be enacted, and sooner rather than later. The government's attempts to maintain both gold and silver backing for the *riyal* was not successful because of fluctuations in gold and silver prices in the international markets. Thus, January 1950 saw the dollar equal to 5.2 *riyals* but by December this had risen to 3.14 *riyals* per dollar. Similarly, the price of 53.5 *riyals* for a sovereign in January had appreciated to 43.3 *riyals* per sovereign in December. The government sought to maintain the value of the sovereign by fixing an artificially high *riyal*–sovereign rate for its own transactions. The intention of the government to create a dollar stabilization fund by using its assets with the US Federal Reserve Bank (FRB) was stymied by the opposition of the State Department, which feared that such a fund would be used primarily as a source of additional funds by the Saudi government rather than as a mechanism for regulating exchange rates. At the same time, the low value of the *riyal* encouraged smuggling and hoarding.[2]

Other ideas bandied about in 1950 included the creation of a Saudi gold pound that would replace the British gold sovereign but have a fixed rate vis-à-vis the *riyal* and could be supplemented by the minting of more *riyals*. The US Treasury also suggested stabilization of the *riyal* with the dollar but at a more realistic weight. In addition, a paper note (controlled by a currency board) could be introduced that would gradually replace the Saudi gold pound as users grew accustomed to it.[3] Al-Sulayman signed an agreement on 29 May for a *riyal*–dollar stabilization fund using the king's special account with the FRB. Dollars would be transferred from the bank and used to purchase *riyals* that would be kept in a special account at the Netherlands Trading Society. They could not be used without US government approval, which would be given only if the coins or their equivalent in silver were paid into the Philadelphia mint (to cancel part of the Lend–Lease silver debt) or if dollars were paid into the king's special account at the FRB.[4] The stabilization fund expired on 27 May 1952 but it was extended for two years with the renewal signed on 9 June.[5]

This step did not, however, put an end to the smuggling problem since the official exchange rate for the *riyal* was so much higher than the market rate and so the stabilization fund was abandoned. As a consequence, attention was returned to the idea of minting a Saudi gold coin with fluctuating exchange rates to be announced by the Ministry of Finance at intervals and the Saudi government sought to purchase a large number of gold sovereigns from the US government until its gold coins were ready.[6]

Even well into the 1950s, the financial construction of the kingdom remained relatively rudimentary. A principal problem was the inability to control government expenditure and it was principally for this reason that Najib Salihah was brought back into the Ministry of Finance in 1949. A related problem was the king's lack of direct control over financial affairs and there was a reluctance to burden him with the intricate details of finance. Although the need for a budget and control of expenditure was indicated to the king during 1950, he seemed to show little interest in financial affairs and even al-Sulayman was unable to convince him. The king was finally persuaded in October to accept financial experts under US Point IV and to create an accounting department in Riyadh to organize the government's budget and control expenditure. The Ministry of Finance formally requested five financial advisers from the US government in December: two customs experts to help reorganize Saudi customs tariffs; two accountants to help establish the new accounting department; and a currency expert to help Najib Salihah introduce the Saudi gold coin.[7]

The first 100,000 gold coins arrived in Jiddah in June 1951.[8] One of the early functions of the Saudi Arabian Monetary Agency (SAMA) was to introduce the coin through the government payroll and sales to ARAMCO, primarily in al-Hijaz. By the end of November 1952, 505,000 were said to have been put into circulation and another 1 million had been ordered (or, more likely, a total of 1 million were ordered, as the source is not clear). Half or 500,000 of these gold coins were to provide the capital for the bank.[9] The idea was to replace the British gold sovereign (the import of which would be made illegal) and the Saudi sovereign (to be known as SS) would be fixed in value against the US dollar. Once it was established, the silver *riyal* would be withdrawn and replaced by a token coin, thus removing the bi-metallic structure of Saudi Arabia's currency.[10]

The credibility of the gold sovereign as the new cornerstone of Saudi currency suffered a blow in the latter part of 1953 when a flood of counterfeit coins hit the country. As head of SAMA, George Blowers wished ARAMCO to continue to accept the coins so as to not undermine confidence in the Saudi monetary system. But al-Sulayman's statement that the government would not accept or give credit for the forged sovereigns dismayed ARAMCO and prompted merchants and money changers to refuse to accept sovereigns. It took a government decree on 7 December to reverse the position by announcing that all sovereigns, real or counterfeit, could be exchanged by SAMA. As a consequence, large numbers of sovereigns were presented for exchange and the government requested the release of silver *riyals* in the *riyal*-dollar stabilization fund in order to redeem the sovereigns. The crisis dealt a death blow to the sovereign's role in Saudi currency.[11]

The only budgetary figures for the year come from an ARAMCO estimate, which guessed roughly that by far the greatest source of income would be royalties (4,755,003 *riyals*), followed by *hajj* (911,000), an ARAMCO loan (550,000), customs (480,000), profit on *riyal* sales (282,000), Pacific Western payment (90,000), and other incidental sources. The largest expenditure was for current salaries (1,615,000 *riyals*) with another 492,000 *riyals* for back salaries. Other major expenditures were reckoned to be "Riyadh allowances"

(830,000), defense (790,000), Syrian loan (550,000), ARAMCO invoices (514,500), Bechtel (327,000), and tribal subsidies (325,000).[12] The *Economist*'s *Confidential Foreign Report* earlier in the year estimated the government's annual income at $87 million and expenditure at about $41 million, with the difference between the two figures being lost to extravagance and misappropriation.[13] In addition, the government relied heavily on loans from local banks as well as ARAMCO to meet its current needs and *riyal* shortages.

In 1951, the Saudi government published its first budget in two-and-a-half years. Covering the period 1 Rajab Awwal 1370 to 1 Rajab Awwal 1371 (8 April 1951–28 March 1952), it was balanced at 490 million *riyal*s. According to an American embassy analysis, the receipts had increased by 256 million *riyal*s while expenditures had increased by 226 million *riyal*s from the AH 1367 budget, but it doubted the accuracy of the figures. Projects and the army accounted for 36 percent of the total budget.[14]

But the existing system of the state's financial administration was coming under increasing pressure from 1950 on. Oil production was growing and the newly agreed 50/50 agreement also added to the kingdom's coffers. At the same time, demands on state revenues were also increasing at an alarming rate. The existing system desperately required modification and institutionalization. Undoubtedly, even the architect of the system, ʿAbdullah al-Sulayman, recognized that changes were needed. As the single individual in charge of finances, under the authority of the king of course, al-Sulayman not only kept track of income and expenditure on the macro level but directly supervised the customs administration, the department of *zakat* (alms tax) and income tax, and the new department of petroleum and mineral affairs. The growing complexity of the Saudi economy guided his efforts to the implementation of currency reforms and the creation of a central bank. Part of the problem was that the entire structure depended on its continued administration by a single individual acting in the name of the king. The finance minister could rely upon few assistants or subordinates at that time who could act independently and competently. Even after his retirement in 1954, many of the same policies that he had initiated and maintained were followed by his successor as minister, Muhammad Surur al-Sabban.[15]

The financial picture for the year 1951 was little changed from that of 1950. Increases in oil production were unable to keep up with continued high levels of expenditure and the growing burden of debt servicing. The continuous Saudi government demands on ARAMCO for additional payments strained the relations between the company and the government, and especially with al-Sulayman, who served as the government's chief negotiator. Matters reached a head when the minister insisted that ARAMCO pay taxes in advance in order to meet claims in the state budget and ARAMCO strongly resisted. Al-Sulayman intimated that he would take the matter to the king and inform him that ARAMCO was not cooperating and offer his resignation. In the end, the king met with ARAMCO officials and sought a compromise. It took several meetings but eventually ARAMCO agreed to make part of the 1951 tax payments, scheduled for 1952, available in installments during the last four months of 1951.[16]

There were other areas of disagreement as well. Al-Sulayman resisted the growing proportion of sterling in ARAMCO's royalty payments since the *riyal*-sterling exchange rate was unprofitable for the government. He also pressed for a Saudi representative on ARAMCO's board of directors, information on the pricing of oil, and relinquishment of part of the concession. Furthermore, it turned out that ARAMCO was paying royalties on the basis of the discounted price for oil ($1.43) rather than the posted price ($1.75). It took another intervention by the king to settle at least some of these disputes.[17]

The basis for al-Sulayman's uncompromising attitude vis-à-vis the company was rooted not only in balancing the budget but in dealing with the ballooning problem of debt servicing. As 1951 wore on, the government's payment commitments grew to include every month: $100,000 to repay the Export-Import Bank loans; between $500,000 and $750,000 to meet current invoices payable to ARAMCO; $1 million for payments for al-Dammam–Riyadh railway; and $750,000 to repay the $6 million loan extended by ARAMCO in January 1950.[18]

Tense relations between the government and ARAMCO also characterized 1952. Royalty payments increased by 24 percent from the previous year but the government was still short of funds. The situation grew worse towards the end of the year as ARAMCO's production levels dropped, thus lowering government revenue. Government income for the year was estimated at $245 million and expenditures, marked at the same amount, were broken down into public projects ($20 million), defense ($49 million), central government expenses and intangibles ($110 million), the Ministries of Health and the Interior ($46 million), and the Ministry of Finance ($20 million).[19]

One bright spot in the arena of financial affairs was tariff reform. While ʿAbdullah al-Sulayman and Najib Salihah had been strongly opposed to any reduction in tariff revenue, they had been persuaded by June 1952 that tariffs should be fewer and cheaper. The king was thought to have been thinking in terms of abolishing all customs duties but had been dissuaded. A new tariff law was promulgated by royal decree on 21 November, embodying a single *ad valorem* duty to be imposed on imports with only five rates of duty.[20]

The Saudi budget for 1371–2 (27 March 1952–15 March 1953) was published in *Umm al-Qura* on 18 April 1952. The budget was balanced at 757,960,158 *riyals* (the equivalent of $189,490,039) with a deficit of 26 million *riyals*. But the US embassy believed that the figures were not accurate and that it included a hidden reserve of 100 million *riyals*, derived from overvaluing the government's debt by 45 million *riyals* and undervaluing revenue by 55 million *riyals*. There was little hope that expenditure would be contained within the budget's levels. The embassy also contended that the Ministry of Finance was responsible for administering over half of the budget.[21] The year 1952 was also notable for King 'Abd al-'Aziz's abolishing of pilgrim dues for the *hajj* on 22 May, thus eliminating what had been the major source of income before oil. This was expected to reduce government revenue by $5 million.[22]

DEVELOPMENT PROJECTS

The government's efforts in the field of development during the early 1950s faced the continuing problem of straitened finances and thus the difficulty of paying for expensive projects. The relationship with its partner in development, Bechtel, was strained by the government's inability to keep current on its payments to the company. In February 1950, the government was reported to owe Bechtel $900,000 for both work completed and for commitments made by the company on behalf of the government.

Many projects had to be postponed and the government sought an additional loan from the Export-Import Bank, which Bechtel negotiated for the government. Many of the projects proposed to the bank had been commenced by Bechtel already but the funding for their completion was missing. The State Department supported the loan but the bank was hesitant. Saudi Arabia's indebtedness to Bechtel grew throughout the year, reaching $2 million in July, and Stephen Bechtel hinted to the State Department that, if the debts were not paid soon, the company would be forced to withdraw gradually from the kingdom. The threat seemed to have an effect on the bank's deliberations, which acted in July to approve a $15 million line of credit. It would expire on 31 May 1953 with the government committed to repayment in installments over 11 years from February 1955. At the same time, the bank attached stipulations designed to allow the bank to keep a close supervision on expenditures and reduce wastage. Bechtel agreed to continue work but only on projects that would be funded by the Export-Import Bank and not performing personal services.[23]

The budget agreed between Saudi Arabia and Bechtel for 1951 called for $7.5 million in expenditure, of which the Export-Import Bank credit would provide $4.8 million and the Saudi government $2.7 million. Despite only providing about one-third of the costs, the government found it hard-pressed to find the funds. American grant aid for some of the projects was discussed but no action taken.[24] One positive development note for 1950 had been the opening of the Jiddah deep-water pier in February. Once subsidiary construction was completed, Hajji Abdullah Alireza and Company took over the operation of the pier.[25] The pier at al-Dammam was also completed during the same year.

Although Bechtel was the government's partner in development, it came under heavy criticism for its charges and for delays in completing projects. For Bechtel's part, it began actively considering a withdrawal from Saudi Arabia because of the inability of the government to pay its debts. In January 1951, the company was owed $430,000, which was an improvement over the $700,000 owed in 1950. However, by June, the government debt to Bechtel had risen to $1.5 million and the company informed the government that if payment was not forthcoming, work would have to stop and it would not seek a renewal of its contract. Negotiations in July proved fruitless and the company identified the Export-Import Bank projects (Jiddah harbor and airport, Jiddah–Makkah road, Riyadh airport, shops in Jiddah, Jiddah electric power extension, a report on the Makkah–al-Ta'if road, and a report on sewage and water in Jiddah) as priorities. A month later, al-Sulayman served official notice of the termination of their contract at the end of the year.

He subsequently signed a new two-year contract with Michael Baker Jr. Inc. (MBJI) in October (effective 1 January 1952) to carry out many of the same projects but with smaller administrative charges. Baker sought to overcome the financial problems by insisting on an American bank account in which the Saudi government would deposit $500,000 for Baker's use and replenish it monthly. In the event, the government could spare only $100,000 for the account and Baker faced the additional problem of finding suitable personnel for its operations.[26]

A number of other development projects were planned and/or carried out during 1951 outside the Bechtel contract. One of these was for establishment of a Saudi company to take over Jiddah's electrical supply and make improvements. Another idea was for a cement factory in Jiddah, to meet the demand occasioned by a Ministry of Finance regulation that all future construction in the city use stone or cement blocks instead of mud. The ministry's Bureau of Mines made preliminary exploration of mining at Muwayli-Dhulm in Najd. Operation of the new Jiddah port was returned to Bechtel from Hajji ʿAbdullah Alireza Company after complaints of excessive charges. A contract was also reportedly signed with an Egyptian company for the construction of a sewage system in Makkah.[27]

As MBJI took over the public works program from Bechtel in 1952, it ran into many of the same problems as its predecessor, most notably a lack of available funds. Furthermore, most of the program was concentrated in al-Hijaz. Still, the completion of the al-Dammam–Riyadh railway had ended Riyadh's isolation and agricultural production at al-Kharj increased by 64 percent although it still only supplied the royal family. Most of the remaining development in the east was carried out by private businessmen with ARAMCO's help.[28]

A team from the Export-Import Bank was sent to assess the situation and it issued a very negative report after its visit to Saudi Arabia in June 1952. In the first place, the team was critical of Export-Import Bank activities in the kingdom, concluding that "A very good case could be made that no credits at all should be extended to the Saudi Arabian Government" since there was little control over spending in the country. The report noted that Bechtel had left three projects unfinished: Jiddah harbor, Jiddah airport, and the Jiddah–Makkah road. Of these, Jiddah harbor would need to be reconsidered since it involved plans for an expansion of facilities. But the bank was also critical of MBJI operations in the country, noting that its top two operations officials were neither engineers nor had a construction background. Changes would need to be made before the company would be allowed to work on Export-Import Bank projects, not just in Saudi Arabia but anywhere: "In other words, Baker would have to make good or get out." Not surprisingly, MBJI promised to make the necessary administrative changes.[29] In the end, the job was too big for the company, a small concern from Pennsylvania that did not seem to have had any overseas work before this contract, let alone serving as virtually the public works department for an entire country.[30]

The company ran into more difficulties with the Saudi government and al-Sulayman in 1953. The latter reportedly signed an agreement with GOVENCO, a German firm, to take over MBJI's work. Michael Baker then approached Prince Saʿud who gave him his support and shortly afterwards MBJI told the embassy that the GOVENCO contract had been cancelled. This was not the end of the story, however, as ʿAbd al-ʿAziz al-Sulayman told MBJI to hand over its installations to GOVENCO. MBJI again appealed to Prince Saʿud, an approach that apparently angered the minister of finance, prompting him to tell Baker that his company's work in the kingdom was now terminated due to their slowness in completing projects and their unduly high administrative costs. Al-Sulayman subsequently informed the US embassy of MBJI's termination.[31]

There were also problems with the Point IV program. It showed little progress from 1951 to 1952 since the 1952 renewal of the agreement was essentially *pro forma* and did not lay out any specific projects. It was left to the Saudi government to make a request for technical cooperation in agriculture, natural resources, communications, and aerial mapping, as well as the training of Saudis in each of these areas, a request that was not fulfilled.[32] Specific improvements during the first half of 1952 included malarial control, the establishment of a commercial school in Jiddah, and the construction of housing for Technical Cooperation Administration personnel. On the other hand, there was a lack of suitable candidates for training and the frequent absence of Saudi government officials hindered coordination.[33]

Indeed, the meager results of the cooperation provoked al-Sulayman to complain about the kingdom's treatment. He noted that Saudi Arabia had been the first Middle Eastern country to conclude a Point IV agreement and that millions of *riyals* had been spent in support of the program but with no visible results. Furthermore, Saudi Arabia had been allocated only $600,000 while other Middle Eastern countries had received much more. When Najib Salihah conveyed these feelings to the US embassy, he pointed out that al-Sulayman had assumed personal responsibility for backing the program even though both the king and Prince Faysal had been neutral. The State Department's response was that allocations were made on the basis of need and not the esteem in which the country was held.[34]

When Edwin Locke visited in July, the finance minister repeated his complaints to him and Locke suggested to the US ambassador that the allocation be increased. Al-Sulayman's intention was not to cancel the program. Rather, he wished to expand it since he felt that the Saudi government should be seen trying to improve the "general welfare of the people as a whole." In particular, he wished to see Point IV assistance extended to health, the provision of water to Riyadh through the building of dams, the development of agriculture in the Jazan area, and road-building.[35] These aims were in addition to the establishment of SAMA and the revision of the customs tariff, of course, as well as education and a railway survey. After further prodding by al-Sulayman, the State Department agreed to contribute another $500,000 in matching funds.[36] By the end of the year, individual agreements for specific sectors had been signed and the director of technical cooperation in Saudi Arabia commented that "The signing of these agreements is indicative of the progress being made in Saudi Arabia towards drawing up a well rounded program under difficult conditions."[37]

In the meantime, Michael Baker spent time in the kingdom in early 1952 to inspect his company's operations. His relations with al-Sulayman were good but Prince Saʿud had said he wished Bechtel was still in charge of public works. This attitude may have been inspired in part by the finance minister's efforts to streamline the public works process and reduce private demands on the company.[38] Meanwhile, Bechtel settled its outstanding account with the government, accepting about one-half of the amount it was owed in hope of being to bid for new contracts in the future. Accordingly, the Ministry of Finance approved the maintenance of a Bechtel office in Jiddah.[39]

Differences had cropped up between ʿAbdullah al-Sulayman and the Technical Cooperation program in 1952, with al-Sulayman threatening in the middle of the year to cancel all Point IV agreements and to hire experts on an individual basis. It took a number of meetings to iron out the differences. The US side was forced to recognize that the Saudi government did not have the funds to carry out all the identified projects. At the same time, the Saudi side was forced to recognize that Point IV aid was limited to technical advice and did comprise a promise to fund and complete projects.[40] A further problem lay with the State Department's intention of reducing the 1954 TCA budget for Saudi Arabia to $1 million, which, as the embassy in Jiddah pointed out, would leave the program unable to meet the minimum criteria identified by the State Department as its purpose, demonstration, and the provision of expertise. While Point IV assistance was successful in identifying water sources and aerial mapping, lack of funding meant that projects in the fields of health, education, and agriculture were left unrealized.[41]

The fact that the Point IV programs achieved little led to more Saudi complaints and finally the Saudi government's termination of the program in 1954.[42] At the same time, the kingdom needed a partner in implementing various development programs. After the negative experiences with Bechtel and Baker, the government turned to a third enterprise. On this occasion, the partners were two German companies—Julius Berger of Wiesbaden and Hansa Stahl of Düsseldorf—who formed the Government Engineering Company of Saudi Arabia (GOVENCO) to take over from Michael Baker Jr. at the end of 1953.

Al-Sulayman was just as involved in the formulation of GOVENCO's contract as he had been with MBJI. GOVENCO was to take over MBJI's projects as well as to survey, design, and construct additional projects. Training for Saudi workers was stipulated, as was preference for Saudi nationals in employment. But because of the Baker experience, the terms of the contract were considerably more detailed and rigid conditions were set for payment for services. The compensation was generous: GOVENCO would receive £30,000 per month and 6.5 percent of turnover for their services. To control demands made on the company by various parties in the kingdom, only al-Sulayman and his nominated deputy were authorized to deal with GOVENCO.[43]

However, al-Sulayman's assumption of tightly held control of dealings with GOVENCO proved to be a liability for him personally. GOVENCO's prospects in Saudi Arabia declined even more rapidly than its predecessors. The company's dismissal of its purchasing manager in July led to his presenting a list of accusations against the company to the Saudi Arabian government and, in particular, to Prince Faysal who took control of GOVENCO and began an investigation with Prince Sultan in charge. GOVENCO stood accused of bribery and fraudulent charges and its operations in Saudi Arabia were constricted by the government. On 4 August, the finance minister informed the company that their work in the kingdom would have to cease. On 7 August, royal decree no. 459 annulled the company's contract.[44]

Toward the end of August, the US embassy reported that GOVENCO's silent Saudi partner and the Saudi government's liaison officer with GOVENCO, had been tried and found guilty by a religious court. The GOVENCO management was brought before the same court soon after. When the parent companies in Germany asked al-Sulayman for information, he replied that it had been proven that "GOVENCO abused the confidence entrusted by conspiring with certain Saudi individuals to rob government funds by certain means and ways." In the embassy's view, however, the issue was cover for a political struggle.[45] Evidence for this view was 'Abdullah al-Sulayman's resignation as minister of finance on 31 August. At the very least, the GOVENCO affair had given ammunition to al-Sulayman's enemies.

THE EXPANSION OF GOVERNMENT ADMINISTRATION

As revenues received by the Saudi government increased and development projects grew in number and expense, the minimalist organization of King 'Abd al-'Aziz's government became increasingly incapable of coping with demands. While a certain number of functions had been split off from the overarching Ministry of Finance—for example, the Ministry of Defense—the Ministry of Finance and 'Abdullah al-Sulayman still maintained control of many of the core bureaucratic functions in addition to financial matters. Because of growing complexity, reorganization was urgently required in the ministry. An early shake-up occurred in May 1951 when a treasury office was established with the finance minister signing all bank deposits and withdrawals personally. In addition, an Income Tax Office was created as was an Office of Riyadh Affairs to handle the Royal Family's funds. Sulayman al-Hamad was entrusted with his father's duties while the latter was abroad and, finally, Najib Salihah was shifted to Public Works and would no longer have financial duties.[46] Not much later, an Office of Economic Affairs with Husayn Jastiniyah at its head was created to deal with economic affairs and matters relating to international organizations, although it seemed to have little substantive power. In addition, al-Sulayman's secretary, Ahmad Mawsili, was authorized to sign routine correspondence on behalf of the minister.[47]

More changes were evident in 1952. After rumors that ʿAbdullah al-Sulayman was ill and expected to take a rest from official duties, Prince Saʿud was reported as confidentially telling James Terry Duce of ARAMCO that he had picked a successor as minister of finance: ʿAbdullah b. ʿAdwan, head of the Ministry of Finance's office in al-Dammam. This of course never took place.[48] However, not long afterwards, it was reported that, at the king's request, al-Sulayman was to establish residence in Riyadh and visit Jiddah only occasionally. This was followed by a royal decree on 15 July appointing Hamad al-Sulayman as vice-minister of finance and Sulayman al-Hamad as deputy minister of finance. In ʿAbdullah's absence, his brother was to be in charge of the ministry and in Hamad's absence, his son was to deputize for him. This left Najib Salihah and Ahmad Mawsili as the next level of officialdom.[49]

Shortly afterwards, it was reported that the role of the Technical Department of the Ministry of Finance was expected to increase. With Najib Salihah at its head, the department would take over the responsibilities of the Development Projects Office and the Public Works Department and supervise large-scale development projects in Riyadh and al-Hijaz.[50]

On a somewhat larger scale, the king had instructed Prince Saʿud to remain in al-Hijaz after the *hajj* to deal with the question of administrative reform. During his stay, the crown prince issued various reform decrees. A decree on 19 October 1952 called for closer adherence to the budget and emphasized the Ministry of Finance's role. It also announced the formation of a State Economic Council with ʿAbdullah al-Sulayman at its head. Furthermore, the Ministry of Finance would be expanded to include a Department of Petroleum Affairs, a Department of Projects, and a National Customs Administration. Prince Saʿud also announced during the *hajj* the creation of a new Department for the Hajj and Broadcasting. This action did little more than formalize the existing machinery for the *hajj* within the Ministry of Finance. Muhammad Surur al-Sabban was appointed general supervisor of the department in December. With Prince Saʿud's departure for Riyadh, al-Sulayman was left with the task of reconciling the reform decree with the existing administration of his ministry.[51]

The General Directorate of Mining and Petroleum was created within the Ministry of Finance in 1372/1952, replacing the Department of Mining and Public Works, which had been created in 1355/1935 when the oil company and the gold-mining firm began operations in the kingdom. It was not until 1960 that a separate Ministry of Petroleum was created with ʿAbdullah al-Turayqi as its first minister.[52]

In 1953, even before the long-anticipated death of King ʿAbd al-ʿAziz, the giant fiefdom administered by ʿAbdullah al-Sulayman from the Ministry of

Finance was experiencing more changes. In May, Prince Sa'ud's instructions to the finance minister to establish the State Economic Council were published in *Umm al-Qura*. The council, apparently part of the Ministry of Finance, included 'Abdullah al-Sulayman as president and Sulayman al-Hamad, Muhammad Surur, and 'Abd al-'Aziz al-Sulayman amongst its members; the only members outside the ministry were Muhammad Buqari and Muhammad 'Alireza. In addition, Prince Sa'ud ordered the abolition of the Office of Economic Affairs and its replacement by a Ministry of the Economy. 'Abdullah al-Sulayman was named to head the new ministry and his title changed to minister of finance and economy to reflect this. His deputy in the new ministry was Ahmad Mawsili, who had been the assistant deputy for economic affairs. The distinction did not seem to involve any major changes.[53]

On 9 October, a royal decree charged Prince Sa'ud with establishing a Council of Ministers. Al-Sulayman's membership in the council was confirmed because of his role as minister of finance and economy. The other ministers in the council were for foreign affairs, defense, health and interior, and communications. By the letter of the decree, the council's decisions were subject to the approval of the king and crown prince and no ministries were allowed to enter into contracts without Prince Sa'ud's approval. ARAMCO sought to interpret this as a restraint on al-Sulayman's actions vis-à-vis the company but this was ignored by Prince Sa'ud.[54]

The creation in 1953 of a number of new administrative entities to take over functions that had previously been handled by the super-Ministry of Finance straddled the change of king. King 'Abd al-'Aziz died on 9 November, 1953. Al-Sulayman was in Europe at the time and the US Air Force provided him with transportation home.[55] The finance minister was understandably concerned at the implications of his majesty's death but, in the event, the accession of Sa'ud b. 'Abd al-'Aziz as the new king was orderly and uneventful.[56] There were, however, more government changes during the last two months of the year. Muhammad Surur was appointed minister of state and given a place in the Council of Ministers.[57] Other ministerial changes appeared with a decree of 24 December, which appointed Prince Fahd b. 'Abd al-'Aziz as the first minister of education and Prince Sultan b. 'Abd al-'Aziz as the first minister of agriculture.[58] Prince 'Abdullah al-Faysal b. 'Abd al-'Aziz had been appointed already in 1951 as minister of the interior. In addition, Prince Talal b. 'Abd al-'Aziz had been appointed as minister of communications in September.[59] Muhammad 'Alireza was appointed a minister of state in December as well as adviser to his close friend al-Sulayman.[60]

Plans to reorganize the Ministry of Finance were also being put into action. Within the sphere of finance, al-Sulayman seems to have managed to maintain his control. Under Prince Saʿud's administrative reforms, al-Sulayman was made president of the State Economic Council and minister of economy. His son, ʿAbd al-ʿAziz al-Sulayman, joined the ministry during 1953 as assistant deputy minister for development projects, mines and foreign companies, replacing Najib Salihah.[61] During ʿAbdullah al-Sulayman's absence in Europe, ʿAbd al-ʿAziz acted for his father in respect of oil negotiations. Other personnel changes included the promotion of ʿAbdullah b. ʿAdwan as assistant deputy minister of finance for the Eastern Region and of Muhammad Ba Harith as director-general of the Ministry of Finance.[62]

But as 1954 opened and King Saʿud moved to put his stamp on the kingdom, ʿAbdullah al-Sulayman's power and influence were trimmed by a series of administrative reforms. There were rumors that changes in the management of government finances were forthcoming, particularly that the Ministry of Finance's monopoly on budgeting was to be replaced by separate budgets for various departments. Such a modification would reduce the Ministry of Finance's control over projects supervised by other departments.[63]

The major effect of the reforms was to empower the Council of Ministers with a wide range of powers, in effect inserting it in the hierarchical chain between the king and all his departments, including the Ministry of Finance. King Saʿud's speech at the inauguration of the Council of Ministers on 7 March dealt with a number of administrative changes, including a reduction of the Ministry of Finance's role to that of simply a Ministry of Finance. The ministry's roles would henceforth be collection of the country's income and authorizing expenditures within the state budget as discussed and approved by the Council of Ministers, instead of being prepared solely by the ministry as in the past.

In addition, a five-year construction plan for larger projects was to be devised, thus removing responsibility for major development projects from the Ministry of Finance. Furthermore, a General Accounting Office, a Grievances Board, and a Department of Experts were to be established within the Council of Ministers, all of which would result in diminished authority for the Ministry of Finance.[64] Finally, al-Sulayman was not included as a member of the new Financial Committee of the Council of Ministers, created to advise the council on its new financial responsibilities.[65]

The council's regulations were published in *al-Bilad al-Saʿudiyah* and *Umm al-Qura*, in elaboration on the king's speech with an explanation of additional powers entrusted to the council. The council was to take over responsibility for concessions and monopoly contracts, the establishment of corporate companies, and the licensing of foreign firms. The General Accounting Office was to "ascertain the accuracy of receipts and expenditures in all ministries, departments and administrations." The comptroller, to whom complaints could be made, was to have a wide range of powers and was to be in direct contact with the king. It was specifically mentioned that this office was in a position to suggest to the Ministry of Finance the most appropriate system of bookkeeping and record keeping, and the records of the Ministry of Finance, like those of all other ministries, were open to the department. In addition to being answerable to the king, the comptroller was to present an annual report to the Council of Ministers in which the performance of the various ministries was to be described.[66]

The creation of other ministries, such as health, education, agriculture, communications, and commerce, also served to reduce the power of the Ministry of Finance and the influence of its minister. This was undoubtedly a natural development, given the sizeable increase in the government's income and the even greater and more complex scope of development projects and expenses. As King Saʿud said in his 7 March address: "The days during which the Ministry of Finance was responsible for all construction, economic, agricultural, industrial and even military projects, have passed. This of course, is quite a burden on a party of powerful men, let alone one person or persons. Therefore, we have taken the responsibility to reduce the burden laid on this Ministry and make it a Ministry of Finance in the true meaning of these words."[67]

As the year wore on, Prince Faysal's increasing status in the government became apparent. As president of the Council of Ministers, appointed by royal decree of 15 August, Prince Faysal was empowered to question any ministry and matters outside of individual ministries' jurisdiction were to be referred to him.[68] The establishment and implementation of a budget under the new arrangement presented difficulties, however, and work on projects was delayed until the budget was put in place at the end of the year. While some suggestion has been made of tension between Prince Faysal and ʿAbdullah al-Sulayman, the bigger problem was working out a division of responsibility between Prince Faysal and the king. King Saʿud's habit of promising development projects during his trips around the country undoubtedly was politically astute but it caused enormous problems for ministries in instituting approved projects and in staying within budget.

THE MINISTRY OF FINANCE IN THE TRANSITION FROM KING ʿABD AL-ʿAZIZ TO KING SAʿUD

Following his accession, King Saʿud took a few months to put his own stamp on the government. In March 1954, he presided over the cabinet's first meeting during his reign. The agenda was expected to include the restructuring of financial management with separate budgets instituted for each of the various departments, rather than an overall budget being implemented by the Ministry of Finance.[69] This was interpreted as an early indicator of the narrowing of al-Sulayman's responsibilities and seemed to receive confirmation by King Sa'ud's first policy speech in inaugurating the Council of Ministers a few days later. In it, he stated that the Ministry of Finance was to submit budgets to the Council of Ministers for their approval, thus constituting a limitation on the ministry's influence.[70]

Other signs included the formation of a Financial Committee of the Council of Ministers, to be led by Prince Faysal and to include Muhammad Surur but not al-Sulayman.[71] The appointment of Muhammad 'Alireza as minister of commerce was regarded as further erosion of al-Sulayman's position. As the American embassy reported it, the formation of another ministry concerned with affairs which had previously been the primary concern of the Ministry of Finance and Economy appeared to be a further indication of the intention of the king to reduce the influence and authority of the minister of finance.[72]

It soon became clear that a number of the powers of the Ministry of Finance were to be transferred to the Council of Ministers. These included the annual budget, dealing with concessions and monopoly contracts, the establishment of corporate entities and the licensing of foreign firms. In addition, a Control of State Accounts was to be created as a subunit of the council with its purpose being to "ascertain the accuracy of receipts and expenditure in all ministries, departments and administrations."[73]

It was also speculated that the king's insistence on having al-Sulayman accompany him on a tour of Bahrain and Pakistan was to permit changes in his sphere of influence to take place during his absence. For one thing, Prince Faysal took over negotiations with ARAMCO during the trip. In addition, Muhammad Surur was named acting minister of finance during al-Sulayman's absence.[74] Nevertheless, the long-time minister of finance continued to soldier on.

After many years in office managing the kingdom's financial affairs along with many other duties, 'Abdullah al-Sulayman resigned as minister of finance in August 1954 and withdrew from government service. There are many theories but no clear explanation as to why he resigned. A logical explanation might lie in the establishment of the Council of Ministers and administrative reforms in March 1954. These pointed to a more developed bureaucratic and administrative structure necessary to cope with the more complex demands being placed on the government. The days of concentration of responsibilities in the hands of a single man and his super-ministry were over.

The idea of personal rifts between King Sa'ud or Prince Faysal and al-Sulayman seems problematic. The GOVENCO affair, which seemed to have been an immediate factor in al-Sulayman's resignation, has been cited as evidence of tension between the two men, as has the SATCO affair. In both cases, al-Sulayman was closely involved in the contractual arrangements with and supervision of the companies in his official capacity as minister of finance while Prince Faysal took charge of matters in both cases when controversy erupted. But there is also some evidence that the finance minister continued to remain on good terms with both sons of King ʿAbd al-ʿAziz, based on a half-century of working with them.[75] While the British concluded that the death of King ʿAbd al-ʿAziz was the primary cause of al-Sulayman's resignation, the GOVENCO affair acted as the trigger and the resignation provided King Saʿud with a face-saving means of extricating himself from the SATCO affair. The latter was thought to have been unlikely to have played a major role in motivating the resignation.[76]

Al-Sulayman's health may have played a major role in his resignation, as his letter of resignation stated. It was reported in mid-September 1953 that he was expected to go to Switzerland for rest and a medical examination.[77] Certainly, the King's Office issued a statement announcing that al-Sulayman had asked to be relieved of his duties due to his critical health condition. Royal decree 6515 of Muharram 1374/August–September 1954 simply announced King Saʿud's acceptance of his minister's resignation and proclaiming his successor as Muhammad Surur al-Sabban. This was soon followed by another decree announcing the merger of the Ministry of Economy into the Ministry of Finance, to be known as the Ministry of Finance and National Economy.[78] It has been suggested as well that after more than 30 years in the king's service, al-Sulayman had grown old and tired. As he explained to people, "As for my resignation from my positions, it is due to my age. I am too old and I need a break. I would always work for my king and my country and I love to do so. It is just the matter of age that tells me to step down and have some rest."[79]

The ministry was left in the hands of al-Sulayman's previous deputy, Muhammad Surur al-Sabban, who apparently had been referred to by King ʿAbd al-ʿAziz as *bashir al-khayr* (messenger of good). He wasted little time in putting his own stamp on the Ministry of Finance and National Economy, shuffling staff around and appointing his own officers and advisers.[80] Furthermore, he asserted the primacy of the ministry in all financial affairs in the kingdom. By a Council of Ministers decree of 9 Dhu al-Hijjah 1373/18 August 1953, a complete statement of indebtedness was ordered prior to settlement of all debts. In order to achieve this, the ministry was given the overall responsibility for the collection of all revenues and for all expenditures, including the posting of a ministry representative in every ministry and major department to ensure that revenue and expenditure were being carried out in compliance with Ministry of Finance and National Economy regulations. This also enabled the ministry to continue executing development projects, such as building factories for margarine and tin, a road to the Jiddah airport and warehouses at Jiddah harbor, and the provision of fresh water to various settlements along the Red Sea.[81]

The disappearance of ʿAbdullah al-Sulayman from the scene marked not only a changing of the economic and financial guard silhouetted underneath the succession of a new king. The explosion of income after World War II produced a prodigious number of ways to spend the new fortune and it had fallen beyond the power of the minister of finance to control expenditures. A single individual, no matter how capable and how trusted by the ruler, clearly could no longer manage the kingdom's finances and oversee its development. The years of King Saʿud's rule and those of King Faysal marked the expansion of the state and its economic and financial apparatus. The transformation did not take place overnight, however. Rationalization of the development process and greater control of spending did not become firmly entrenched until the bonanza of the 1973–4 oil price explosion.

It is no exaggeration to assert all that has been achieved since 1953 was made possible only by the stringencies of the three previous decades and the gradual steps taken to ameliorate them. It may seem difficult to reconcile the burgeoning economy, comprehensive state administration, and standards of living and education with the Saudi Arabia of the pre-oil and early oil eras. Nevertheless, the ubiquitous Ministry of Finance and its enduring minister created the foundations of the modern economy, financial organization, and administrative structure of Saudi Arabia. The man and the institution provided the essential bridge between proto-state at the beginning of the twentieth century and the developed system of today.

Notes

1 SAUDI ARABIA IN THE TWENTIETH CENTURY

1. The full details are included in the National Archives, Kew, London, Foreign Office (FO) Records, FO/371/31451/E655, F.H.W. Stonehewer Bird to Anthony Eden, the Secretary of State for Foreign Affairs, 6 January 1942.
2. Among the better standard references on the modern history of Saudi Arabia are Alexei Vassiliev, *The History of Saudi Arabia* (London: Al Saqi Books, 2000), and Madawi Al-Rasheed, *A History of Saudi Arabia* (2nd ed.; Cambridge: Cambridge University Press, 2002). The numerous and voluminous books by H. St. John B. Philby, listed in the bibliography, provide considerable detail and more general "popular" works include David Holden and Richard Johns, with James Buchan, *The House of Saud: The Rise and Rule of the Most Powerful Dynasty in the Arab World* (New York: Holt, Rinehart and Winston, 1982), and Robert Lacey, *The Kingdom: Arabia and the House of Saud* (New York: Harcourt Brace Jovanovich, 1982). The best known account in Arabic is probably Khayr al-Din al-Zirkali, *Shibh al-jazirah fi ʿahd al-malik ʿabd al-ʿaziz* (4 vols, Beirut, 1970).
3. The Ikhwan (Brotherhood) consisted of a movement of bedouin who had been religiously imbued with Wahhabi beliefs and sought to spread Wahhabi ideals throughout the Arabian Peninsula. Initially operating in the service of Ibn Saʿud, the Ikhwan later turned against him and had to be vanquished.
4. ʿAbdullah Mannaʿ, *ʿAbdullah al-Sulayman: sanawat al-taʾsis* (unpublished manuscript, 2001), p. 51, citing Muhammad al-Mani, "Unification of Saudi Arabia," p. 265 (no further details and incident is not present in Mohammed Almana, *Arabia Unified: A Portrait of Ibn Saud* [London: Hutchinson Benham, 1980, rev. 1982]).
5. University of Essex interview with Muhammad Ba Harith (c.1982).
6. University of Essex first interview with Shaykh ʿAbd al-ʿAziz al-Sulaiman (c.1982).
7. University of Essex interview with Salih b. Shilhub (c.1982).
8. Mannaʿ, *sanawat al-taʾsis*, p. 42.
9. University of Essex first interview with Shaykh ʿAbd al-ʿAziz al-Sulaiman.
10. Ḥamad al-Jasir, *Min sawaniḥ al-dhikriyat* (ed. & arranged by ʿAbd al-Raḥman al-Shubayli; Riyadh: Dar al-Yamamah, 1327/2006), pp. 699–706.
11. As ʿAbdullah al-Sulayman told a Western visitor years later. George Bilainkin, *Cairo to Riyadh Diary* (London: Williams & Norgate, 1950), p. 90.
12. University of Essex first interview with Shaykh ʿAbd al-ʿAziz al-Sulaiman; University of Essex interview with Salih b. Shilhub.

13. Manna', *sanawat al-ta'sis*, p. 73.
14. *Ibid.*, p. 74.
15. *Ibid.*, p. 77.
16. FO/371/11432, E363/11/91, S.R. Jordan, Acting Consul, Jiddah, to Sir Austen Chamberlain, 28 December 1925, enclosing "Report of Negotiations with King Ali and the Sultan of Nejd whilst acting as Intermediary for the Submission of the Jeddah Garrison and Town."
17. FO/371/11431, E2287, Acting British Consul, Jiddah, to FO, Tel. 37, 7 April 1926.
18. FO/371/11436, E5283/155/91, S.R. Jordan, Vice-Consul, Jiddah, to Sir Austen Chamberlain, 26 August 1926, enclosing "Pilgrimage Report 1926"; FO/371/11442, E4434/367/91, Jordan to Chamberlain, 5 July 1926, enclosing Jiddah Report for 1–30 June 1926.
19. FO/371/11436, E5283/155/91, Jordan to Chamberlain, 26 August 1926, enclosing "Pilgrimage Report 1926." Apparently there was another incident at Mina when Egyptians celebrated the *'id* (festival) by playing music and thereby incurred Wahhabi wrath.
20. FO/371/12250, E2849/644/91, F.H.W. Stonehewer Bird, Acting Consul, Jiddah, to Sir Austen Chamberlain, 31 May 1927, enclosing Jiddah Report for 26 April–31 May 1927.
21. It was not until April 1936 that discussions began on settling problems between the two countries. Even then disagreement over whether the Egyptians would resume providing the *mahmal* remained a problem. In the end, the matter was dropped and the *mahmal* was not mentioned in the treaty of friendship signed between the two countries on 7 May 1936. See the correspondence in FO/371/20061 as well as endnote 27 below.
22. FO/371/12250, E4115/644/91, Jiddah Report for 1–31 August 1927; Ḥusayn 'Abdullah Ba Salamah, *Tarikh al-ka'bah al-mu'azzamah* (2nd ed.; Jiddah: al-kitab al-'Arabi al-Sa'udi, 1402/1982), p. 293. Apparently part or all of the *kiswah* for the 1928 *hajj* was woven in India. FO/371/13010, E3332/484/91, Jiddah Report for 1–31 May 1928.
23. R/15/1/567, E5981/4309/91, C.G. Hope-Gill, Jiddah, to A. Henderson, 18 October 1930, summarizing Umm al-Qura article listing Hijaz-Najd accomplishments over prior 12 months.
24. Ba Salamah, *Tarikh al-ka'bah*, p. 295. A detailed description of the *kiswah* and the inscriptions upon it is given in *ibid.*, pp. 296–7.
25. FO/371/13741/E6285, W.L. Bond, Jiddah to A. Henderson, FO, 2 November 1929.
26. FO/371/16857/E4704, A.S. Calvert, Jiddah, to Sir John Simon, 29 July 1933.
27. FO/371/20061/E7752, Bullard to Eden, 25 November 1936, enclosing an exchange of notes regarding the *kiswah* and the *mahmal* between Egyptian Prime Minister Mustafa El Nahas Pasha and Saudi Under-Secretary for Foreign Affairs Fu'ad Hamza. The agreement was based on a compromise, however. The Egyptian escort for the *mahmal* would accompany it to Jiddah but the onward journey of the *kiswah* to Makkah would be with a Saudi escort. In addition, Egypt would resume *waqf* (religious endowment) and charitable payments for the Holy Places. FO/371/200161/E7300, Sir Miles Lampson, Cairo, to the FO, tel. no. 1042 of 21 November 1936.
28. FO/371/11442, E1399/367/91, Jordan to Chamberlain, 4 February 1926, enclosing Jiddah Report for 1–31 January 1926.
29. FO/371/11442, E6016/367/91, Norman Mayers, Acting Vice-Consul Jiddah, to Chamberlain, 3 October 1926, enclosing Jiddah Report for 1–30 September 1926.

30. FO/371/11442, E4937/367/91, Jordan to Chamberlain, 31 July 1926, enclosing Jiddah Report for 1–31 July 1926. As examples of the payments made to delegates, Rashid Rida of Egypt was reported to have received £2000 and Amin al-Husayni of the Palestinian delegation £1000. *Ibid.* The loan was offered principally by the three main merchant families of Jiddah: Zaynal ʿAlireza, Banajah, and Sulayman Gabil. *Ibid.*
31. FO/371/11442, E6655/367/91, Mayers to Chamberlain, 3 November 1926, enclosing Jiddah Report for 1–31 October 1926.
32. FO/371/13010, E1460/484/91, Stonehewer Bird to Chamberlain, 1 March 1928, enclosing Jiddah Report for 1–28 February 1928.
33. University of Essex interview with Salih b. Shilhub.
34. India Office Records, L/P&S/12/2074, W.L. Bond, Jiddah, to A. Henderson, FO, 1 October 1929; copy in FO/371/13741/5017.
35. Shaykh ʿAbdullah al-Sulaiman Papers, privately held, Jiddah, Miscellaneous Correspondence, letter from Shaykh ʿAbdullah al-Sulaiman to unknown, n.d. (c.1931–2).
36. ʿAbd al-Rahman b. Sulayman al-Ruwayshid, *ʿAbdullah al-Sulayman al-Hamdan: ṣafḥah mushriqah fi tarikh al-mamlakah al-ʿarabiyah al-saʿudiyah AH 13021385/AD 18851965* (Riyadh: Dar al-shil, 1421; 2nd ed., 2009), p. 60.
37. Jasir, *Min sawanih al-dhikriyat*, pp. 699–706.
38. University of Essex second interview with Shaykh ʿAbd al-ʿAziz al-Sulaiman (c.1982).

2 THE ORGANIZATION OF STATE FINANCES

1. United Kingdom, National Archives, Kew, Foreign Office (FO) Records, Political Department, General Correspondence, FO/371/12250, E644/644/91, Norman Mayers, Acting Consul, Jiddah, to Sir Austen Chamberlain, 8 January 1927, enclosing Jiddah Report for 1–31 December 1926.
2. The following summary is drawn largely from United Kingdom, British Library, India Office Records (IOR), Political Residency in the Persian Gulf Records (R/15), various correspondence in R/15/1/319 and R/15/1/480.
3. Various correspondence in R/15/2/74 and R/15/1/559.
4. H. St.J. B. Philby, *Arabian Jubilee* (New York: John Day, 1953), p. 226. Sharif Sharaf was described as the Hijaz finance minister in late 1927. FO/371/12997/E1130, C. Walker, Admiralty, to the Foreign Office (FO), 1 March 1928, enclosing "Proceedings of HMS 'Clematis' in the Red Sea," Report of 28 December 1927.
5. Kingdom of Saudi Arabia, Ministry of Finance and National Economy, National Center for Economic and Financial Information, *al-tarikh al-iqtiṣadi lil-mamlakah al-ʿarabiyah al-saʿudiyah* (Riyadh, 1420/2000), pp. 38–9.
6. FO/371/16878/E3745, Sir Andrew Ryan, Jiddah, to Sir John Simon, 7 October 1933, enclosing "Personalities in Arabia."
7. *Ibid.*
8. Ibrahim al-Muslim, *Rijal min al-Qaṣim* (Vol. 4; Riyadh: dar al-thiqafiyah lil-nashr, 2000), p. 44.
9. FO/371/13010, E4956/484/91, F.H.W. Stonehewer Bird, Consul, Jiddah, to Chamberlain, 30 September 1928, enclosing Jiddah Report for 1–30 September 1928.
10. FO/371/20063/E5458, Calvert to Eden, 26 June 1936, enclosing "Economic Survey of Saudi Arabia."

11. FO/371/13728, E489/94/91, H.J. Jakins, Consul, Jiddah, to Chamberlain, 1 January 1929, enclosing Jiddah Report for 1–31 December 1928. One of al-Sulayman's predecessors as "minister of finance" during the Sharifian period was Ahmad Banajah of Jiddah. FO/371/17935/E3550, Jiddah Report for April 1934.
12. University of Essex first interview with Shaykh ʿAbd al-ʿAziz al-Sulayman (c.1982).
13. IOR, India Office, Political (External) Files & Collections, L/P&S/12/2074, 1929, W.L. Bond, Jiddah, to A. Henderson, FO, 1 October 1929.
14. L/P&S/12/2085, Sir A. Ryan, Jiddah, to A. Henderson, FO, 18 April 1931, "Annual Report for Hejaz–Nejd, 1930."
15. Al-Ruwayshid, *safhah mushriqah*, p. 67.
16. George Blake, *Gellatly's, 1862–1962: A Short History of the Firm* (London: Blackie, 1962), pp. 137–8. In later years, Gellatly's also took on the construction of a water pipeline to Jiddah from the hills about 25 miles distant. *Ibid.*, p. 141. One example of the requests occurred in August 1929 when Gellatly, Hankey in London received a telegram from their Jiddah agent reporting a request for a loan of £10,000 to pay the Government of India for arms delivered to the King. FO/371/13741/E4281, FO memorandum by G.W. Rendel, 26 August 1929, "Hejazi Government's request for financial assistance from Messrs. Gellatly Hankey & Company."
17. FO/371/13728, E4713/94/91, W.L. Bond, Consul, Jiddah, to Henderson, 22 August 1929, enclosing Jiddah Report for 1–31 July 1929.
18. FO/371/13728, E6289/94/91, Bond to Henderson, 8 November 1929, enclosing Jiddah Report for 1–31 October 1929.
19. Al-Ruwayshid, *safhah mushriqah*, pp. 65–6; Muhammad Rifʿat al-Mahami, *asad al-jazirah qal li* (arranged and annotated by Ḥamad b. Nasir al-Dukhayyal; 2nd ed.; Riyadh: maktabat al-malik ʿabd al-ʿaziz al-ʿammah, 1419/1999), p. 176.
20. The adviser left Saudi Arabia in May 1933 and died in the Netherlands on 7 July. FO/371/16857/E4704, Calvert, Jiddah, to Sir John Simon, 29 July 1933. Commenting on his departure, the British minister, Andrew Ryan, remarked that "It was to be foreseen that no adviser could reorganise the finances of this country in a year, least of all in a year so inauspicious as one beginning in April 1932, when they were already in a desperate condition and the whole world as well was in a mess." FO/371/16867/E3133, Ryan to Simon, 20 May 1933.
21. Ministry of Finance and National Economy, *al-tarikh al-iqtisadi*, pp. 43 and 94–6. The citation for the expenditures is Muhammad al-Qahtani, "The Political and Administrative Role for Planning and Budgeting in the Kingdom of Saudi Arabia: Adaptation to Rapid Changes" (Ph.D. Dissertation, University of North Texas, 1989), p. 83.
22. Ministry of Finance and National Economy, *al-tarikh al-iqtisadi*, pp. 38–9.
23. Carlo Alfonso Nallino, ed. by Maria Nallino, *Raccolta di scritti editi e inediti*; Vol. 1: L'Arabia Saʿudiana (Rome: Istituto per l'Oriente, 1939), pp. 26–7.
24. Ministry of Finance and National Economy, *al-tarikh al-iqtisadi*, p. 43.
25. Shaykh ʿAbdullah al-Sulaiman Papers, privately held, Jiddah, Miscellaneous Correspondence, Shaykh ʿAbdullah al-Sulaiman to Shaykh Hamad al-Sulaiman, n.d. (c.1931–2).
26. FO/371/12243/E365, Perry, for Comptroller General, Department of the Treasury, to FO, 12 January 1927.
27. FO/371/12250/E3204, Jiddah Report for 1–30 June 1927.
28. FO/371/12250, E5083/644/91, Jiddah Report for 28 September–31 October 1927. Ottoman currency was based on the Ottoman gold pound divided into 100 gold

piasters. The Ottoman gold pound was slightly less in value than the English gold pound, which superseded the former as the basis for the value of the Saudi currency. Unfortunately, the Saudi *riyal* fluctuated widely through the 1930s in its value vis-à-vis the gold pound. FO/371/20063/E2106, Ryan to Eden, 29 March 1936.

29. FO/371/13010, E3901, Stonehewer Bird to the British High Commissioner in Iraq, 19 July 1928.
30. Kingdom of Saudi Arabia, Ministry of Finance, *mu'assasat al-naqd al-'arabi al-sa'udi* (Makkah: matbu'at al-hukumah, 1371/1952). A detailed report on the monetary history of the kingdom is to be found in United States, National Archives and Records Administration, Department of State General Records, RG59, 890f.002/7-2546, J. Rives Childs, US Minister in Jiddah, to State, "Some Monetary Notes on Saudi Arabia," 30 July 1946.
31. FO/371/13010, E994/484/91, Stonehewer Bird to Chamberlain, 1 February 1928, enclosing Jiddah Report for 1–31 January 1928. Presumably the mint responsible was the Mint Birmingham Ltd., not the Royal Mint, as was stated in a British inquiry about a 1936 order for new *riyal* coins similar to the Indian rupee. FO/371/20061/E1682, Herbert Brittain, Treasury, to G.W. Rendel, FO, 27 March 1936.
32. FO/371/13010, E5700/484/91, Stonehewer Bird to Chamberlain, 1 November 1928, enclosing Jiddah Report for 1–31 October 1928. A summary of the new regulations was reported in FO/371/13010, E614, Stonehewer Bird to the Secretary of State, 20 January 1928.
33. FO/371/13010, E3901, Stonehewer Bird to the British High Commissioner in Iraq, 19 July 1928.
34. FO/371/20063/E5458, Calvert to Eden, 26 June 1936, enclosing "Economic Survey of Saudi Arabia."
35. FO/371/20064/E1538; Annual Report on Saudi Arabia. Another currency, although rare, in circulation in al-Ahsa' before unification was the *tawilah*, equal to 1/150th of the Maria Theresa dollar. Shaped like the letter V, it derived from the Persian *larin*. Riyadh Chamber of Commerce and Industry, Research Department, *al-iqtisad al-sa'udi bayna al-madi wal-ḥadir* (Riyadh: n.d.), p. 70.
36. FO/371/20063/E5458, Calvert to Eden, 26 June 1936, enclosing "Economic Survey of Saudi Arabia."
37. FO/371/13727/E5605, British Agency, Jiddah, to FO, tel. 159 of 30 October 1929.
38. FO/371/13728, E6289/94/91, Bond to Henderson, 8 November 1929, enclosing Jiddah Report for 1–31 October 1929.
39. FO/371/16024, E2304, translation of an extract from *Umm al-Qura* of 15 January 1932, enclosed in the Jiddah Report for January–March 1932.
40. Remarks by the former mayor of Riyadh, 'Abdullah al-'Ali al-Nu'aym, at an appreciation of Shaykh 'Abdullah al-Sulayman in 'Unayzah, *Paris Najd*, No. 13 (1/1/1431H), p. 92.
41. FO/371/15299/E6307, translation of extract from *Umm al-Qura*, No. 364, 24/7/1350/4 December 1931. See also Ministry of Finance and National Economy, *al-tarikh al-iqtisadi*, pp. 42–3.
42. FO/371/15299/E6307, translation of extract from *Umm al-Qura*, No. 363, 17 Rajab 1350/27 November 1931.
43. Al-Ruwayshid, *safhah mushriqah*, pp. 67–8.
44. Ministry of Finance and National Economy, *al-tarikh al-iqtisadi*, p. 43.
45. FO/371/20063/E5458, Calvert to Eden, 26 June 1936, enclosing "Economic Survey of Saudi Arabia."

46. FO/371/15298/E4167, Ryan to Henderson, 12 July 1931.
47. Gerald De Gaury, "Memories and Impressions of the Arabia of Ibn Saud," in R.B. Serjeant and R.L. Bidwell, ed., *Arabian Studies*, No. 2 (London: Hurst, 1975), p. 24.
48. Nallino, *Raccolta di scritti*, p. 27.
49. Karl S. Twitchell, *Saudi Arabia* (3rd ed.; Princeton: Princeton University Press, 1958), p. 213.
50. Muhammad ʿAli al-Maghrabi, *aʿlam al-Hijaz fi al-qarn al-rabiʿ ʿashar, 1301–1400h/1883–1980m* (2nd ed., 1405/1985), pp. 115–16.
51. FO/371/15289/E4180, Jiddah Report for May–June 1931.
52. FO/371/15289/E4180, Jiddah Report for May–June 1931; FO/371/15299/E3889, Ryan to Henderson, 1 July 1931.
53. FO/371/15289, E6029, Jiddah Report for September–October 1931.
54. The British Legation ascribed even this partial payment to an entreaty to Fu'ad Hamza and the absence of al-Sulayman in Najd. FO/371/15289, E6029, Jiddah Report for September–October 1931.
55. FO/371/15298/E5141, C.G. Hope–Gill, Jiddah to the Marquess of Reading, 30 September 1931.
56. FO/371/15298/E5141, Hope–Gill to the Marquess of Reading, 30 September 1931.
57. FO/371/15289, E6029, Jiddah Report for September–October 1931; FO/371/15299/E5799, Hope–Gill to the Marquess of Reading, 2 November 1931.
58. FO/371/15299/E5807, Hope–Gill to Sir John Simon, FO, 9 November 1931.
59. FO/371/15299/E4911, Hope–Gill to the Marquess of Reading, 9 September 1931. Nevertheless, the Saudi government did not trust the Soviet Union. As an internal intelligence report noted, "The Soviets do not give money to anyone till they know you are really loyal to them and you follow their policy and ideas. They also want to sell their products on the one hand, and ruin the relationship with the neighboring countries on the other. The transaction between Russia and the government of Najd and al-Hijaz ended in a misunderstanding that the Russians took advantage of and succeeded in selling the fuel for a big profit." Shaykh ʿAbdullah al-Sulaiman Papers, privately held, Jiddah, Intelligence Summary, Jiddah, 19 Rajab, 1350/25 February 1932.
60. FO/371/16024/E4944, Jiddah Report for July–August 1932. ʿAbdullah al-Sulayman also employed a relative, Muhammad, as director of the condensers at Jiddah. FO/371/16878/E3745, Ryan to Simon, 7 October 1933, enclosing "Personalities in Arabia." Hamad al-Sulayman was utilized in a number of ways. As examples, he was part of the delegation to treat with Imam Yahya of Yemen before the two countries went to war and he was chosen to be a Saudi delegate for the 1935 conference on Bahraini transit dues. FO/371/19004/E1383, Ryan to FO, tel. of 28 February 1935. Amongst other officials in the ministry, Muhammad Tawil served as the financial director of the Eastern Province in the 1930s but was replaced by a new director of finance, ʿAbdullah Qadi, in April 1936. FO/371/20062, Jiddah Report for April 1936; Jiddah Report for August 1936.
61. FO/371/16875/E904, Ryan to Simon, 1 February 1933.
62. FO/371/20842/E7045, Jiddah Report, October 1937.
63. R/15/2/312, Bahrain Intelligence Report, 15 November 1936.
64. Al-Muslim, *Rijal min al-Qaṣim*, p. 44.
65. Georgetown University Library, Special Collections Division, William E. Mulligan Papers, Box 9, Folder 1.

66. FO/371/14460, E3036/92/91, Bond to Henderson, 3 May 1930, enclosing Jiddah Report for 1–30 April 1930.
67. FO/371/15289/E81, Jiddah Report for September, October, November 1930. But when the time came due for repayment in 1931 of the arms debt, the king directly and through Yusuf Yasin begged for another year's grace, arguing it was better to be indebted to the British government than to others. See the correspondence in FO/371/15297.
68. FO/371/20063/E5458, Calvert to Eden, 26 June 1936, enclosing "Economic Survey of Saudi Arabia."
69. FO/371/15289/E528, Ryan to FO, 17 January 1931, enclosing Jiddah Report for December 1930.
70. Elizabeth Monroe, *Philby of Arabia* (London: Faber and Faber, 1973), p. 173. The king instructed his finance minister in October 1945 to repay all the debts to Sharqieh and al-Sulayman did so using 400 gold pieces worth £4 apiece. *Ibid.*, p. 239.
71. *Ibid.*, pp. 202–3. See the discussion of the search for oil and signing of a concession, including Philby's role, in the following chapter.
72. Shaykh ʿAbdullah al-Sulaiman Papers, privately held, Jiddah, Shaykh ʿAbdullah al-Sulaiman Correspondence with King ʿAbd al-ʿAziz, Letters 1 and 3, Shaykh ʿAbdullah to King ʿAbd al-ʿAziz, 22 Ramadan 1349/9 February 1931.
73. FO/371/15289E/2221, Jiddah Report for January–February 1931; FO/371/15299/E2064, Ryan to Henderson, 23 March 1931.
74. FO/371/15299/E3024, Ryan to Henderson, 15 May 1931.
75. FO/371/15289/E3462, Jiddah Report for March–April 1931.
76. FO/371/15289/E4180, Jiddah Report for May–June 1931. About this time, Ibn Saʿud sent ʿAbd al-Rahman al-Qusaybi to London to approach British banks, including the Eastern Bank and the Ottoman Bank. FO/371/15299/E3931, C.M.J. Jones, FO memorandum, 24 July 1931. Having been unable to raise any British interest, al-Qusaybi was reported by the Hijaz–Najd representative in London, Hafiz Wahba, to have gone on to the Netherlands where a Dutch bank was interested. FO/371/15299/E4576, G.W. Rendel, FO Memorandum, 4 September 1931.
77. FO/371/15299/E4677, Hope–Gill to the Marquess of Reading, 29 August 1931
78. FO/371/16012/E166, Ryan to Simon, 29 December 1931.
79. FO/371/20063/E5458, Calvert to Eden, 26 June 1936, enclosing "Economic Survey of Saudi Arabia."
80. FO/371/16024/E1197, Jiddah Report for November–December 1931. Other budget items included frontier forces, headquarters of justice and *sharīʿah* courts, communications and transports, viceroy's office and sections, Legislative Council and administrative councils, Ministry for Foreign Affairs and sections, public health and quarantines, water condensers and sections, public Department of Education, Customs Department and sections, Finance Departments, government press, committees of virtue, miscellaneous allotments, posts, telegraphs, wireless, and telephones, and the two holy sanctuaries and *awqaf*. *Ibid.*
81. FO/371/16024, E2304, Jiddah Report for January–March 1932.
82. *Ibid.*
83. FO/371/16024, E3903, Jiddah Report for May–June 1932.
84. *Ibid.*
85. Shaykh ʿAbdullah al-Sulaiman Papers, privately held, Jiddah, Intelligence Summary, Jiddah, 19 Rajab 1350/25 February 1932.

86. The breakdown of debts was put at £50,000 to the Poles, £25,000 to the al-Qusaybis in Bahrain, £30,000 to the Soviets, £15,000 to the Shell Company, £15,000 to Standard Oil, £15,000 to Marconi, £10,000 to the Government of India, £10,000 to German firms, £5,000 to the Nederlandische Handel-Maatschappij (Netherlands Trading Society), £2,500 to the Eastern Telegraph Company, and £1,700 to the British government. FO/371/16024, E6396, Jiddah Report for September–October 1932.
87. FO/371/20063/E5458, Calvert to Eden, 26 June 1936, enclosing "Economic Survey of Saudi Arabia." Over the years, a certain amount of speculation about the possibility of reviving the al-Hijaz Railway, constructed by the Ottomans to al-Madinah before World War I, persisted although nothing concrete came of the talk. See, for example, the discussion in FO/371/20843. For more details on the railway, see James Nicholson, *The Hejaz Railway* (London: Stacey International; Riyadh: Al Turath, 2005).
88. FO371/16875/E902, Jiddah Situation Report, 1–31 January 1933.
89. FO/371/16857/E4704, Calvert to Simon, 29 July 1933.
90. FO/371/16868/E7969, Calvert to Simon, 5 December 1933.
91. FO/371/16875/E3469, Jiddah Situation Report for May 1933.
92. FO/371/16868/E5923, note by K.R. Johnstone, 11 September 1933 {sic}, on minute by Andrew Ryan, 4 October 1933, on his conversation with Philby.
93. FO/371/16868/E3661, G. Ogilvie-Forbes, Baghdad, to Sir Andrew Ryan, Jiddah, 19 June 1933, and Ryan's reply (E3969).
94. FO/371/16857/E4704, Calvert to Simon, 29 July 1933.
95. FO/371/16867/E743, Chancery, Jiddah, to FO, 6 January 1933; FO/371/16868/E6951, Calvert to FO, tel. 196, 15 November 1933. See FO/371/16867 and FO/371/16868 for further British internal discussion of how to deal with this outstanding debt and the inability of the Saudi government to repay it. Philby, in a conversation with the British minister, estimated the total Saudi government debt at about £150,000 gold, of which debt to his own concerns constituted about £50,000 gold. Furthermore, Philby was disappointed that the government was not using any of the payments from Standard Oil of California against these debts. FO/371/16868/E5923, minute by Andrew Ryan, 4 October 1933. The manager of the Dutch Bank confirmed his belief that the king was keeping the bulk of the £35,000 in gold received from the oil company in reserve. Calvert to FO, *ibid.*
96. FO/371/17941/E3126, Ryan to FO, 28 April 1934, enclosing "Annual Report for Saudi Arabia, 1933."
97. FO/371/20063/E5458, Calvert to Eden, 26 June 1936, enclosing "Economic Survey of Saudi Arabia."
98. FO/371/17921/E7799, Calver to Simon, 11 December 1934.
99. FO/371/14468/E6755, Hope-Gill to Fu'ad Bey Hamza, Acting Minister of Foreign Affairs, 4 November 1930; Fu'ad Hamza to Hope-Gill, 28.6.1349/19 November 1930; Hope-Gill to Fu'ad Hamza, 29 November 1930. This debt was eventually settled up to the end of December 1930 although other debts remained outstanding. FO/371/14484/E6987. A detailed background précis on telegraphs in the kingdom is contained in FO/371/19000/E1463, "Note on the position in regard to the External Telegraphic Communications of Saudi Arabia," British Legation, Jiddah, 15 February 1935. Comment on and the text of a new agreement on the Jiddah–Port Sudan cable are contained in FO/371/19000/E2955, Ryan to Simon, 18 April 1935.

100. FO/371/19014/E557, Jiddah Report for December 1934.
101. FO/371/19019/E3607, Ryan to Simon, 18 May 1935, "Saudi Arabia Annual Report, 1934."
102. FO/371/20064, E1538/1538/25, Ryan to Mr. Eden, FO, 29 February 1936, "Saudi Arabia Annual Report, 1935."
103. FO/371/17935/E5333, Jiddah Report for July 1934.
104. FO/371/19002/E5154, Calvert to FO, 4 August 1935, enclosing "Report on 1935 Pilgrimage to the Hejaz."
105. FO/371/20063/E5458, Calvert to Eden, 26 June 1936, enclosing "Economic Survey of Saudi Arabia."
106. Kermit Roosevelt, *Arabs, Oil, and History: The Story of the Middle East* (New York: Harper, 1949), p. 162.
107. L/P&S/12/2085, E1810/1810/25, Sir R. Bullard to Viscount Halifax, 12 February 1939, "Annual Report on Saudi Arabia for 1938."
108. FO/371/17935/E5976, Jiddah Report for August 1934.
109. FO/371/17935/E6983, Jiddah Report for October 1934.
110. FO/371/20063/E5458, Calvert to Eden, 26 June 1936, enclosing "Economic Survey of Saudi Arabia."
111. Shaykh ʿAbdullah al-Sulaiman Papers, privately held, Jiddah, Shaykh ʿAbdullah al-Sulaiman Correspondence with King ʿAbd al-ʿAziz, King ʿAbd al-ʿAziz to California Arabian Standard Oil Company, 25 Dhu al-Hijjah 1354/20 March 1936.
112. FO/371/24585/E2988, Stonehewer Bird to FO, 28 September 1940, enclosing "Annual Report on the Hejaz Pilgrimage."
113. FO/371/20841/E1634, Jiddah Report for February 1937; FO/371/20839/E1859, Bullard to Eden, 11 March 1937; *ibid.*, E2425, Bullard to Eden, 18 April 1937.
114. FO/371/21908/E2338, Bullard to Viscount Halifax, 26 March 1938, enclosing "Saudi Arabia Annual Report, 1937." One bright note was the promise to repay a seven-year-old debt of £30,000 to the Soviet Union, although the Soviet minister was not sanguine about it actually happening. FO/371/21908/E2778, Bullard to Viscount Halifax, 17 April 1938, enclosing "Economic Report, Saudi Arabia 1937."
115. FO/371/21908/E2778, Bullard to Viscount Halifax, 17 April 1938, enclosing "Economic Report, Saudi Arabia 1937."
116. FO/371/23268/E2928, "Saudi Arabia Annual Report, Economic (A), for 1938."
117. R/15/2/422; Lenahan, Jiddah, to Ohliger, ARAMCO, tel. 162 of 30 December 1938, copied to Edward Skinner, San Francisco. The telegram had been intercepted by British censors and the contents reported by the Political Agent, Bahrain, to the Political Resident, 4 January 1940.
118. FO/371/23268/E3695, Bullard to FO, tel. no. 5 saving of 25 April 1939.
119. FO/371/23271/E8088, Jiddah Report for November 1939.
120. L/P&S/12/2085, E/1293/1293/25, S.R. Jordan to Anthony Eden, 15 February 1944, "Annual Report on Saudi Arabia for 1943."
121. L/P&S/12/2085, E/952/952/25, Jordan to Eden, 27 January 1945, "Annual Report on Saudi Arabia for 1944." At the same time, the king replaced Najib Salihah as director of mines and public works with ʿIzz al-Din Shawa. *Ibid.*
122. L/P&S/12/2085, E/952/952/25, Jordan to Eden, 27 January 1945, "Annual Report on Saudi Arabia for 1944." Additional assistance included the British provision of £10,000 a month to cover the cost of Saudi missions abroad and American provision of 10 million *riyal*s on credit Lend–Lease. These amounts were in addition to the subsidy of £450,000 and gift of 200,000 sovereigns paid at the beginning of the year. *Ibid.*

3 THE 1933 OIL CONCESSION AND OIL AFFAIRS TO WORLD WAR II

1. This brief survey has been drawn largely from Daniel Yergin, *The Prize: The Epic Quest for Oil, Money, and Power* (New York: Simon & Schuster, 1991); Stephen Longrigg, *Oil in the Middle East: Its Discovery and Development* (3rd ed.; London: Oxford University Press, for the Royal Institute of International Affairs, 1968); and H. St.J. B. Philby, *Arabian Oil Ventures* (Washington: Middle East Institute, 1964).
2. Archibald H.T. Chisholm, *The First Kuwaiti Oil Concession Agreement: A Record of the Negotiations, 1911–1934* (London: Frank Cass, 1975), pp. 5–6 and 93–5n15. Additional material on Holmes is drawn from his biography by Aileen Keating, *Mirage: Power, Politics, and the Hidden History of Arabian Oil* (Amherst, NY: Prometheus Books, 2005).
3. Chisholm, *The First Kuwaiti Oil Concession*, pp. 5–6 and 93–5n15; Keating, *Mirage*, p. 57. E&GS was incorporated in London on 6 August 1920 with an authorized capital of £50,300 and with principal shareholders being the Chartered and General Exploration and Finance Company Ltd., Allen and Hanburys Ltd. (Pharmaceutical Chemists), and Adeni merchant B.M. Messa. The first directors were Edmund Davis, F.W. Gamble, E.W. Janson, P.C. Tarbutt, and J.E.H. Lomas. According to the initial directors' report, the company first opened an office in Aden along with a chemist's and druggist's business. Chisholm, *The First Kuwaiti Oil Concession*, p. 95n16. Janson was the first chairman of the Board, with William Pocock, secretary. Janson's son Rex T. Janson subsequently became an officer of the syndicate. On Rex T. Janson's death in 1962, his son Jonathan became chairman of the board. E&GS sold its share of Bahrain royalties to Berry-Wiggins and Company in 1972 and changed its name to Cavandish Land Company. University of Wyoming, American Heritage Center, Thomas Edward Ward Papers, Box 3; University of Utah, J. Willard Marriott Library Special Collections, Wallace Earle Stegner Papers, Box 86, Folder 9. Stegner wrote of Holmes that "He was on the trail of a big idea very early, but as it happened, arrived just a little too early and in not quite the right way." Wallace Stegner, *Discovery! The Search for Arabian Oil* (Beirut: Middle East Export Press, 1971; reprinted Vista, CA: Selwa Press, 2007), p. 7.
4. Keating, *Mirage*, pp. 97–8.
5. Chisholm, *The First Kuwaiti Oil Concession*, pp. 5–6; various correspondence in British Library, Oriental and India Office Collection, Persian Gulf Political Residency Records, R/15/1/559 and R/15/2/74. The question of whether ʿAbdullah al-Sulayman was involved in the negotiations even at this early date is undetermined, although one contemporary was adamant that he was. University of Essex interview with Salih b. Shilhub (c. 1982).
6. Reproduced from Chisholm, *The First Kuwaiti Oil Concession*, p. 98n21.
7. United Kingdom, National Archives, Kew, Foreign Office (FO) Records, Political Department, General Correspondence, FO/371/16871/E3106; "Petroleum in Sa'udi Arabia," FO memorandum by Sir Andrew Ryan, Jiddah, 16 May 1933. Holmes contended that the failure to make the payments of £3,000 to Ibn Saʿud were due to the latter being at war and impossible to reach. Ward Papers, Holmes to Thomas Ward, 23 September 1926.
8. Stegner Papers, Box 86, Folder 19, Eastern and General Syndicate to Standard Oil of California, 8 May 1933.
9. Ward Papers, Box 3, Holmes to Ward, 23 September 1926. Holmes added that there were also some interests in the Mosul area but nothing definite had been arranged yet. *Ibid.*

10. Ward Papers, Box 3, H.T. Adams, Secretary, Eastern and General Syndicate, to Thomas Ward, 9 June 1927.
11. Ward Papers, Box 3, Adams to Ward, 14 September 1927.
12. Ward Papers, Box 3, Adams to Ward, 15 November 1929.
13. Stegner, *Discovery!*, p. 9.
14. FO/371/13729/E281, Williams, Colonial Office, to Petroleum Department, Board of Trade, 12 January 1929, enclosing Eastern and General Syndicate to the Colonial Office, 19 December 1928; FO/371/13730/E1697, untitled FO memorandum by "L. O.", 3 April 1929, enclosing memorandum by US chargé d'affaires Atherton 3 April 1929; "Note of meeting of Inter-departmental Committee on Tuesday, 7th May, 1929, to consider the policy of H.M. Government in regard to the control of companies prospecting for oil on Crown Lands in the Colonies," Petroleum Department; "Bahrein Oil Concession and U.S. Interests," FO memorandum by G.W. Rendel, 30 May 1929. The interdepartmental meeting based its conclusions on a letter from Shaykh ʿIsa b. ʿAli Al Khalifah, Ruler of Bahrain, to Major A.P. Trevor, Political Agent, Bahrain, 18 Jumada al-Thani 1332/14 May 1914 (copy in FO/371/13730), which merely states that Shaykh ʿIsa would inform the Political Agent, Bahrain, about any possibilities regarding oil in his territory and would not make any arrangements for exploration without the approval of the British government.
15. FO/371/13731/E6076, Williams, Colonial Office, to FO, 21 November 1929, enclosing F.A. Ledvy, Eastern Gulf Oil Company, to Eastern and General Syndicate, 24 October 1929; see also the correspondence between the Colonial Office and Eastern and General Syndicate in FO/371/14454/E726. This led in subsequent years to a rather confusing situation during the competition for a Saudi Arabian concession. Frank Holmes served as the chief representative of the Bahrain Petroleum Company (BAPCO), owned by SOCAL, at the insistence of the British government, but he was also representing E&GS in a competing bid for a Saudi concession. FO/371/16871/E3106, "Petroleum in Sa'udi Arabia," memorandum by Sir Andrew Ryan, Jiddah, 16 May 1933. E&GS reappeared at the beginning of 1934 seeking a concession for the Kuwait–Saudi Neutral Zone, in partnership with ʿAbd al-Ghani Ydlibi. FO/371/17918/E313, Sir Andrew Ryan to FO, tel. no. 4 of 13 January 1934. Ydlibi was a naturalized British Syrian merchant based in Manchester. FO/371/17934/E1101, Jiddah Report for January 1934. It was also suggested that Saudi official Fu'ad Bey Hamza (of Egyptian origin) had commercial connections with Ydlibi and his partners in this concession. FO/371/17919/E6145; Memorandum by Sir Andrew Ryan, 2 October 1934.
16. FO/371/16870/E965, E.H.C. Elkington, APOC Abadan Refinery, to Col. Fowle, 3 January 1933. Elkington also speculated that it might be best to approach the king's representative in Kuwait as rival Frank Holmes was already dealing with the king's Bahrain representative. *Ibid.*
17. FO/371/16870/E1498, Ryan to C.F.A. Warner, FO, 28 February 1933.
18. Ward Papers, Box 3, Frank Holmes to Ibn Saʿud, 23 December 1927. In his reply, Ibn Saʿud equivocated on the question of an audience. *Ibid.*; translation of Ibn Saʿud to Holmes, 20 Rajab 1346/16 January 1928.
19. Stegner Papers, Box 84, Folder 22, Stegner interview with Fred Davies, President of the Board, Dhahran, 21 November 1955; *ibid.*, Box 86, Folder 9, "Negotiation of the Concession—Chronology." Hafiz Wahba, Ibn Saʿud's minister in London, finally wrote to Holmes on 28 November 1930 conveying Ibn Saʿud's regrets

that he could not allow geologists to visit Saudi Arabia at that time. *Ibid.*, Chronology.

20. Stegner papers, Box 86, Folder 19, unsigned memorandum of 5 September 1930 found in ARAMCO files and ascribed by Stegner to Lombardi.
21. Stegner Papers, Box 86, Folder 9, "Negotiation of the Concession—Chronology."
22. H. St.J. B. Philby, *Saudi Arabia* (London: Ernest Benn, 1955; reprinted Beirut: Librairie du Liban, 1968), pp. 329–30.
23. C.B. Squire, "Charles Richard Crane." *Middle East Forum* (American University of Beirut), Vol. 30, Nos. 10–11 (October–November 1955), pp. 8–12 and 34–8. As Crane spoke no Arabic, he frequently took George Antonius along as his translator and Crane's Institute of Current World Affairs financially supported the writing of Antonius' *Arab Awakening*. Crane died in 1939. Among his other philanthropic interests in the Middle East were payment of the daily bread bill of the Russian Orthodox convent in Jerusalem until his death, financing the work of John Whittemore in restoring the St. Sophia mosque in Istanbul, and financially supporting Roberts College in Istanbul. *Ibid.*
24. FO/371/12250/E644, Jiddah Report for 1–31 December 1926. Ibn Saʿud's translator contends that Crane first contacted Ibn Saʿud by cabling "I am interested in Arabia and desire to meet Your Majesty if permitted." Ibn Saʿud was said to have no idea who Crane was and therefore not interested in a meeting. He instructed a reply saying, "The time is not propitious as His Majesty is busy with the approaching hajj season and internal affairs." Mohammed Almana, *Arabia Unified: A Portrait of Ibn Saud* (London: Hutchinson Benham, 1980; rev. ed., 1982), p. 218. According to this account, Crane was undeterred and attempted to drive to Najd from Basra, Iraq, but his party was attacked by the Ikhwan as they passed through Kuwaiti territory. John Van Ess, an American missionary in Basra accompanying Crane, was killed. His perseverance impressed the king, who wrote to him in Cairo and agreed to meet him in Jiddah in February 1931. *Ibid.*, p. 219. Other accounts tell a slightly different story.
25. Twitchell was an engineer and a geologist, with degrees from the Kingston School of Mines in Ontario and work experience with mining companies first in the United States and later Europe, Africa, South America, and the Middle East. Princeton University, Seeley Mudd Manuscript Library, "Karl S. Twitchell Papers, 19111967: Finding Aid," MC171, http://arks.princeton.edu/ark:/88435/pr76f3413.
26. Twitchell Papers, Box 11, Folder 7, "Summary of Gifts of Chas. R. Crane Administered by K.S. Twitchell," manuscript written by Twitchell, n.d. but about 1938.
27. FO/371/13718, E144, R.S. Champion, Aden, to Colonial Office, 7 December 1928, enclosing Aden Political Intelligence Summary.
28. Twitchell Papers, Box 5, Folder 4, Twitchell to King Ibn Saʿud, 14 November 1927. This earlier episode does not seem to have generated much response from the Saudi ruler since Twitchell does not mention it in his book, which begins instead with the 1930–1 activities. Twitchell, *Saudi Arabia*, pp. 211–12.
29. FO/371/15289E/2221; Jiddah Report for January–February 1931; FO/371/15297/E1601; Sir Andrew Ryan, Jiddah, to A. Henderson, 6 March 1931. During this visit, Ibn Saʿud presented Crane with three Arabian horses. The background of these gifts and of the horses was outlined in a letter from Fawzan El-Sabak of the Saudi Ministry of Foreign Affairs to Karl Twitchell, 20 August 1931, in Twitchell Papers, Box 19, Folder 5.

30. Twitchell Papers, Box 5, Folder 4, Twitchell to King Ibn Sa'ud, 20 April 1931; Twitchell, *Saudi Arabia*, pp. 211–12. Saudi Arabia's search for water and Twitchell's role is also discussed in Toby Craig Jones, *Desert Kingdom: How Oil and Water Forged Modern Saudi Arabia* (Cambridge, MA: Harvard University Press, 2010), particularly Ch. 2, "Imperial Geology."
31. Twitchell Papers, Box 6, Folder 2, Twitchell, Jiddah, to Crane, Paris, 14 May 1931; enclosing Saudi Reports 1 and 2. Initially, Twitchell dealt with "Halid Bey, the King's representative."
32. FO/371/15289/E3462, Jiddah Report for March–April 1931. Crane wrote to the king, saying: "Greetings I'm taking liberty of sending Twitchell to test drill for water and gold gravel subject to your approval but entirely my expense so asking you defer general development program approximately six months as I do not wish any connection with subsequent commercial exploitation stop writing fully Twitchell will arrive October with empire driller salaams." Twitchell Papers, Box 5, Folder 4, copy of undated telegram.
33. FO/371/15289/E4180, Jiddah Report for May–June 1931; FO/371/15300/E3536, translation from *Umm al-Qura*, No. 355, 5 May 1931. A further lengthy summary of a later account in *Umm al-Qura* of 28 August 1931 is found in FO/371/15300/ E5033, C.G. Hope-Gills, Jiddah, to Secretary of State for Foreign Affairs, 12 September 1931.
34. FO/371/15300/E3536, Ryan to Secretary of State for Foreign Affairs, 16 June 1931.
35. Twitchell Papers, Box 6, Folder 2, Twitchell, Jiddah, to Crane, Paris, 18 May 1931, Letter No. 11; Twitchell to Crane, 2 June 1931, Letter No. 12.
36. Twitchell Papers, Box 11, Folder 7, "Summary of Gifts of Chas. R. Crane Administered by K.S. Twitchell."
37. Twitchell Papers, Box 5, Folder 4, Twitchell to King Ibn Sa'ud, 5 Muharram 1350/24 May 1931.
38. Twitchell, *Saudi Arabia*, p. 214.
39. Twitchell Papers, Box 5, Folder 4, Twitchell to King Ibn Sa'ud, 5 Muharram 1350/24 May 1931.
40. Twitchell Papers, Box 19, Folder 5, translation of 'Abdullah al-Sulayman al-Hamdan to Charles Crane, 6 Rabi' al-Awwal 1350/21 July 1931.
41. Twitchell Papers, Box 19, Folder 5, translation of 'Abdullah al-Sulayman al-Hamdan to Karl Twitchell, n.d. but late July 1931. Al-Sulayman's letter was in reply to Twitchell's letter to him of 15 July 1931. *Ibid.*
42. FO/371/15300/E5034, Hope-Gills to Secretary of State for Foreign Affairs, 12 September 1931, quoting from *Umm al-Qura* of 31 July 1931. Hope-Gills also notes that Twitchell was on his way to New York to buy the necessary equipment, as provided in a contract signed with al-Sulayman.
43. FO/371/15300/E6203, G.W.F., Jiddah, memorandum of 25 November 1931.
44. Twitchell Papers, Box 5, Folder 4, Twitchell to Ibn Sa'ud, 20 October 1931.
45. Twitchell Papers, Box 5, Folder 4, Twitchell to Ibn Sa'ud, 20 October 1931 (additional letter).
46. FO/371/16024/E2304, Jiddah Report for January–March 1932.
47. Twitchell Papers, Box 5, Folder 4, 'Abd al-'Aziz b. 'Abd al-Rahman al-Faysal to Charles Crane, 10 Ramadan 1350/18 January 1932. Mohammed Almana contends that Ibn Sa'ud instructed him to give a copy of Twitchell's report on oil prospects to Amir Faysal who then handed it to British authorities during his trip to the UK. Shortly afterwards, the British mission in Jiddah contacted the king to thank him for the report but that HMG was not interested. Almana, *Arabia Unified*, p. 221.

48. Twitchell, *Saudi Arabia*, p. 219. According to Almana, Twitchell was asked to form a national oil company, for which he would receive a 10 percent share. Upon his refusal, the offer was upped to 15 percent and then 20 percent before it was realized that Twitchell actually had no interest in the venture. Almana, *Arabia Unified*, p. 222.
49. Twitchell Papers, Box 5, Folder 4, ʿAbd al-ʿAziz b. ʿAbd al-Rahman al-Faysal to Charles Crane, 28 Jumada al-Thani 1350/8 November 1931.
50. Twitchell Papers, Box 5, Folder 4, Twitchell, "Notes for Sheikh Abdullah Suleiman," 5 March 1932.
51. FO/371/16024, E3903; Jiddah Report for May–June 1932.
52. Twitchell Papers, Box 11, Folder 7, "Summary of Gifts of Chas. R. Crane Administered by K.S. Twitchell," manuscript written by Twitchell, n.d. but about 1938. As in the case of the oil concession later, Crane was offered free participation in the Saudi Arabian Mining Syndicate concession but refused on the grounds that "he wished no connection in any way in any commercial enterprise founded on his philanthropy." *Ibid.* The assertion is repeated in Twitchell, *Saudi Arabia*, p. 219. The Saudi government published the mineral concession agreement in Kingdom of Saudi Arabia, Ministry of Finance, *Ittifaqat sharikat istithmar al-bitrul wa-mustakhrajatihi wal-maʿadin* (1st ed., 1359/1940–1).
53. FO/371/17935/E4334, Jiddah Report for May 1934; FO/371/17941/E4624, Ryan to Simon, 2 July 1934.
54. FO/371/19014/E557, Jiddah Report for December 1934.
55. FO/371/17935/E6983, Jiddah Report for October 1934.
56. Twitchell Papers, Box 10, Folder 6, Twitchell to John F. Park, General Manager, SAMS, Mahd al-Dhahb, 22 August 1940.
57. Twitchell Papers, Box 18, Folder 4, Twitchell to ʿAbdullah al-Sulayman, 16 November 1953. Earlier improvements to the harbor by way of erecting beacons and laying down buoys had been carried out by SAMS under Twitchell's supervision in 1938, since SAMS would benefit the most after the construction of its pier outside the port. FO/371/23268/E161, "Saudi Arabia Annual Report, Economic (B), for 1938." Twitchell also asked for permission to bring in movies for the entertainment of Western employees at SAMS's Mahd al-Dhahab mine. In another aside, Twitchell was acquainted with the British military officer and political agent Gerald de Gaury and the two men reached an agreement in 1943 for Twitchell to act as de Gaury's agent for the American publication of the latter's books. One of these apparently was to be translated into Arabic by ʿAbdullah al-Turayqi, who later became the Saudi minister of oil. For the latter point, see Twitchell Papers, Box 11, Folder 8, typed note to Imprimerie Misr, 24 April 1943, signed by both de Gaury and Twitchell.
58. Twitchell, *Saudi Arabia*, pp. 216–17.
59. This paragraph is based on Stegner Papers, Box 86, Folder 9, "Negotiation of the Concession—Chronology."
60. Twitchell, *Saudi Arabia*, pp. 220–2. Daniel Yergin asserts that SOCAL had been interested in a concession for al-Ahsaʾ even before discovering oil in Bahrain. According to Yergin, Twitchell contacted SOCAL first, which was "immediately receptive." *The Prize*, p. 289.
61. Twitchell Papers, Box 11, Folder 4, M.E. Lombardi, Standard Oil Company of California, to Karl S. Twitchell, 10 January 1933. The agreement was transferred subsequently to the California Arabian Standard Oil Company on 9 April 1934. *Ibid.*

62. Twitchell Papers, Box 11, Folder 7, "Summary of Gifts of Chas. R. Crane Administered by K.S. Twitchell," manuscript written by Twitchell, n.d.
63. Stegner Papers, Box 86, Folder 9, "Negotiation of the Concession—Chronology."
64. FO/371/16870/E1498, Ryan to C.F.A. Warner, FO, 28 February 1933.
65. FO/371/16870/E1498, minute regarding letter of Ryan to Warner, 28 February 1933.
66. Stegner Papers, Box 86, Folder 9, "Negotiation of the Concession—Chronology."
67. FO/371/16870/E1615, Ryan to FO, tel. 55 of 26 March 1933. Ryan added that "Holmes has hitherto been believed to be distasteful to Ibn Saud" but offered no explanation for this observation. *Ibid.* The IPC representative was Major Stephen Longrigg, who had served previously in the Iraqi Ministry of the Interior and who arrived in Jiddah on 12 March. Longrigg told Ryan that IPC and APOC were working together, with APOC approaching King ʿAbd al-ʿAziz from the Gulf side and IPC via Jiddah. FO/371/16870/E1750, Ryan to Warner, 15 March 1933. Longrigg confirmed the king's distaste for Holmes, surmising that it was because the king had claimed payments from the previous concession that were never paid. *Ibid.* FO sleuthing turned up a telegram stating that the problem was due to the refusal of then-Sultan ʿAbd al-ʿAziz to alter a clerical error of a date in the concession and that the backers E&GS were not prepared to finance the concession until British diplomatic representation was present in the country. FO/371/16870/E1948, PRPG to the Colonial Office, tel. of 31 October 1925.
68. FO/371/16870/E1750, Ryan to Warner, 15 March 1933. Al-Sulayman generally was accompanied during these negotiations by Fu'ad Hamza, the Deputy Foreign Minister, and Yusuf Yasin, Ibn Saʿud's confidential secretary. "Hardheaded, smart, patient, tenacious, wary, they were bargainers worthy of anyone's steel, and Hamilton was handicapped in his negotiating by his ignorance of Arabic and of the Arab character and culture." Stegner, *Discovery!*, p. 21.
69. Stanford University, Hoover Institution Archives, Philip C. McConnell Papers, Box 2, "Historical background based on interview with Mr. M.E. LOMBARDI." (No other identification other than "CONFIDENTIAL".)
70. The acrimony between SOCAL and E&GS continued throughout the negotiations until the latter wrote SOCAL on 19 July 1933 breaking off relations with SOCAL. Stegner Papers, Box 86, Folder 9, "Negotiation of the Concession—Chronology."
71. Stegner Papers, Box 86, Folder 11, Hamilton to Holmes, 11 April 1933 (copy of original letter with notation "As originally written and handed to Holmes at Jedda").
72. Stegner, *Discovery*, p. 22. Almana indicates that ʿAbdullah al-Sulayman negotiated as the head of a committee that also included ʿAbdullah Muhammad al-Fadl and Hasan al-Qusaybi and the committee was lodged in Bayt al-Baghdadi in Jiddah. *Arabia Unified*, p. 223.
73. Stegner Papers, Box 84, Folder 22, Stegner interview with William Burleigh, Washington, DC, 30 November 1955.
74. FO/371/16870/E1792, Ryan to FO, tel. no. 3 (saving) of 22 March 1933; Elizabeth Monroe, *Philby of Arabia* (London: Faber and Faber, 1973), p. 205, citing her interview with Longrigg. Frank Holmes remained in the picture, reportedly preparing to visit Jiddah and King ʿAbd al-ʿAziz at the latter's invitation to discuss an oil concession. FO/371/16870/E1558, PRPG to the Colonial Office, tel. of 21 March 1933; FO/371/16870/E1792, minute by K.R. Johnstone (7 April 1933) on Ryan's telegram. Holmes did come to Jiddah but left after three days without seeing the king. It was supposed that his objective was only an oil concession in

the Saudi–Kuwaiti Neutral Zone. FO/371/16870/E1945, Ryan to FO, tel. of 12 April 1933; and FO/371/16871/E2172, Ryan to FO, tel. no. 6 (saving) of 11 April 1933. Ryan subsequently surmised that Holmes had left so suddenly because there was no prospect of a Neutral Zone concession and "He may also have discovered however that he was not persona grata for any purpose except apparently enlargement of field of competition for Hasa concession." FO/371/16871/E3073, Ryan to FO, tel. no. 10 (saving) of 1 June 1933. Twitchell had known Holmes from mining experiences in Abyssinia prior to both being introduced to Arabia. Keating, *Mirage*, p. 93.

75. Stegner Papers, Box 86, Folder 11, Stegner's synopses of letters by Philby to Hamilton on 14 and 17 March 1933.
76. FO/371/16871/E2172, Ryan to FO, tel. no. 6 (saving) of 11 April 1933.
77. "The general impression ... was that Hamilton was consciously bargaining for a prize of great value. I think he was bargaining all right but we should remember that he and people whom he knew intimately in Standard of California had been and were bargaining all over the world for concessions, many of which were and are extremely disappointing. He had been told to get a piece of real estate and he did his best to get it on the most favorable terms. Nevertheless, I am inclined to believe that if Longrigg could have had at his disposal an additional half-million or possibly even a quarter-million dollars, this concession might well have been held by IPC." Stegner Papers, Box 85, Folder 2, Tom Barger, ARAMCO Dhahran, to Stegner, 26 May 1958. This view was confirmed by ARAMCO's public relations department upon viewing the first draft of Stegner's book *Discovery!*. "[T]he present text makes it seem as though the early negotiators were a bunch of sharpies who through devious methods were out to take the Saudis. The talk of strategy and tactics, of maneuvering, of poker game handling all tend to leave a bad taste. Moreover, one gets the impression that Hamilton knew in 1931 there were 35 billion barrels of oil in Al Hasa—that he was well aware of the high stakes awaiting if he could only pull off the deal. This, to me, seems to destroy the contribution made by the 'ten men' and others who had to work hard to build the foundation for the present-day operation." Stegner Papers, Box 85, Folder 3, W. Jack Butler, Public Relations Department, ARAMCO, Dhahran, to H.O. Thompson, ARAMCO, New York, 11 January 1958.
78. Monroe, *Philby of Arabia*, p. 205. Hamilton told SOCAL that al-Sulayman had told Philby that IPC had offered £100,000 for an exploration concession without a development obligation. By contrast, Vane cabled Hamilton on 12 April that they did not wish to offer more than £25,000. Stegner Papers, Box 86, Folder 9, "Negotiation of the Concession—Chronology."
79. Stegner Papers, Box 86, Folder 9, "Negotiation of the Concession—Chronology."
80. The terms as sent by Hamilton to Vane on 21 February 1933. Stegner Papers, Box 86, Folder 9, "Negotiation of the Concession—Chronology."
81. Stegner, *Discovery*, pp. 23–6. Part of the difficulty lay in how the exchange rate between the US dollar and the British gold sovereign should be calculated. Stegner Papers, Box 86, Folder 9, "Negotiation of the Concession—Chronology." Philby later wrote that the British were shocked by the terms of the contract and felt that SOCAL had made a bad bargain. St. Antony's College, Oxford, Middle East Center Archives, H. St. John B. Philby Papers, GB165 0229, Box 34, Folder 3, "Oil Negotiations," July 1944.
82. H. St. J. B. Philby, *Arabian Oil Ventures* (Washington: Middle East Institute, 1964), p. 124. Philby also relates that as al-Sulayman read out the text of the agreement,

the king fell asleep, awakening only when al-Sulayman had stopped. Philby interprets this as both a recognition that the king already knew the contents of the agreement, since he had approved them all, and an implicit vote of confidence in his finance minister. *Ibid.*

83. R. Narayanan, "A Review of Oil Contract Negotiations By Saudi Arabia With Aramco," *International Studies*, Vol. 7, No. 4 (April 1966), p. 570. The text of the agreement was published as Decree No. 1135 in *Umm al-Qura*, 17 Rabiʿ al-Awwal 1353/14 July 1933, with a translated copy in FO/371/16871/E4699 and again in FO/371/16871/E7646 along with the text of the agreement. An original version of the decree signed by the king is contained in the Shaykh ʿAbdullah al-Sulaiman Papers, privately held, Jiddah. Wallace Stegner noted that "Prior to 1939 Casoc was administered as a division of Socal rather than as a subsidiary, with the department heads of Socal handling the respective problems from San Francisco. Arabian Government relations and operational matters were, however, cleared through Casocol (California Arabian Standard Oil Company, Limited), the London Office, and the officials there, being in closer contact with Saudi Arabia, usually made recommendations in both directions." The introduction of an interest in the producing company by the Texas Company, however, necessitated administrative changes. Stegner Papers, Box 86, Folder 13, "Company Organization." It was subsequently noted that the printed text omitted the precise territory that the concession covered. FO/371/16871/E4699, FO minute by K.R. Johnstone, 2 September 1933. A corrected version as supplied by the Saudi government, along with the 1939 agreement, is contained in FO/371/35152/E8031, S.R. Jordan, Jiddah, to Eden, FO, 28 November 1943. The Saudi government also published the agreement in Kingdom of Saudi Arabia, Ministry of Finance, *Ittifaqat sharikat istithmar al-bitrul wa-mustakhrajatihi wal-maʿadin* (1st ed., 1359/1940–1). The actual site of the negotiations was in Khazam Palace in Nazlah, outside Jiddah. Najib Salihah acted as the sole interpreter and secretary. Hamilton left after the signing but SOCAL required Twitchell to stay on for the next phase and permitted him to accept a "reward" from the Saudi Arabian government. Twitchell, *Saudi Arabia*, p. 222. After settling the Saudi Arabian concession, Hamilton undertook negotiations for concessions in India, Egypt, and Baluchistan, but had to abandon the schemes when war broke out. Stegner Papers, Box 84, Folder 22, Stegner interview with Spike Spurlock, Associate General Counsel, Dhahran, 17 November 1955. Lombardi apparently was responsible for choosing the name of the California Arabian Standard Oil Company. Stegner Papers, Box 86, Folder 10, "Exploration of the Concession, 1933–1935 Inclusive—Chronology."
84. FO/371/16871/E7646. The FO noted that the royalty in Bahrain was just over 5s per ton. FO/371/16871/E6078, Starling, Petroleum Department, to George Rendel, FO, 10 October 1933.
85. FO/371/17918/E28, Calvert, Jiddah, to Warner, FO Eastern Department, 12 December 1933. Other terms of the agreement included the proviso that the second loan and subsequent rental payments could be made in a currency of SOCAL's choice; the company was bound to begin exploration within three months and it could not abandon drilling and keep the concession; drilling would begin within three years and continue until commercial production was enabled or the company abandoned the concession; the Saudi government would receive a royalty advance of £50,000 upon the determination of commercial production, followed by another £50,000 in a year; the concession would cover the entire

eastern area of the country with an understanding in a parallel private agreement that SOCAL would have the right to match any competing offers for other areas, including the Saudi–Kuwaiti Neutral Zone; and it would remain in force for 60 years. Stegner, *Discovery*, pp. 26–7.

86. McConnell Papers, Box 2, "Historical background based on interview with Mr. M. E. LOMBARDI." SOCAL was not entirely happy with the terms Hamilton had negotiated and Lombardi advised Hamilton in June that the company might modify the royalty and advance on royalty provisions. Hamilton replied that the APOC contract had provided a share in net profits (even though the royalty was lower) and warned that he believed that further negotiations would result in a worse deal. Stegner Papers, Box 86, Folder 9, "Negotiation of the Concession—Chronology."
87. Twitchell, *Saudi Arabia*, p. 224. SOCAL's ability to produce the 35,000 gold sovereigns ran into difficulty because of the new American policy on gold and so the company turned to a British bank to obtain them shortly before the deadline. This decision was providential since SOCAL's application for the export of the gold from the US was denied by the US Treasury only a few days after the London arrangements had been made. Stegner, *Discovery*, pp. 28–9; and Stegner Papers, Box 86, Folder 9, "Negotiation of the Concession—Chronology."
88. FO/371/16871/E5330, Calvert to Sir John Simon, 23 August 1933. Guaranty Trust in London obtained the gold, packed in seven boxes, for SOCAL from the Royal Mint. FO/371/16871/E5455, Chancery, Jiddah, to FO, 24 August 1933.
89. Twitchell, *Saudi Arabia*, p. 224.
90. Monroe, *Philby*, pp. 202–3. See also Philby's handwritten account of the negotiations written in 1944, in Philby Papers. In this account, Philby claims to have convinced the king to allow foreign exploitation of oil and minerals, as well as having introduced the king to Charles Crane. This was confirmed by one of the company's early officials. Stegner Papers, Box 84, Folder 22, Stegner interview with Floyd Ohliger, Dhahran, 15 and 21 November 1955. The same account is repeated in Stegner, *Discovery!*, p. 14, presumably using Philby's books as his source.
91. Philby, *Arabian Oil Ventures*, p. 127. Leonard Mosley mistakenly attributes the statement to al-Sulayman in incorrectly citing Philby. Mosley, *Power Play: The Tumultuous World of Middle East Oil, 1890–1973* (London: Weidenfeld and Nicholson, 1973), p. 51. SOCAL was said to have paid Philby $1000 a month, $10,000 if SOCAL won the concession, a further $25,000 if commercial oil was found, and a royalty of 50 cents per ton exported until a second $25,000 was reached. Philby also discussed assistance to IPC but this fell through when IPC sent Longrigg. In addition, Philby reported much of what he knew to both Ibn Saʿud and the British minister, as well as passing on what Longrigg had told him to Hamilton. Monroe, *Philby of Arabia*, p. 204. Philby also admitted in 1933 that he had acted in an unofficial but advisory capacity at the "Cabinet" meeting that finally examined the concession, clause by clause, and approved it. FO/371/17918/E28, Calvert to Warner, 12 December 1933. One of the early oil men, Floyd Ohliger, later general manager and vice-president of the company in Dhahran, told an interviewer years afterward that "Twitchell and Philby were both promoters and their accounts of the concession agreements are unreliable. The British have always perpetuated the notion that they are the Middle Eastern experts. Neither Philby or Twitchell was as close to Ibn Saud as he pretended to be. Philby was actually a pretty good man and certainly the better of the two." Stegner Papers, Box 84, Folder 22, Stegner interviews with Ohliger,

Dhahran, 15 and 21 November 1955. Soon after his arrival in Jiddah, Lloyd Hamilton wrote Lombardi that "I am not yet prepared to say how much the prestige of Twitchell is likely to help us in a business way. Just at the moment I am inclined to think that the need for money on the part of the Government is the most important factor, and that the Government being so desperately in need of cash might deal with the highest bidder, despite its protestations that it does not care to have any oil company here which is associated with a foreign government, or which for that matter is continental or English. However, I shall reserve my final opinion on that point. Meanwhile I do feel that the alliance with Mr. Philby will be very helpful, if for no other reason than that his opposition would, I think, be a serious obstacle." Hamilton went on to say that "From one or two discussions with Mr. Philby I am far from sure that his ethics are all that could be desired, but nothing so far has occurred to cause any alarm on our part. Furthermore, being new to this part of the world, and not well acquainted with conditions as they exist here, I am not yet prepared to levy too heavy a criticism about ethics. The standard may necessarily be a little different. I think we are getting Mr. Philby's full cooperation, and I think he is quite pleased over his alliance with us. Like everyone else these days especially, he is in need of money, and he expressed real appreciation over the promptness with which the Company deposited his first two months' retainer in the bank at Cairo. If and when our competitors, the Irak people arrive here, Mr. Philby can undoubtedly keep us well informed about the terms that may propose to the government; he has offered to do so, with such confidence as to assure me that he will be able to do so. . . ." Stegner Papers, Box 86, Folder 11, Hamilton to Lombardi, 27 February 1933. There were also rumors circulating that Philby had been paid by SOCAL to bribe Saudi officials. Both Hamilton and Lenahan categorically denied the rumors to Fu'ad Hamza, who had originally brought the rumors to Philby's attention. Stegner Papers, Box 86, Folder 10, "Exploration of the Concession" (text).

92. R/15/2/422, Political Agent, Bahrain, to the PRPG, 19 January 1940.
93. FO/371/23271/E6626, Jiddah Report for August 1939. In August 1934, Najib Salihah, 'Abdullah al-Sulayman's assistant who had been acting as translator, approached the company for remuneration for his interpreting and translating work. Accordingly, the company paid him £50 gold for his services in August 1934. Salihah continued to provide assistance to the company, for which he was paid an additional £60 in January 1935 and regular payments followed on a semi-annual basis for some time. Stegner Papers, Box 86, Folder 10, "Exploration of the Concession" (text).
94. FO/371/16871/E7094, Calvert, Jiddah, to Simon, FO, 31 October 1933; FO/371/16875/E7249, Jiddah Report for October 1933. Other sources indicate that Twitchell was accompanied by R.P. Miller and S.K. Henry in the first party landing at al-Jubayl on 23 September 1933. Miller was the first field manager and was replaced by Floyd Ohliger, who had been in charge of drilling and construction, when Miller left Dhahran after two years, while Max Steineke became the chief geologist in 1934. Stegner Papers, Box 86, Folder 4, "Misc. handwritten notes that eventually become character sketches." More details about Steinecke are in G.C. Gester, "Max Steineke, Sidney Powers Memorial Medalist," by G. C. Gester, *Bulletin of the American Association of Petroleum Geologists*, Vol. 35, No. 7 (July 1951), pp. 1694–7; copy in Stegner Papers, Box 86, Folder 6.
95. Stegner Papers, Box 86, Folder 10, "Exploration of the Concession, 1933–1935 Inclusive—Chronology."

96. Narayanan, "Oil Contract Negotiations," p. 570n6. Almana says that "Everybody in the Court was glad that the Americans seemed likely to get the concession, for we all felt that the British were still tainted by colonialism. If they came for our oil, we could never be sure to what extent they would come to influence our government as well. The Americans on the other hand would simply be after the money, a motive which the Arabs as born traders could readily appreciate and approve." Almana, *Arabia Unified*, p. 223.
97. Narayanan, "Oil Contract Negotiations," pp. 572–3.
98. The event is covered well in Stegner, *Discovery!*, particularly on pp. 114–19.
99. Mosley, *Power Play*, p. 84. Hamilton, Rob Lebkicher, and Gary Owen apparently compiled a history of the company's operation up to 1940 "for the confidential use of the State Department." It is not known what happened to this history. Stegner Papers, Box 84, Folder 22, Stegner interview with Roy Lebkicher, Dhahran, 18 November 1955.
100. Narayanan, "Oil Contract Negotiations," pp. 572–3.
101. Organization of Petroleum Exporting Countries, *Selected Documents of the International Petroleum Industry: Saudi Arabia—pre-1966* (Vienna: OPEC Information Department, April 1976); *Foreign Relations of the United States, 1947*, 890F.6363/7–947, Childs, US Minister, Jiddah, to Secretary of State, tel. of 9 July 1947. See Stanford University, Hoover Institution Archives, Harley C. Stevens Papers, Box 1, for texts of many of these agreements.
102. Stegner Papers, Box 86, Folder 12, "The Negotiation of the Supplemental Agreement, 1938–1939" (text and chronology).
103. Twitchell, *Saudi Arabia*, p. 231; Stegner, *Discovery!*, pp. 124–8.
104. Narayanan, "Oil Contract Negotiations," p. 572; Stegner, *Discovery!*, p. 141. The decree ratifying the agreement was published in *Umm al-Qura*, No. 760 (19 Jumada al-Awal 1358/7 July 1939), and was also published subsequently in *Ittifaqat sharikat istithmar al-bitrul*. The terms of the new agreement provided for a payment at once to the government of £140,000 gold, an annual rent of £20,000, and a further £100,000 upon the discovery of oil in commercial quantities. In addition, the company would supply to the government supplies of petrol and kerosene until the discovery of oil, when the amounts would be increased. FO/371/13273/E5620, A.C. Trotter, Jiddah, to Viscount Halifax, 23 July 1939.
105. Stegner Papers, Box 86, Folder 12, "The Negotiation of the Supplemental Agreement, 1938–1939: Chronology."
106. The concession was first pursued by a pair named Urquhart and Cooper who apparently had the sponsorship of Sir Arnold Wilson and thus were supposed to have a connection with the Anglo-Persian Oil Company. See the correspondence in FO/371/11447/E2660 in April 1926, including the translation of a concession dated 1 March 1923 by the Idrisi ruler to Urquhart and Cooper for the Farasan Islands. An even earlier concession of some sort had been secured by Eastern and General Syndicate from the Idrisi earlier in 1926 but it was superseded by a concession granted on 26 September 1926 to Cooper, who marketed it to the Anglo-Saxon Petroleum Company (part of the Royal Dutch-Shell Group). The company thereupon formed Red Sea Petroleum Company to work the concession but it quickly ran into political difficulties between the Idrisi and Ibn Saʿud. The latter, who by this time had gained control over the Idrisi, demanded a new concession but Red Sea Petroleum decided to withdraw from the islands completely in September 1928. FO/371/16871/E3106, "Petroleum in Sa'udi Arabia," memorandum by Sir Andrew Ryan, Jiddah, 16 May 1933.

107. FO/371/13010, E4770/484/91, Stonehewer Bird to Chamberlain, 31 August 1928, enclosing Jiddah Report for 1–31 August 1928.
108. FO/371/16871/E2957, Ryan to FO, tel. 111 of 4 June 1933, together with jacket minutes; FO/371/16871/E3340, Starling, Petroleum Department, to FO, 21 June 1933. Ryan later explained that the abandonment of the concession was not due to either problems with the Idrisi or Italian intrigues but rather because King ʿAbd al-ʿAziz did not want it. FO/371/16871/E4308, Ryan to Simon, 12 July 1933. Enclosed is an extract of an article by Fu'ad Bey Hamza on "The History of Tihamat ʿAsir," published in *Umm al-Qura*, 7 July 1933.
109. FO/371/20063/E3528, memorandum by Sir Andrew Ryan, "Red Sea Oil Concession," 21 May 1936; FO/371/20064/E3952, Ryan to Eden, 9 June 1936. A few days after this memorandum was written, IPC informed the Saudi government that it had broken off relations with Etherton and Ydlibi. While the Saudis were keen on IPC, they also intended to play the company off against French oil interests. FO/371/20063/E3147, Ryan to FO, tel. no. 76 of 2 June 1936. It later became clear that the French interests were in fact Compagnie française des Pétroles (CFP), which, as a partner in IPC, would act in concert with Petroleum Concessions Ltd. in its efforts to secure the Red Sea concession. If, however, as seemed likely, that the Farasan Islands would lie outside this concession, then CFP would be free to pursue a separate concession. Longrigg was expected to leave for Jiddah momentarily. FO/371/20063/E3307, "Record of a Conversation at the Foreign Office on Friday, June 5th, between Mr. Skliros, of Petroleum Concessions Limited, who was accompanied by Major Longrigg, and Mr. Rendel."
110. FO/371/20063/E3634, "Record of Conversation at the Foreign Office between Colonel E.T. Etherton and Mr. Brenan," 24 June 1936.
111. FO/371/20062/E4594, Jiddah Report for June 1936.
112. FO/371/20064/E5003, Calvert to Eden, 13 July 1936. The French representative was ill during the entire negotiations and died in Jiddah after their conclusion. The agreement was published in *Umm al-Qura* on 10 July 1936. A subsidiary company was formed to operate the concession: Petroleum Development (Western Arabia) Limited. FO/371/20062/E7326, Jiddah Report for October 1936.
113. FO/371/24590/E1827, H.H. Wheatley, Petroleum Development (Western Arabia) Limited, to L. Baggallay, FO, 23 April 1940; *ibid.*, E1950, Stonehewer Bird to FO, tel. no. 85 of 13 June 1940.
114. Shaykh ʿAbdullah al-Sulaiman Papers, privately held, Jiddah, correspondence of Shaykh ʿAbdullah al-Sulaiman with King ʿAbd al-ʿAziz, letter from King ʿAbd al-ʿAziz to Shaykh ʿAbdullah, 29 Jumada al-Thaniyah 1357/25 August 1938. The other student was Muhanna Muʿabid. Yusuf b. Muhammad al-Qablan also cites the letter in *Paris Najd*, No. 13 (1 Ramadan 1431H), p. 102.

4 EARLY ADMINISTRATIVE ARRANGEMENTS

1. Shaykh ʿAbdullah al-Sulaiman Papers, privately held, Jiddah, Internal Ministry of Finance Affairs, "The Opinion of the Minister of Finance on the Formation of an Audit Agency for Official Departments," 10 Safar 1355/2 May 1936.
2. United Kingdom, National Archives, Kew, Foreign Office (FO) Records, Political Departments, General Correspondence, FO/371/16024/E2304, Jiddah Report for January–March 1932.
3. FO/371/17922/E6498, A.S. Calvert, Jiddah, to Sir John Simon, 2 October 1934. Surprisingly, the announcement of the appointment was made in *Sawt al-Hijaz*

(on 24 September) instead of *Umm al-Qura*. Although the *wikalat al-difa'* had been formed in the early 1930s, it became the Ministry of Defense (*wizarat al-difa'*) only in 1944. Madawi Al-Rasheed, *A History of Saudi Arabia* (Cambridge: Cambridge University Press, 2002), p. 90.

4. Richard H. Sanger, *The Arabian Peninsula* (Ithaca, NY: Cornell University Press, 1954), pp. 36–7.
5. FO/371/17932/E5550, Calvert to FO, 11 August 1934, enclosing the Annual Report for the Pilgrimage for 1934.
6. FO/371/17941/E4001, Sir Andrew Ryan, Jiddah, to the Principal Secretary of State for Foreign Affairs, 30 May 1934.
7. FO/371/17943/E71515, Calvert to Simon, 3 December 1934.
8. FO/371/20062/E1704, Jiddah Report for February 1936. The report cast the difference in terms of "considerable rivalry" and "The struggle appears to turn partly on the wish of each of them to control both the army and the police .... The roots of the quarrel probably go much deeper." *Ibid.*
9. FO/371/20842/E2126, R.W. Bullard, Jiddah, to Anthony Eden, Secretary of State for Foreign Affairs, 30 March 1937.
10. See, for example, University of Oxford, St. Antony's College, Middle East Center Archives, GB165–0229, H. St. John B. Philby Papers, Box 34/3, Sharqieh Ltd., Correspondence with Sir A.E. Dunbar 1940–6.
11. The Ministry of Defense, after its creation in the 1940s, also included a department of aviation that embraced both the small air force and commercial airplanes owned by the government, as well as supervised the training schools for pilots at al-Ta'if and for airport personnel at Dhahran. Sanger, *Arabian Peninsula*, pp. 36–7. Until the mid-2010s, it was still known as the Ministry of Defense and Aviation.
12. Reader W. Bullard letter to FO, 26 June 1938, reproduced in Reader Bullard, ed. by E.C. Hodgkin, *Two Kings in Arabia: Sir Reader Bullard's Letters from Jeddah* (Reading: Ithaca Press, 1995), p. 235.
13. FO/371/14454/E6942, *Umm al-Qura*, 14 November 1930.
14. FO/371/17941/E7514, Calvert to Simon, 17 December 1934.
15. *Umm al-Qura*, No. 684 (14 January 1938).
16. University of Essex second interview with Shaykh 'Abd al-'Aziz al-Sulaiman (c.1982).
17. FO/371/13728, E4134/94/91, Bond to Henderson, 22 July 1929, enclosing Jiddah Report for 1–30 June 1929. It required prolonged negotiation to ensure that some 30 British-protected subjects would be removed from the conscription. *Ibid.*
18. FO/371/13728, E6790/94/91, Jiddah Report for 1–30 November 1929.
19. FO/371/17941/E4802, Ryan to Simon, 6 July 1934.
20. FO/371/20841/E2691, Jiddah Report for July 1937.
21. Philby Papers, 38/39; letters to his wife Dora, 19 March, 5 July, and 10 July 1938.
22. FO/371/23268/E161, "Saudi Arabia Annual Report, Economic (B), for 1938."
23. FO/371/16875/E1488, Ryan to Simon, 28 February 1933.
24. FO/371/24588/E1811, Jiddah Report for March 1940.
25. FO/371/20843/E1637/1637/25, Bullard to Eden, 28 February 1937, "Saudi Arabia Annual Report, 1936"; FO/371/21905/E5600, Jiddah Report for August 1938.
26. FO/371/21905/E7803, Jiddah Report for November 1938. At the same time, however, Philby also alleged that the Ministry of Finance could produce no accounts about the approximately £100,000 owed Sharqieh for Ford motor cars. He attributed this "great deterioration in the Saudi administration" in part to the

"gradual elimination" of Muhammad Surur, the director of finance, in favor of a young Syrian, Najib Salihah. *Ibid.*

27. Letter of 6 February 1939, Bullard, *Two Kings in Arabia*, p. 252.
28. University of Essex interview with Muhammad Ba Harith (c.1982).
29. University of Essex first and second interviews with Shaykh ʿAbd al-ʿAziz al-Sulaiman. Apparently al-Sulayman discussed the poor state of relations between King ʿAbd al-ʿAziz and King Fuʾad of Egypt with Haykal and then invited the Egyptian to make the *hajj* as his personal guest. After Haykal's arrival, al-Sulayman arranged for him to meet King ʿAbd al-ʿAziz who spoke forcefully about the refusal of King Fuʾad of Egypt to recognize Saudi Arabia. With this meeting, the ball started rolling towards the normalization of Saudi–Egyptian relations. *Ibid.*
30. FO/371/16878/E7639, Calvert to Simon, 22 November 1933; E7970, Calvert to Simon, 5 December 1933.
31. University of Essex first interview with Shaykh ʿAbd al-ʿAziz al-Sulaiman.
32. FO/371/17922/E7512; Calvert to Simon, 27 November 1934; *ibid.*, E7545; Calvert to Simon, 4 December 1934.
33. University of Essex first interview with Shaykh ʿAbd al-ʿAziz al-Sulaiman. It is not clear whether the hotel was government-owned or a private venture. Other schemes that Shaykh ʿAbdullah discussed with Talʿat Harb included the construction of a date-processing plant, the provision of electricity and water supply for Makkah, and the repair of existing roads. The date-processing plant was never built while the other schemes were implemented far later. University of Essex interview with Ahmad al-Jaffali (c.1982).
34. *Umm al-Qura*, No. 636 (12 February 1937).
35. FO/371/20061/E2980, Miles W. Lampson, High Commissioner, Cairo, to Anthony Eden, Secretary of State for Foreign Affairs, 12 May 1936.
36. FO/371/20841/E580, Jiddah Report for December 1936. The reports indicated that Egypt was to share in the revenues from these schemes and the Egyptian share would then be distributed to the poor. By the end of 1936, however, only the Makkah hotel and air services between Egypt and Hijazi cities had been completed. But Banque Misr arranged for the dredging of Jiddah harbor and agreed on a sharing of the costs of the public works schemes, estimated at £250,000. FO/371/21908/E2778, Bullard to Viscount Halifax, 17 April 1938, enclosing "Economic Report, Saudi Arabia 1937." Final agreement on Saudi acceptance of the Egyptian role in road-building appeared to have been reached in 1939. FO/371/23272/E1108 and E1109.
37. FO/371/23272/E7407, A.C. Trott (for the Minister, Jiddah) to Viscount Halifax, 17 October 1939.
38. University of Essex second interview with Shaykh ʿAbd al-ʿAziz al-Sulaiman.
39. FO/371/23270/E2429, G.T. Havard, British Consul–General, Beirut, to the Secretary of State for Foreign Affairs, 10 March 1939.
40. Grobba first visited the kingdom in early 1939 and unsuccessfully sought to pursue an arms deal. The official Saudi attitude after the outbreak of World War II was decidedly anti-German, although public opinion in al-Hijaz was more pro-German. FO/371/24589/E2720, Stonehewer Bird to Viscount Halifax, 18 July 1940, enclosing "Political Review of Events in Saudi Arabia for the Year 1939." The king did send Khalid al-Qarqani to Berlin but he stressed to the British this was only in an effort to purchase arms and that the deal had fallen through because of German demands for Saudi neutrality. The British subsequently offered financing for arms and a cartridge factory. FO/371/23271/E6626, Jiddah Report for August 1939.

41. Lukacz Hirszowicz, *The Third Reich and the Arab East* (London: Routledge and Kegan Paul, 1966), p. 69n. See also Fahd Abdullah al-Semmari, "Saudi Arabian–German Political and Economic Relations 1926–1939" (Ph.D. dissertation, University of California, Riverside, 1989; tr. into Arabic with additions and published as *al-malik ʿabd al-ʿaziz wa-almaniya: dirasah tarikhiyah lil-ʿalaqat al-saʿudiyah al-alamaniyah 1344–1358/1926–1939* [n.p., n.d.]).
42. University of Essex second interview with Shaykh ʿAbd al-ʿAziz al-Sulaiman.
43. *Umm al-Qura*, Nos. 681 (24 December 1937) and 685 (21 January 1938).
44. Muhammad Tawfiq Sadiq, *Tatawwur al-hukm wal-idarah fi al-mamlakah al-ʿarabiyah al-saʿudiyah* (Riyadh: Maʿhad al-idarah al-ʿammah, 1385/1965), p. 117. The Directorate of Hajj Affairs was transferred to the Ministry of the Interior in 1961 and two years later became the Ministry of Hajj Affairs and Awqaf. *Ibid.*
45. Karl S. Twitchell, *Saudi Arabia* (3rd ed.; Princeton: Princeton University Press, 1958), pp. 213–15.
46. Twitchell, *Saudi Arabia*, p. 245. The Saudi government also published the agreement in Kingdom of Saudi Arabia, Ministry of Finance, *Ittifaqat sharikat istithmar al-bitrul wa-mustakhrajatihi wal-maʿadin* (1st ed., 1359/1940–1). A summary of developments regarding oil and mining was published in *Umm al-Qura*, No. 1320 (19 July 1950), pp. 10–12 (cited by Sadiq, *Tatawwur al-hukm wal-idarah*, p. 113n1). Daniël Van Der Meulen, in *The Wells of Ibn Saʿud* (London: John Murray, 1957), pp. 137–8, postulated that Twitchell had been convinced that there was gold in Arabia because it had been mentioned in the Bible.
47. FO/371/20061/E601, Ryan to Anthony Eden, Secretary of State for Foreign Affairs, 3 February 1936.
48. FO/371/23271, Jiddah Report for August 1939.
49. A typed list of shareholders at 27 November 1953 is contained in Twitchell Papers, Box 20, Folder 2. ʿAbdullah al-Sulayman owned 40,720 shares by himself and another 8000 shares jointly with his brother Hamad. Twitchell published a survey of the mine's history and its current operations in the *ASARCO News Letter*, Vol. 3, No. 12 (December 1950). Copy in Twitchell Papers, Box 19, Folder 6. A note from A.S. Calvert in Jiddah in 1936 indicated that a controlling interest in SAMS was at that time held by the Mining Trust (Limited) although the Jiddah manager of the syndicate declared that "the American Smelting Company" owned SAMS. Calvert also reported that work on the company's terminal in Jiddah was underway and a landing ground for its airplane had been cleared near the compound, but no work had begun on the jetty. FO/371/20061, Calvert to Aden, 28 July 1936.
50. Twitchell Papers, Box 10, Folder 5, Saudi Arabian Mining Syndicate, Limited, Report of the Directors, 1 August 1940.
51. FO/371/40283/E1293, Annual Report on Saudi Arabia for 1943; copy in United Kingdom, British Library, Oriental and India Collection, India Office, Political (External) Files & Collections, L/P&S/12/2085, E/1293/1293/25. The American Smelting Corporation's requests for shipping space were denied in January. In May, the SAMS director in Jiddah was instructed by Allied war authorities to inform the minister of finance of this decision and to prepare to close down operations once existing stocks were exhausted. The minister was to be informed 30 days prior to shut down in order to take advantage of the *force majeure* clause in the contract. However, the US position softened slightly in December to permit a small allocation of operational supplies as a measure of "moderate political expediency." NARA, Records of the Foreign Economic Administration, RG169 E445, Box 2769, Middle East Supply Committee, Committee Meeting Minutes,

19 January 1943; *ibid.*, MESC Meeting Minutes, 10 May 1943; *ibid.*, E445, Box 2759, meetings with Landis, 13 December 1943. The efforts of Twitchell and al-Sulayman to keep the mine going were founded on the impact of its closing on the Saudi workers as much as income. An American employee of SAMS wrote home to his sister that "I'm afraid the workmen here are going to have a tough time when we close down .... Even on the good wages we pay, they have found it hard lately to more than just get by." RG169, Bureau of Areas, Box 187, SAMS 1943, B.L. Cope to Miss M. Cope, 24 December 1943.

52. RG59, 890f.24/56, George Kirk, American minister, Cairo, to W. Murtery (?), State Department, 14 May 1943; RG59, 890f.24/47, Moose, Jiddah, to the Secretary of State, 2 July 1943.
53. RG169 Bureau of Areas Box 187, SAMS 1944, P. Dawson, Middle East Division, to J.W. Angell, memorandum of 24 April 1944.
54. RG59, 890f.6341/4–845, Eddy to Secretary of State, 8 April 1945; 890f.63/3/2645, R.F. Goodwin, American Smelting & Refining Company, to Richard Sanger, State Department, 26 March 1945.
55. FO/371/62103/E5274, "Annual Economic (A) Report on Saudi Arabia, 1946," 19 June 1947.
56. Twitchell Papers, Box 19, Folder 6, Saudi Arabian Mining Syndicate, Limited, Report of the Directors, 20 June 1951.
57. Correspondence in Twitchell Papers, Box 18, Folder 6. The Saudi mine had lingered on, despite stiff competition from richer South African mines, only because the price of gold soared during World War II and made Mahd al-Dhahab competitive. Van Der Meulen, *The Wells of Ibn Sa'ud*, p. 138. This was not quite the end of Twitchell's mining interests in the kingdom, as 'Abdullah al-Sulayman's successor as minister of finance asked him in late 1954 to investigate the possibility of diamond drilling at another ancient mine, al-Hablah, north-east of Mahd al-Dhahab. As SAMS was in the process of liquidation, Twitchell sought to create the Saudi Arabian Development Group to exploit the mine but there is no evidence that anything came of the venture. Twitchell Papers, Box 18, Folder 6, Twitchell to to James MacPherson, vice-president and general manager, Independent Oil Company, Kuwait, 15 November 1954.
58. Twitchell Papers, Box 19, Folder 6, Twitchell to R.F. Goodwin, vice-president, American Smelting and Refining Company, 8 April 1951; and Saudi Arabian Mining Syndicate, Limited, Report of the Directors, 20 June 1951. On the company's opposition to being subjected to the tax, see RG59, 886A for 1951
59. Twitchell Papers, Box 20, Folder 3, Frank Cameron, general manager, SAMS, to Twitchell, 12 November 1953. The results of the liquidation of the company can be found in Twitchell Papers, Box 20, Folder 4, "Saudi Arabian Mining Syndicate, Limited, In Voluntary Liquidation," 15 October 1955.
60. University of Oxford, St. Antony's College, Middle East Centre Archive, H. St. John B. Philby Papers, Box 30, Folder 5, various letters between Philby and Dudler.
61. FO/371/14460/E1385, W.L. Bond, Consul, Jiddah, to A. Henderson, 2 March 1929, enclosing memorandum on "Proposed Scheme for supplying Jedda and Mecca with Electricity."
62. University of Essex interview with Ahmad al-Jaffali (c.1982); University of Essex third interview with Shaykh 'Abd al-'Aziz al-Sulaiman (c.1982).
63. FO/371/13010, E484/484/91, Stonehewer Bird to Sir Austen Chamberlain, 4 January 1928, enclosing Jiddah Report for 1–31 December 1927; FO/371/13010,

E1460/484/91, Stonehewer Bird to Chamberlain, 1 March 1928, enclosing Jiddah Report for 1–28 February 1928.

64. FO/371/17920/E73, Calvert to Simon, 9 December 1933. A later examination of the conduit revealed that the water was not as unsanitary as believed earlier. FO/371/17921/E1635, Ryan to FO, 13 March 1934.
65. Twitchell, *Saudi Arabia*, pp. 215–16.
66. FO/371/16875/E5724, Jiddah Situation Report for August 1933.
67. FO/371/17935/E7516, Jiddah Report for November 1934.
68. FO/371/21905/E661, Jiddah Report for December 1937.
69. NARA, RG165, War Department General and Special Staffs, E77, G-2 Regional File, Arabia, Jiddah, CASOC 20 December 1938.
70. FO/371/23268/E2928, "Saudi Arabia Annual Report, Economic (A), for 1938." While the search was carried out in Riyadh, al-Sulayman was reported to spend hours in the afternoon watching the drilling activities. Philip C. McConnell, *The Hundred Men* (Peterborough, NH: Currier Press, 1985), pp. 149–50.
71. University of Utah, J. Willard Marriott Library Special Collections, Wallace Stegner Papers, Box 84, Folder 4, Tom Barger Letters, July–December 1938, Barger letters to family from Riyadh, 20 and 29 September 1938. Barger noted that "In the valley [around Yamamah] are the remains of many old irrigation works, far greater gardens they must have had in the old days. Round about on the hills are many tumuli, mounds of stones apparently graves—there are hundreds of them on Bahrain ...". *Ibid.*, 29 September 1938.
72. University of Essex interview with Glen Brown, Washington, DC, 4 November 1985.
73. FO/371/23268/E161, "Saudi Arabia Annual Report, Economic (B), for 1938."
74. FO/371/24588/E230, Jiddah Report for December 1939.
75. Sadiq, *Tatawwur al-hukm wal-idarah*, pp. 127–8.
76. FO/371/11442, E7077/367/91, Norman Mayers, for S.R. Jordan, Acting Vice-Consul Jiddah, to Chamberlain, 5 December 1926, enclosing Jiddah Report for 1–30 November 1926. A royal decree from King Husayn of al-Hijaz in 1925 permitted Prince Habib Lutfallah to establish the Arabian National Bank of al-Hijaz, enabling it to carry out such banking business as note issues, loans, the discounting of bills, and accounts. This permission was confirmed by Ibn Sa'ud in 1926 and the bank was established with its headquarters in Jiddah and branches in Egypt, working at first in connection with Barclays Bank. At the beginning of 1926, Lutfallah had made a proposal for financing the *hajj* by issuing paper currency guaranteed by customs receipts and other government sources of revenue. The Egyptian Department of the Foreign Office, however, was of the opinion that Ibn Sa'ud would be foolish to listen to any Lutfallah proposal. Nevertheless, the bank went ahead with its plans and printed its first issue of notes, equal to £200,000, about 1929, hoping to get permission to put them into circulation. FO/371/11440, E704, Henderson, Cairo, to Jiddah, 19 January 1926; FO/371/11442, E7077/367/91, Mayers to Chamberlain; FO/371/13741/E5528, Cecil L'Estrange Malone, MP, to Arthur Henderson, FO, 24 October 1929. Lutfallah's scheme apparently never got off the ground. The king again approached the British for help in attracting a British bank to serve as a sort of state bank, for which British officialdom advised a neutral response. FO/371/15299/E3559, R.V.N. Hopkins, Treasury, to the under-secretary of state at the Foreign Office, 8 July 1931. It should be noted that the Ottoman Bank had operated in Hashimi al-Hijaz as well. FO/371/20063/E5458, Calvert to Eden, 26 June 1936, enclosing "Economic Survey of Saudi Arabia."

77. FO/371/20063/E5458, Calvert to Eden, 26 June 1936, enclosing "Economic Survey of Saudi Arabia."
78. FO/371/17921/E911, Ryan to FO, tel. no. 19 of 8 February 1934.
79. FO/371/23271/E6626, Jiddah Report for August 1939; FO/371/23268/E7679, John S. Cook, Treasury, to H.L. Baggallay, FO, 21 November 1939.
80. FO/371/21905/E7803, Jiddah Report for November 1938. As Shaykh ʿAbdullah was said to have insisted on "impossible conditions" throughout the four months of negotiation, the Gray Mackenzie representative left Jiddah in March 1939 without an agreement. Nevertheless, the company was able to take on activities in practice that were never arranged on paper. FO/371/23271/E3188, Jiddah Report for March 1939.
81. FO/371/21904, various correspondence.
82. King ʿAbd al-ʿAziz Foundation (Darat ʿAbd al-ʿAziz), Riyadh, selected telegrams from King ʿAbd al-ʿAziz, 1930s. In another message to his financial adviser, the king wrote: "Regarding the guests and what you mentioned about them—I see that as a duty and in reality I am very grateful to you in this respect. This is something that merits God's support, *inshallah*. Again, I am very very grateful to you. May Allah bless you! It is not possible to keep a record of these people; the best thing to do is to continue feeding them. Taking care of the younger and needy members of the group is better—it is a form of religious obligation. A meal of millet should be prepared for them, as you have suggested. Then you should provide 4,000 to 5,000 pieces of clothing for both men and women, of all sizes, small, medium and large, and distribute it among them. If this is not enough, then supplement it. Hasten to have this done soon! They should be given clothing, and be accompanied by pious, compassionate and trustworthy men. A course of action like this is indeed very good and God elevates people's status with such acts, *inshallah*. It is also part of your blessed acts." King ʿAbd al-ʿAziz Foundation, King ʿAbd al-ʿAziz to Shaykh ʿAbdullah al-Sulayman, tel. no. 8879 of 1/10/?; *ibid.*, tel. no. 8689 of 20 Ramadan 1360/11 October 1941.
83. Shaykh ʿAbdullah al-Sulaiman Papers, privately held, Jiddah. Some of these letters appear to be addressed to ʿAbdullah's brother Hamad. See also the correspondence in the archival database of the King 'Abd al-'Aziz Public Library, Riyadh.

5 BRITISH WARTIME ASSISTANCE AND THE EMERGENCE OF ANGLO-AMERICAN RIVALRY

1. United Kingdom, National Archives, Kew, Foreign Office (FO) Records, Political Department, General Correspondence, FO/371/23271/E7018, Jiddah Report for September 1939.
2. United States, National Archives and Records Administration (NARA), General Records of the Department of State, RG59, 890f.404/25, Jiddah to State, 17 August 1943.
3. FO/371/23271/E6508, W.L. Gorell Barnes, Export Credits Guarantee Department, to M.R. Zada, Secretary, Saudi Arabian Legation, London, 12 September 1939; *ibid.*, Lacy Bagallay, Foreign Office (FO), to Sir Reader Bullard, Jiddah, 21 September 1939.
4. FO/371/23271/E4380, Jiddah Report for May 1939; FO/371/23271/E7242, Gorell Barnes to Baggallay, 27 October 1939.
5. FO/371/24587/E945, F.H.W. Stonehewer Bird to Viscount Halifax, 6 February 1940. Stonehower Bird immediately applied to London for a credit of £200,000 and

a promise of further aid if necessary. *Ibid.*, Treasury subsequently approved this request, provided that all purchases be made within the sterling area. FO/371/24587/E780, C.G. Syers, Treasury, to Baggallay, 21 February 1940.

6. FO/371/24587/E1039, FO to Stonehewer Bird, tel. no. 20 of 7 March 1940. The British minister reported that the minister of finance had expressed the king's appreciation of the offer and also outlined a list of commodities required and their approximate cost. ʿAbdullah al-Sulayman asked that sums to meet these expenses be placed in India, Singapore, and possibly Egypt for Saudi Arabia's credit, with the remainder of the credit deposited to the kingdom's credit in India or Egypt to meet further requirements for equipment. FO/371/24587/E1168, Stonehewer Bird to Gellatly, Hankey, tel. no. 44 of 14 March 1940. Beginning in the 1930s, Britain maintained a neo-mercantilist policy of regulating trade in its empire and related states through strict exchange controls intended to protect its economy and currency. Growing American concern with the burgeoning international petroleum industry during World War II and in the following years, combined with its promotion of the Bretton Woods international monetary system, caused Washington to oppose the continuation of what had become known as the sterling area. Britain finally abandoned its sterling policy with the devaluation of 1967. Steven G. Galpern, *Money, Oil, and Empire in the Middle East: Sterling and Postwar Imperialism, 1944–1971* (New York: Cambridge University Press, 2009), pp. 23–4.
7. FO/371/24588/E1509, FO to Stonehewer Bird, tel. no. 33 of 12 April 1940. The *riyals* were minted in India in 1941 but paid for by London. FO/371/27265/E3180, FO to Jiddah, tel. of 20 June 1941.
8. FO/371/27261/E1766, Stonehewer Bird to Anthony Eden, Secretary of State for Foreign Affairs, 28 April 1941.
9. FO/371/24590/E2694, FO to Stonehewer Bird, tel. no. 158 of 4 October 1940.
10. FO/371/27265/E2984, Washington embassy to Gellatly, Hankey, tel. no. 2874 of 20 June 1941.
11. FO/371/31460/E4326, Summary of Events in Saudi Arabia During 1941. The Saudi government at first requested $10 million from CASOC, due to the sudden fall in pilgrimage and customs revenues, as well as a great increase in payments to be made to tribes. The minister of finance was pushed to admit that the amount could be reduced to $8 million under strict economies but CASOC's president countered with a maximum offer of $6 million. The demand by Yusuf Yasin of the Foreign Ministry for a minimum of $6 million in royalties nearly derailed the discussions but agreement was finally reached on the $3 million to be advanced by CASOC with a request to the parent companies to advance a further $3 million. In return, CASOC received an extension of two years to their concession. Nevertheless, Yasin was dispatched to report to the British minister in Jiddah that even if all $6 million were received from the oil companies, the Saudi deficit would be at least $2 million after including the British subsidy. Therefore, the king asked for a loan of £1 million instead of the £400,000 promised. FO/371/27264/E276, Stonehewer Bird to Gellatly, Hankey, tel. no. 42 of 22 January 1941. The Foreign Office response was frosty, noting that a few years previously the total income of Saudi Arabia was about £600,000 gold while rising expenditures growing out of increased revenues from oil had boosted current expenditure to £2 million in gold. Stonehewer Bird's orders were to convey London's regretful inability to loan the larger sum, particularly since the British government had already offered an advance of £800,000, of which £400,000 had been paid already and two installments of £200,000 each were scheduled for 1941. *Ibid.*, FO to Stonehewer

Bird, tel. no. 42 of 6 March 1941. Al-Sulayman also approached the Saudi Arabian Mining Syndicate for a loan against customs and royalties and the latter apparently made a payment of $150,000. FO/371/27265/E2133, Khartoum Periodical Report No. 34, 7–21 March 1941, containing Saudi Arabian Mining Syndicate telegram intercepts.

12. FO/371/27266/E5189, Jiddah to FO, tel. of 30 August 1941.
13. RG59, 890f.51/48–1/2, J.A. Moffett, CASOC, to President Roosevelt, 16 April 1941; *ibid.*, Murray, State Department Near East Division (NEA), to the Secretary of State, 21 April 1941; RG59, 890f.51/31, various correspondence, May 1941. Even Karl Twitchell added his voice, warning that if Saudi Arabia did not receive timely aid, it might be forced to turn to Germany for help. RG59, 890f.00/60, Twitchell to Murray, State Department, 14 May 1941.
14. RG59, 890f.51/37, J. Jones, Federal Loan Agency, to the Secretary of State, 6 August 1941, enclosing President Roosevelt's note to Jones. The news was relayed to SOCAL (Standard Oil of California, CASOC's parent), in a conversation between State Department NEA officials and Davies and Lloyd Hamilton of SOCAL on 7 August 1941 (RG59, 890f.51/38) and by State to the embassy in Cairo on 22 August 1961 (RG59, 890f.51/29). Ambassador Kirk in Cairo passed the information on to Prince Faysal on 11 October 1941 (RG59, 890f.51/41).
15. NARA, General Records of the Department of Commerce, RG40, 103022, Jesse Jones, Secretary of Commerce, to W.S.S. Rodgers, 28 May 1941.
16. FO/371/27266/E7373, Stonehewer Bird to Gellatly Hankey, tel. no. 332 of 10 November 1941.
17. *Ibid.*
18. *Ibid.*, E7387, Stonehewer Bird to Gellatly, Hankey, tel. of 11 November 1941; *ibid.*, FO to Jiddah, tel. of 23 November 1941. One of al-Sulayman's ideas for savings was for the Saudi government to buy foodstuffs directly from the Government of India and he asked permission that part of the British loan for 1942 take the form of a credit with the Government of India. FO/371/27266/E8288, Stonehewer Bird to Gellatly, Hankey, tel. of 15 December 1941.
19. FO/371/2764/E1054, intercepted letter from Gellatly, Hankey in Jiddah to their office in Khartoum, 2 February 1941; *ibid.*, 1 March 1941.
20. FO/371/31460/E4326, Summary of Events in Saudi Arabia During 1941. A pilgrim ship in Jiddah harbor was mistakenly targeted by a British aircraft as an Italian destroyer but it was not hit, nor was a British legation launch hit despite being machine-gunned. *Ibid.*
21. RG59, 890f.51/45, memorandum of conversation, 27 November 1941.
22. FO/371/31451/E655, Stonehewer Bird to Eden, 6 January 1942.
23. RG59, 890f.6363, Standard Oil Co/137, Cairo to State Department, drawing on a Roy Lebkicher memorandum on Saudi Arabian financial conditions, 28 February 1942.
24. FO/371/31451/E166, Stonehewer Bird to FO, tel. of 8 January 1942.
25. FO/371/31451/E1379, Stonehewer Bird to the Government of India, tel. of 28 February 1942; *ibid.*, E831, Stonehewer Bird to FO, tel. no. 33 of 28 February 1942.
26. FO/371/31448/E2591, Stonehewer Bird to FO, 31 March 1942, enclosing memorandum on "Supplies for Saudi Arabia"; FO/371/31451/E1797, FO to Jiddah, tel. no. 95 of 26 March 1942; *ibid.*, E1797, Stonehewer Bird to Gellatly, Hankey, tel. of 1 April 1942.
27. FO/371/35147/E140, Stonehewer Bird to Eden, 13 December 1942.
28. FO/371/31451/E2138, Stonehewer Bird to FO, tel. of 6 April 1942.

29. FO/371/31451/E2165, Stonehewer Bird to FO, tel. no. 118 of 7 April 1942.
30. FO/371/31452/E2644, Stonehewer Bird to the Government of India, 27 April 1942.
31. FO/371/31448, various correspondence.
32. FO/371/31448 and FO/371/31452, various correspondence.
33. FO/371/35155/E1102, Annual Summary of Events in Saudi Arabia During 1942.
34. FO/371/35141/E690, Director of Gellatly, Hankey, & Co., to Eyres, FO, 1 February 1943, containing a complete breakdown of receipts and payments. Many of these transactions were also recorded elsewhere in FO/371/35141.
35. FO/371/31452/E6625, Stonehewer Bird to FO, tel. no. 335 of 9 November 1942.
36. FO/371/31451 and 31452, various correspondence.
37. FO/371/35147/E469, "Record of audiences granted to Lord Moyne by King Ibn Saud, December 1942." In mid-1943, al-Sulayman asked the British whether credit could be obtained for the purchases of medicine or other government supplies in India. The British considered the possibility of crediting the sum to Saudi Arabia's account with Gellatly's as a means of repaying the king for the commandeering of the Ford cars without causing him embarrassment after he had said he wanted to give the cars as a gift. FO/371/35154/E4062, Cairo to FO, telegram of 7 July 1943.
38. RG59, 890f.51/52, Cairo to State Department, telegram of 24 October 1942.
39. FO/371/31452/E6625, Stonehewer Bird to Gellatly Hankey, tel. no. 335 of 9 November 1942. A thorough analysis of the famine conditions caused by the drought in Najd and surrounding areas was compiled by Harold Dickson as "Note on the Food Situation in Central and North Eastern Saudi Arabia," 1 December 1942. University of Oxford, St. Antony's College, Middle East Center Archives, H.R.P. Dickson Papers, GB165–0085, Box 3, File 8.
40. FO/371/35144/E6396, Minister of State, Cairo, to Young, Treasury, with enclosure of budget, 7 September 1943.
41. FO/371/40283/E1293, Annual Report on Saudi Arabia for 1943; copy in United Kingdom, British Library, India Office Records, India Office, Political (External) Files & Collections, L/P&S/12/2085, E/1293/1293/25. The actual amount of the subsidy was adjusted for a reduction of £60,000 because of the unexpected increase of about 40 percent in overseas pilgrims on the *hajj* during that year.
42. FO/371/35144/E6346, E.M.H. Lloyd, Office of the Minister of State, Cairo, to C.H.M. Wilcox, Treasury, 12 October 1943.
43. FO/371/40267/E364, S.R. Jordan, British minister, Jiddah, to Baxter, FO, 31 December 1943.
44. FO/371/40283/E1293, Annual Report on Saudi Arabia for 1943; copy in L/P&S/12/2085, E/1293/1293/25; FO/371/45546, Annual Report on Saudi Arabia for 1944.
45. FO/371/35143/E4810, FO to Jiddah, tel. of 9 September 1943.
46. FO/371/45546, Annual Report on Saudi Arabia for 1944.
47. FO/371/40283/E1293, Annual Report on Saudi Arabia for 1943; copy in L/P&S/12/2085, E/1293/1293/25. Additional assistance included the British provision of £10,000 a month to cover the cost of Saudi missions abroad and the American supply of 10 million *riyal*s on credit Lend–Lease. These amounts were additional to the subsidy of £450,000 and gift of 200,000 sovereigns paid at the beginning of the year. *Ibid.*
48. FO/371/45546, Annual Report on Saudi Arabia for 1944; NARA, Records of the Foreign Economic Administration (RG169), E129, Box 819, Saudi Arabia, M. Maerlik (?) to Frank Coe, memorandum of 31 August 1944. Britain's

contribution was additional to the £450,000 paid as subsidy at the beginning of the year, the gift of 200,000 sovereigns, and payment of the remaining Saudi debt due to the UK Commercial Corporation after deducting the 1943 *hajj* revenue. *Ibid.* The Saudi foreign missions that were covered by subsidy in 1944 included Shaykh Hafiz Wahbah in London, legations in Baghdad, Damascus, Ankara, and Cairo, and consulates in Jerusalem and Basrah. See, for example, the Gellatly's accounts for 1944 in FO/371/40262.

49. FO/371/45546, Annual Report on Saudi Arabia for 1944.
50. It is a matter of speculation whether Jordan's fulminations and warnings to King ʿAbd al-ʿAziz resulted in the late 1943 communiqué prohibiting government officials from undertaking private commercial activities and from utilizing their official position for their private gain. FO/371/40279/E605, Wikely to Eden, 12 January 1944, enclosing translated text of Official Communiqué No. 83, *Umm al-Qura*, 31 December 1943. In any case, Jordan's figures on the budget were unreliable. Lend–Lease silver designated for 1943 was included as income for 1944, and a stock of grain was assumed whereas the Saudi government claimed that grain stocks had been depleted during 1943. RG59, 890f.51/70, Jiddah to State, 13 April 1944.
51. FO/371/40267/E1292, Jordan to Eden, 14 February 1944.
52. FO/371/40267/E1292, Jordan to Eden, 14 February 1944. The letter enclosed the reply of King ʿAbd al-ʿAziz setting out the justifications for the kingdom's increased expenditure, including persistent drought, the need to import increased amounts of supplies, and the rising prices of commodities.
53. FO/371/40268/E1566, "Record of a Conversation between His Majesty's Minister and Shaikh Abdullah Suleiman, Minister of Finance, on 15th February, 1944."
54. FO/371/40270/E3840, Ellison, Jiddah, to FO, tel. no. 214 of 29 June 1944.
55. FO/371/40271/E4535, draft decree dated 14 Ramadan 1363/5 July 1944.
56. FO/371/40259/E7857, Jordan to FO, tel. no. 499 of 23 December 1944. The telegram contains the draft of the note to be sent to the Saudi government but the file contains no confirmation that the note was delivered.
57. FO/371/40267/E364, FO to Jiddah, tel. no. 23 of 16 February 1944. See also the reworked and reduced budget estimates produced in Cairo in FO/371/40268/E2036, A.W. France, FO memorandum, 22 March 1944.
58. RG59, 890f.5018/5, William Eddy, "Memorandum on Malnutrition and the Cost of Food Among the Mutayr Tribe in the Hejaz," 14 April 1944.
59. NARA, Records of the Office of Strategic Services, RG226, 85959, G4514, "Saudi Arabia: Economic Threat of Starvation," 26 July 1944.
60. RG59, 890f.515/115, Jiddah to State, tel. of 17 June 1944; 890f.515/116, Jiddah to State, tel. of 18 June 1944.
61. RG59, 890f.24/188, Jiddah to State, tel. of 22 June 1944; 890f.24/6–2244, Jiddah to State, tel. of 22 June 1944.
62. RG59, 890f.24/7–744, Jiddah to State, tel. of 1 July 1944, and Jiddah to State, tel. of 7 July1 944.
63. RG59, 890f.24/7–744, Cairo to Treasury, tel. of 7 July 1944; 890f.24/7–1744, Cairo to State, tel. of 24 July 1944.
64. RG59, 890f.24/8–344, Jiddah to State, tel. of 3 August 1944. Another result of the meeting was an additional plea to ARAMCO by al-Sulayman for more aid. 890f.24/8–644, Jiddah to State, tel. of 6 August 1944.
65. RG59, 890f.24/8–1144, Jiddah to State, tel. of 11 August 1944. The US minister in Jiddah, James S. Moose, sparred with Jordan over the latter's contentions. *Ibid.*

66. FO/371/402067/E1160, FO to Jiddah, tel. no. 39 of 16 March 1944.
67. FO/371/40268/E2324, "Translation of Aide-Mémoire prepared by Shaikh Yusuf Yasin and submitted to King Ibn Saud regarding the financial discussion which took place between Mr. Jordan and His Majesty's counsellors," 2 April 1944. At the king's request, Jordan laid out the terms of British assistance in a subsequent letter. FO/371/40269/E3058, Jordan to King ʿAbd al-ʿAziz, 10 May 1944.
68. FO/371/40009/E2206, Jiddah to FO, tel. of 10 April 1944; FO/371/40009/E7519, "Middle East Financial Conference, Cairo, Proceedings, 24–29 April 1944."
69. FO/371/40009/E2206, Jiddah to FO, tel. of 10 April 1944; FO/371/40009/E7519, "Middle East Financial Conference, Cairo, Proceedings, 24–29 April 1944"; FO, Records of the Minister Resident in Cairo, FO/921/270, ʿAbdullah al-Sulayman to Lord Moyne, 6 Jumadi al-Awwal 1363/29 April 1944, including both Arabic original and English translation.
70. *Ibid.*
71. The British monthly subsidy payments were arriving late, forcing the government to draw £200,000 from Gellatly's. Furthermore, Britain had not transferred the 1943 *hajj* revenues, worth £1,200,000, and Jordan had threatened to apply the whole amount to Saudi Arabia's debt to the UKCC. RG59, 890f.51/63, Jiddah to State, 9 March 1944.
72. FO/921/273, Jordan memorandum, "Normal Saudi Joint Revenue," 3 May 1944. He also recommended again that the 1943 *hajj* revenues should go towards paying debts to the UKCC and not handed over to the Saudis. *Ibid.*
73. "Budget of Saudi Arabia," 8 May 1944, copy in FO/371/40269/E3057. See also the figures presented in FO/921/273, which makes clear that the exercise was carried out by Moose and Landis.
74. FO/921/192, various correspondence.
75. FO/921/272, various correspondence.
76. FO/371/40265/E1671, Jordan to Minister Resident, Cairo, tel. no. 3 of 29 February 1944, enclosing translation of telegram from al-Sulayman to King ʿAbd al-ʿAziz. Al-Sulayman's telegram seems to have been prompted by a telegram to him from Najib Salihah in Cairo, complaining that the MESC was being kept in ignorance of Saudi Arabia's need for vehicles because Jordan had told them that there was no urgent need for vehicles. Salihah had been able to press the Saudi case upon James M. Landis, the American director of economic operations in the Middle East at the MESC, who agreed to supply 100 vehicles. Furthermore, Salihah asserted that Jordan had exhibited a "mean and obstinate attitude" by refusing use of Locust Mission vehicles for the transportation of foodstuffs within the kingdom. He added that Landis had expressed his "indignation at this mean behaviour and promised that they would do their utmost to have Locust mission vehicles employed for transport of foodstuffs." *Ibid.*, Jordan to Minister Resident, Cairo, tel. no. 1 of 1 March 1944 and tel. no. 2 of 2 March 1944. Shortly afterwards, Jordan complained to King ʿAbd al-ʿAziz about Salihah and a month after these telegrams, Salihah was replaced as director of mines and supplies.
77. FO371/40265/E1871, Jordan to Eden, 15 March 1944.
78. *Ibid.* Al-Sulayman had been in India to receive medical treatment.
79. FO/371/40271/E4821, Jordan to C.W. Baxter, FO, 25 July 1944; *ibid.*, Baxter to Jordan, 18 August 1944.
80. FO/371/40266/E4820, memorandum by Wikeley, 29 July 1944.
81. FO/371/40266/E5502, Jordan to Baxter, 31 August 1944.
82. FO/371/40265/E3105, British embassy, Washington, to FO, tel. of 21 May 1944.

83. RG59, 890f.50/61744, Eddy to Merriam, State Department, 17 June 1944.
84. RG59, 890f.00/6–2644, Memorandum of conversation between Hull and Halifax on "U.S.–British Relations in Saudi Arabia," 26 June 1944.
85. FO/371/40265/E3398, FO to Washington, tel. no. 209 saving of 8 June 1944. In answers to more specific points, London assured the US that Jordan had not in fact suggested that the king should ask for a Sunni Muslim military mission or financial adviser; rather, the initiative had come from the king. Furthermore, Britain had not intervened against the Americans in the matter of road construction; Jordan had simply remarked to the king when he met him in Riyadh on the poor state of the road from Jiddah and the king had asked on his own initiative for temporary British assistance. While it was admitted that Jordan had asked the British Council to help secure entrance for Saudi Arabian boys to British secondary schools in Khartoum, it was not meant as a competition with the US. British injunctions against the continual supply of silver was based on the fear that it would simply lead to inflation and was not a resentment of American supplies. *Ibid.*
86. RG59, 890f.24/127, Landis, Cairo, to State, tel. of 11 March 1944.
87. RG59, 890f.6363, Jiddah to State, tel. of 30 March 1944.
88. RG59, 890f.24/153, Jiddah to State, tel. of 13 April 1944; 890f.51/69, Jiddah to State, tel. of 21 April 1944.
89. RG59, 890f.24/194, Eddy to G.P. Merriam, NEA, State, 18 May 1944. Eddy added his observation that supplies to SAMS had ceased while supplies to British companies continued, presumably due at least in part to the actions of Jordan. *Ibid.*
90. RG59, 890f.24/9–144, Jiddah to State, tel. of 1 September 1944.
91. RG59, 890f.24/9–444, Eddy, Jiddah, to State, tel. of 4 September 1944; 890f.24/9–544, Eddy to State, tel. of 5 September 1944.
92. RG59, 890f.51/1–145, Eddy to State, 1 January 1945.
93. FO/371/52823/E2249, Annual Report on Saudi Arabia for 1945.
94. FO/921/272, France, memorandum on "Saudi Arabian Subsidy 1945," 24 November 1944. A detailed memorandum (unsigned) prepared for the new minister resident in Cairo in 1945 laid out the history of the British subsidies since the beginning of the war. FO/922/4, 16 February 1945.
95. FO/921/271 and FO/921/272, various correspondence.
96. FO/371/52823/E2249, Annual Report on Saudi Arabia for 1945.
97. A copy of the budget, as well as the British memorandum on it, is contained in FO/371/45523/E1014. The memorandum is unsigned but, judging from the date, it is likely to have been prepared by Jordan. See also FO/371/45524/E1923, Jiddah to FO, 2 March 1945. Eddy reported back to Washington that he was convinced that Jordan's budget figures were "fantastic" and that he was awaiting al-Sulayman's return to the kingdom for a clearer statement of the kingdom's *riyal* needs. RG59, 890f.51/3–845, Eddy to State, 8 March 1945.
98. FO/371/52823/E2249, Annual Report on Saudi Arabia for 1945. See also the discussion in FO/371/45523 and FO/371/45524.
99. Al-Sulayman made it clear that a loan at the previous year's figure of £100,000 would not be sufficient. The British minister in Jiddah, L.B. Grafftey Smith, concluded that "The loan is obviously required to enable the Finance Minister as Court juggler to satisfy pressing claims from money-lenders, officials and other creditors ...." The company was not keen on the idea, since it would probably require it to cover part of the loan from outside sources, but it was anxious to keep the goodwill of the Saudi government. Grafftey Smith suggested that Gellatly's

offer £100,000 credit on items that it would import. FO/371/45535/E5054, Grafftey Smith to FO, tel. no. 195 of 18 April 1945.

100. FO/371/45525/E2942, Grafftey Smith to Baxter, FO, 28 April 1945.
101. FO/371/45537/E5746, Jiddah to FO, tel. of 5 August 1945. The loan was intended to cover the cost of goods previously expected under the subsidy, Ramadan expenses, and the expenses of the king's visit to Egypt; it was to be secured by 1945 pilgrim dues. FO/371/45528/E6000, Gellatly Hankey Khartoum to Gellatly Hankey London, tel. of 8 August 1945.
102. FO/371/52823/E2249, Annual Report on Saudi Arabia for 1945; FO/371/45528/E5830, Jiddah to FO, 30 July 1945.
103. FO/371/45529/E9285, Grafftey Smith to FO, tel. no. 553 of 28 November 1945.
104. RG59, R and A 1206, 10 January 1944.
105. NARA, Records of the War Department General and Special Staffs, RG165, OPD 336, Arabia, Sec–1, H.L. Stimson, secretary of war, to the secretary of state, 1 May 1944. See also the correspondence in NARA, Records of the State Department Interdepartmental and Intradepartmental Committees, RG353, State War Navy Coordination Committee, on the discussions about how to finance Saudi Arabian development through the War Department.

6 THE BEGINNINGS OF THE US–SAUDI PARTNERSHIP

1. National Archives, Kew, London, Foreign Office Records (FO), FO/371/15298/E1110; Atherton to Oliphant, 25 February 1931.
2. FO/371/15298/E2421; George Rendel, "Recognition of Ibn Saud by U.S. Government," FO memorandum, 7 May 1931.
3. National Archives and Records Administration (NARA), Department of State General Records, RG59, 890f.7962/45, Kirk, Near East Affairs (NEA) memorandum on the visit, 18 June 1942.
4. *Foreign Relations of the United States* (FRUS), 1942, vol. 4, pp. 560–1.
5. RG59, 890f.51/67, Jiddah to State, tel. of 13 April 1944. A translation of the king's order to al-Sulayman to request the aid is in RG59, 890f.515/99, Jiddah to State, tel. of 13 April 1944.
6. RG59, 890f.515/97A, State to Jiddah, tel. of 13 April 1944.
7. RG59, 890f.515/99, Jiddah to State, tel. of 15 April 1944.
8. RG59, 890f.24, various correspondence in July 1944.
9. RG59, 890f.51/7–1244, State to Jiddah, 12 July 1944, enclosing "Extension of Increased Financial and Economic Assistance to Saudi Arabia," Policy Committee Meeting, 28 June 1944.
10. RG59, 890f.24/9–2544, Jiddah to State, tel. of 25 September 1944.
11. RG59, Petroleum Division, Saudi Arabia, various correspondence, October 1944. Much of the rationale for this planning rested on a letter from King ʿAbd al-ʿAziz stating that he wanted "an assurance from us that we are prepared on a long range basis to help him to establish a sound economy and to improve the living standards of his people in return for the oil we are going to get from his country." RG59, Miscellaneous Office Files, File 570–178, NEA/NE, 13 October 1944.
12. FO/371/52823/E2249, Annual Report on Saudi Arabia for 1945.
13. Undoubtedly the most authoritative sources on this subject are Irvine H. Anderson, *Aramco, the United States, and Saudi Arabia: A Study of the Dynamics of Foreign Oil Policy, 1933–1950* (Princeton, NJ: Princeton University Press, 1981), and Aaron David Miller, *Search for Security: Saudi Arabian Oil and American Foreign*

Policy, 1939–1969 (Chapel Hill: University of North Carolina Press, 1980). See also Barry Rubin, *The Great Powers in the Middle East, 1941–1947* (London: Frank Cass, 1980), pp. 42–67.

14. FO/371/40283/E1293, Annual Report on Saudi Arabia for 1943.
15. NARA, Records of the Foreign Service Posts of the Department of State, RG84, 800.1–1943, State to Cairo, tel. of 22 July 1943, enclosing the text of a note from President Franklin D. Roosevelt to King ʿAbd al-ʿAziz. The invitation came in the context of correspondence between the two heads of state on the matter of Palestine.
16. State Department press release on impending arrival of Prince Faysal, 25 September 1943, 890F.0011/74, in FRUS, 1943, vol. 8, pp. 841–2; 890F.0011/102, "Memorandum, of Conversation, by the Chief of the Division of Near Eastern Affairs"; 890F. 0011/103, "Memorandum, of Conversation, by the Chief of the Division of Near Eastern Affairs: Various Economic Questions in Saudi Arabia"; 890F.0011/101, "Memorandum of Conversation, by the Chief of the Division of Near Eastern Affairs"; and "890F.0011/99, "Memorandum of Conversation, by the Chief of the Division of Near Eastern Affairs: Possible Government Participation in Casoc"; all taking place on 1 November 1943 and reproduced in *FRUS*, 1943, vol. 8, pp. 845–51. During this trip, Prince Faysal signed an agreement on 3 October 1943 by which the US would loan enough silver for 15 million *riyals*, enough to meet Saudi Arabia's needs to the end of 1943 and to be repaid in full within five years after the end of the war. *Ibid.*
17. RG59, 890.00/12–2044, Hart to the Secretary of State, 20 December 1944.
18. The translated text of the declaration of war is contained in FO/371/45542/E1613, Grafftey Smith to FO, tel. no. 114 of 28 February 1945. A State Department analysis of the decision to declare war concluded it was driven by realization that only those countries at war with the Axis would be invited to the San Francisco conference on the UN and it followed closely the king's meetings with Roosevelt and Churchill. RG59, R&A 2963S, Research and Analysis Report, 9 March 1945.
19. Personal details of the meeting are drawn from the most detailed source, William Eddy's *F.D.R. Meets Ibn Saud* (Washington: American–Mideast Educational & Training Services, 1954). The account of the meeting itself is derived from the official memorandum of the conversation prepared by Eddy and Yusuf Yasin in RG59, 711.90F/2–1445, "Memorandum of Conversation Between the King of Saudi Arabia (Abdul Aziz Al Saud) and President Roosevelt, 14 February 1945, Aboard the U.S.S. 'Quincy.'" Reproduced in *FRUS*, 1945, Vol. 8, p. 23.
20. Eddy, *F.D.R. Meets Ibn Saud*, p. 31.
21. FO/371/45220/E3689, Report of the Proceedings of the HMS *Aurora*, 18 February 1945. The members of the Saudi entourage included the Princes ʿAbdullah, Muhammad, and Mansur, as well as ʿAbdullah al-Sulayman, Dr. Rashad Pharaon, and Hafiz Wahbah. *Ibid.*
22. RG59, 890f.24/21, W. Murray to Dean Acheson, 15 December 1942.
23. RG59, 890f.24/20 to 21A and 890f.24/30, correspondence between Acheson and Stettinius, January–February 1943; RG169, E9, Box 178, E.R. Stettinius, Jr. to President F.D. Roosevelt., 1 February 1943.
24. RG59, 890f.24/32, Stettinius to Acheson, 20 February 1943; RG169, E47, Box 422, Roosevelt to Stettinius, 18 February 1943.
25. RG59, 890f.24/23, State Department to Cairo, tel. of 6 March 1943; RG59, 890f.24/26, Kirk, Cairo, to secretary of state, tel. of 5 April 1943; 890f.24/27, Cairo to State Department, tel. of 13 April 1943.

26. RG59, 890f.24/23, State Department to Cairo, tel. of 6 March 1943. The king was not happy with delays in the supply of the trucks or the provision of three-tonners instead of ten-tonners, and the question was raised of whether they had been modified for desert use. Kirk indicated that the timing and size of the trucks was based on availability and he confirmed that they had indeed been modified. *Ibid.* Negotiations with the Saudi government over the terms of Lend–Lease lasted a number of months. 890f.24, various correspondence between April and August 1943. See also FO/371/40283/E1293, Annual Report on Saudi Arabia for 1943, on the subject, and Lend–Lease materials contained in University of Virginia Library, Special Collections, E.R. Stettinius Jr. Papers, 2723.
27. RG59, 890.51/7–1043, NEA memorandum, 10 July 1943.
28. FO/371/40266/E6177, Lord Moyne to Eden, 29 September 1944.
29. RG59, 890f.50/1–145, memorandum of conversation between M. Wright, Counselor of British Embassy, Murray of NEA, Alling of NEA, and Parker of NE, 1 January 1945; 890f.51/1–145, memorandum from Collado, FMA to Clayton, EA, 1 January 1945.
30. Stettinius Papers, 2723, Box 721, Stettinius to US Legation, tel. of 24 December 1944. Stettinius also instructed the Legation to not inform the British ambassador "because of his apparently deliberate failure to cooperate with you regarding similar matters." *Ibid.*
31. RG59, Petroleum Division, C. Raynor to Murray, NEA. 2 January 1945. See also the discussion during 1944 and 1945 in RG169.
32. RG165 OPD 400.3295, memorandum from State Department to the President, "Long Range Financial Assistance to Saudi Arabia," January 1945.
33. See also various correspondence for 1945 in RG165; Harry S. Truman Presidential Library, R.K. Davies Papers, Box 15, memorandum for files, 6 April 1945, as well as other adjacent files; Library of Congress, Harold Ickes Papers, Diary 9703, 6 May 1945; Library of Congress, Robert P. Patterson Papers, 161, Senate, June 1945; University of Virginia, Stettinius Papers, 2723/734, 5 and 8 January 1941. Harold Ickes resigned over the issue of oil policy regarding Saudi Arabia, noting in his draft letter of resignation that "As you know, I have been particularly interested in the proposed Anglo-American Oil Agreement with respect to the tremendously rich deposits of petroleum in Saudi Arabia. I haven't had from other members of the Administration the help that I should have in pressing for this Agreement. I do not believe that it can be successfully contended that, especially at the beginning, I had the help in bringing about an understanding with the British, with the acquiescence of the Government of Saudi Arabia, that the best interest of the country demanded. Even after I had persuaded President Roosevelt of the transcendent importance, from the point of view of world peace, of this issue, I found indifference, obstruction and even sabotage ...." Davies Papers, Box 15, Conference Correspondence 1940–8, Ickes resignation draft, 2 July 1945.
34. RG59, 711.90f/4–1147, State Department, 11 April 1947.
35. FO/371/24589/E1636, Bullard to Viscount Halifax, 29 November 1939.
36. RG59, 890f.20/6, Kirk to the secretary of state, tel. of 2 December 1942.
37. RG59, 890f.6363/44, Jiddah to State Department, tel. of 14 September 1942.
38. RG59, 890f.7962, Cairo to State Department, tel. of 19 May 1942; 890f.7962/45, Ambassador Kirk, NEA memorandum on his conversations during his visit to Saudi Arabia, 18 June 1942.
39. RG59, 890f.7962/26, various correspondence on the subject between July and September 1942.

40. RG59, 890f.7962/31, Jiddah to State, tel. of 2 September 1942.
41. NARA, Records of the Army Air Forces, RG18, E300, Central Decimal File, October 1942–4, Foreign Files, 686.6, Cairo to the secretary of state, tel. of 14 July 1942.
42. FO/371/40283/E1293, Annual Report on Saudi Arabia for 1943; copy in British Library, India and Oriental Collection, India Office Records (IOR), India Office: Political and Secret Department Records, L/P&S/12/2085, E/1293/1293/25.
43. FO/371/35154/E7886, Jordan to Gellatly's, tel. no. 527 of 15 December 1943.
44. RG59, 890f.20 Missions/4, Moose to Secretary of State, enclosing report on American Military Mission by US Legation, Jiddah, 12 January 1944.
45. RG59, 890f.24/2–444, G. Olmsted, General Staff Corps, to P. Alling, NEA State, 4 February 1944, enclosing a War Department directive regarding the supply of military equipment to Saudi Arabia, and Brig. Gen. G.X. Cheves to War Department.
46. RG59, 890f.20 Mission/7, Kirk, Jiddah, to secretary of state, tel. of 14 March 1944.
47. RG59, 890f.20 Mission/7–2844, Moose to secretary of state, 28 July 1944.
48. RG59, 890f.20 Mission, various correspondence August–October 1944. An outline of US Army activities in Saudi Arabia for February 1943–September 1944 is contained in NARA, Records of the Army Staff, RG319, E47 350.03 to 350.08, 24 October 1944.
49. RG59, 890f.20 Mission/10–1644, Nils E. Lind, Legation Attaché, "Graduation Exercises of the 1st Student Class of the U.S. Military Mission—Taif," 16 October 1944.
50. FO/371/52823/E2249, Annual Report on Saudi Arabia for 1945. The British, unaware of the scope of the requests, thought the US had taken undue advantage of the Combined Chiefs of Staff recommendation for approval and felt that King ʿAbd al-ʿAziz would not have agreed had London not signaled its approval. Indeed, the British minister reported the king's reaction as "Now that Berlin has fallen they turn on me!" *Ibid.*
51. RG59, 890f.248, various correspondence, March–April 1945.
52. RG59, 890f.6363/6–2945, E.E. Roth, Navy Department, to Parker, Near East Division, State Department, and Parker's reply to Roth, both 29 June 1945.
53. RG59, 890f.002/1–645, State to US Legation, Jiddah, tel. of 6 January 1945; 890f.002/1–845, Eddy to State, tel. of 8 January 1945. With the creation of the Ministry of Defense, ʿAbdullah al-Sulayman gave up his role as deputy minister of defense and consequently was able to concentrate his attention on the growing complexity of finances. *Ibid.*
54. NARA, Records of the US Joint Chiefs of Staff (RG218), JCS 42–45, Geographic, 381, "Report of Negotiations with Ibn Saud re Dhahran Air Base and Military Mission," prepared by Voris H. Connor, 23 May 1945.
55. RG353 SWNCC 19/13, State Department memorandum on construction of Dhahran air base, 14 June 1945; SWNCC 19/14, Grew, Acting Secretary of State to the President, 28 June 1945; RG218 JCS 42–45, Geographic, 381, "Report of Negotiations with Ibn Saud re Dhahran Air Base and Military Mission," prepared by Voris H. Connor, 23 May 1945; *ibid.*, Dhahran to secretary of state, tel. of 4 July 1945; RG218 JCS 42–45, Geographic, 381 Saudi Arabia, "Reappraisal of Dhahran Air Base," SWNCC Study, 23 August 1945. See also NARA, State Department Post Files, RG84 Jiddah, 030–850, Eddy to Secretary of State, 8 August 1945. The rationales for the consideration of the Dhahran base as being in the national interest were: ① US demonstration of American interest in Saudi Arabia and

thereby strengthening the political integrity of the kingdom and thus safeguarding American oil interests; ② the postwar commercial use of the field would be a major asset to American civil aviation; ③ if negotiations to build the field should be abandoned, the king would undoubtedly regard American policies towards him as being of a "wavering character." *Ibid.*

56. RG165/OPD 475.4/Sec 5/Cases 89–90:5/8, Eddy to Yusuf Yasin, 5 August 1945; RG84 Jiddah, 030–850, Eddy to secretary of state, 8 August 1945. A copy of the agreement, signed by Yusuf Yasin on behalf of the kingdom, is contained as an enclosure.
57. RG165/ABC 679/5/2/43/Sec 5, US minister Jiddah, to Saudi Arabian Foreign Ministry, 20 December 1945, and Yusuf Yasin's reply agreeing to new terms, January 1946.
58. R/15/2/317, Bahrain Intelligence Report No. 1, 15 January 1946.
59. FO/371/62103/E5274, "Annual Economic (A) Report on Saudi Arabia, 1946," 19 June 1947.
60. RG59, military adviser to the Office of Near Eastern, South Asian, and African Affairs, Boxes 1,2, and 4, February–March 1950.
61. RG218/CCS 381/Saudi Arabia (2/7/45)BP, JUSSGSA Report of Joint Survey Group (the "O'Keefe Report"), 3 January 1950; NARA, Records of the Office of the Secretary of Defense, RG330, CD 6–2–5, Numeric File Sept–47–June'50, "JUSSGSA Field Report with Final Recommendations for the Saudi Arabian Army, Navy, and Air Force," 1950 (a summary of the O'Keefe Report); RG218/CCS 381/Saudi Arabia/2/7/45/Sec 6:7/8, memorandum to the secretary of defense from General Bradley for the Joint Chiefs of Staff, 7 August 1950. The O'Keefe Report also sought to estimate the income of the Saudi government, which it put at $95 million to $100 million in fiscal year AH 1368.

7 ADMINISTRATIVE DEVELOPMENTS

1. United States, National Archives and Records Administration (NARA), Records of the War Department General and Special Staffs, RG165, G2 Regional File, Saudi Arabia box 3208, 3000–3799, Fish to the Secretary of State, 11 March 1940.
2. RG165, E77, G–2 Regional File, Col. H.R. Snyder, "Description of Saudi Arabia's Armed Forces," based on information supplied by F.A. Kettaneh, 28 June 1942.
3. United Kingdom, National Archives, Kew, Foreign Office, Political Department, General Correspondence, FO/371/52823/E2249, Annual Report on Saudi Arabia for 1945. Some of these comments were derived from FO/371/45524/E1958, Grafftey-Smith to FO, tel. no. 155 of 21 March 1945. The annual report went on to describe Shaykh ʿAbdullah's methods of finance: "These methods are by any standards unusual. The occasional short-term loans obtained from Messrs. Gellatly, Hankev and Co. are backed by a pledge of pilgrimage revenues; but the more frequent and considerable advances of millions of *riyal*s, made by Sadaka Kakl and other local money-changers, have less orthodox collateral and are deviously refunded. American gold bullion, at a Jedda market rate, is one means of repayment. More common, and more ruinous, is the Finance Ministry's practice of compelling its creditors to accept cereals, piece-goods and sugar (supplied to the Government gratis under subsidy) at inflated values, and to recoup themselves in the black market. The short-sighted policy of charging outrageously high pilgrimage dues reflects the same mentality; and it is, of course, a commonplace of local

administration for the salaries of Government officials and the army to be three months in arrears. Sheikh Abdullah Sulaiman, as the man who is expected to produce up to a million *riyals* at a moment's notice, has to try everything at least once." *Ibid.*

4. University of Oxford, St. Antony's College, Middle East Center Archives, H. St. John B. Philby Papers, GB1650–0229, Box 14, Folder 2, report prepared for Hugh Scott, August 1945.
5. NARA, Records of the Foreign Economic Administration, RG169, Bureau of Areas Box 193, Arthur Paul to Executive Policy Committee, "Al Kharj Agricultural Project," early 1944. Some observers felt that al-Sulayman played a secondary role in the project because of the king's great personal interest in it. University of Essex interview with Edwin Locke, New York, 17 November 1985.
6. Princeton University, Seeley G. Mudd Manuscript Library, Karl S. Twitchell Papers, Box 10, Folder 6, Twitchell, Riyadh, to ʿAbdullah al-Sulayman, al-Kharj, 17 August 1940.
7. RG59, 890F.00/73, J.F. Carter, "Memorandum on Saudi Arabia," with the notation that it was "based on an interview with a reliable informant (American) recently returned from there." 28 October 1941.
8. Twitchell Papers, Box 9, Folder 7, R.A. Bramkamp, T.C. Barger, and L.M. Snyder, "Report on Development of Saudi Arabian Government's Irrigation Project at Al Kharj, Saudi Arabia," California Arabian Standard Oil Company, Dhahran, 29 June 1941.
9. The first drive took place in the winter of 1941–2. All of them started in Yemen and took some four to five months to cross the Peninsula to Dhahran via al-Kharj. The 1944–5 winter was exceptionally dry and the 200 head of cattle at the beginning of the drive had fallen to only 20–40 survivors by the time it reached al-Kharj. The oil company had to send trucks to bring them the rest of the way into Dhahran. University of Utah, J. Willard Marriott Library, Wallace Stegner Papers, Box 84, Folder 22, Stegner interviews with Bill Eltiste, Dhahran, 16 November 1955, and Steve Furmen, Dhahran, 19 November 1955. See also Philip C. McConnell, *The Hundred Men* (Peterborough, NH: Currier Press, 1985), pp. 181–2.
10. Twitchell Papers, Box 9, Folder 7, Bramkamp et al., "Report on Development of Saudi Arabian Government's Irrigation Project at Al Kharj."
11. British Library, India Office Records, R/15/2/314, Bahrain Intelligence Report, No. 12, 30 June 1941.
12. RG59, 890f.611A/3, memorandum of conversation between the State Department and the Department of the Interior, 14 May 1941, discussing Twitchell's proposal of the previous day; 890f.61A/7, Twitchell to State, 21 September 1941, enclosing letter from Twitchell to King ʿAbd al-ʿAziz; 890f.51/29, Twitchell to King ʿAbd al-ʿAziz, telegram of 20 September 1941; 890f.51/44, Cairo to State, telegram of 15 December 1941; RG59, 890f.51/44, Cordell Hull, secretary of state, to H. Ickes, secretary of the interior, and C. Wickard, secretary of agriculture, 12 January 1942; 890f.61A/9, State Department to Cairo, tel. of 26 February 1942; 890f.61/17, Cairo to State Department, tel. of 12 May 1942.
13. RG59, 890f.61A/33, US Agricultural Mission to Saudi Arabia, Report 1 (1 June 1942); 890f.61A/48, Report 2 (15 July 1942); 890f.61A/52, Report 3 (1 September 1942); 890f.61A/61, Report 4; 890f.61A/68, Report 5 (10 December 1942). Another of Twitchell's brainstorms while working on the agricultural project was the idea of giving the inactive al-Hijaz Railway as scrap to the Allied Powers in return for a promise to build a highway along the same route after the war. Al-Sulayman did

not like the idea, arguing that the railway had been paid for by the global Muslim community and belonged to them rather than to the Saudi Arabian state, and he also cited negotiations that were in progress towards its rehabilitation. The head of the US mission in Jiddah, James Moose, scolded Twitchell for having presented the proposal to the Saudi government without consulting with him. *Ibid.*, Report 4; *ibid.*, 890f.61A/72, Jiddah to State Department, 5 November 1942. Some of the reports and additional information were provided to Washington by the oil company. See RG169 E58, Box 463, CASOC S.A.–PB173–81–PC, Davies, CASOC, to the Board of Economic Warfare, 22 May 1942.

14. RG59, 890f.65A/95, Twitchell to the Secretary of State, copied to ʿAbdullah al-Sulayman, 14 June 1943; 890f.65A/106, Twitchell to al-Sulayman, enclosed in Jiddah to State Department, tel. of 18 June 1943; 890f.65A/109, Twitchell to Parker, State Department, enclosing letter from Twitchell to King ʿAbd al-ʿAziz, 9 August 1943; 890f.61/98, Jiddah to State Department, enclosing letter from King ʿAbd al-ʿAziz to Twitchell, 26 June 1943; 890f.61A/18a, Twitchell to King ʿAbd al-ʿAziz, 6 November 1943.
15. RG59, 890f.24/66A, State Department to US Legation, Jiddah, tel. of 9 October 1943.
16. RG59, 890f.61A/107, Jiddah to the State Department, tel. of 22 July 1943. CASOC also informed the State Department that it felt it necessary to increase its personnel at al-Kharj to seven Americans and 100 other company men in order to ensure the project's completion. RG165 E77, G–2 Regional Files, Saudi Arabia, Box 3210, 4115, Jiddah to State, 22 July 1943.
17. RG59, 890f.24/39, Kirk to the Secretary of State, 4 June 1943; 890f.24/39, State Department to US Legation, Cairo, tel. of 9 December 1943.
18. RG165, E77, G–2 Regional File, Box 3209, 14120–4599, cited in BBC Monitoring Arab News Bulletin, 15 March 1943.
19. RG59, 890f.61A/86, Jiddah to the State Department, 26 April 1943. A year later, William Eddy, after his visit to al-Kharj, described the Egyptian Agricultural Mission as ineffective and working only when al-Sulayman was present. NARA, Records of the Office of Strategic Services, RG226, 77641, Eddy, "Memorandum on Visit to Rodat at Tinhat, el Riyadh, and el Kharj, April 23–30, 1944," 3 May 1944.
20. RG59, 890f.61A90, Jiddah to the State Department, 13 May 1943, enclosing a translation of the interview, published on 13 March 1943.
21. NARA, Records of the Foreign Service Posts of the Department of State, RG84, 851, Garry Owen, CASOC, Jiddah, to CASOC, San Francisco, 10 January 1943, enclosing a translated text of the interview.
22. FO/371/45546, Annual Report on Saudi Arabia for 1944.
23. RG59, 890f.24, various correspondence, January–February 1944.
24. Muhammad Rifʿat al-Mahami, *Asad al-jazirah qal li* (arranged and annotated by Hamad b. Naṣir al-Dukhayyal; 2nd ed.; Riyadh: maktabat al-malik ʿAbd al-ʿAziz al-ʿammah, 1419/1999), p. 179.
25. RG169, Bureau of Areas Box 193, Arthur Paul to Executive Policy Committee, "Al Kharj Agricultural Project," early 1944. A detailed assessment of Saudi Arabia's agricultural possibilities was made about the same time. RG169, Bureau of Areas Box 187, J.G. Hamilton, Chief, Regional Agronomy Division, Albuquerque, to Volorus H. Hougen, Acting Agricultural Adviser, Office of Economic Warfare, Washington, 3 February 1944.
26. University of Essex interview with Glen Brown, Washington, DC, 4 November 1985.

27. *Ibid.*
28. *Ibid.*
29. RG84, 124.8/Dhahran 44–49, Wing Commander Dunstan Skillbeck, MESC, "The Future Development of the State Farms at Al Kharg," March 1944; RG59, 890f.61A/8–344, Jiddah to State, tel. of 3 August 1944; 890f.24/8–644, Jiddah to State, tel. of 6 August 1944.
30. RG59, 890f.61A/9–2044, Eddy to Yusuf Yasin, 7 September 1944. Negotiations continued during this period on the Saudi government's responsibilities for the US Agricultural Mission, which included rent-free accommodation, visas, and exemption from import duties. RG169 E448, Box 2779, Incoming Cables, Jiddah, 25 September 1944.
31. RG59, 890f.61A/8–2244, Twitchell to Yusuf Yasin, Daniël van der Meulen, and Cyril Ousman, 22 August 1944.
32. RG59, 890f.62222/12–2744, report by William Eddy, 27 December 1944.
33. FO/371/52823/E2249, Annual Report on Saudi Arabia for 1945; RG169 E448, Box 2753, Incoming Telegrams Jiddah, Jiddah to State, tel. of 15 April 1945.
34. RG84 121.8, Dhahran 44–49, AAMSA, Eddy to State, 18 April 1945, enclosing "Report on U.S. Agricultural Mission Al Kharj by Nils E. Lind, Legation Attaché," March 1945; RG59, 890f.61, J.P. Dawson, "Visit to El Kharj Agricultural Project, 11–17 August 1945." Lind also noted that because a locust plague had struck Najd, it was likely there would be a serious food shortage during the summer and extra food imports would be required. *Ibid.*, Eddy also praised the work of the mission but noted that any further expansion of its work would have to wait until a long-range economic aid program had been agreed. RG169 E448, Box 2793, Incoming Cables Jiddah, Eddy to State, 16 June 1945.
35. RG59, 890f.61/6–1446, P.T. Hart, Dhahran, to Secretary of State, 14 June 1946; 890f.61/7–1746, Richard Sanger, NE, to Henderson, NEA, memorandum on history of US aid to al-Kharj, 17 July 1946.
36. RG59, 890f.61/5–2846, Nils E. Lind, N.E. Lind Import-Export Company, to Sanger, NEA, 28 May 1946. See also al-Sulayman's activities regarding agriculture during his 1946 visit to the US, as described in Chapter 9.
37. RG59, 890f.61/10–3047, President Truman to King ʿAbd al-ʿAziz, 29 October 2011.
38. RG59, 890f.61/10–3147, "Report of Al-Kharj Agricultural Project for September 1947, prepared by S.T. Logan, Assistant Director, and submitted to H.E. Shaikh Abdullah Salaiman," 3 October 1947; 890f.61/1–348, "Report of Al-Kharj Agricultural Project for November 1947, prepared by S.T. Logan, Assistant Director, and submitted to H.E. Shaikh Abdullah Salaiman," 7 December 1947; RG84, Dhahran 44–49, R.P. Davies, 3rd Secretary, US Legation, "Irrigation Planning in Saudi Arabia," 25 April 1947.
39. University of Essex interview with Glen Brown, Washington, DC, 4 November 1985.
40. Ibrahim al-Muslim, *Rijal min al-Qaṣim* (Vol. 4; Riyadh: Dar al-thiqafiyah lil-nashr, 2000), p. 45.
41. Examples and mentions of the ministry's role in foreign affairs are contained in FO/371/16875/E904, Ryan to Simon, 1 February 1933; Reader Bullard, *The Camels Must Go: An Autobiography* (London: Faber and Faber, 1961), p. 214; FO/371/27261, 27263, 31445, and 31460, various correspondence.
42. RG165, E77, G–2 Regional File, Saudi Arabia, Box 3210, 5990–9899, OSS Report 1652, "The Position of Saudi Arabia Within the Arab World," 4 February 1944.

43. FO/371/40251/E5941, Major Anderson, "Report on Plan to Obtain Armoured Cars for Riyadh," 6 September 1944.
44. FO/371/40251/E7947, Jiddah to FO, tel. of 9 December 1944.
45. FO/371/40251/E6888, translation of letter from Eddy to al-Sulayman, 21 October 1944; *ibid.*, E6986, Jiddah to FO, tel. of 13 November 1944.
46. Philby Papers, Box 14, Folder 2, report prepared for Hugh Scott, August 1945.
47. ʿAbd al-Raḥman b. Subayt al-Subayt et al., ed., *Kunt maʿa ʿAbd al-ʿAziz* (n.p., 2nd ed. 1415/1994), pp. 125–7.
48. *Ibid.*, pp. 237, 270–1.
49. FO/371/31451/E739, Stonehewer Bird to FO, tel. no. 49 of 2 February 1942. Stonehewer Bird also requested that a financial expert be sent from Cairo by plane to confirm his belief that Saudi finances were in "an appalling financial muddle," as well as to affirm that the country required gold sovereigns to ease its currency woes. He continued by recommending discussions between the financial expert and himself, the minister of finance, and the manager of CASOC. FO/371/31451/E1003, 11 February 1942. The mission was never acted upon as no suitable candidate could be found in Cairo.
50. FO/371/31451/E1395, FO to Jiddah, tel. no. 82, 7 March 1942.
51. FO/371/35155/E1102, Annual Summary of Events in Saudi Arabia During 1942. King ʿAbd al-ʿAziz was adamant about not mixing currencies, which seemed curious in light of his long-standing practice of exchanging *riyal*s for rupees in Najd.
52. FO/371/31451/E1053, Stonehewer Bird to FO, tel. no. 6 of 25 February 1942.
53. FO/371/35141/E424, Wikeley, Chargé d'Affaires, Jiddah, to FO, tel. no. 33 of 21 January 1943.
54. FO/371/40283/E1293, Annual Report on Saudi Arabia for 1943.
55. FO/371/35141, draft telegram to Sir H. MacMichael, High Commissioner for Palestine, consisting of points for discussion of the Accountant-General for Palestine with Saudi Authorities, n.d.; FO/371/35142/E1311, FO to Washington Embassy, tel. no. 1635 of 14 March 1943.
56. FO/371/35142/E1704, Wikeley, Chargé d'Affaires, Jiddah, to FO, tel. of 22 March 1943; *ibid.*, E2012, Peters to Wikeley, 22 March 1943; *ibid.*, E1738, FO to US Embassy, London, 9 April 1943. See also the summary of British views about arrangements for a Saudi Arabian currency formulated after discussions with Washington in FO/371/35144/E5936, FO to Jiddah, tel. of 16 October 1943.
57. FO/371/35143/E3064, Wikeley to FO, tel. of 20 May 1943; *ibid.*, E3713, Wikeley to the State Department, 31 May 1943.
58. FO/371/35161/E3293, Jiddah to Cairo, tel. of 5 June 1943; FO/371/35143/E459, Wikeley to R.M.A. Hankey, FO, 17 July 1943. As usual, Hamad al-Sulayman served as acting minister of finance during his brother's absence and Hamad's son, Sulayman al-Hamad, was sent to Cairo on official business. FO/371/35161/E3317, Hankey to Wikeley, 13 June 1943; *ibid.*, E459, Wikeley to Hankey, 17 July 1943.
59. FO/371/35145/E6727, British embassy in Washington to FO, tel. of 5 November 1943.
60. RG59, 890f.51/55, memorandum of conversation between the State Department and the Treasury, 24 November 1943.
61. RG59, 890f.5151/9, Thornburg to Corbess, Financial Division, State Department, 9 July 1943. See also the discussion in RG59, 890f.515/3–15, February–April 1943.
62. RG59, 890f.51/51–1/4, Moose, report on "General Considerations in Connection with Economic or Financial Assistance to Saudi Arabia," 3 April 1943.

63. RG59, 890f.51/52–1/2, Thornburg to Collado, 5 July 1943.
64. RG59, 8909f.51/51–1/2, memorandum of conversation between the State Department, the Treasury Department, and CASOC, 11 August 1943; 890f.515/27, Treasury to Livesey, for Gunter (the Treasury representative in Jiddah), 25 August 1943; *ibid.*, State Department to Cairo, tel. of 26 August 1943; 890f.515/38, Jiddah to the State Department, tel. of 9 September 1943; 890f.515/44B, State Department to Cairo for Gunter, tel. of 11 September 1943; 890f.515/50, Jiddah to the State Department, tel. of 5 October 1943.
65. FO/371/35145/E6738, Jordan to FO, tel. no. 450 of 6 November 1943.
66. FO/371/35145/E6738, Jordan to FO, tel. no. 450 of 6 November 1943. Jordan's belief that the US was pushing for a central bank may have arisen over the approach of the Eastern Bank, a British firm, to the Ministry of Finance for permission to open a branch in al-Khubar. The State Department instructed Moose to dissuade al-Sulayman from allowing this since the US hoped to establish a US bank in the kingdom in conjunction with the proposed currency reform. Moose was successful as al-Sulayman postponed his decision. RG59, 890f.516/2, Jiddah to State and State to Jiddah, tels. of 2 November 1943; 890f.516/3, Jiddah to State, tel. of 15 December 1943.
67. FO/371/35145/E6813, British embassy, Washington, to FO, tel. of 9 November 1943.
68. Apparently on his own initiative, the king contracted a three-man Syrian financial team in March 1944. Although the head of the team subsequently fell ill and returned home, accompanied by another of the team, it had been able to prepare a pension law and was hoped later to draw up a civil service law and help prepare a budget. FO/371/40270/E3667, "I.D.," "Syrian Finance Commission to Hedjaz," 8 June 1944.
69. National Archives, Kew, FO Records, Records of the Minister Resident, Cairo, FO/921/271/E3025, Maurice Peterson, FO, to Howard Bucknell, US Embassy, London, 8 June 1944.
70. The State Department considered offering Col. William Eddy as a joint military and financial adviser but concluded it would not be fortuitous at the time. 890f.51A/31A, 18 April 1944. Eddy of course was subsequently appointed as the first US resident minister in Jiddah.
71. FO/921/271, various correspondence.
72. FO/371/40283/E1293, Annual Report on Saudi Arabia for 1943; copy in United Kingdom, British Library, India Office Records (IOR), India Office, Political (External) Files & Collections, L/P&S/12/2085, E/1293/1293/25.
73. FO/371/45546, Annual Report on Saudi Arabia for 1944.
74. *Ibid.*, On the Eastern Bank's activities, see also IOR, R/15/2/470.
75. FO/371/40273/E5725, Ellison, Jiddah, to FO, tel. no. 363 of 18 September 1944.
76. FO/371/75505/E1949, "Saudi Arabia: Annual Review for 1948," 9 February 1949. The Dutch bank clawed back at least some of its favored position when an assistant manager from Indonesia, Sayyid Husayn al-Attas, was transferred to Jiddah and proved to be very active and established close links with contacts in the government. University of Essex interview with W. D. Brewer, Pasadena, CA, 6 December 1985.
77. RG59, 890f.515/83, Jiddah to State, tel. of 25 January 1944; 890f.515/85, Jiddah to State, tel. of 16 February 1944.
78. RG59, 890f.51/56, Jiddah to State, 12 January 1944.

79. RG59, 890f.515/89, Jiddah to State, tel. of 6 March 1944; 890f.515/90, Jiddah to State, tel. of 9 March 1944; 890f.515/404, Cairo to State, Kermit Roosevelt report on trip to Jiddah, 20 March 1944. See also Roosevelt's account in his *Arabs, Oil, and History: The Story of the Middle East* (New York: Harper, 1949).
80. RG59, 890f.515/7–744, US–UK Joint Financial Aide Memoire regarding Saudi Arabia and 1944 budget, 7 July 1944. Years later, an American diplomat who had been stationed in Jiddah during that period noted that much of the oil income went to the king. The preponderant amounts handed over to the king were meant for payment as tribal subsidies. "I remember during several visits to Riyadh, at the Ministry of Finance office there, seeing tribal Sheikhs from all over the country coming in and receiving bags of money that were paid to them on the basis of the number of armed tribesmen they could theoretically produce if needed. It was in lieu of a more standing army. An army had begun to be built, but the reliance was still on tribal levies, and this required a great deal of money." This, he added, was usually paid in silver *riyals*. University of Essex interview with Hermann Eilts, Boston, 19 November 1985.
81. RG59, 890f.515/96, Jiddah to State, tel. of 9 April 1944; 890f.515/91, State to Jiddah, tel. of 12 April 1944; 890f.515/109, Jiddah to State, tel., Moose to Prince Faysal, and Prince Faysal to Moose, 26 April 1944.
82. RG59, 890f.515/8–1444, Jiddah to State, tel. of 14 August 1944; 890f.515/10–2344, Dhahran to State, 23 October 1944. Nearly half a century later, a maritime expedition funded by a group of Omani businessmen raised the *John Barry* from off the coast of Oman and recovered the *riyals*. An account of the recovery is given in John Beasant, *Stalin's Silver* (London: Bloomsbury, 1995).
83. RG59, 890f.51/7–2744, State Department memorandum, Division of Financial and Monetary Affairs, 27 July 1944; 890f.24/8–2644, Acheson to FEIA, 26 August 1944.
84. RG59, 890f.515, various correspondence, October–November 1944.
85. See RG169, correspondence for 1945 and, in particular E448, Box 2753, Incoming Cables Jiddah, Eddy to Secretary of State, 20 January 1945.
86. RG59, 890f.51 and 890f.515, various correspondence, February–November 1944.
87. RG59, 890f.5034/9–1344, various correspondence between the American Eastern Corporation and NEA of the State Department, September 1944; 890f.85/11–2844, Marcel Wagner, American Eastern Corporation, to Merriam, State Department, 28 November 1944. The British view of American Eastern involvement in Saudi Arabia also placed the instigating factor on the shoulders of Karl Twitchell. The British minister in Jiddah reported that Twitchell proposed the creation of a Saudi Arabian American Development Company (SAADCO) to al-Sulayman. The company would have a capital of $4 million with 45 percent of the shares available to the Saudi government or nationals (including 15 percent allotted free of charge to the government) while 55 percent would be available to Americans. A board of nine directors (five of them American) was proposed with presumably al-Sulayman as president, Marcel Wagner of American Eastern as chairman, and Twitchell as vice-chairman. Proposed schemes included: quays and wharves at Jiddah, Jiddah and Makkah town-lighting, a water supply for Jiddah, an electric railway between Jiddah and Makkah, fish-drying and canning, the manufacture of carpets and camel-hair work, agricultural developments, a sugar-corn plantation at Jazan, a sugar refinery, a steamship company, weaving and glass factories, flour mills, and road building. British antipathy was raised partly because of the American nature

of the proposed enterprise but also because American Eastern had a sordid history in Iraq. FO/371/45545/E5025, Grafftey Smith to Eden, 1 July 1945. On the company's Iraq activities, see FO/371/45543/E3010, Baghdad to FO, 1 May 1945, and *ibid.*, E3650, "Intelligence Report on the American Eastern Company," 21 May 1945.

88. RG59, Shipping Policy Files, Box 8, File "Saudi Arabia," Twitchell to al-Sulayman, 29 January 1945; *ibid.*, State Department memorandum of conversation, 2 August 1945. For earlier reservations, see RG59, 890f.85/12–244, NEA memorandum, 2 December 1944; 890f.80/12–544, NEA memorandum, 5 December 1944.
89. RG59, 890f.51/3–345, Eddy to State, 3 March 1945, enclosing Karl Twitchell to Marcel Wagner, President, American Eastern Corporation, 28 February 1945. The latter project seemed to interest ʿAbdullah al-Sulayman in particular because of his love of fishing and he pointed out that there were "several localities in which there are great quantities of sardines or similar fish." *Ibid.*
90. RG59, 890f.6363/4–1145, Eddy to State, tel. of 11 April 1945, for Marcel Wagner from Karl Twitchell.
91. RG59, 890f.50.7–1545, CS/SMS, Twitchell to G.P. Merriam, NEA, State Department, 15 July 1945.
92. RG59, 890f.51/7–3045, memorandum of Young to Henderson, NEA, 30 July 1945.
93. RG59, 890f.50/8–2945, D.M. Phelps, Office of Financial and Development Policy, to M.H. Wagner, American Eastern, 29 August 1945.
94. RG169 E448, Box 2793, Incoming Cables, Jiddah, Sands, Jiddah to State, and State to Jiddah, both of 7 November 1945.
95. RG59, 890f.50/1–446, Twitchell, to Merriam, State, 4 January 1946; 890f.6363/5–1346, Eddy to State, 13 May 1946; 890f.6363/5–1646, Eddy to State, 16 May 1946; and 890f.6363/6–646, M.F. Wagner, American Eastern Corporation, to Henderson, State Department NEA, 6 June 1946.
96. RG59, 890f.00/12–1245, Jiddah to State, 12 December 1945. This dispatch covered a number of personnel changes, including replacement of the mayor of Makkah, ʿAbbas Qattan, by ʿAbd al-Raʿuf al-Sabban (formerly director-general of awqaf), and replacement of Tahir al-Dabbagh as director-general of education by Imam Muhammad b. Manʾya. *Ibid.*
97. FO/371/40276/E1873, Jiddah to FO, 16 March. 1944. Not surprisingly, the State Department regarded the British offer as an attempt to counteract US plans for road-building based on an aerial survey. RG59, 890f.24/102, Jiddah to State, tel. of 5 Feburary 1944; 890f.24/124, Moose to Jiddah, tel. of 14 March 1944.
98. FO/371/40265/E3398, FO to the British embassy in Washington, tel. no. 209 saving of 8 June 1944.
99. FO/371/52823/E2249, Annual Report on Saudi Arabia for 1945; FO/371/45551/E8447, Jiddah to Cairo, tel. of 5 November 1945.
100. FO/371/40271/E4543, Jordan to FO, tel. no. 272 of 27 July 1944.
101. FO/371/42440, various correspondence.

8 OIL EMERGES AS THE FINANCIAL ENGINE

1. For examples of positive recapitulations of ARAMCO's work, see M.S. Cheney, *Big Oilman from Arabia* (London, 1958); Kermit Roosevelt, *Arabs, Oil, and History: The Story of the Middle East* (New York: Harper, 1949); G.C. Butler, *Kings and Camels* (New York: Devin-Adair, 1960); and Anthony Cave Brown, *Oil, God and Gold: The Story of ARAMCO and the Saudi Kings* (Boston: Houghton Mifflin, 1999). ARAMCO

itself hired the prominent American writer Wallace Stegner to write its official history but was so dismayed with the result that it buried the manuscript. It was published years later in only a bowdlerized edition as *Discovery! The Search for Arabian Oil* (Beirut: Middle East Export Press, 1971; reprinted Vista, CA: Selwa Press, 2007). A later self-publication by ARAMCO is Arthur P. Clark and Muhammad A. Tahlawi, ed., *A Land Transformed: The Arabian Peninsula, Saudi Arabia and Saudi Aramco* (Dhahran, Saudi Arabia: Saudi Arabian Oil Company [Saudi ARAMCO], 2006). A standard academic treatment is Irvine H. Anderson, *Aramco, the United States, and Saudi Arabia: A Study of the Dynamics of Foreign Oil Policy, 1933–1950* (Princeton, NJ: Princeton University Press, 1981). A condemnation of the ARAMCO experience as one example of the unjust labor practices of US multinational corporations in the extractive sector around the world is given by Robert Vitalis in *America's Kingdom: Mythmaking on the Saudi Oil Frontier* (Stanford: Stanford University Press, 2006).

2. R. Narayanan, "A Review of Oil Contract Negotiations By Saudi Arabia With Aramco," *International Studies*, Vol. 7, No. 4 (April 1966), pp. 573–4.
3. United States, National Archives and Records Administration (NARA), General Records of the Department of State, RG59, 80f.504/6, Jiddah to State Department, 14 September 1942.
4. United Kingdom, National Archives, Kew, Foreign Office (FO) Records, Political Departments: General Correspondence, FO/371/24588/E2806, F.H.W. Stonehewer Bird to FO, tel. no. 242 of 19 October 1940; *ibid.*, Stonehewer Bird to FO, tel. no. 246 of 20 October 1940; *ibid.*, Stonehewer Bird to FO, tel. no. 247 of 21 October 1940; *ibid.*, E2879, Stonehewer Bird to FO, tel. no. 259 of 3 November 1940.
5. United Kingdom, British Library, India Office Records (IOR), Political Residency in the Persian Gulf, Political Agency, Bahrain, R/15/2/442, Political Agent, Bahrain (PAB), to Political Resident in the Persian Gulf (PRPG), 16 January 1940, enclosing intercept of CASOC telegram, 30 December 1939.
6. R/15/2/314, Bahrain Intelligence Reports, Nos. 6 (31 March 1941) and 7 (15 April 1941).
7. IOR, Political Residency in the Persian Gulf (R/15/1), R/15/1/66, Sir Rupert Hay, PRPG, to the External Affairs Department of the Government of India, reporting on his visit to CASOC in al-Ahsa', 19 November 1941; FO/371/31453/E2314, Stonehewer Bird to FO, telegram of 13 April 1942.
8. RG59, 890f.6363 Standard Oil Co/133, Davies to Hull, 17 January 1942.
9. NARA, Records of the War Department General and Special Staffs, RG165, E77, G-2 Regional File, various correspondence, 1942.
10. NARA, Records of the U.S. Joint Chiefs of Staff, RG218, JCS 42–45, Geographic, 660.2, Arabia (8–13–42), report prepared by Floyd Ohliger of CASOC, 22 October 1942. There was also a US military report in which the manager of CASOC reportedly stated that the Saudi Arabian government had authorized the company's execution of preliminary steps to plug oil wells and provide the means for their destruction. The manager was said to have added that the company would not adopt a "scorched earth" policy without specific orders from the Saudi government. NARA, Records of the Army Staff, RG319, E47, Box 162, 350.03–350.08, Army Intelligence Project Decimal File, Military Attaché report, 29 May 1942.
11. FO/371/35159/E6310, British embassy, Washington, to Ministry of Fuel and Power, tel. of 12 October 1943. The impetus for the US government's desire to own oil interests in Saudi Arabia came from the US military. The Joint Administrative

Committee proposed the construction of a 50,000 b/d refinery to support operations in India, Burma, and China, while the vice-chief of Naval Operations wrote to the Joint Chiefs of Staff urging that a government corporation should be created to acquire Saudi Arabian oil reserves, as well as building a refinery there. The Joint Chiefs of Staff sent their approval for the action to the Petroleum Reserves Corporation for action. RG165, ABC, 679 Sec–1A, various correspondence over 1943.

12. RG59, 890f.6363/52, Feith to the secretary of state, relating the former's meeting with President Roosevelt on the matter, 3 July 1943; *ibid.*, Cordell Hull to President Roosevelt, 6 July 1943.
13. RG59, 890f.6363, various correspondence between July and December 1943. Harold Ickes was a strong proponent of US government action regarding the Saudi oilfields, propelled in part because of his perception of British oil interests constituting a dangerous rival. Ickes presented his arguments to President Roosevelt: "I objected again that we had no international oil policy and pointed out that England never overlooked an opportunity to get in where there was oil. Here is probably the greatest and richest oil field in all the world (Saudi Arabia) and American oil companies have concessions in these fields but everyone here suspects that the British are trying to edge their way in and we have given them a great opportunity. The British have advanced some 20 million dollars to the king of Arabia and we have not found it possible to give him a thing. I told the President that the government ought to have a financial interest in these American oil concessions in Arabia and there would probably never be a better time to do it than now." Library of Congress, Harold Ickes Papers, Diary/7462–3:20/2. The Petroleum Reserve Corporation was established in early July 1943 with Ickes as its president, despite the State Department's desire to have its secretary, Cordell Hull, hold that position. Ickes Papers. The proposal to take over the Saudi Arabia concession came in the context of growing American concern over the control of vital petroleum supplies, which also prompted an attempt to resolve common concerns regarding American- and British-owned petroleum resources—including sales in dollars and in the sterling area—through inconclusive bilateral talks in 1944 and 1945. Steven G. Galpern, *Money, Oil, and Empire in the Middle East: Sterling and Postwar Imperialism, 1944–1971* (New York: Cambridge University Press, 2009), pp. 35–48.
14. NARA, Records of the Reconstruction Finance Corporation, RG234, E225, Box 1, various correspondence over 1943. See also the correspondence in RG165 ABC, 679 Sec–1A and the Cordell Hull Papers for 1943 at the Library of Congress. Ickes' position seems to have been dictated by practical concerns such as opposition by the oil companies, rather than personal conviction. Ickes in his diary cites Hull's call for a stop to "discussions with reference to the interests of our nationals in oil in the Middle East" by regarding Hull's priority as discussions with the British over postwar interests. Ickes writes that the original purpose of the PRC was to gain "100 percent (government) control of CASOC!" In addition, he asserts to himself that he is prepared to make a fight of it right up to the president. Ickes Papers, Diaries pp. 8533–5, 9 January 1944.
15. Ickes Papers, Diaries pp. 8581–2, 29 January 1944.
16. RG59, 890f.6363/97A, State Department to Jiddah, tel. of 28 January 1944.
17. RG59, PRC, Petrol Division, Arabian Pipeline, 24 January 1944; RG169, E129, Box 757, SA.000.999, Harold Ickes to Crowley, FEA. 14 February 1944; *ibid.*, Sumner Pike to Laughlin Currie, memorandum on "Contract for the Construction of Arabian Pipeline," 28 February 1944. Not surprisingly, this arrangement was

attacked as a form of "industrial imperialism." RG169, E129, Box 757, SA.000.999, S. Sherwood to L.T. Cowley, memorandum of 26 February 1944.

18. Ickes Papers, Diaries p. 9621, 24 March 1945. See also the unsigned memorandum on "Petroleum Reserve Corporation, Middle Eastern Agreement," 15 February 1944, contemplating postwar implications of the pipeline on Anglo-American relations, in the University of Virginia, E.R. Stettinius Jr. Papers, 2723, Box 744, Petroleum Reserve Corporation.
19. University of Utah, J.W. Marriott Library Special Collections, Wallace Stegner Papers, Box 86, Folder 8, "Discussions in Riyadh June 14th & 15th, 1943"; "General Relations with Saudi Arab Government, Labor Regulations", Roy Lebkicher, Dhahran, 26 June 1943.
20. NARA, Records of the Foreign Service Posts of the Department of State, RG84, Dhahran 44–49, 800.1, William Sands, Dhahran consulate, to secretary of state, tel. of 6 May 1945. Al-Sulayman was accompanied by Yusuf Yasin and the new local *amir* (governor), Khalid al-Sudayri. Al-Sudayri's role was also to take over responsibilities of liaison between the government and the company, a role formerly played by Sami Kutbi, the representative of the Bureau of Mines and Public Works in Dhahran. When a rivalry developed between al-Sudayri and the powerful *amir* of al-Ahsa' Province, Sa'ud b. Jiluwi, the king entrusted al-Sulayman with resolution of the problem and sent him to Dhahran to work things out. RG84, Dhahran, 800, C16, Dhahran to State, 3 December 1945. Kutbi had been a minor official in the Ministry of Finance and received the position because he knew some English and got on well with the oil company officials. However, because the ARAMCO presence continued to grow, it was recognized that the Saudi representative needed to be of higher rank. Kutbi was then called back to Jiddah. University of Essex interview with Parker T. Hart, Washington, DC, 30 October 1985.
21. R/15/2/316, Bahrain Intelligence Report, 31 August 1945.
22. RG59, 890f.5045/8–345, Dhahran consulate to State, 3 August 1945.
23. A comprehensive review of ARAMCO's labor relations is contained in Vitalis, *America's Kingdom*, and is also discussed in Toby Craig Jones, *Desert Kingdom: How Oil and Water Forged Modern Saudi Arabia* (Cambridge, MA: Harvard University Press, 2010), especially Ch. 5, "The Black Gold Coast."
24. RG84, Dhahran 44–49, 863.6, memorandum on ARAMCO by Dhahran consulate, 18 October 1945; RG84, Dhahran 863.6, ARAMCO to 'Abdullah al-Sulayman, 1 December 1945.
25. FO/371/62103/E5274, "Annual Economic (A) Report on Saudi Arabia, 1946," 19 June 1947; Stephen Longrigg, *Oil in the Middle East: Its Discovery and Development* (3rd ed.; London: Oxford University Press, for the Royal Institute of International Affairs, 1968), pp. 201–2 and 206–8.
26. See the various correspondence in RG59, 890f.6363 during July 1947, as well as RG84, Dhahran 44–9, 864, Childs to secretary of state, 9 July 1947. The text of the pipeline agreement was published in Kingdom of Saudi Arabia, Ministry of Finance, *Ittifaqiyat khatt al-anabib 'abra al-bilad al-'Arabiyah al-Sa'udiyah* (Makkah: matbu'at al-hukumah, 1369/1949–50).
27. RG59, 886A.2553 for January–April 1951. The mission consisted of Muhammad al-Sudayri, 'Abdullah al-Turayqi, and 'Abdullah b. 'Adwan. *Ibid.*
28. As a preliminary to the negotiations, ARAMCO suggested expert advisers to the Saudi Arabian Government. The government then engaged Manley Hudson of the Harvard Law School, and his associate, Richard Young. Hudson had been a judge

on the World Court. University of Essex interview with James Knight, Washington, DC, 8 November 1985.

29. See various correspondence during 1948 in RG59, 890f.6363 and RG59, R and A 7607, "Concessionary Agreements Relating to Islands or the Sea Bed in the Persian Gulf," 5 November 1957, as well as in FO/371/68325, various correspondence, for more details. Further material about ARAMCO's discussions with the government is in RG59, 8990f.6363, various correspondence in January–March 1949.
30. University of Essex, Interview with William Mulligan, 1985; copy in Georgetown University Special Collections Division, William Mulligan Papers, Box 8, Folder 4. Gary Owen was ARAMCO's representative to the government at this time, so he handled negotiations with al-Sulayman. Contacts at the next level down were handled between James Knight of ARAMCO and Ahmad Fakhri, head of the Office of Mines and Companies, later ʿAbd al-ʿAziz ʿAbdullah al-Sulayman, and still later ʿAbdullah al-Turayqi. University of Essex interview with James Knight, Washington, DC, 8 November 1985.
31. Discussion of the gold dispute is based on RG59, 890f.6363/2–2647, Childs to secretary of state, 26 February 1947, which gives a detailed history of the dispute since its beginning in 1940, drawing heavily on a 47-page ARAMCO memorandum by Roy Lebkicher, 5 August 1946; and other 890f.51 and 890f.6363 correspondence for 1947.
32. RG59, 890f.51/2–1748, Childs to secretary of state, tel. of 18 February 1948.
33. RG59, 890f.5151/4–248, G.W. Ray, Jr., ARAMCO, to G. Merriam, Department of State, 2 April 1948.
34. *Ibid.*
35. RG59, 890f.51/4–348, enclosure in Childs to secretary of state, 3 April 1948.
36. RG59, 890f.6363/4–148, Childs to secretary of state, 1 April 1948; 890f.5151/4–648, Childs to secretary of state, 6 April 1948.
37. RG59, 890f.5151/3–3148, Childs to secretary of state, 31 March 1948; 890f.5151/4–148, memorandum of conversation between A.P. Merriam and R.H. Sanger, NE, H.L. Deimal, NEA, E.W. Doherty, FN, and Gary Owen, ARAMCO, 1 April 1948.
38. RG59, 890f.5151/4–1448, Childs to secretary of state, 14 April 1948. The Jiddah manager of the Banque de l'Indochine, Delaby, recognized the gold/*riyal*/dollar arbitrage profit, although it did not last after the Argentine sovereigns dried up and Delaby was fired by the Paris home office. University of Essex interview with Hermann Eilts, Boston, 19 November 1985; University of Essex interview with William Crawford, Philadelphia, 1 November 1985. By one account, Delaby used the bank's working capital to mint Saudi gold sovereigns in Switzerland without any guarantee that the Saudi government would buy them. This led to Delaby's firing. University of Essex interview with W.D. Brewer, Pasadena, CA, 6 December 1985.
39. RG59, 890f.5151/2–1648, Childs to secretary of state, 16 February 1948; 890f.51/2/1848, Childs to secretary of state, 18 February 1948. Fortunately, al-Sulayman was able to dispose of considerable numbers of sovereigns through commercial banks, particularly the Banque de l'Indochine and the Netherlands Trading Society; in fact so many that the exchange rate soon rose to $13 per sovereign. RG59, 890f.515/7–1248, Childs to secretary of state, 12 July 1948.
40. RG59, 890f.5151/6–548, Childs to secretary of state, 5 June 2011, enclosing report on "Saudi Arabia's Financial Position" by Judd Polk, 31 May 1948.
41. RG59, 890f.5151, various correspondence through 1949.

42. RG59, International Trade Policy, Petrol Division, 1943–9, Box 2, Near East Oil, 1949, 18 August 1949; *ibid.*, 20 December 1949.
43. RG59, 890f.5151, various correspondence through 1949.
44. Leonard Mosley, *Power Play: The Tumultuous World of Middle East Oil, 1890–1973* (London: Weidenfeld and Nicholson, 1973), pp. 146–7 and 153–4. As early as 1941, al-Sulayman had telegraphed ARAMCO demanding an increase in royalty payments. *Ibid.*, pp. 109–10.
45. RG59, 890f.6363/1–1049, Childs to State, tel. of 10 January 1949.
46. RG59, 890f.6363/9–249, various correspondence.
47. RG59, 890f.6363/11–2649, various correspondence in November 1949.
48. "[M]y understanding was that he just considered that his job was to get more and more and more, squeeze the goose. There were times when, I am sure that it was reported, we couldn't make him seem to understand our point but I think more often than not he was just being plain obstinate rather than dumb." University of Essex interview with William Mulligan. This and following paragraphs depend heavily on Anderson, *Aramco, the United States, and Saudi Arabia*, pp. 188–97, as well as State Department documents at the US National Archives and those included in the *Foreign Relations of the United States* series.
49. Narayanan, "Oil Contract Negotiations," p. 574.
50. This discussion depends on RG59, 886A for 1950.
51. *Foreign Relations of the United States* (FRUS), 1948, Vol. 5, Part 1, pp. 238–41; Childs, Jiddah, to secretary of state, 6 May 1948, tel. no. 129. This matter is discussed in more detail earlier in this chapter.
52. The terms of the concession agreement not only stipulated "an increase of 5 cents per barrel of royalty payments, but incorporated an income-tax levy of 25 per cent on the Company's net profits accrued after deducting the total expenditure from gross receipts." Narayanan, "Oil Contract Negotiations," p. 575. Thus the royalty price per barrel was raised to 55¢ and a minimum annual royalty amount of $1 million was agreed upon. "Agreement Between the Government of the kingdom of Saudi Arabia and Pacific Western Oil Corporation, dated February 20, 1949."
53. There had been some suggestion that Getty had simply bought up the concession as a kind of reserve or as an investment to be sold off later at profit. However, Getty's Jiddah representative later told an interviewer that "I never had any impression at all that they didn't mean to get in there and find the biggest oilfield in the world. They were very anxious for it to be exploited. Any more money coming in would be welcome. I don't think there was anything mysterious about Getty's getting the concession. He just paid more than anyone else was willing to pay." University of Essex interview with William Peyton, London, 10 October 1985.
54. RG59, 890f.6363, various correspondence during January–February 1949; RG59, International Trade Policy, Petrol Division, Box 2, Near East Oil, 18 August 1949.
55. A thorough discussion of the 50/50 Agreement is contained in Narayanan, "Oil Contract Negotiations," pp. 574–9.
56. Anderson, *Aramco*, pp. 189–90.
57. Mosley, *Power Play*, p. 155.
58. RG59, 886A.2553/5–2550, Childs to State, 23 May 1950; 886A.2553/6–1350, Childs to secretary of state, tel. of 13 June 1950.
59. Arthur N. Young, *Saudi Arabia: The Making of a Financial Giant* (New York: New York University Press, 1983), p. 21; Mosley, *Power Play*, pp. 155–6.

60. RG59, 886A for November–December 1950.
61. RG59, 886A for December 1950; Mosley, *Power Play*, pp. 155–6. Young, *Saudi Arabia*, p. 21, says the decree was issued on 27 December 1950 but RG59 documents indicate it was simply published in *Umm al-Qura* on that date. It should be noted that this decree followed an earlier decree published in *Umm al-Qura* on 4 November that established income tax obligations on individuals (apparently including Saudi citizens, although they were later excepted because they were subject to *zakat* [alms tax]) and companies. FO/82667/ES1172, Scott–Fox to Bevin, 14 November 1950.
62. "[T]he introduction in Venezuela of the Law of Hydrocarbons in 1943 and of the Additional Tax of 1948 enhanced the Venezuelan Government's share to at least 50 per cent of the net income of oil companies. All the four of ARAMCO's owning companies had subsidiaries in Venezuela which had accepted the plan of the local government's participation in oil profits on this new basis. Nearer to Saudi Arabia, in Iran, a new profit-sharing agreement which envisaged the sharing of the net profits between the Iranian Government and the company on a fifty-fifty basis was being examined by the Anglo-Iranian Oil Company." Narayanan, "Oil Contract Negotiations," pp. 574–5. The 50/50 agreement also enabled King ʿAbd al-ʿAziz to order *hajj* fees to be reduced by half and to make additional military purchases to strengthen the army. Muhammad ʿAli Maghrabi, *aʿlam al-hijaz fi al-qarn al-rabiʿ ʿashar, 1301–1400h/1883–1980m* (2nd ed., 1405/1985), p. 117; remarks by the former mayor of Riyadh, ʿAbdullah al-ʿAli al-Nuʿaym, at an appreciation of ʿAbdullah al-Sulayman in ʿUnayzah, *Paris Najd*, No. 13 (1/1/1431H), p. 93.
63. The loss of revenue to the US government by the ARAMCO agreement—and similar ones with other oil-producing countries—seems to have been a major impetus for the opening of investigations by the US Department of Justice and the US Congress on alleged antitrust activity by US oil companies. See, *inter alia*, Burton I. Kaufman, *The Oil Cartel Case* (Westport, CT: Greenwood Press, 1978).
64. Narayanan, "Oil Contract Negotiations," p. 579. Not all payment issues were settled by the 50/50 agreement, however. Differences over calculation of the government's share continued until February 1952 when the 50/50 agreement was revised to place profit-sharing before, rather than after, US taxation. Then in March 1956, an understanding was reached over the recalculation of the price per barrel sold by ARAMCO to its parent companies to reflect the posted price, rather than privately agreed discounts. *Ibid.*, pp. 578–9.
65. RG59, 886A.2553/2–1051, "Economic Report for January 1951," 10 February 1951.
66. Vitalis, *America's Kingdom*, p. 138; citing RG59, 886A.2553/98–1551, Dhahran to State, incoming tel. 83, 15 August 1951.
67. *Ibid.*, p. 138; citing Princeton University, Seeley Mudd Manuscript Library, William A. Eddy Papers, Box 6, Folder 4, William Eddy to Mary Eddy, 18 August 1951.
68. *Ibid.*, pp. 139–40; citing RG59, 886A.2553/8–2151, Awalt's Memo to File, 21 August 1951.
69. *Ibid.*, p. 140; citing RG59, 986A.512/3–3152, Awalt, Memorandum of Conversation, 31 March 1952, with Duce and others.
70. RG59, 886A for 1950.
71. RG59, 886A.2553 for 1952.
72. RG59, 886A.10 for 1953.
73. RG59, 886A.131/1–752, Hare to secretary of state, 7 January 1952.
74. RG59, 886A.2553 for 1952.
75. RG59, 886A.2553 for 1953.

76. RG59, 986A and 886A.2553 for 1953.
77. The affair is discussed in many popular sources on Saudi Arabia, such as David Holden and Richard Johns, with James Buchan, *The House of Saud: The Rise and Rule of the Most Powerful Dynasty in the Arab World* (New York: Holt, Rinehart and Winston, 1982), and Robert Lacey, *The Kingdom: Arabia and the House of Saud* (New York: Harcourt Brace Jovanovich, 1982). Discussion in this and following paragraphs is based largely on a thorough account in Nicholas Fraser et al., *Aristotle Onassis* (London: Weidenfeld and Nicolson, 1980), pp. 185–213, Narayan, "Oil Contract Negotiations," and various US NARA archival sources, including the records of the State Department (RG59 and RG84), the National Security Council (RG273), and the Joint Chiefs of Staff (RG218). Other details were provided by an affidavit written by Spyridon Catapodis in Cannes on 18 September 1954. A copy of the affidavit is in FO/371/110124/ES1533 and was supplied to the FO by Stavros Niarchos on 21 September 1954. It should be noted that the affidavit was meant to give Catapodis' side of the story, particularly his falling out with Onassis, and therefore is not necessarily trustworthy. Citations of the affidavit have been made when Catapodis' account is the only source of the information. A scholarly analysis was published by Nathan Citino, "Defending the 'Postwar Petroleum Order': The U.S., Britain and the 1954 Saudi–Onassis Tanker Deal," *Diplomacy and Statecraft*, Vol. 11, No. 2 (July 2000), pp. 137–60; and recapitulated in his *From Arab Nationalism to OPEC: Eisenhower, King Sa'ud, and the Making of U.S.–Saudi Relations* (Bloomington: Indiana University Press, 2002), pp. 65–9 and 74–6.
78. RG59, 986A.53/7–2054, J.T. Duce, ARAMCO, to S. Dorsey, NEA, 20 July 1954. The affair is also covered in FO/371/110122 and FO/371/110123.
79. Narayan, "Oil Contract Negotiations," p. 581.
80. *Ibid.*
81. RG59, 886A.2553/2–2454, Standard Oil of California to assistant secretary of state, 24 Feburary 1954, enclosing Shaykh ʿAbdullah al-Sulayman to ARAMCO, 23 January 1954.
82. RG84, Dhahran 50–54, 510.1, Dhahran consulate to State, 15 April 1954.
83. RG59, 510.1 File, Onassis Agreement, State to Jiddah, tel. of 23 April 1954.
84. *Ibid.*, Jiddah to State, 20 April 1954.
85. *Ibid.*, J.J. Jones, III, Jiddah, to State, 25 April 1954.
86. Fraser et al., *Aristotle Onassis*.
87. In addition, the agreement stipulated that a maritime school would be established to train Saudis for employment in SATCO, the Saudi government would have 50,000 tons of oil shipped free of charge, port fees and a tax per ton would be imposed on SATCO in lieu of income taxes, and a guarantee was included that a fleet of a minimum of 500,000 tons deadweight would be established under the Saudi flag. RG59, 886A.2553/7–1354, J.J. Jones III, Jiddah, to State, 13 July 1954, enclosing translation of the text of the agreement between the Saudi Arabian government and Onassis and two letters between Onassis and al-Sulayman dated 7 April 1954, as well as the Arabic text as it appeared in the July issue of *al-Riyad* magazine. For the text of the agreement, see "The Onassis Agreement," *Egyptian Economic and Political Review* (January 1955), pp. 42–4.
88. RG84, Dhahran 50–55, 510.1 (SAG–Onassis), Dhahran to State, 3 November 1954.
89. Fraser et al., *Aristotle Onassis*. The State Department feared that Getty's Pacific Western Oil, despite having objected to the Onassis agreement, had entered into a deal with Onassis to use his new ship, the *King Saʿud I*, to transport oil. RG59,

886A,2553/7–1554, State Department memorandum on the Onassis agreement, 15 July 1954. Pacific Western, however, although contending that the agreement contravened its concession, was prepared to load the King Saʿud I if charges were competitive. In fact, Pacific Western seemed to be playing for time in avoiding a decision, hoping that ARAMCO would win its arbitration case first. RG59, 886A.2553/12–2354, memorandum of conversation between David Hecht, lawyer representing Pacific Western, and Eakers, PED, 23 December 1954.

90. RG59, 886A,2553/7–1554, State Department memorandum on the Onassis agreement, 15 July 1954.
91. NARA, RG273, NSC Report 5428, 23 July 1954, and National Security Council Progress Report 155/1, 30 July 1954.
92. Fraser et al., *Aristotle Onassis.*
93. RG59, 886A.2553/12–1354, Nelson, Jiddah, to Secretary of State, 13 December 1954. Leonard Mosley in *Power Play*, p. 312, ascribes the resolution of the dispute to a coordinated boycott of Onassis tankers by ARAMCO's parent companies, rather than the threat of legal action. An alternative account of the affair alleging CIA involvement is given in J. Hougan, *Spooks: The Private Use of Intelligence Agents* (London: W.H. Allen, 1979), pp. 280–303. In November, Catapodis held a press conference attacking Onassis. The two sued and counter-sued in both France and the US. The Paris case was dismissed when Catapodis could not produce a signed copy of his original agreement with Onassis (he claimed that Onassis had used disappearing ink). The American case eventually ended inconclusively. Ensuing arbitration at The Hague finally passed judgment in favor of ARAMCO in 1958.
94. Anthony Sampson, *The Seven Sisters: The Great Oil Companies and the World They Shaped* (New York: Viking Press, 1975); Daniel Yergin, *The Prize: The Epic Quest for Oil, Money, and Power* (New York: Simon & Schuster, 1991).
95. Citino, "Postwar Petroleum Order," p. 152.
96. FO/371/110124/ES1533, H. Phillips, Jiddah, to FO Eastern Department, 21 November 1954.

9 POSTWAR STRINGENCIES AND THE PUSH FOR DEVELOPMENT (1945–9)

1. United Kingdom, National Archives, Kew, Foreign Office (FO) Records, Political Department, General Correspondence, FO/371/62095/E1095, L.W. Grafftey-Smith to Aneurin Bevin, "Saudi Arabia Annual Report for 1946," 5 February 1947.
2. FO/371/62103/E5274, "Annual Economic (A) Report on Saudi Arabia, 1946," 19 June 1947.
3. United States, National Archives and Records Administration (NARA), General Records of the Department of State, RG59, 890f.50/7–3047, 30 July 1947; Petrol Division 1945–6, 2 April 1947.
4. NARA, Records of the Office of Strategic Services, RG226, XL 49635, McGuire, FN, to L. Jones, NE, memorandum of 25 March 1946. US policy towards the kingdom was stated in 1947 "to provide such assistance as may be necessary and feasible to strengthen and maintain Saudi Arabia as a sound sovereign state, free from internal and external disturbances which might threaten its stability." In particular, the US sought to ① prevent control of Saudi oil falling into unfriendly hands and to guide the development of the oil industry in line with US and world security and economic interests; ② to secure sea, air and land routes; ③ to develop closer ties with the king and Saudi political and religious leaders because of their influence in the larger Arab world; and ④ to "influence the tremendous economic

development which is beginning so that Saudi Arabia may become a bulwark against Communism and an example to the whole Arab world of the benefits of cooperation with the United States." NARA, Records of the War Department General and Special Staffs, RG165, ABC 400.336/20/3/47/Sec 1-b:13/8, State War Navy Coordination Committee (SWNCC) "Country Study on Long-Range Assistance, Saudi Arabia," 13 August 1947.

5. RG226, XL40463, Fred. H. Awalt, Economic Analyst, US Legation, Jiddah, "Technical Industrial Information and Advisory Services in Saudi Arabia," 31 January 1946.
6. David Holden and Richard Johns, with James Buchan, *The House of Saud: The Rise and Rule of the Most Powerful Dynasty in the Arab World* (New York: Holt, Rinehart and Winston, 1982), p. 156.
7. Parker T. Hart, *Saudi Arabia and the United States: Birth of a Security Partnership* (Indianapolis: Indiana University Press, 1998), pp. 250–1.
8. NARA, Records of the Foreign Service Posts of the Department of State, RG84, Dhahran, Parker T. Hart Personal File, 29 July, 1 and 8 August 1947.
9. RG84, Dhahran, Hart Personal File, 12 and 20 September 1947. Other construction projects favored by the king were said to be road construction around Riyadh, the improvement of Riyadh's landing strip, the improvement of Jiddah harbor, and a railway between Jiddah, Makkah, and al-Madinah. FO/371/62097/E3617, Grafftey Smith to Bevin, 21 April 1947.
10. In July 1946 it was reported that Senator Hugh Butler, a Republican from Nebraska, was calling for a full inquiry into the air base after being told by the base's commander that "This airport is the biggest farce in the world. I frankly don't know why we are here." Butler seemed to regard the base as a purely diplomatic measure and an extravagance given it handled only four flights a week. NARA, Records of the Army Air Forces, RG18, Air Adjutant General, Box 677, Vol. II, Foreign Miscellaneous, 000–8000, 23 July 1946. There was also some discussion about sending a military attaché to the kingdom. The State Department proposed that he entered the kingdom in disguise because of the king's objection but the War Department felt that the secret would escape and embarrass everyone and, furthermore, an attaché was not really needed. RG165, Army OCS, E13, Box 270, 091Arabia:, "Ibn Saud's Secret Approval of a U.S. Military Attaché Entering Saudi Arabia as a State Department Official," 22 January 1946.
11. RG59, 890f.7962/10–2947, Bailey, Jiddah, to secretary of state, 29 October 1947.
12. Point IV assistance to Saudi Arabia began in 1951. It was the first Arab state to sign a technical assistance agreement and the first to participate in the Mutual Defense Assistance Program. Aid in that year amounted to $97,300 and was expected to rise in 1952 to $690,000. Truman Presidential Library, Harry N. Howard Papers, Box 3. But it appears that aid to Saudi Arabia never reached the upper figure and that the program was largely symbolic. "The Point Four aid was just a gesture, $24,000,000 is nothing. A country got maybe $100,000 to hire a consultant, that sort of thing. They didn't need that and that amount is well within the competence of any of these countries and these consultants were available anywhere. We had the Williamstahl firm which was offering its services, we had Bechtel who would build them anything they want, they don't need Government. Point IV had some mild usefulness but it was on such a small scale. I mean, we very quickly went into the Mutual Security Programme which provided money in hundreds of millions. The Point IV was a very good concept and it bought time until we could come in with a more substantial programme but it couldn't be expected to bring about a

great deal of change .... Saudi Arabia never got anything but $150,000 from it." University of Essex interview with George McGhee, Washington, DC, 29 October 1985. The American official negotiating the Point IV agreement later noted that al-Sulayman and the other Saudis were eager to sign the agreement and did not seem to pay much attention to any of the finer points that did not interest them. University of Essex interview with W.D. Brewer, Pasadena, CA, 6 December 1985. Another American official involved with the program commented on the inexperience that many of the program's employees had with the Middle East and their unsuitability for the assignment. University of Essex interview with Edward Betzig, Washington, DC, 20 December 1985. See also McGhee's account of his trip to Saudi Arabia as assistant secretary of state in March 1950 in his *Envoy to the Middle World: Adventures in Diplomacy* (New York: Harper & Row, 1969), pp. 181–204.

13. Ahmad ʿAbdullah al-Sulaiman, Jiddah, April 2012. The State Department had reported that the delegation included Hamad al-Sulaiman, Ahmad Kanali, ʿAli ʿAbdullah Reza, Husayn al-ʿAwaym, Sayyid Matuk Hasanayn, Khalid al-Hamad, Sadam Kaʿki, and ʿAli Hamrani. RG59, 809f.002/7–2456, Childs to State, tel. of 25 July 1946; 890f.51/8–2046, Childs to Secretary of State, 20 August 1946.
14. RG59, 890f.002/8–1446, "Meeting of Abdullah Sulaiman with the President of the United States," 14 August 1946. Al-Sulayman was accompanied at the meeting by the Saudi minister to the US, Asʿad al-Faqih, and ʿAli ʿAlireza (who served as interpreter). *Ibid.* See also Truman Presidential Library, Official File 508 (1945–7), R.D. Muir, Protocol, to Connelly, 13 August 1946; President's Secretary's Files (PSF), Presidential Appointment File, June–November 1946, August 1946 Daily Slate, Memorandum for President, 14 August 1946. The meeting took place at 11:30am and Edwin J. Locke and Admiral W.D. Leahy were also present. *Ibid.* Locke, who was a special assistant to President Truman at the time, accompanied al-Sulayman on the part of the trip involving Arizona and southern California. This itinerary was meant to show the minister the date plantations and irrigation activities in an arid part of the US. University of Essex interview with Edwin Locke, New York, 17 November 1985.
15. Truman Presidential Library, Nathaniel P. Davis Papers, August 1946. A memorandum for the president before his meeting with al-Sulayman outlined the minister of finance's objectives in his mission as: "To obtain a $10,000,000 line of credit in order to buy much needed wheat, flour, textiles, medical supplies, automotive equipment, etc. The repayment of this $10,000,000, has been underwritten by the Arabian American Oil Company and the loan has been made by the Export-Import Bank. To work out certain details connected with internal Saudi Arabian finance such as (a) purchase of gold and silver; (b) minting additional coins; (c) stabilizing the Rial in relation to the dollar. Discussions on these points are progressing satisfactorily between members of the Suleiman Mission and officials of the State and Treasury Departments. To explore American financial and technical aid for certain Saudi Arabian development projects, particularly (a) A railroad or highway from Riyadh, the capital, to the Persian Gulf; (b) The electrification of Riyadh; (c) A deep water pier at Jidda, on the Red Sea; and (d) A series of hospitals throughout the country. Future loans from the Export-Import Bank or from the International Bank will be needed for these developments. To give the Finance Minister and his chief aides a chance to travel in the United States and to observe some of our irrigation projects, railways, airways, steel plants, auto plants, hospitals, hydro-electric developments, etc. and

our way of thinking." Truman Presidential Library, President's Secretary's Files, memorandum from the State Department, 14 August 1946.

16. Truman Presidential Library, Edwin Locke Papers, Box 3, Special Assistant to the President (Personal), May–November 1946, invitation to tea party, 14 August 1946; *ibid.* Locke dinner menu; Truman Presidential Library, PPF 2810, Lock to W.D. Hassett, 3 September 1946.
17. RG59, 890f.51/12–2845, State to Jiddah, 4 January 1946; 890f.51/12–2845, Jiddah to State, 31 January 1946; 890f.51/21646, Jiddah to State, 16 February 1946.
18. More details of the deliberations are contained in RG59, 890f for 1945 and 1946. During deliberations with the US Legation, King ʿAbd al-ʿAziz insisted that the loan was to help the poor, to provide public works and services, and to service internal debts. 890f.51/3–2146, Eddy to Secretary of State, 21 March 1946, and Eddy to Secretary of State, tel. of 21 March; 890f.51/3–2246, Eddy to Secretary of State, 22 March 1946.
19. RG59, 890f.51/10–1046, office memorandum from Henderson, NEA, to Acheson, 10 October 1946; *ibid.*, memorandum from Ness, OFD, to Clayton, UE, 14 October 1946; 890f.51/10–1446, Ness to Clayton, 14 October 1946; 890f.51/10/2246, State to US Legation, Jiddah, 22 October 1946. A slightly garbled account by the Associated Press was printed in the *New York Times* on 15 August 1946. According to it, al-Sulayman, during his call on President Truman, "was reported to have told the President that his Government's request for a loan of $10,000,000 from the Export-Import Bank stemmed from a remark made by President Roosevelt to King Ibn Saud in February, 1945. Mr. Roosevelt is reported to have told Ibn Saud that if he was ever interested in building a railroad line the United States might be able to help him out."
20. University of Essex interview with Muhammad Ba Harith, Jiddah, c.1982.
21. One of those officials later recounted that "At the time the telegram arrived I happened to be with Sheikh Abdallah and he was rather crushed by it but he recognized the order and proceeded to push and ultimately to get a railroad." University of Essex interview with Edwin Locke, New York, 17 November 1985. Locke's quotation of the telegram's contents is presumably a paraphrase.
22. Truman Presidential Library, PSF, Foreign Affairs, Box 189, King ʿAbd al-ʿAziz to President Truman, tel. of 6 October 1946. One scholar cites St. John Philby and unspecified others as reporting that "Ibn Saud regarded trucks 'as enemies, like the Germans and Russians.' The second reason the king gave for wanting a railroad is that highways provided advantages to enemies close by, leaving his capital vulnerable to invasion. 'A railroad could be controlled—and if need be—blown up.'" Robert Vitalis, *America's Kingdom: Mythmaking on the Saudi Oil Frontier* (Stanford: Stanford University Press, 2006), pp. 74–5.
23. Al-Sulayman's purpose in making the call was said to be "to thank [Acheson] for the courtesies Sheikh Abdulla had received from the Government of the United States during his two-months' stay in this country .... The meeting was a brief one lasting less than 10 minutes and was largely devoted to compliments and pleasantries." RG59, 890f.77/10–1046, State Department memorandum of conversation, 10 October 1946.
24. RG59, 890f.51/8–2946, memorandum of conversation between ʿAbdullah al-Sulayman, and Paul F. McGuire, 29 August 1946.
25. RG59, 890f.6374/10–2146, State to US Legation, Jiddah, tel. of 21 October 1946; 890f.6371/11–246, Giles, Jiddah, to State, tel. of 2 November, and State to Giles,

tel. of 7 November 1946; 890f. 6374/11–846, Childs to State, tel. of 8 November 1946. A few months after al-Sulayman returned to Saudi Arabia, the White House sent him a number of films with an agricultural emphasis, including several on Boulder Dam, as well on reclamation in the arid Western states, irrigation, weed fighting, and water measurement. Truman Presidential Library, Official File.508 (1945–7), E.E. Mills to Saudi Arabia Legation, Washington, 24 January 1947.

26. Truman Presidential Library, PSF, memorandum from the State Department, 14 August 1946.
27. RG59, 711.90f/11–1046, Childs to secretary of state, 10 November 1946. Around the time of this trip, al-Sulayman apparently sponsored A. Yusuf Ali's seminal translation of the Qur'an.
28. The final wrap-up of the program as regards Saudi Arabia required disposition of the kingdom's remaining debt. While Saudi Arabia had been given $12.1 million in Lend-Lease assistance, it had also received $15.5 million in silver that it was obliged to return. However, since early 1943, it had been assumed in Washington that no "tangible benefits in settlement" would be received from the kingdom and that it would be "unrealistic and impolitic" to request payment. In fact, the king had been led to believe that Lend–Lease was part of the UK–US subsidy program. Consequently, it was agreed that no payment demand be made to Saudi Arabia. RG165 400.3295 (7–31–42) Sec. 1–C, US Lend–Lease and Surplus Settlement Committee, Middle East and Turkey Working Group, minutes, 28 June 1946.
29. George Bilainkin, *Cairo to Riyadh Diary* (London: Williams & Norgate, 1950), pp. 89–90.
30. RG59, FW890f.51/2–2265, SWNCC Ad Hoc Committee, 1 March 1945.
31. RG59, 890f.6363/3–2745, State Department office memorandum by Collado, OFD, to Clayton, A–C, 27 March 1945.
32. RG59, 890f.51/4–445, Dean Acheson, Department of State, to Dunn, 4 April 1945; 890f.51/4–745, Clayton, A/C, to Dunn, A/D, 7 April 1945.
33. RG59, 890f.51/5–1745, State Department memorandum by Dean Acheson, 17 May 1945.
34. RG59, 890f.51/5–2945, State Department memorandum for the president, 23 May 1945, and Truman's approval in principal, 29 May 1945.
35. RG59, 890f.51/6–1845, McGuire, State, to Eddy, Jiddah, tel. of 18 June 1945; 890f.51/6–2145, Eddy to secretary of state, 21 June 1945.
36. RG59, 890f.6363/6–145, James T. Duce, ARAMCO, to P. McGuire, State Department, 1 June 1945; *ibid.*, Duce to McGuire, 9 June 1945.
37. RG59, 890f.51/8–745, State to Collado, US Embassy, London, 8 August 1945.
38. RG59, 890f.51/3–1645, Eddy to State, 16 March 1945; 890f.51/3–1845, Eddy to State, tel. of 18 March 1945.
39. RG59, 890f.515/6–2345, Eddy to secretary of state, 23 June 1945; 890f.51/1–1145, State to US Legation Jiddah, 11 January 1945; 890f.51/3–2445, State to Jiddah, 24 March 1945.
40. FO/371/52814/E4030, FO minutes, 6 and 12 April 1946.
41. RG59, 890f.77/8–246, Parker Hart, Consul, Dhahran, to Secretary of State, 2 August 1946. The debate between railway and road system was associated with problems in cross-country transport and the government garage. The State Garage had been established in Jiddah in 1942, replacing a smaller garage, but mismanagement prompted the government to bring in a team of British mechanics to run the garage. Frustrated, the mechanics resigned and the garage was sold in August 1946 to the Arabian Car Company. This company had begun as

a largely government-owned entity but its shares were gradually transferred to the company in lieu of payment of debts. The general inefficiency of the car company and the garage was advanced as another reason for the king's insistence on a railway. RG59, 890f.70/8–1446, Childs to Secretary of State, 14 August 1946. In 1948, ʿAbdullah al-Sulayman was elected president of the Arabian Motor Car Company and he then appointed Sulayman al-Hamad to administer the company on his behalf. *al-Bilad al-Saʿudiyah*, Rabiʿ al-Awwal 1367/ 12 January 1948, summarized in RG84, Dhahran 44–49, 891, 16 February 1948.

42. FO/371/52811/E12526, Jiddah to FO, tel. of 29 December 1946. Their survey recommended a route from Dhahran through Abqayq (Buqayq), al-Ahsa', Hilal, and al-Kharj, and terminating in Riyadh. *Ibid.*
43. RG59, 890f.1111/9–546, memorandum of conversation, Snodgrass, Nichols, and Duba of Bechtel, Sanger of NE and O. Donnell of CP, 5 September 1946; 890f.61/ 9–1046, J. Shaw, Bechtel, California, to E.F. English, Bechtel, Washington, 10 September 1946; 890.f248/12–1846, Snodgrass, Bechtel International, to R.H. Sanger, State Department, 18 December 1946.
44. RG 890f.77/12–1646, Childs to secretary of state, "Survey of the Proposed Dammam Riyadh Railway and other Projects in Saudi Arabia by International Bechtel Inc.," 16 December 1946; 890f.70A/10–2846, C.S. Snodgrass, vice-president, Bechtel Brothers McCone, to Sanger, State Department, 28 October 1946.
45. RG 890f.51/9–646, Childs to secretary of state, 6 September 1946.
46. RG59, 890f.51/10–146, Eddy to Sanger, NE, 1 October 1946.
47. RG59, 890f.51/1–1648, memorandum from Merriam, NE, to Henderson, NEA, 16 January 1947; 890f.51/2–1847, memorandum of conversation between Amir Saʿud, Fu'ad Bey Hamza, the Saudi minister to Washington, Sulayman al-Hamad, the secretary of state, Loy Henderson of NEA, and R.H. Sanger of NE, 18 February 1947; 890f.51/2–2447, Childs to State, 24 February 1947; 890f.51/3–647, Childs to State, tel. of 6 March 1947.
48. RG59, 890f.51/3–1347, Jiddah to State, 13 March 1947. ʿAbdullah al-Sulayman had been concerned enough about the country's financial interests being correctly represented on Prince Saʿud's trip that he requested that his nephew, Sulayman al-Hamad, be included in the prince's entourage. RG84 Dhahran 44–49, 800.1, Bailey, Jiddah, to Secretary of State, 9 January 1947.
49. RG59, 890f.24–6–447, Childs to secretary of state, 4 June 1947.
50. RG59, 890f.51/2–2447, Childs to State, 24 February 1947 (second letter of same date); 890f.24 FLC/12–447, Childs to State, 4 December 1947.
51. RG59, 890f.002/12–1247, Childs to secretary of state, 12 December 1947.
52. RG59, 890f.002/12–1247, Childs to secretary of state, 12 December 1947. The question of health arose again on 7 November 1948 when St. John Philby wrote to his wife that ʿAbdullah al-Sulayman had had a serious heart attack on the previous day and that he was seriously ill. Philby Papers, Wife 47/48, 7 November 1948.
53. RG59, 890f.002/12–3148, Childs to State, tel. of 31 December 1948.
54. FO/371/75505/E1949, "Saudi Arabia: Annual Review for 1948," 9 February 1949.
55. RG59, 890f.77/4–1647, Childs to secretary of state, 16 April 1947.
56. RG59, 890f.5151/6–548, Childs to secretary of state, 5 June 2011, enclosing report on "Saudi Arabia's Financial Position" by Judd Polk, 31 May 1948.
57. RG59, 890f.51/2–2748, Childs to secretary of state, 27 February 1948; 890f.51/ 3–148, Childs to secretary of state, 1 March 1948; 890f.51/3–1548, R.H. Sanger, NE, to E. Doherty, FN, 15 March 1948.

58. RG59, 890f.51/4–248, Childs to secretary of state, 2 April 1948. The budget was published as well in the Egyptian newspaper *Misr Infitah*, 10 December 1948 and examined in detail in FO/371/68786/E7811, Trott to Bevin, 29 May 1948.
59. FO/371/68786/E7811, Trott to Bevin, 29 May 1948. The American diplomat in Jiddah who was responsible for reporting on economic matters voiced his skepticism to Washington that the budget figures were reliable and that it had not gone through the normal process of budgetary preparation but officials in the US capital were just happy to get any figures at all. University of Essex interview with W. D. Brewer, Pasadena, CA, 6 December 1985.
60. RG59, 890f.51/7–648, Childs to State, tel. of 6 July 1948.
61. FO/371/68772/E4439, Jiddah Economic Report, January–February 1948; *ibid.*, E9521, Jiddah Economic Report, May–June 1948; FO/371/68872/E14801, Jiddah Economic Report, September–October 1948.
62. RG59, 890f.002/5–1548, Childs to secretary of state, 15 May 1948; 890f.002-5/1748, Childs to secretary of state, 17 May 1948. The two other bureaux named in this announcement were the Bureau of Development Projects (a reorganization of the former Office of the Minister of State for Development Projects that Fu'ad Hamza had headed) and the Bureau of Mines and Companies that Sami Kutbi had headed. Both men resigned at this time. *Ibid.*
63. FO/371/68786/E7812, A.C. Trott, Jiddah, to Bevin, 30 May 1948.
64. RG59, 890f.515/11–548, Bergus, Jiddah, to State, 5 November 1948; 890f.5151/1–649, Jiddah to State, 6 January 1949. At the time, Mikesell was retired from the US Treasury and acting as a consultant on Middle Eastern economic affairs for the State Department. Eddy stayed longer and was primarily responsible for the team's report to the Saudi Arabian government. University of Essex interview with Raymond Mikesell, Eugene, Oregon, 26 November 1985. The British Treasury representative in Cairo, Waight, visited Jiddah in November for the same purpose and, in conversations with al-Sulayman and Muhammad Surur, recommended the linking of the *riyal* to sterling (at an approximate rate of 10 to £1) and the creation of a Currency Board. FO/371/75505/E1949, "Saudi Arabia: Annual Review for 1948," 9 February 1949.
65. The following discussion is based on RG59, 890f.515 and 890f.5151, various correspondence for January–July 1949.
66. The following summary is drawn from various correspondence in RG59, 890f.00, 890f.12, 890f.50, 890f.5151, and 890f.6363 for 1949.
67. The loan had been agreed in 1949 by the king on purely political grounds with Saudi Arabia securing commercial loans to cover it. However, the kingdom's financial difficulties and internal Syrian political troubles forestalled it until al-Sulayman routinely signed the loan agreement in his capacity as minister of finance, together with a trade agreement, on 29 January 1950 with the Syrian minister of national economy. Unfortunately, the Saudi government had already spent the loan proceeds and al-Sulayman was forced to obtain fresh funds. An approach to the Export-Import Bank about applying part of the remaining $15 million credit to the Syrian loan was futile and finally ARAMCO stepped in and loaned the necessary amount to the Saudi government. Not surprisingly, the matter drew considerable criticism inside Saudi Arabia. At the same time, the Saudi government informed ARAMCO that it had no intention of paying back this loan. FO/371/82663, FO/371/82657, FO/371/82659, and FO/371/82647, various correspondence. The first of three installments of $2 million was paid after the 1950 signing but the remainder was left unpaid until August 1951 when the Syrian chief

of staff visited King ʿAbd al-ʿAziz and was given the remainder of the loan. The government could only pay the $4 million by taking out a loan from the Netherlands Trading Society, guaranteed by anticipated tax payments from ARAMCO. FO/371/9167/ES1101, Jiddah Economic Report, 5 September 1951.

68. FO/371/82638/E1011, "Saudi Arabia: Annual Review for 1949," 28 February 1950.
69. RG59, 890f.50/7–149, Bechtel to State Department, 1 July 1949.
70. *Ibid.*
71. RG59, 890f.64/11–2447, Childs to secretary of state, 24 November 1947.
72. RG84 Dhahran 44–49, 864BMC, Childs to secretary of state, 21 February; *ibid.*, 7 June 1947. Bechtel was also hired to repair the king's palace in Riyadh, which had been destroyed by fire at the beginning of September 1947. Reconstruction was expected to cost more than $1.6 million. Dhahran 44–49, 864, Bailey, Jiddah, to secretary of state, 30 October 1947.
73. FO/371/75505/E1949, "Saudi Arabia: Annual Review for 1948," 9 February 1949.
74. RG59, 890f.6363/12–2249, Jiddah to State, 22 December 1949.
75. FO/371/13010, E994/484/91; F.H.W. Stonehewer Bird, Consul, Jiddah, to Sir Austen Chamberlain, 1 February 1928, enclosing Jiddah Report for 1–31 January 1928.
76. Richard H. Sanger, *The Arabian Peninsula* (Ithaca, NY: Cornell University Press, 1954), pp. 3–4.
77. FO/371/68872/E14801, Jiddah Economic Report, September–October 1948.
78. RG59, 890f.5151/6–548, Childs to secretary of state, 5 June 1948.
79. RG59, 890f.51/4–348, Childs to secretary of state, 3 April 1948, enclosing a summary of the interview with ʿAbdullah al-Sulayman in *al-Bilad al-Saʿudiyah*. In the same interview, al-Sulayman stated that work was progressing with both the al-Dammam Pier and the railway, with hope that both projects would be completed by 1950.
80. See various correspondence in RG84 Dhahran 44–49 during 1948 for more details on these and smaller projects.
81. RG59, 890f.50/7–149, Bechtel to State Department, 1 July 1949.
82. RG59, 890f.15/4–949, Jiddah to State, 9 April 1949.
83. As a Bechtel official described the situation, "recently Sheikh Abdallah Sulaiman had returned from Riyadh and expressed to him his dissatisfaction the fact that Bechtel was hauling a large quantity of equipment from Dhahran to Riyadh for the use of 'various persons' rather than for basic development projects. Borman replied that it was a fact that he was hauling much cargo for such purposes and that the fact annoyed him greatly but that he did so on the direct written order of Sheikh Abdallah bin Adwan, who in turn obtained his order from the king and the crown prince. Sheikh Abdallah Sulaiman reflected, then said, 'Well of course you have to take their orders.'" RG59, 890f.15/8/849, Childs to State, 8 August 1949.
84. RG59, 890f.50/7–149, Bechtel to State Department, 1 July 1949.
85. FO/371/82638/E1011, "Saudi Arabia: Annual Review for 1949," 28 February 1950.

10 THE BROAD REMIT OF THE POSTWAR MINISTRY OF FINANCE

1. United States, National Archives and Records Administration (NARA), General Records of the Department of State, RG59, 890f.01/9–3047, Waldo E. Bailey, chargé d'affaires, Jiddah, to secretary of state, "A List of Saudi Arabian Government Officials and Local Officials in Jeddah and Medina," 30 September 1947.
2. Interview with Abdullah al-Sulayman in *al-ʿAlam al-ʿArabi*, 10 June 1948, p. 16.

3. Interview with Abdullah al-Sulayman in *al-Hajj* (Makkah), Vol. 1, No. 8 (Safar 1367/December 1947), pp. 10–16.
4. United Kingdom, National Archives, Kew, Foreign Office (FO) Records, Political Department: General Correspondence, FO/371/62103/E5274, "Annual Economic (A) Report on Saudi Arabia, 1946," 19 June 1947.
5. United Kingdom, British Library, India Office Records, India Office, Political (External) Files & Collections, L/P&S/12/2085, E/1293/1293/25; S.R. Jordan, British minister in Jiddah, to Anthony Eden, 15 February 1944, "Annual Report on Saudi Arabia for 1943. There was an even earlier trial balloon in 1938 regarding a currency board, first in conjunction with Iraq and then separately for the kingdom. Abdullah al-Sulayman approached the British for advice on the scheme and was told that it was not believed to be feasible. FO/371/21907/E4797, British memorandum to the Saudi Ministry of Foreign Affairs, undated; *ibid.*, E5093, al-Sulayman, on behalf of the Ministry of Foreign Affairs, to the chargé d'affaires, Jiddah, 6 August 1938. The proposal may well have been introduced by the Syrians in the Ministry of Foreign Affairs and al-Sulayman simply used the British advice to kill a proposal he did not favor.
6. *Foreign Relations of the United States* (FRUS), 1948, Vol. 5, Part 1, pp. 238–41; Childs, Jiddah, to secretary of state, tel. 129 of 6 May 1948. At the same time, al-Sulayman was soliciting advice from a British Treasury representative sent from Cairo. For more details on the possibility of issuing notes from the British point of view, see FO/371/68787 and FO/957 for 1948.
7. RG59, 886A.14/11–1751, Embassy Jiddah to State, 17 November 1951.
8. Truman Presidential Library, Oral History Interview, Arthur N. Young, 21 February 1974.
9. Occidental College, Library, Special Collections & College Archives, Arthur N. Young Papers, Box 3, Young to Awalt, State Department, 10 July 1952. Young published his account of SAMA's founding in Arthur N. Young, *Saudi Arabia: The Making of a Financial Giant* (New York: New York University Press, 1983).
10. Young Papers, Box 2, "Preliminary Memorandum on Establishment of a Government Bank in Saudi Arabia," 30 September 1951.
11. RG59, 886A.14/11–1751, Embassy Jiddah to State, 17 November 1951. The report is contained in Young Papers, Box 2, Government Bank to 4–20–52, "Preliminary Report on Establishment of Government Bank in Saudi Arabia," 14 November 1951.
12. Truman Presidential Library, Oral History Interview, Arthur N. Young, 21 February 1974. More details can be found in the Young Papers. The text of the agreement was published as Kingdom of Saudi Arabia, Ministry of Finance, *Mu'assasat al-naqd al-ʿArabi al-Saʿudi* (Makkah: Matbuʿat al-hukumah, 1371/1952). One source claims that "the establishment in 1952 of a Currency Board with an American director and powers to supervise the budget was an attempt to strengthen the hand of the minister of finance against the royal family's raids on the bait ul-mal." Peter Calvocoressi, *Survey of International Affairs—1952* (London: Oxford University Press, 1955), p. 202n.
13. Young Papers, Box 3, Monetary Agency 4–20–52 to 11–4–55, Young, "The Saudi Arabian Monetary Agency and Monetary Policy," 11 August 1952. Details about the establishment of SAMA are also to be found in the reports of the new British ambassador, Pelham, in FO/371/98836. By a royal decree on 6 August 1952, Khalidi was included as a board member. FO/371/99836/ES1114, Pelham to Eden, 30 August 1952.

14. Young Papers, Box 3, Monetary Agency 10–4–52 to 12–31–53, Alex McLeod to Young, 3 August 1953. Despite official reluctance to issue paper currency, such a move was bound to be received with popular approval. The physical weight of the silver *riyal* meant that shopping required carrying a stout riyal bag, capable of carrying several pounds of silver. Large payments could be made only using the British sovereign or foreign banknotes, which raised the risk of unfavorable conversion rates. But even sovereigns posed a physical problem: the 40 *riyal*s required to buy one sovereign weighed a little more than one pound of silver, but 100 sovereigns (worth about $1000 or less than £400) weighed about one pound and 12 ounces. Alex N. McLeod's written responses to questions from the University of Essex team about SAMA (2 January 1987), p. 3.
15. RG59, 886A.413 for May–July 1953; 886A.10/8–2753, Jiddah to State, 27 August 1953.
16. Young Papers, Box 3, Blowers to Young, 28 November 1953. The receipts were originally issued in a 10 riyal denomination but five riyal receipts were added in 1954 and both notes incorporated greater security measures. There was some idea of issuing 100 riyal notes but SAMA was advised against it because the design would be too vulnerable to counterfeiting. McLeod written response to University of Essex team.
17. Elizabeth Monroe, *Philby of Arabia* (London: Faber and Faber, 1973), p. 266.
18. RG59, 886A.2531/3–1953, Embassy Jiddah to State, 19 March 1953.
19. RG59, 890f.77/1–1747, Childs to secretary of state, 17 January 1947; 890f.6363/2–1747, Childs to secretary of state, tel. of 17 February 1947.
20. RG59, 890f.77/3–2047, Childs to secretary of state, tel. of 20 March 1947.
21. RG59, 890f.77/4–1647, Childs to secretary of state, 16 April 1947; 890f.6363/6–647, memorandum of conversation between W.F. Moore and J.T. Duce of ARAMCO, and L.W. Henderson and R.H. Sanger of the State Department, 6 June 1947.
22. RG59, 986A.512/10–1351, G.A. Abbey, Jiddah, to State, 13 October 1951; 986A.512/10–1851, Rutherford, Dhahran, to secretary of state, tel. of 18 October 1951.
23. RG59, 986A.512/1–1453, Hare to State, 14 January 1953.
24. RG59, 886A.00–TA for 1952.
25. Interview with al-Sulayman in *al-'Alam al-'Arabi*, 10 June 1948, p. 14. See also the interview with him in *al-Mokattam*, as reproduced by *Journal du Commerce et de la Marin*e and summarized in R/15/2/483, 1 May 1948.
26. *al-Minhal*, Vol. 11, No. 3 (December 1950–January 1951), pp. 174–6.
27. RG59, 886A.2612/1–1250, Embassy Jiddah to State, 12 January 1950; 886A.2612/5–2750, Embassy Jiddah to State, 27 May 1950. More details on the Jiddah–al-Madinah road project, from Philby's point of view, are contained in his papers, 36/1 and 40/3.
28. RG59, 886A.2612/1–753, Embassy Jiddah to State, 7 January 1953.
29. FO/371/62103/E5274, "Annual Economic (A) Report on Saudi Arabia, 1946," 19 June 1947.
30. Interview with al-Sulayman in *al-'Alam al-'Arabi*, 10 June 1948, p. 14.
31. FO/371/62107/E7042, Guy H. Clarke, Jiddah, to Bevin, 28 July 1947.
32. Interview with al-Sulayman in *al-'Alam al-'Arabi*, 10 June 1948, p. 16.
33. RG 890f.42/3–447, State to Jiddah, 21 March 1947, enclosing Garry Owen to James Terry Duce, both of ARAMCO, 13 March 1947.

34. University of Utah, J.W. Marriott Library Special Collections, Wallace Earle Stegner Papers, MS 676, Box 83, Folder 11, Typed Notes, entry for November 7, 1955.
35. Muhammad Tawfiq Sadiq, *Tatawwur al-hukm wal-idarah fi al-mamlakah al-'Arabiyah al-Sa'udiyah* (Riyadh: Ma'had al-idarah al-'ammah, 1385/1965), pp. 115–16.
36. Interview with 'Abdullah al-Sulayman in *al-'Alam al-'Arabi*, 10 June 1948, p. 12.
37. RG59, 890f.61, various correspondence throughout 1948; NARA, Records of the Foreign Service Posts of the Department of State, RG84, Dhahran 44–49, "Reports for 1949," 16 April 1949.
38. RG59, 890f.61/4–549, Childs to secretary of state, tel. of 5 April 1949; 890f.61/5–1249, Bergus, Jiddah, to secretary of state, 12 May 1949.
39. RG59, 890f.61, monthly reports of al-Kharj Agricultural Project for 1949.
40. RG59, 890f.61/6–1649, report on al-Kharj by H.V. Geib, US Department of Agriculture, 16 June 1949.
41. RG59, 890f.12/549, US Embassy, Jiddah, to State, 5 December 1949.
42. RG59, 890f.61/4–749, Childs to secretary of state, 7 April 1949; 890f.50/5–749, Childs to secretary of state, 7 May 1949; 890f.61/5–2049, Childs to secretary of state, 20 May 1949. In his 7 May letter, Childs noted that al-Sulayman had been experimenting with a particular tractor at the Hadda agricultural preserve.
43. RG59, 886A.20/2–1550, Embassy Jiddah to State, "Agricultural Program in Saudi Arabia," 15 February 1950.
44. RG59, 886A.00TA for 1950. The Point IV initiative also become involved with customs administration and the Ministry of Health (particularly in developing an effective quarantine program for the *hajj*). University of Essex interview with James Knight, Washington, DC, 8 November 1985.
45. University of Essex interview with Glen Brown, Washington, DC, 4 November 1985.
46. RG59, 890f.6363/5–1646, Eddy to State, tel. of 16 May 1946; 890f.70/8–1446, Childs to secretary of state, 14 August 1946. Like many projects in Saudi Arabia, the Jiddah water supply improvement scheme was characterized by hold-ups and postponements. 'Abdullah al-Sulayman contended that the project was postponed because of ARAMCO's attempt to supply inferior equipment. ARAMCO, on the other hand, claimed that "the minister of finance, who owns most of the land in the Wadi Fatma, was very seriously alarmed at the proposal to seek the supply of water for Jidda from sources which might have affected the supply of water for the irrigation of his own lands and he consequently influenced the Government to drop the project." In the end, the matter was left for al-Sulayman's discussions in the US. RG84 815.1 Dhahran 44–9, Childs to secretary of state, 16 August 1946. ARAMCO's claims against al-Sulayman were undoubtedly influenced by his demands on behalf of the king for better concession terms and his requests for further loans to the government. Furthermore, al-Sulayman never owned land in Wadi Fatimah and the Hadda farm was owned by the government and used frequently by the king to meet non-Muslims who could not travel to Makkah. Shaikh Ahmad, 'Abdullah al-Sulaiman, Jiddah, April 2012.
47. RG59, 890f.151/11–1347, Jiddah to State, 13 November 1947; 890f.151/12–1247, Jiddah to State, 12 December 1947.
48. RG59, 886A.2614/12–2050, Embassy Jiddah to State, 20 December 1950.
49. Interview with 'Abdullah al-Sulayman in *al-'Alam al-'Arabi*, 10 June 1948, p. 13.
50. Badr Ahmad Karim, *Nashah wa-tatawwur al-idha'ah fi al-mujtama' al-sa'udi* (Jiddah: al-kitab al-'Arabi al-Sa'udi, 1402/1982), pp. 37–9 and 56–8. See also RG59, 986A.00, 986A.30, and 886A.00 for 1950.

51. RG59, 986A.81/1–1953, Hare to State, 19 January 1953.
52. FO/371/68779/E2805, Annual Report on Saudi Arabia for 1947, 12 February 1948. Innovations introduced in 1947 included the transport of pilgrims to al-Madinah by Saudi Arabian Airlines and the introduction of a microphone and speakers at the mosque in ʿArafat, thus enabling all the pilgrims to hear the imam leading the prayers and delivering his sermon. *Ibid.*
53. Interview with ʿAbdullah al-Sulayman in *al-ʿAlam al-ʿArabi*, 10 June 1948, p. 14.
54. *Ibid.*, p. 11.
55. RG59, 896A.2614/9–353, Embassy Jiddah to State, 3 September 1953.
56. RG59, 890f.51A/9–1748, M.E. Wagner, President, American Eastern Corporation, to secretary of state, 17 September 1948; 890f.51A/10–1848, Wagner to secretary of state, 18 October 1948. It was also noted that Twitchell would continue to be employed by American Eastern.
57. RG59, 890f.12/2–449, Jiddah to State, 4 February 1949; 890f.143/4–1449, Jiddah to State, 4 April 1949.
58. RG59, 890f.6363/3–249, Childs to secretary of state, 2 March 1949. This was the same Edwin A. Locke, Jr., who had served as special assistant to President Truman during 1946–7 and with whom al-Sulayman had dealt during his 1946 visit to the US. His interest in SARINCO derived from his position as a vice-president of Chase National Bank, which saw opportunities for the investment of funds that otherwise would be liable to US taxes. However, the firm's success in Saudi Arabia was limited to the establishment of a Coca-Cola factory in Jiddah. In January 1952, Locke was appointed US economic and technical assistance administrator for the Middle East. FO/371/98276/E11343, Hugh-Jones to Eden, 6 January 1952.
59. SARINCO was developed as a collaboration between American, Swiss, and Saudi investors. As a first step, the company received an informal commitment from the Export-Import Bank for a $4 million loan to buy equipment and provide part of the working capital. But when the Korean War broke out, the American investors grew nervous and pulled out. This brought an end to the project and al-Sulayman agreed to reimburse the company $50,000 for its expenses. University of Essex interview with Edwin Locke (17 November 1985). Locke and his fellow investors subsequently established a Coca-Cola bottling plant in Jiddah, as well as an ice plant. *Ibid.*, p. 13.
60. RG59, 886A.26A and 886A.3972 for 1953.

11 THE EMERGENCE OF PROSPERITY (1950–4)

1. University of Virginia Library, Special Collections, J. Rives Childs Papers, 9256/6, undated.
2. United States, National Archives and Records Administration (NARA), General Records of the Department of State (RG59), 886A for January–April 1950. See also the correspondence on currency during 1950 in United Kingdom, National Archives, Kew, Foreign Office (FO) Records, Political Departments: General Correspondence, FO/371/82661.
3. RG59, 886A for 1950.
4. RG59, 886A.13/5–30–50, Jiddah to State, 30 May 1950.
5. RG59, 886A.13/7–652, Jiddah to State, with text of renewal, 6 July 1952.
6. RG59, 886A for 1950.

7. RG59, 886A for 1950 and 1951. The tariff experts presented a preliminary report on changes in the tariff schedule to al-Sulayman in December 1951. He was angered because of his impression that certain items would be omitted from duty and feared that this would lessen government revenues. The team assured him that the possibility of omitting items had been discussed but not decided upon. Furthermore, they could not estimate the impact of the changes upon revenue because of a lack of economic data. RG59, 886A.00TA/12–2751, Hare to State, 27 December 1951.
8. RG59, 886A for 1951.
9. RG59, 886A and 786A for 1952; Occidental College, Library, Special Collections & College Archives, Arthur N. Young Papers, Box 3, Government Bank to 4–20–52, Young to George A. Blowers, International Monetary Fund, 23 March 1952.
10. FO/37/99836/ES1114, Pelham to Eden, 1 May 1952.
11. RG59, 886A.133/11–1953, Embassy Jiddah to State, 19 November 1953, and further 886A correspondence in December 1953. More details are contained in University of Essex interviews, Alex N. McLeod written responses to questions about SAMA, 2 January 1987.
12. RG59, 886A.10/9–850, J.T. Duce, ARAMCO, to Awalt, State Department, 8 September 1950.
13. FO/371/82659/ES1111, Chancery Jiddah to Eastern Department, FO. The figures from the Economist reporting were also published in an article in *al-Misri* (Cairo). RG59, 886A.10/4–850, Childs to State, two letters, both dated 8 April 1950.
14. RG59, 886A.10/5–951, Jiddah to State, 9 May 1951; 886A.10/5–1351, Jiddah to State, 13 May 1951; 886A.10/7–751, Jiddah to State, 7 July 1951. The budget was published in *al-Bilad al-Sa'udiyah* on 17 June 1951 and *Umm al-Qura* on 23 June 1951.
15. George A. Lipsky, *Saudi Arabia: Its People, Its Society, Its Culture* (New Haven, CT: Human Relations Area Files Press, 1959), p. 181.
16. RG59, 886A for 1951. By the 50/50 agreement, royalties were paid to the Saudi government one month in arrears while taxes were paid in the following year. The total income tax due during 1950 was estimated by ARAMCO first at $44 million and then later at $50 million. *Ibid.*
17. RG59, 886A for 1951.
18. RG59, 886A.2553 for 1951.
19. RG59, 886A.00/4–1253, Saudi Arabia Annual Economic and Financial Review for 1952, 12 April 1953.
20. RG59, 886A.00 for 1952; RG84, Dhahran Post, 832843/511.2, Dhahran to State, 17 November 1952.
21. RG59, 886A.10/5–552, Embassy Jiddah to State, 5 May 1952.
22. RG59, 886A for May–July 1952.
23. RG59, 886A for 1950.
24. RG59, 886A for December 1950.
25. RG59, 986A.541 for 1950.
26. RG59, 886A.2553 for 1951.
27. RG59, 886A for 1951.
28. RG59, 886A.00/8–2052, Glenn Abbey, Jiddah, to State, 17 March 1952.
29. Truman Presidential Library, William B. Gates, Jr., "Some Comments on the Loan Problem in Saudi Arabia," memorandum for files, 2 July 1952; Sidney Sherwood and Karl O. Kohler, Jr., memorandum, "Meeting with Baker Officials, 2 July 1952; Sidney Sherwood Papers, Exim Bank Trip to Middle

East, April–May 1952, "Exim Bank Operations in Saudi Arabia, Report," 8 July 1952.

30. University of Essex interview with Edward Betzig, Washington, DC, 20 December 1985.
31. RG59, 886A.2553 for October–December 1953. Details on the negotiations between MBJI and the Saudi government that eventually allowed the company to depart completely from the kingdom in 1954 are in RG84, Dhahran 1950–4.
32. RG59, 886A.00 for March–April 1952.
33. RG59, 886A.00–TA/6–1552, Samuel Stratton, US director, TCA, to State, "Point IV May Report—Saudi Arabia," 15 June 1952.
34. RG59, 886A.00–TA/7–1352, Awalt to Stabler, State Department, and Embassy Jiddah tel. to State, both of 13 July 1952.
35. RG59, 886A.00–TA/7–2952, Embassy Jiddah to State, 29 July 1952.
36. RG59, 886A.00–TA/9–952, "Point IV August Report—Saudi Arabia," 9 September 1952.
37. RG886A.00–TA/9–952, "Point IV November Report—Saudi Arabia," 7 December 1952.
38. RG59, 886A.2553/5–2652, memorandum of conversation between the State Department and Michael Baker, 26 May 1952.
39. R59 886A.2553/4–452, memorandum of a conversation between the State Department and Bechtel representatives, 4 April 1952. Bechtel's English complained that Najib Salihah had refused him access to al-Sulayman and insisted on handling the matter personally. *Ibid.*
40. RG59, 786A.5MSP/1–1053, Embassy Jiddah to State, 10 January 1953.
41. RG59, 786A.00–TA for 1953.
42. It should be noted that al-Sulayman was unhappy that an end to the mapping and geological operations of the US Geological Survey was one undesired aspect of the Point IV termination. RG59, 786a.022/8–1454, Jones, Jiddah, to State, 14 August 1954. At the same time, the finance minister seems to have taken the opportunity, while on his 1953 trip to Germany, to engage prominent German geologists to undertake surveys for oil and minerals. FO/371/110125, various correspondence, March–April 1954.
43. RG59, 886A.19/4–2554, J.J. Jones, III, Jiddah, to secretary of state, 25 April 1954.
44. RG59, 886A.19/8–1054, Wadsworth to secretary of state, tel. of 11 August 1954; 886A.19/8–1754, C.C.R. Nelson to secretary of state, 17 August 1954.
45. RG59, 886A.19/8–2954, Wadsworth to State, tel. of 29 August 1954; 886A.19/9–154, Wadsworth to secretary of state, tel. of 1 September 1954; 886A.19/9–754, Embassy Jiddah to State, 7 September 1954.
46. RG59, 886A.10/5–1651, Hare to State, 16 May 2011.
47. RG59, 786A.13/9–2951, Embassy Jiddah to Secretary of State, 29 September 1951; 786A.13/10–1851, Embassy Jiddah to State, 18 October 1951; Young Papers, Box 2, memorandum by Young, 27 October 1951. The ministerial decision was published in *Umm al-Qura*, No. 1378, 5 Dhu al-Hijjah 1370/7 September 1951.
48. RG59, 986A.512/3–3152, memorandum of conversation between Duce and State Department NEA officials G.L. Jones, N.E. Funkhauser, Stabler, Langanecker, and Awalt, 31 March 1952. Bin ʿAdwan apparently had studied to be a *qadi* in Najd. He later became a director of the electric company in Riyadh. University of Essex interview with James Knight, Washington, DC, 8 November 1985.
49. RG 786A.13/7–1752, Hare to State, tel. of 17 July 1952; 786A.13/7–1952, G.A. Abbey, Jiddah, to State, 19 July 1952.

50. RG59, 886A.00/8–3152, Glenn Abbey, Jiddah, to State, 31 August 1952.
51. RG59, 786A.00/11–1652, Hare to State, 16 November 1952; 786A.1/11–2452, Jiddah to State, 24 November 1952; 786A.11/12–2052, Hare to State, 20 December 1952; 786A.1/12–2252, Jiddah to State, 22 December 1952.
52. Muhammad Tawfiq Sadiq, *Tatawwur al-hukm wal-idarah fi al-mamlakah al-'Arabiyah al-Sa'udiyah* (Riyadh: Ma'had al-idarah al-'ammah, 1385/1965), pp. 113–14; citing *ARAMCO Handbook*, p. 241; royal decree no. 140 of 29–1–1372, published in *Umm al-Qura*, no. 1436, 12/2/1372–31/10–1952; royal decree no. 37 of 3/7/1380, published in *Umm al-Qura*, no. 1850, 5/8/1380–23/12/1960.
53. RG59, 786A.13/7–1953, Embassy Jiddah to State, 19 July 1953.
54. RG59, 786A.00/10–1253, Embassy Jiddah to secretary of state, 12 October 1953; 786A.13/11–153, J.J. Jones, Jiddah, to State, 1 November 1953.
55. RG59, 786A.13 during November 1953. Al-Sulayman and his family had departed Jiddah for Beirut in September 1953. His departure sparked a frantic round of rumors. Philby noted that "Abdullah Sulaiman has departed on indefinite leave of absence on the grounds of ill-health, and it is rumoured that he is not likely to return, while this is supported by the fact that two planes were required to transport him and his family and his chattels to Beirut. At any rate his absence will be prolonged, though as yet no successor has been appointed, while it is rumoured that one of the king's sons, Khalid, may be the new Minister, with Muhammad Surur as his number one man; and Tubaishi, the king's chamberlain, has also been tipped for the post. The position of Sulaiman al Hamad and 'Abdul-'Aziz ibn Sulaiman is not yet clear, and it is on the cards that there may be a clean sweep of the whole family and of all the officials employed by it." Philby Papers, 13/6, diary entry for 14 September 1943; 36/4, Philby to Wood, 21 September 1953. Philby also noted in his diary that the king had given al-Sulayman 5 million *riyal*s for his sick-leave holiday. Philby Papers, 13/6, 29 September 1953.
56. Philby noted in his diary that al-Sulayman had tendered his resignation but that King Sa'ud had not accepted it for the time being. Philby Papers, 13/6, diary entry for 28 November 1953.
57. Muhammad Surur's appointment led to more rumors that he would replace al-Sulayman in the near future, or that a prince would take al-Sulayman's place and Muhammad Surur would serve as his deputy. RG59, 786A.11/12–653, J.J. Jones, Jiddah, to State, 6 December 1953.
58. RG786A.13/12–2953, Jiddah to State, 29 December 1953.
59. RG59, 786A.13/9–953, Jiddah to State, 9 September 1953.
60. RG59, 786A.11/12–1753, Jones, Jiddah, to State, tel. of 18 December 1953.
61. RG59, 786A.13/2–1953, G.A. Abbey, Jiddah, to State, 19 February 1953. Salihah apparently had been out of the country at the time of 'Abd al-'Aziz al-Sulayman's appointment. Upon his return, and the discovery that he would not get his job back, he left Saudi Arabia after only one week, presumably for good. FO/371/104879/ES153, Pelham to Greenhill, 3 August 1953. An American diplomat in the early 1950s remembered years later a trip he made to Lebanon that included a stop in Salihah's village of origin. According to this description, Salihah returned to his home village as one of the wealthiest men in Lebanon. University of Essex interview with William Crawford, Philadelphia, 1 November 1985.
62. RG59, 786A.13/3–253, Hare to State, 2 March 1953.
63. RG 59 786A.00/3–454, Wadsworth, Jiddah, to secretary of state, tel. of 5 March 1954.

64. RG59, 786A.00/3–1054, Wadsworth, Jiddah to State, 10 March 1954; 786A.11/3–1554, Wadsworth, Jiddah, to secretary of state, tel. of 15 March 1954.
65. RG59, 786A.00/3–1754, Wadsworth to secretary of state, tel. of 17 March 1954. Prince Faysal was to head the committee and Muhammad Surur was named a member. *Ibid.*
66. RG59, 786A.00/4–654, J.J. Jones III, to State, 6 April 1954.
67. RG59, 786A.11/3–1554, Wadsworth, Jiddah, to secretary of state, tel. of 15 March 1954.
68. RG59, 786A.13/9–454, Nelson, Jiddah, to State, 4 September 1954; enclosing the decree and King Saʿud's letter to Prince Faysal on the appointment, as published in *al-Bilad al-Saʿudiyah* of 16 August 1954.
69. Other expected agenda topics included the Onassis Agreement and British proposals regarding al-Buraymi affair. RG59, 786A.00/3–454, Wadsworth, Jiddah, to secretary of state, 5 March 1954.
70. RG59, 786A.00/3–1054, Wadsworth, Jiddah, to State, 10 March 1954; 786A.00/3–1554, Wadsworth, Jiddah, to secretary of state, 15 March 1954.
71. RG59, 786A.00/3–1754, Wadsworth, Jiddah, to secretary of state, 17 March 1954.
72. RG59, 786A.13/3–2154, Wadsworth, Jiddah, to secretary of state, tel. of 21 March 1954. Wadsworth also noted that the new minister of commerce had been a very influential figure in the recent Ministry of Finance agreement with Onassis. *Ibid.*
73. RG59, 786A.00/4–654, J.J. Jones III, Jiddah, to State, 6 April 1954. See also the description of changes in FO/371/110098/ES1017, Pelham to Eden, 20 April 1954.
74. RG59, 786A.13/4–1954, Embassy Jiddah, to State, 19 April 1954.
75. Earlier anecdotes indicate good relations between Prince Faysal and al-Sulayman. One story relates that probably in the early 1930s, al-Sulayman accompanied the king on a motor tour around Jiddah. They came into al-Kandarah quarter where the finance minister told the king he was living in some small houses there. When they moved onto al-Madinah Road, the king spotted a large house and asked who the owner was. When he discovered it belonged to Muhammad ʿAlireza, the king asked him to give it to al-Sulayman. However, al-Sulayman told the king that Prince Faysal did not have a house in which to stay when he came to Jiddah and that Prince Faysal was more worthy of the house, and so the house passed to Prince Faysal. Years later, when King Saʿud ascended the throne, he presented himself in Jiddah. Although the new king had a palace in Jiddah, Prince Faysal still had the same house in al-Kandarah. Al-Sulayman realized that Prince Faysal had need of an office in Jiddah and so he presented him with the house of his wife to use as an office. When the prince refused, al-Sulayman went to King Saʿud and prevailed upon him to accept the house for Prince Faysal's use. Muhammad ʿAli Maghrabi, *aʿlam al-Hijaz fi al-qarn al-rabiʿ ʿashar, 1301–1400h/1883–1980m* (2nd ed., 1405/1985), pp. 121–2.
76. Further evidence that al-Sulayman's removal was simply an inevitable transition to retirement came from the British ambassador: "Abdullah Sulaiman was for many years Ibn Saud's minister of finance and chief adviser, and the power he wielded was second only to the king's. Somewhat irrationally, he came to symbolise in the eyes of the younger men who now fill the ministerial posts all that was unsatisfactory in the old regime. With much face-saving he was gently removed from power and his placed filled by Sheikh Mohammed Surur, a competent man, but one who depends on Faisal for major decisions. Thus the reins of government passed to one who, though no more experienced than Abdullah Sulaiman, yet realises more clearly that Saudi Arabia can no longer be ruled in the arbitrary

manner of the good old days." FO/371/114872/E1011, Pelham to Eden, 6 January 1955. This interpretation was confirmed by an ARAMCO official, James Knight, who told an interviewer that "I have no feeling of his being ousted or anything like that. Thinking back on it I guess at the time we must have all thought it was just a normal transition. He had been around for a long long time and the fact that he was no longer in that position, my recollection is that that came as no great surprise to people." University of Essex interview with James Knight, 8 November 1985, p. 20. This was also the view of Parker T. Hart, who had known al-Sulayman when he served in the US embassy in Jiddah in 1944–6 and again as ambassador in 1961–5. "I assumed he retired because of age and because of some infirmities. He had also acquired enough wealth. You see, the old King made his Royal retainers wealthy men, when he had the money to make them that way. When he didn't have the money he gave them land, which later became tremendously valuable. That was the way he rewarded, that was the pension, only the pension started before you retired frequently." University of Essex interview with Parker T. Hart, Washington, DC, 30 October 1985, p. 19. Hart also speculated that working under King Sa'ud must have been a tremendous headache for al-Sulayman due to the king's lack of financial resolve and tendency to hand out money without any accounting. *Ibid.*, pp. 20–2.

77. Princeton University, Seeley G. Mudd Manuscript Library, Karl S. Twitchell Papers, Box 18, Folder 4, Bill Burleigh, ARAMCO, Dhahran, to Twitchell, 14 September 1953.
78. The texts of the announcement and the decrees was printed in *al-Mirhal* (Muharram–Safar 1374/October 1954), pp. 2–4.
79. Shaykh 'Abdullah al-Sulaiman Papers, privately held, Jiddah, 'Abdullah al-Sulayman letter to Sulayman al-Naniyah, 1/23/1374.
80. "Saudi Arabia's Finance—The Achievements of the Ministry of Finance," *Islamic Review*, Vol. 43 (December 1955), p. 33.
81. *Ibid.*

Bibliography

PRIMARY SOURCES

Arabic

Darat al-Malik ʿAbd al-ʿAziz, Riyadh.
King ʿAbd al-ʿAziz Library Documentary Archives, Riyadh.
Shaykh ʿAbdullah al-Sulaiman Papers, privately held, Jiddah.
Umm al-Qura, semi-official gazette, Makkah. Darat al-Malik ʿAbd al-ʿAziz. *al-kashaf al-tahliliyah li-sahifat umm al-qura*. 2 vols Riyadh, 1419/1999.

English

United Kingdom Government.
British Library, London.
India and Oriental Collection.
India Office Records (IOR).
L/P&S, India Office: Political and Secret Department Records, 1756–c1950.
R/15, Records of the Political Residency in the Persian Gulf, and the Bushire, Bahrain, Kuwait, Muscat and Trucial States Agencies, 1763–1951.
National Archives, Kew, London.
Foreign Office (FO).
FO/371, Political Departments: General Correspondence (1906–66).
FO/905, Foreign Office Post Files: Jiddah Legation.
FO/921, Minister Resident, Cairo.
FO/922, Middle East Supply Centre.
FO/957, British Middle East Office, Cairo.
FO/967, Legation, Hejaz.
FO/1016, India Office and successors: Political Residencies and Agencies, Persian Gulf: Correspondence and Papers.
Ministry of Power, POWE 33.

United Kingdom Private Papers
Oxford University, St. Antony's College, Middle East Centre Archives, Oxford.
H.R.P. Dickson Papers.
H. St. John B. Philby Papers.
Sir Andrew Ryan Papers.

Royal Geographical Society, London.
H. St. John B. Philby Papers.

United States Government
Foreign Relations of the United States, annually. Online at <http://digital.library.wisc.edu/1711.dl/FRUS>.
National Archives and Records Administration (NARA), College Park, MD. Record Groups (RG).
RG18, Records of the Army Air Forces, 1903–64.
RG38, Records of the Office of the Chief of Naval Operations, 1875–1989.
RG40, General Records of the Department of Commerce, 1898–1996.
RG59, General Records of the Department of State, 1756–1999.
RG84, Records of the Foreign Service Posts of the Department of State, 1788–1964.
RG151, Records of the Bureau of Foreign and Domestic Commerce, 1904–63.
RG165, Records of the War Department General and Special Staffs, 1860–1952.
RG169, Records of the Foreign Economic Administration, 1939–47.
RG208, Records of the Office of War Information, 1926–51.
RG218, Records of the U.S. Joint Chiefs of Staff, 1941–78.
RG226, Records of the Office of Strategic Services, 1919–48
RG234, Records of the Reconstruction Finance Corporation, 1928–68.
RG273, National Security Council Reports.
RG304, Records of the Office of Civil and Defense Mobilization, 1947–62.
RG319, Records of the Army Staff, 1903–2006.
RG330, Records of the Office of the Secretary of Defense, 1921–2005.
RG353, Records of Interdepartmental and Intradepartmental Committees (State Department), 1917–81. State War Navy Coordination Committee.
Presidential Libraries.
Dwight D. Eisenhower Presidential Library, Abilene, Kansas.
Franklin Delano Roosevelt Presidential Library, Hyde Park, New York.
Harry S. Truman Presidential Library, Independence, Missouri.

United States Private Papers
Georgetown University Library, Special Collections Division, Washington, DC.
William Mulligan Papers.
Library of Congress, Washington, DC.
Cordell Hull Papers.
Harold Ickes Papers.
Robert P. Patterson Papers.
Occidental College, Library, Special Collections and College Archives, Los Angeles, California.
Arthur N. Young Papers.
Princeton University, Mudd Manuscript Library, Princeton, New Jersey.
William A. Eddy Papers.
Karl S. Twitchell Papers.
Stanford University, Hoover Institution, Palo Alto, California.
Raymond H. Close Papers.
Phillip C. McConnell Papers.
Izzedine Shawa Papers.
Harley C. Stevens Papers.

University of Utah, J. Willard Marriott Library, Special Collections, Salt Lake City, Utah.
Wallace Earle Stegner Papers.
University of Virginia Library, Special Collections, Charlottesville, Virginia.
J. Rives Childs Papers.
E.R. Stettinius Papers.
University of Wyoming, American Heritage Center Archives, Laramie, Wyoming.
Parker T. Hart Papers.
Richard Sanger Papers.
C. Stribling Snodgrass Papers.
Thomas E. Ward Papers.

Interviews

"American Perspectives of ARAMCO, the Saudi-Arabian Oil-Producing Company, 1930s to 1980s." Unpublished manuscript of interviews. Berkeley: University of California, Bancroft Library, Regional Oral History Office, 1995. Interviews with: Frank Jungers; Paul and Elizabeth Arnot; Baldo Marinovic; William L. Owen; R. W. "Brock" Powers; Peter Speers; Ellen Speers. With an Introduction by Frank Jungers.

Saudi Arabia
Shaykh Abd al-Aziz al-Sulaiman (4 interviews) (c.1982)*
Shaykh Abd al-Aziz al-Sulaiman (2010)
Shaykh Abd al-Rahman Aba al-Khayl (2010)
Dr. Abd al-Rahman al-Shobaily (2009 and 2010)
Shaykh Ahmad al-Jaffali (c.1982)*
Shaykh Ahmad al-Sulaiman (2010–12)
Shaykh Ibrahim al-Hamrani (c.1982)*
Shaykh Kanan al-Khatib (c.1982)*
Shaykh Muhammad Ba Harith (c.1982)*
Shaykh Salih b. Shilhub (c.1982)*

United Kingdom and United States
Edward Betzig, US Agency for International Development (Point IV) in Saudi Arabia, mid–1952 to late 1954 (1985)*
Glen Brown, US Geological Survey in Saudi Arabia, 1944 and early 1950s (1985)*
W.D. Brewer, US diplomat in Saudi Arabia, late 1940s until 1951 (1985)*
William Crawford, US diplomat in Saudi Arabia, early 1950s (1985)*
Hermann Eilts, American diplomat in Saudi Arabia, early 1950s (1985)*
Raymond Hare, American diplomat in Saudi Arabia, early 1950s (1985)*
Parker T. Hart, American diplomat in Saudi Arabia, mid–1940s, early 1950s, ambassador 1961–5 (1985)*
J.M. Heath, British diplomat in Saudi Arabia, the late 1940s (1985)*
John Hewitt, Locust Survey in Saudi Arabia, 1940s (1985)*
Sir Hugh Jones, British diplomat in Saudi Arabia, 1949–52 (1985)*
James Knight, ex-ARAMCO official (1985)*
Edwin Locke, US government official and later private entrepreneur in Saudi Arabia, 1940s and 1950s (1985)*
George McGhee, US government official in negotiations in Saudi Arabia, early 1950s (1985)*
Raymond Mikesell, involved with the creation of the Saudi Arabian Monetary Agency, early 1950s (1985)*

William Mulligan, ARAMCO Government Relations Department, 1950s (1985)*
William Peyton, Jiddah representative of Pacific Western Oil Company, early 1950s (1985)*
George Rentz, ARAMCO Government Relations Department, 1950s (1985)*
(* = interview conducted by University of Essex team; see Preface)

UNPUBLISHED MANUSCRIPTS AND ACADEMIC DISSERTATIONS AND THESES

Awaji, Ibrahim Mohamed. "Bureaucracy and Society in Saudi Arabia." Ph.D. dissertation, University of Virginia, 1971.
Hamad, Turki Hamad Turki Al-. "Political Order in Changing Societies; Saudi Arabia: Modernization in a Traditional Context." Ph.D. dissertation, University of Southern California, 1985.
Khunaizi, Tayseer Baquir. "Economic, Social, and Political Development in Saudi Arabia: A Historical Analysis." Ph.D. dissertation, University of Kansas, 1993.
Mana', 'Abdullah. *'Abdullah al-Sulayman: sanawat al-ta'sis*. Unpublished manuscript, 2001.
Mazyed, Sulaiman M. al-. "The Structure and Function of Public Personnel Administration in Saudi Arabia." Ph.D. dissertation, The Claremont Graduate University, 1972.
Nuaim, Mishary Abdalrahman Al-. "State Building in a Non-Capitalist Social Formation: The Dialectics of Two Modes of Production and the Role of the Merchant Class, Saudi Arabia 1902–1932." Ph.D. dissertation, University of California, Los Angeles, 1986.
Parker, Chad. "Transports of Progress: the Arabian American Oil Company and American Modernization in Saudi Arabia, 1945–1973." Ph.D. dissertation, Indiana University, 2008.
Rawaf, Othman Yasin al-. "The Concept of the Five Crises in Political Development—Relevance to the Kingdom of Saudi Arabia." Ph.D. dissertation, Duke University, 1980.
Samore, Gary Samuel. "Royal Family Politics in Saudi Arabia (1953–1982)." Ph.D. dissertation, Harvard University, 1983.
Sultan, Ali Ahmed Al-. "Class Structure in Saudi Arabia." Ph.D. dissertation, Michigan State University, 1988.
"'The Minister': The Life and Times of Sheikh Abdallah Alsulaiman". Documentary survey in 12 vols researched and prepared by members of the Department of History, University of Essex, Colchester, Essex, England. Project Directors: Dr. Frederick Stanwood, Dr. Fiona Venn. Research Officers: Andre Noor, Julian Putkowski. Project Secretary: Doreen Waller. 30 April 1987.

PUBLISHED MATERIALS

Arabic

Ba Salamah, Husayn 'Abdullah. *Tarikh al-ka'bah al-mu'azamah*. 2nd ed., Jiddah: al-kitab al-'Arabi al-Sa'udi, 1402/1982.
Hafiz, 'Ali. *Nafhat min tayyibah*. Jiddah: Tihama, 1404/1984.
Jasir, Hamad al-. Ed. & arranged by 'Abd al-Rahman al-Shubayli. *Min sawanih al-dhikriyat*. Riyadh: Dar al-Yamamah, 1327/2006.
Karim, Badr Ahmad. *Nashah wa-tatawwur al-idha'ah fi al-mujtama' al-Sa'udi*. Jiddah: al-kitab al-'Arabi al-Sa'udi, 1402/1982.

Kingdom of Saudi Arabia. Ministry of Finance. *Ittifaqat sharikat istithmar al-bitrul wa-mustakhrajatihi wal-ma'adin.* 1st ed., 1359/1940–1.

———. *Ittifaqiyat khatt al-anabib 'abra al-bilad al-'Arabiyah al-Sa'udiyah.* Makkah: matbu'at al-hukumah, 1369/1949–50.

———. *Mu'assasat al-naqd al-'Arabi al-Sa'udi.* Makkah: matbu'at al-hukumah, 1371/1952.

Kingdom of Saudi Arabia. Ministry of Finance and National Economy. *Taqwim umm al-qura.* Riyadh: musallahat matabi' al-hukumah, 1413.

———. *Wizarat al-maliyah wal-iqtisad al-watani wa-marahil tatawwur al-nizam al-mali fi al-mamlakah al-'Arabiyah al-Sa'udiyah.* Riyadh, 1419/1999.

Kingdom of Saudi Arabia. Ministry of Finance and National Economy. National Center for Economic and Financial Information. *Al-tarikh al-iqtisadi lil-mamlakah al-'Arabiyah al-Sa'udiyah.* Riyadh, 1420/2000.

Maghrabi, Muhammad 'Ali. *A'lam al-Hijaz fi al-qarn al-rabi' 'ashar, 1301–1400h/1883–1980m.* 2nd ed., 1405/1985.

Mahami, Muhammad Rif'at al-. *Asad al-jazirah qal li.* Arranged and annotated by Hamad b. Nasir al-Dukhayyal. 2nd ed.; Riyadh: Maktabat al-malik 'Abd al-'Aziz al-'ammah, 1419/1999.

Mayman, Thamir Muhammad al-. *Shakhsiyat fi dhakirat al-watan.* Riyadh: Dar al-marsah, 1424/2003.

Mu'ammar, Faysal b. 'Abd al-Rahman b., general supervisor, and Fahd b. 'Abdullah al-Sammari, scientific editing and revision. *Al-malik 'Abd al-'Aziz: qa'imat bibliyujrafiyah iqtina'iyah; King Abdulaziz: A Collective Bibliography.* Vol. I: al-matbu'at bil-lugh'ah al-'Arabiyah; Vol. II: Foreign Languages Documents. Riyadh: King Abdulaziz Public Library, 1423/2002.

Muslim, Ibrahim al-. *'Abd al-'Aziz ibn Sa'ud wa-shakhsiyat fi al-dhakirah.* Riyadh?: al-Dar al-thiqafiyah lil-nashr, 1422/2001.

———. *Rijal min al-Qasim.* Vol. 4; Riyadh: Dar al-thiqafiyah lil-nashr, 2000.

Paris Najd, No. 13 (1431/2011), entire issue.

Qablan, Yusuf Muhammad al-, and Khalid 'Abdullah al-Qablan. *'Unayzah al-insan.* Riyadh: Dar al-asdiqa', 1430/2009.

Rafi', Muhammad 'Umar, ed. *Makkah fi al-qarn al-'ashar al-hijri.* Makkah: Manshurat nadi Makkah al-thiqafi, 1401/1981.

Riyadh Chamber of Commerce and Industry, Research Department. *Al-iqtisad al-Sa'udi bayna al-madi wal-hadir.* Riyadh, n.d.

Ruwayshid, 'Abd al-Rahman b. Sulayman al-. *'Abdullah al-Sulayman al-Hamdan: safhah mushriqah fi tarikh al-mamlakah al-'Arabiyah al-Sa'udiyah AH 1302–1385/AD 1885–1965.* Riyadh: Dar al-shil, 1421. 2nd ed., 2009.

Sadiq, Muhammad Tawfiq. *Tatawwur al-hukm wal-idarah fi al-mamlakah al-'Arabiyah al-Sa'udiyah.* Riyadh: Ma'had al-idarah al-'ammah, 1385/1965.

Semmari, Fahd Abdullah al-. *al-malik 'Abd al-'Aziz wa-Almaniya: dirasah tarikhiyah lil-'alaqat al-Sa'udiyah al-Alamaniyah 1344–1358/1926–1939.* N.p., n.d. Translation with additions of "Saudi Arabian–German Political and Economic Relations 1926–1939." Ph.D. dissertation, University of California, Riverside, 1989.

Shubayli, 'Abd al-Rahman al-. *Safhat watha'iqiyah min tarikh al-i'lam fi al-jazirah al-'Arabiyah.* Riyadh, 1423/2002.

Subayt, 'Abd al-Rahman b. Subayt al-, et al., eds. *Kunt ma'a 'Abd al-'Aziz.* N.p., 2nd ed. 1415/1994.

Tawiyan, 'Abdullah Zayid al-. *Aysar al-dala'il li-ba'd ansab asr al-Qasim wa-Ha'il.* Riyadh: Darat al-malik 'Abd al-'Aziz, 1361/2000.

———. *Rijal fi al-dhakirah: sayyar datiyah li-ba'd rijal Najd al-mu'asirin.* Vol. 1; 1418.

Tuwayjiri, ʿAbd al-ʿAziz b. ʿAbd al-Muhsin al-. *Li-surat al-layl hataf al-sabah, al-malik ʿAbd al-ʿAziz: dirasah witha'iqiyah.* Beirut: Al-dar al-ʿArabiyah lil-ʿulum nashirun, 1429/2008.

ʿUnayzah Community Organization. *Maʿrad sur maʿali al-Shaykh ʿAbdullah al-Sulayman, bi-munasibit takrim abna' maʿali al-Shaykh ʿAbdullah al-Sulayman, rahmat Allah.* ʿUnayzah: Markaz Salih b. Salih al-ijtimaʿi, 28 Dhu al-Hijjah, 1430.

ʿUthaymin, ʿAbdullah al-Salih al-. *Tarikh al-mamlakah al-ʿArabiyah al-Saʿudiyah.* Part Two: *ʿahd al-malik ʿAbd al-ʿAziz.* 8th ed.; Riyadh: maktabat al-ʿubaykan, 1428/2007.

Zirkali, Khayr al-Din al-. *Shibh al-jazirah fi ʿahd al-malik ʿAbd al-ʿAziz.* 4 vols, Beirut, 1970.

Western Languages

Aburish, Said. *The Rise, Corruption and Coming Fall of the House of Saud.* London: Bloomsbury, 1994.

Alice, Princess of Great Britain. *For My Grandchildren: Some Reminiscences of Her Royal Highness Princess Alice, Countess of Athlone.* London: Evans Brothers, 1966.

Alireza, Marianne. *At the Drop of a Veil.* Boston: Houghton Mifflin, 1971.

Almana, Mohammed. *Arabia Unified: A Portrait of Ibn Saud.* London: Hutchinson Benham, 1980; rev. ed., 1982.

Anderson, Irvine H. *Aramco, the United States, and Saudi Arabia: A Study of the Dynamics of Foreign Oil Policy, 1933–1950.* Princeton, NJ: Princeton University Press, 1981.

Armstrong, Harold C. *Lord of Arabia: Ibn Saud, an Intimate Study of a King.* London: Penguin, 1938; reprinted London: Kegan Paul for the King Abdulaziz Foundation, 2005.

Assah, Ahmed. *Miracle of the Desert Kingdom.* London: Johnson, 1969.

Belgrave, Charles D. *Personal Column.* London: Hutchinson, 1960.

Bilainkin, George. *Cairo to Riyadh Diary.* London: Williams & Norgate, 1950.

Blake, George. *Gellatly's, 1862–1962: A Short History of the Firm.* London: Blackie, 1962.

Brown, Anthony Cave. *Oil, God and Gold: The Story of ARAMCO and the Saudi Kings.* Boston: Houghton Mifflin, 1999.

Brown, E.H. *The Saudi-Arabia–Kuwait Neutral Zone.* Beirut, 1963.

Bullard, Reader. *The Camels Must Go: An Autobiography.* London: Faber and Faber, 1961.

Bullard, Reader. Ed. by E.C. Hodgkin. *Two Kings in Arabia: Sir Reader Bullard's Letters from Jeddah.* Reading: Ithaca Press, 1995.

Carter, J.R.L. *Leading Merchant Families of Saudi Arabia.* London: Scorpion Publications, 1979.

Champenois, Lucien, and Jean-Louis Soulie. "Chronologie du royaume d'Arabie Saoudite." In Paul Bonnenfant, ed., *La Péninsule Arabique d'aujourd'hui* (Paris: Centre National de la Récherche Scientifique, 1982), pp. 597–603.

Cheesman, R.E. *In Unknown Arabia.* London: Macmillan, 1926.

Cheney, M.S. *Big Oilman from Arabia.* London: Heinemann; New York: Ballantine, 1958.

Childs, J. Rives. *Foreign Service Farewell: My Years in the Near East.* Charlottesville: University Press of Virginia, 1969. Published for Randolph-Macon College.

Chisholm, Archibald H.T. *The First Kuwaiti Oil Concession Agreement: A Record of the Negotiations, 1911–1934.* London: Frank Cass, 1975.

Citino, Nathan J. *From Arab Nationalism to OPEC: Eisenhower, King Sa'ud, and the Making of U.S.–Saudi Relations.* Bloomington: Indiana University Press, 2002.

———. "Defending the 'Postwar Petroleum Order': The U.S., Britain and the 1954 Saudi–Onassis Tanker Deal." *Diplomacy and Statecraft,* Vol. 11, No. 2 (July 2000), pp. 137–60.

Clark, Arthur P., and Muhammad A. Tahlawi, eds. *A Land Transformed: The Arabian Peninsula, Saudi Arabia and Saudi Aramco.* Dhahran, Saudi Arabia: Saudi Arabian Oil Company (Saudi ARAMCO), 2006.

Clayton, Gilbert F. Ed. and introduced by Robert O. Collins. *An Arabian Diary*. Berkeley: University of California Press, 1969.

Crary, Douglas D. "Recent Agricultural Developments in Saudi Arabia." *Geographical Review*, Vol. 41, No. 3 (July 1951), pp. 366–83.

Davies, Rodger P. "The Organization of the Government of Saudi Arabia." Jiddah: American Legation, February 16, 1948. Report No. 3.

Davis, Simon. "Keeping the Americans in Line? Britain, the United States, and Saudi Arabia, 1939–1945: Inter-Allied Rivalry in the Middle East Revisited." *Diplomacy and Statecraft*, Vol. 8, No. 1 (March 1997), pp. 96–136.

De Gaury, Gerald. "Memories and Impressions of the Arabia of Ibn Saud." R.B. Serjeant, and R.L. Bidwell, ed., *Arabian Studies*, No. 2 (London: Hurst, 1975), pp. 19–31.

Dequin, H.F.E. *The Challenge of Saudi Arabia*. Hufuf: privately printed, October 1976.

Dialdin, Ali M., and Muhammad A. Tahlawi, ed.; researched and written by Thomas A. Pledge. *Saudi Aramco and Its People: A History of Training*. Dhahran: Saudi Arabian Oil Company (Saudi Aramco), 1998.

Eddy, William A. *F.D.R. Meets Ibn Saud*. Washington: American-Mideast Educational & Training Services, 1954.

Eilts, Hermann Frederick. "Ameen Rihani and the Hijaz–Najd Conflict: An Abortive Peace Mission." In James Piscatori and George S. Harris, ed., *Law, Personalities, and Politics of the Middle East: Essays in Honor of Majid Khadduri* (Boulder, CO: Westview Press; Washington, DC: Middle East Institute, 1987), pp. 93–123.

Farsy, Fouad al-. *Modernity and Tradition: The Saudi Equation*. London: Kegan Paul International, 1991.

Field, Michael. *The Merchants: The Big Business Families of Saudi Arabia and the Gulf States*. New York: Overlook Press, 1985.

Fraser, Nicholas, et al. *Aristotle Onassis*. Philadelphia: Lippincott, 1977; London: Weidenfeld and Nicolson, 1980.

Galpern, Steven G. *Money, Oil, and Empire in the Middle East: Sterling and Postwar Imperialism, 1944–1971*. New York: Cambridge University Press, 2009.

Godfried, Nathan. *Bridging the Gap Between Rich and Poor: American Economic Development Policy Toward the Arab East, 1942–1949*. New York: Greenwood, 1987.

Habib, John S. *Ibn Sa'ud's Warriors of Islam: The Ikhwan of Najd and Their Role in the Creation of the Sa'udi Kingdom, 1910–1930*. Leiden: E.J. Brill, 1978.

Harrington, Charles W. "The Saudi Arabian Council of Ministers." *Middle East Journal*, Vol. 12, No. 1 (1958), pp. 1–19.

Hart, Parker T. *Saudi Arabia and the United States: Birth of a Security Partnership*. Indianapolis: Indiana University Press, 1998.

Helms, Christine Moss. *The Cohesion of Saudi Arabia: Evolution of Political Identity*. London: Croom Helm; Baltimore: Johns Hopkins University Press, 1981.

Hirszowicz, Lukacz. *The Third Reich and the Arab East*. London: Routledge and Kegan Paul, 1966.

Holden, David, and Richard Johns, with James Buchan. *The House of Saud: The Rise and Rule of the Most Powerful Dynasty in the Arab World*. New York: Holt, Rinehart and Winston, 1982.

Hougan, J. *Spooks: The Private Use of Intelligence Agents*. London: W.H. Allen, 1979.

Howarth, David. *The Desert King: A Life of Ibn Saud*. London: Collins, 1964.

Jones, Toby Craig. *Desert Kingdom: How Oil and Water Forged Modern Saudi Arabia*. Cambridge, MA: Harvard University Press, 2010.

Kaufman, Burton I. *The Oil Cartel Case*. Westport, CT: Greenwood Press, 1978.

Keating, J. "Mission to Mecca: The Course of the Murphy." *US Naval Institute Proceedings*, Vol. 102, No. 1/875 (January 1976), pp. 54–63.

Kennedy, W.J., ed. *Secret History of the Oil Companies in the Middle East.* 2 vols; Salisbury, NC: Documentary Publications, 1979.

Kheirallah, G. *Arabia Reborn.* Albuquerque: University of New Mexico Press, 1952.

Kostiner, Joseph. *The Making of* Saudi *Arabia, 1916–1936: From Chieftaincy to Monarchical State.* New York: Oxford University Press, 1993.

Lacey, Robert. *The Kingdom: Arabia and the House of Saud.* New York: Harcourt Brace Jovanovich, 1982.

Leatherdale, Clive. *Britain and Saudi Arabia, 1925–1939: The Imperial Oasis.* London: Frank Cass, 1983.

Lipsky, George A. *Saudi Arabia: Its People, Its Society, Its Culture.* New Haven, CT: Human Relations Area Files Press, 1959.

Long, David E. *The Kingdom of Saudi Arabia.* Gainesville: University Press of Florida, 1997.

Longrigg, Stephen. *Oil in the Middle East: Its Discovery and Development.* 3rd ed.; London: Oxford University Press, for the Royal Institute of International Affairs, 1968.

McConnell, Philip C. *The Hundred Men.* Peterborough, NH: Currier Press, 1985.

McGhee, George. *Envoy to the Middle World: Adventures in Diplomacy.* New York: Harper & Row, 1969.

Mikesell, Raymond F. "Monetary Problems of Saudi Arabia." *Middle East Journal* (April 1947), pp. 169–79.

Miller, Aaron David. *Search for Security: Saudi Arabian Oil and American Foreign Policy, 1939–1969.* Chapel Hill: University of North Carolina Press, 1980.

Monroe, Elizabeth. *Philby of Arabia.* London: Faber and Faber, 1973.

Mosley, Leonard. *Power Play: The Tumultuous World of Middle East Oil, 1890–1973.* London: Weidenfeld and Nicholson, 1973.

Musil, Alois. *Northern Nejd.* New York: American Geographical Society, 1928.

Nallino, Carlo Alfonso. Ed. by Maria Nallino. *Raccolta di scritti editi e inediti*; Vol. 1: L'Arabia Sa'udiana. Rome: Istituto per l'Oriente, 1939.

Narayanan, R. "A Review of Oil Contract Negotiations By Saudi Arabia With Aramco." *International Studies*, Vol. 7, No. 4 (April 1966), pp. 568–88.

Nawwab, Ismail I., Peter C. Speers, and Paul F. Hoye, eds. *Aramco and Its World: Arabia and the Middle East.* Dhahran: Aramco, 1980. Rev. ed. edited with additional material by Arthur P. Clark, James P. Mandaville, William Tracey, and Jane Waldron Grutz and published as *Saudi Aramco and Its World: Arabia and the Middle East.* Dhahran, Aramco, 1995.

"Onassis Agreement, The." *Egyptian Economic and Political Review*, January 1955, pp. 42–4.

Peterson, J.E. *Historical Dictionary of Saudi Arabia.* Metuchen, NJ: Scarecrow Press, 1993; rev. ed., 2003.

Philby, H. St.J. B. *Arabia of the Wahhabis.* London: Constable, 1928.

———. *A Pilgrim in Arabia.* London: Robert Hale, 1946.

———. *Arabian Days.* London: Robert Hale, 1948.

———. "The Golden Jubilee in Saudi Arabia." *Journal of the Royal Central Asian Society*, Vol. 37 (April 1950), pp. 122–3.

———. *Arabian Jubilee.* New York: John Day, 1953.

———. *Forty Years in the Wilderness.* London: Robert Hale, 1957.

———. *Arabian Oil Ventures.* Washington: Middle East Institute, 1964.

———. *Saudi Arabia.* London: Ernest Benn, 1955. Reprinted Beirut: Librairie du Liban, 1968.

Rasheed, Madawi Al-. *A History of Saudi Arabia.* Cambridge: Cambridge University Press, 2002; rev. ed., 2010.

Rashid, Ibrahim al-. *Documents on the History of Saudi Arabia*. 3 vols; Salisbury, NC: Documentary Publications, 1976.

Rihani, Ameen Fares. *Ibn Saud of Arabia: His People and His Land*. London: Constable, 1928.

Robertson, Nelson, ed. *Origins of the Saudi Arabian Oil Empire–Secret U.S. Documents, 1923–1944*. Salisbury, NC: Documentary Publications, 1979.

Roosevelt, Kermit. *Arabs, Oil, and History: The Story of the Middle East*. New York: Harper, 1949.

Rubin, Barry. *The Great Powers in the Middle East, 1941–1947*. London: Frank Cass, 1980.

Rutter, Eldon. *The Holy Cities of Arabia*. 2 vols; London and New York: G.P. Putnam's Sons, 1928.

Ryan, Andrew. *The Last of the Dragomans*. London: G. Bles, 1951.

Sadhan, Abdulrahman M. al-. "The Modernisation of the Saudi Bureaucracy." In Willard A. Beling, ed., *King Faisal and the Modernisation of Saudi Arabia* (London: Croom Helm; Boulder CO: Westview Press, 1980), pp. 75–90.

Sadleir, George Forster. *Diary of a journey across Arabia from El Khatif in the Persian Gulf, to Yambo in the Red Sea, during the year 1819*. Bombay: Government of Bombay, 1866. Reprinted Naples: Falcon; New York: Oleander, 1977.

Sampson, Anthony. *The Seven Sisters: The Great Oil Companies and the World They Shaped*. New York: Viking Press, 1975.

Sanger, Richard H. *The Arabian Peninsula*. Ithaca, NY: Cornell University Press, 1954.

———. "Ibn Saud's Program for Arabia." *Middle East Journal*, Vol. 1, No. 1 (1947), pp. 180–90.

Sarhan, S., ed. *Who's Who in Saudi Arabia*. Jiddah: Tihama, 1978.

"Saudi Arabia's Finance—The Achievements of the Ministry of Finance." *Islamic Review*, Vol. 43 (December 1955), pp. 33–4.

Sheean, Vincent. *Faisal: The King and His Kingdom*. London: Tavistock, 1975.

Squire, C.B. "Charles Richard Crane." *Middle East Forum*, Vol. 30 (October–November 1955), pp. 8–12.

Stegner, Wallace. *Discovery! The Search for Arabian Oil*. Beirut: Middle East Export Press, 1971; reprinted Vista, CA: Selwa Press, 2007.

Toy, Barbara. *A Fool Strikes Oil*. London: John Murray, 1957.

Troeller, Gary. *The Birth of Saudi Arabia: Britain and the Rise of the House of Sa'ud*. London: Frank Cass, 1976.

Twitchell, Karl S. *Saudi Arabia*. 3rd ed.; Princeton: Princeton University Press, 1958.

United Kingdom. Admiralty. Naval Intelligence Division. *Western Arabia and the Red Sea*. Oxford: HMSO, 1946. Geographical Handbook Series, B.R. 527.

Van Der Meulen, Daniël. *The Wells of Ibn Sa'ud*. London: John Murray, 1957.

Vassiliev, Alexei. *The History of Saudi Arabia*. London: Al Saqi Books, 2000.

Vitalis, Robert. *America's Kingdom: Mythmaking on the Saudi Oil Frontier*. Stanford: Stanford University Press, 2006.

———. "Aramco World: Business and Culture on the Arabian Oil Frontier." In Robert Vitalis and Madawi al-Rasheed, ed., *Counter-Narratives: History, Contemporary Society, and Politics in Saudi Arabia and Yemen* (New York: Palgrave, 2004), pp. 151–82.

Wahba, Hafiz. *Arabian Days*. London: Arthur Barker, 1964.

Ward, Thomas Edward. *Negotiations for Oil Concessions in Bahrain, El Hasa (Saudi Arabia) the Neutral Zone, Qatar and Kuwait: A Story Dedicated to Those Who Worked with Heart, Hand, and Mind in Uncovering and Developing the Petroleum Resources of the Persian Gulf Area*. New York: Ardlee Service,1965.

Watt, D.C. "The Foreign Policy of Ibn Saud, 1936–39." *Journal of the Royal Central Asian Society*, Vol. 50 (April 1963), pp. 152–60.

Wilmington, Martin W. *The Middle East Supply Centre*. Albany: State University of New York Press, 1971; London: University of London Press, 1972.

Yergin, Daniel. *The Prize: The Epic Quest for Oil, Money, and Power*. New York: Simon & Schuster, 1991.

Young, Arthur N. *Saudi Arabia: The Making of a Financial Giant*. New York: New York University Press, 1983.

Index

www.ingramcontent.com/pod-product-compliance
Ingram Content Group UK Ltd.
Pitfield, Milton Keynes, MK11 3LW, UK
UKHW020244290926
15470UKWH00002B/720

9 781784 539009